Confronting Power,
Theorizing Gender

To
Juliette Knight

From

With
love and
respect

Confronting Power, Theorizing Gender

Interdisciplinary Perspectives in the Caribbean

Edited by

Eudine Barriteau

University of the West Indies Press
Jamaica • Barbados • Trinidad and Tobago

University of the West Indies Press
1A Aqueduct Flats   Mona
Kingston 7   Jamaica
www.uwipress.com

07 06 05 04 03   5 4 3 2 1

CATALOGUING IN PUBLICATION DATA

Confronting power, theorizing gender: interdisciplinary perspectives in the
Caribbean / edited by Eudine Barriteau.
p. cm.
Includes bibliographical references.

ISBN: 976-640-136-5

1. Feminist psychology – Caribbean, English-speaking. 2. Sex differences
(Psychology) – Caribbean, English-speaking. 3. Sex role – Caribbean,
English-speaking. 4. Power (Social Sciences) – Caribbean, English-speaking.
5. Women in development – Caribbean, English-speaking. I. Barriteau, Eudine.

BF201.4.C66 2003   155.3'33

Cover and book design by Robert Harris
Set in Sabon 10.5/14.5 x 27
Printed in Canada

Dedicated to the memory
of
my beloved nephew

René Wilbur Barriteau
15 September 1973–11 October 2001
Gone too soon . . .

For René

Maybe the body's husk
is but a chrysalis we weave
and wrap to warm
our naked spirit, that at
some point undresses,
and we burn into the depths
as stars

Maybe our varied and temporary beauty
is but grass;
is harvested some importunate
and utterly impetuous day
Only to scatter the seeds of our bright souls
into the welcoming and everlasting
nebulae

– Margaret D. Gill

Contents

Part III
Theorizing Historiography,
Historicizing Gender and Sexuality

Part IV
Gender, Genre and Cultural/Literary Discourse

Part V

*Gender and Power in the Public Domain:
Feminist Theorizing of Citizenship*

Part VI

*Gender and Power in the Public Domain:
Deconstructing Masculinity and Marginality*

Acknowledgements

The idea for this volume of essays in Caribbean feminist theorizing and scholarship on gender came from a desire to explore why the Caribbean appears as an anomaly in terms of differential outcomes and vastly different interpretations of social change for women and men. The contributors to this volume know that Caribbean gender relations have been changing rapidly and are equally aware that some theoretical explanations and conceptual tools have not kept pace with societal developments and thus were in danger of losing their explanatory powers.

Towards probing these ongoing transformations the Centre for Gender and Development Studies at the Cave Hill campus of the University of the West Indies invited about twenty-five colleagues to present papers at a one-day symposium in June 1999. The majority of the chapters here had their genesis in the papers presented at that consultation. I thank each of my colleagues for their participation, contribution and final submission. I also apologize to you for the incubation period between conceptualization and publication. An edited, peer-reviewed collection poses its own challenges, but I accept full responsibility for undue delays in your ideas being published and contributing to that growing body of Caribbean feminist scholarship.

Through its project of support for teaching, research and outreach at the Centre for Gender and Development Studies, University of the West Indies, the Dutch government provided financial support for the mounting of the workshop and the various activities of the editing and publications process. They correctly saw the output of this project as contributing a body of research available for undergraduate and postgraduate teaching and thus contributing to the generation of new curricula. We thank them for their vital support.

Many colleagues, staff members and friends gave generously of their time, energy and intellect. I thank Linden Lewis, Rhoda Reddock, David

Berry, Richard Clarke, Cynthia Burack, Mindie Lazarus-Black, Ann Denis, Barbara Bailey, Elaine Savory, Bridget Brereton and Louraine Emmanuel. As the first research assistant to work on the manuscript, Jacqueline Morris worked tirelessly to ensure that contributors received the comments of reviewers and that deadlines and schedules were kept. She was succeeded by Carmen Hutchinson-Miller and Deborah Deane, research assistant and administrative assistant respectively. They continued the pattern of giving of their best. Yet all staff members past and present contributed to the project. Veronica Jones helped to plan the symposium, Olivia Birch undertook many secretarial assignments and Susan McEachrane, graduate assistant, provided additional administrative support.

Through their generous support and numerous conversations, across a range of intellectual spaces and sites, my friends and colleagues nurtured the idea and the need for this volume. I thank Andaiye, Peggy Antrobus, Keturah Babb, Christine Barrow, Cynthia Barrow-Giles, Jeanette Bell, Joan Brathwaite, Roberta Clarke, Joan Cuffie, Diane Cummins, Aviston Downes, Leith Dunn, Joyce Endeley, Marlene Hamilton, Pansy Hamilton, Richard Goodridge, Don Marshall, Joycelin Massiah, Patricia McFadden, Folade Mutota, Verna St Rose Greaves, Letnie Rock, Sheila Stuart, Linnette Vassell and Joy Workman. Other friends nurtured me in so many different ways, especially during a very rough period of family losses. Maxine McClean, Celia Pollard-Jones, Elizabeth Bernard, Jennifer Woodroffe, Sandra Baptiste, Randy Hallett, Colin Bellamy, Marcia Martindale, Mark Cadogan, Harold Codrington and Benita Holder, thank you.

My family continues to encircle me with their unconditional love and branches of the clan continue to grow. I welcome Sumaya in London, and Michael Jr in New York. I give thanks for my brothers, sisters, nieces, nephews and cousins. Ma, I miss you so; René, I wish I was at home when you called; and Daddy, I miss your gentle, caring voice. I know all of you continue to be proud of me. Cabral, you try so hard to understand why I have yet another project and I am just blessed to see you grow and challenge me with a teenager's take on contemporary gender relations. Al, you continue to make the journey so much easier, and the victories so much sweeter. I am blessed by your love and support.

Abbreviations

AWID	Association of Women in Development
CARICOM	Caribbean Community
CIDA	Canadian International Development Agency
DAWN	Development Alternatives with Women for a New Era
GAD	Gender and Development
UNDP	United Nations Development Programme
UNIFEM	United Nations Development Fund for Women
UWI	University of the West Indies
WAD	Women and Development
WAND	Women and Development Unit, University of the West Indies
WICP	Women in the Caribbean Project
WID	Women in Development
WIRC	West India Royal Commission

⁂ Part 1 ⁂
Introduction

⇥ Chapter 1 ⇤

Confronting Power, Theorizing Gender in the Commonwealth Caribbean

> Including power in an analysis of gender allows us to see how gender is con-
> structed through the practices of power. "Female" and "male" are shaped
> not only at the micro-level of everyday social interaction but also at the macro
> level as social institutions control and regulate the practices of gender. (Radtke
> and Stam 1994, 13)

Some eleven years ago the conjuncture of power that inheres in dominating relations of gender and its influence over the emergence of an
embryonic Caribbean feminist epistemology appeared as a subtext in my
work on constructing a post-modernist feminist theory to guide social
science research. I was then attempting to carve the contours of an
indigenous feminist theory informed by post-modernist feminist insights
(Barriteau 1992). I was dissatisfied with imported theoretical constructs
that did not stimulate critiques of epistemologies, methodologies and
practices, and therefore reinforced and maintained exclusions and invisibility around key dimensions of women's lives. I argued that unless these
received knowledges were deconstructed, dominating relations of gender
would continue to permeate feminist research and scholarship in the
Caribbean (Barriteau 1992, 14). I stated that, to be relevant, a new

theoretical construct should guarantee women equal access to power (Barriteau 1992, 7). Implicitly I recognized that a distinguishing feature of women's lives was the absence of power, and spoke of power in two ways. I stated that knowledge represented a critical source of power and underscored the urgency of creating new knowledges through building more meaningful feminist theoretical constructs. I also conceptualized power as the capacity to affect access to resources and, to a lesser extent, as a generalized stream of influence to alter outcomes, to define situations and to shape belief systems. Eleven years later, after a decade of contestations over feminists' attempts to create knowledges about women's lives, the contributors maintain that there is still much work to be done in Caribbean feminist theorizing around the complications of power in – and of – gender. This book seeks to shift the terrain in Caribbean feminist scholarship by excavating and interrogating the nexus of power and gender in Caribbean scholarship and society.

Although earlier I used a Foucauldian understanding of power as existing in myriad layers and multiple sites, with productive and positive dimensions to transcend the negative and coercive common understandings of power, I did not illustrate the implications of the power of dominating relations of gender. The contributors provide ample evidence of the power of gender, ranging from how it circumscribes indigenous feminist theorizing and inhibits the strengthening of feminist epistemology, to its effect on women involved in student politics at the University of the West Indies.

I theorized that an absence of power characterized many dimensions of women's lives and indicated what that absence meant to theorizing dominating relations of gender. I had not interrogated the *relations of power* within relations of gender, nor how the experience of gendered identities was grounded in asymmetrical practices of power. I noted that gendered relations were characterized "as the ways in which social relations between women and men are socially constituted to perpetuate male dominance" (Barriteau 1992, 15). Yet, although I was ostensibly attempting to construct a new theoretical frame that recognized both women and men as equally gendered, but with significantly differing and asymmetrical material and psychological outcomes, at the foundation of that work was the subterranean but effervescent desire to expose power in relations of gender.

Using a feminist understanding of the social relations of gender, I claim that one of the shortcomings of the existing discourse on gender in the Caribbean is our failure to confront the raw power dynamics impinging on our ongoing attempts to expose and alter the systemic character of women's multiple experiences of material and ideological subordination. What has been visibly absent in feminist scholarship in the anglophone Caribbean is an explicit acknowledgement that in theorizing relations of gender we are confronting one of the more repressive expressions of power. Our collective reluctance or reservations about naming and examining how oppressive power is inscribed in the rituals and practices of gendered relations have increasingly forced a shift from feminist engagements with patriarchal practices to theoretical skirmishes at the borders of women's subjectivity. This volume seeks to remedy that. The contributors draw on the existing feminist discourse but advance feminist scholarship by making explicit how relations of power work within relations of gender.

Collectively the investigations reveal and demonstrate that power relations underwrite and complicate all relations of gender in the Caribbean. The contributors recognize that to consider gender is to engage in an analysis of the many dimensions of power. Earlier discussions have focused on gender relations without examining how they constitute another configuration of power in the contemporary Caribbean, much as the power relations of race and class have been and continue to be theorized (Beckles 1989a; Lewis 2001; Gray 2001; Watson 1990; Boxill 2002). The book confronts and exposes the perverse operations of relations of power in gendered discourses and practices. Whether the analyses flow from history, literary studies, sociology, political science or feminist studies, all the contributors engage in revealing the relations of power in gender. The book engages with several new research questions from the perspective of destabilizing existing theory and issuing new epistemological challenges.

In the last twenty-five years several excellent works have been published about the lives of women in the Caribbean, or about women in developing countries that include a focus on the Caribbean. These continue to be relevant (see, for example, Tinker and Bo Bramsen 1976; Steady 1981; Nash and Fernandez-Kelly 1983; *Social and Economic Studies* 1986a, 1986b; Sen and Grown 1987; Momsen and Townsend

1987; Mohammed and Shepherd 1988; Hart 1989b; Tinker 1990; Bush 1990; Senior 1991; Mohanty, Russo and Torres 1991; Beneria and Feldman 1992; Momsen 1993; Reddock 1994; Safa 1995; Shepherd, Brereton and Bailey 1995; and Marchand and Parpart 1995).

Three of the more recent works contributing to Caribbean feminist theorizing include Parpart, Connelly and Barriteau 2000; Barrow 1998b; and López Springfield 1997. Parpart, Connelly and Barriteau explain the relevance of theory; this volume constructs theory. This collection brings Caribbean theorizing to the body of feminist knowledge rather than making available Caribbean case studies for feminist analysis. Both Barrow (1998b) and López Springfield (1997) provide comprehensive essays on gender issues in the contemporary Caribbean.

Barrow (1998b) makes a solid contribution to Caribbean feminist scholarship, with a focus on gender ideology and identity. The objective of that collection was not to theorize material relations of gender or to critique the theoretical frameworks that have been used to analyse women's work, as Ann Denis does in chapter 12. The contributors here engage with the work published in Barrow and López Springfield but move beyond it. Throughout the work there is a sustained, coherent theme of gender relations as relations of power that create disproportionate, asymmetric benefits and burdens for women and men in Caribbean societies. It examines how material and ideological relations of gender are constructed and maintained to keep women in disadvantageous positions relative to men. Whether the analysis deconstructs Caribbean constitutions to reveal how women have been theoretically excluded from citizenship (Robinson, chapter 11) or undertakes a dissection of the gendered, hierarchical, unequal experiences of young women with political power (Leo-Rhynie, chapter 13) or offers an incisive historical and contemporary dissection of the theorization of sexual relations in the Caribbean (Kempadoo, chapter 8), this work exposes how relations of gender constitute another manifestation of power relations underwriting the resiliency and fluidity of patriarchal legacies and practices.

In the introduction to a 1994 edited collection of essays, Radtke and Stam begin by acknowledging that the authors bring their individual views of power to bear on the conceptions, problems, cases and analyses of gender (Radtke and Stam 1994, 2). The writers explore the multifaceted problems posed by problematizing power from multiple angles, points, practices and disciplines.

The grounding in this collection is somewhat different. Starting from different disciplinary locations, each of the contributors engages with the theoretical challenges and possibilities that gender poses to the social relations and practices they examine. The anchor becomes relations of power embedded in gender. With the exception of a few, the majority did not isolate and interrogate power explicitly. Yet all these essays grapple with the intersections of power and gender. They simultaneously underscore a previously unacknowledged tension in feminist scholarship and practice in the Caribbean. To date we have not questioned the power/gender confluence as representing a major hurdle to unravelling the enduring practices that maintain inequalities and the absence of gender justice.

In a 1999 review of six of the then current works on Caribbean women, Riva Berleant-Schiller states that Caribbeanist scholars have garnered a trove of empirical data, both qualitative and quantitative, on women and gender. However, she identifies a lacuna in this scholarship by advising that comparison, synthesis and theoretical ferment ought to follow. Berleant-Schiller criticizes several contributions in López Springfield for exhibiting a kind of historical amnesia by displaying an unawareness of Caribbean research before the 1980s (Berleant-Schiller 1999).

This book contributes to the genesis of that overdue theoretical and intellectual ferment in Caribbean feminist scholarship. It offers a rigorous, incisive and very compelling examination of the epistemological, theoretical, conceptual and practical issues and implications that emerge when the study of the multiple dimensions of the social relations of gender intersects with history, law, political economy, politics and policy in the Commonwealth Caribbean. It theorizes emerging issues in feminist, masculinity and gender studies from several interdisciplinary perspectives.

At this juncture in the genesis of Caribbean feminist thought, we need to probe deeper into examining the power relations surrounding the generation of knowledge about women and the asymmetrical practices of power that shape everyday life. Caribbean feminists have completed the earlier stocktaking and data analysis that the Women in the Caribbean

Project represented. We are advancing ethnographic studies exploring the lives of women and men in the Caribbean and its diaspora (Thomas 2001; Bolles 2001). We are moving beyond confronting the fathers in the Caribbean literary canons and critiquing women writers and their treatment of female subjectivity (Davies and Savory-Fido 1990; Barnes 1999; Edmondson 1999a). We are proving that the process by which education as a public good is made available is gendered and deeply problematic (Leo-Rhynie, Bailey and Barrow 1997). We are conducting exploratory studies on women's sexuality (Mohammed 2000a, 2000b; Kempadoo 1999b) and tentatively crossing boundaries into studying, reflecting and ceasing to avoid creating a discourse on lesbian and homosexual sexual orientations (Silvera 1992; Alexander 1997; Cave and French 1995; Atluri 2001). We are dissecting the global economy to expose women's continuously precarious insertions (Freeman 2000; Jayasinghe 2001).We are taking on the state and exposing its patriarchal character (Alexander 1997; Barriteau 2001). We have moved beyond documenting how existing laws treat women and we are now using feminist legal theory to interrogate the law, revealing it as deeply problematic even as we theorize citizenship as a Caribbean feminist project (Robinson 2000). That partial sketch of the diverse body of feminist work is pointing us to new knowledges that demand a rethinking of Caribbean society from feminist perspectives.

As feminists we ought to challenge the patriarchal practices and deployments of power, but we have been reluctant to explicitly theorize the absence of power as a constraining factor in women's lives. The pairing of women and power continues to be problematic from both androcentric and feminist perspectives. The former is perhaps more easily understood, since phallocentric discourses are vested in keeping women powerless. It is feminism's ambiguity in grappling with power that is more challenging, since the goal of feminism is changing both the "conceptual practices of power" (Smith 1990) and the material outcomes of the deployment of power in everyday life.

Feminists are increasingly constrained in our attempts to examine and expose the multiple, contradictory and often harsh realities of women's lives. One of the several reasons that this becomes more difficult to accomplish is that as feminists we have an ambivalent relationship with power and with acknowledging our need for it. The history of the ambivalence that women have had to admitting we are powerful (Moglen 1983) and can be powerful (Pohlmann 1995) coexists with and is complicated by adverse gendered societal practices. Consequently, because we are not confronting power and the relations of power in the discourse on gender, we are not devising meaningful strategies of intellectual and activist engagement with the institutions and practices opposed to the ideals of gender justice. Instead, within both the academy and the women's movement, we are becoming embedded with a feminism of moralism, rather than with a feminism that continues to develop a politics of epistemological and activist engagement with societal institutions and practices.

Additionally, internalizing but simultaneously wrestling with patriarchy's ancient wish that women display courage in obeying rather than commanding (Aristotle 1885, quoted in Agonito 1977, 54), many women as leaders will tie themselves in knots before they will admit that the particular posts or responsibilities they hold are in fact powerful (Statham 1987; Pohlmann 1995; Moglen 1983; Kitzinger 1991).

Exposing Gender Relations as Regimes of Power

By interrogating the interface of power and gender, this work offers several distinctive features. It departs from the earlier literature by becoming the first work in Caribbean feminist theorizing that explicitly and deliberately confronts gender relations as regimes of power that produce significantly different material and ideological outcomes for women and for men. By investigating the intersection of gender and power both historically and in contemporary society, the contributors remove a popular but misguided understanding of relations of gender in the region as benign socialization that can be corrected by well-intentioned, but often poorly conceptualized, policy initiatives.

Consolidating and Advancing Indigenous Feminist Theorizing

The work underscores the further maturing of Caribbean scholarship in feminist and gender studies. Christine Barrow notes that "Caribbean Feminist scholarship has, since the late 1970s, moved rapidly to become established as an exciting field of epistemological, theoretical and methodological advance" (1998b, xi). While recognizing the significance of earlier and other research, the writers critique Caribbean scholarship in this field, document weaknesses and gaps in earlier theoretical formulations and policy prescriptions, and formulate or suggest new theoretical constructs while delineating the implications of these. In doing so the work consolidates and advances what Caribbean feminist theorizing offers to feminist epistemology as a critical body of knowledge. Yet these attempts to create new intellectual infrastructures are not driven by any need to create "abstractions about abstractions" (Stacey 2001, 99). Instead, these are grounded in the theory/praxis nexus of rapid economic and social changes in Caribbean societies.

Theorizing the Historical and Contemporary Terrain of Feminism and Gender in Caribbean Societies

Although the volume of literature on Caribbean feminist and gender studies has grown significantly in the last quarter of the twentieth century, none of the existing works has explicitly set out from interdisciplinary perspectives to theorize the historical and contemporary terrain and suggest a way forward. This book does that. These chapters display an intellectual restlessness, revealing dissatisfaction with the status quo. Several contributors engage with the works of others and identify strengths and weaknesses, even as they ask new questions of existing understandings or unearth new areas for interrogation.

Interrogating and Deconstructing Marginality and Masculinity in the Caribbean

This volume of essays, more than any other previous text in Caribbean feminist/gender studies, interrogates masculinity. In the majority of the chapters, the work examines issues and questions about the construction of masculinity and the content of gender identities for Caribbean men. Richard Goodridge argues persuasively for examining Islamic masculinity, particularly in theorizing contemporary gender relations. Jane Bryce exposes the pervasiveness of hegemonic masculinity in the black Caribbean diasporic identity. Kamala Kempadoo calls attention to the theoretical closures surrounding the construction of black male sexuality.

Part 6 is devoted to interrogating and deconstructing the "marginalization of the black male" thesis. The widespread acceptance of this thesis has been particularly influential in debate and in altering policies on women and gender in the Commonwealth Caribbean. Yet the thesis does not advance an understanding of what is ontologically different in the lives of Caribbean men, and while it has been presented as a definitive theory and its methodology and conclusions widely criticized, its core assumptions have not previously been subjected to a sustained, rigorous examination. The adoption of this thesis as a priority area for government intervention was narrowly defeated at the Commonwealth Meeting of Ministers of Women's Affairs in New Delhi, India, 6–9 April 2000 (Chadha 2000). This section concludes by stating that

> The male marginalization thesis is a deeply flawed, one-dimensional reading of manhood in the region. It gives us Caribbean man as victim, with a wounded, regressive masculinity. It does a disservice to understanding the many manifestations of Caribbean masculinity, and therefore it is inadequate in providing guidelines for further research and policy on issues affecting and affected by Caribbean men in relation to changing gender identities and roles. (Barriteau, chapter 15)

Contributions to Constructing and Critiquing Contemporary Feminist Theorizing from the Perspective of the South

Another significant feature of this volume is that, although Caribbean states, economies, societies, social relations and practices form the terrain against which the analyses are constructed, the epistemological, theoretical and policy issues raised are immediately relevant to ongoing debates about what is feminist theory, and to reflecting on social life in societies in the North and South. Judith Stacey advises that "just when feminist theory appears to be assimilated, coopted, or just plain fatigued in the centers of the western 'metropole,' . . . closer attention to the diverse sources and character of the flourishing of non-western feminist practice and thought might do more to revitalize western feminist theory" (Stacey 2001, 101).

Finally, many works in feminist studies originating in the South – as opposed to having a Southern sensibility – do not actively engage with constructing or critiquing theory. Instead they tend to focus on what appears to be the more pressing concerns of programme and policy design and implementation. This work recognizes that theoretical biases are embedded in and influence all policy prescriptions and programme design. It deliberately interrogates and deconstructs theoretical constructs and advances ongoing feminist theorizing as a priority for the Caribbean and other Southern regions.

The subject of post-modernism floats in and out of the narratives of most of these texts. Some writers are more comfortable with the idea of the post-modern, employing its deconstructive tools and vocabulary as part of their methodologies of analysis. Others take a more critical stance, even when they employ some of its discursive techniques. This is not new to feminist scholarship in the South. Jane Parpart and Marianne Marchand provide an extensive, informed review of post-modernism, post-modernist feminist thought, and their complications, attractions and criticisms for feminists in the South (Parpart and Marchand 1995, 1–22). Still, post-modernism and post-modernist feminist thought represent a theoretical space not yet fully captured in terms of what they offer or fail to offer in the growth of Caribbean feminist scholarship.

A popular tendency in the region, as elsewhere, is to use "post-modernist" almost as a metaphor for the inexplicable, the bizarre, all that is undesirable and incomprehensible. The quest for truth, sources, origins and definitive answers is compelling. In a region indisputably carved out by a multiplicity of exploitative relations, many of which continue to haunt our daily lives, the desire to infuse with the correct interpretation, reveal the accurate historical experience, devise the definitive set of policy prescriptions, make the true reading of Caribbean masculinity, identify the essential Caribbean woman, is overpowering and seductive. Post-modernism's claim that there is no authentic, singular truth is deeply disturbing to our need to establish authority, authenticity and origins. So, while it may prove useful for discursive strategies, the idea that, epistemologically, post-modernism can assist in generating relevant sources of knowledge for Caribbean feminist scholarship awaits further exploration.

Part 2, Epistemological Inquiries, Theoretical Restlessness, centres on three essays located in three differing conceptual approaches. The

writers enter the messy multiplicity of the intersection of women's subjectivity and feminist scholarship through encounters with different feminist theoretical questions. Yet they share a common strategy and an
understanding of the responsibilities of feminist scholarship. Donna St
Hill, Michelle Rowley and I undertake an internal critique of feminist
theoretical engagements, and we maintain a critical stance on the obligations of feminist scholarship to the development of the discipline.

A central concern of this project is the question, In what ways
has feminism failed to critique itself in its advocacy of an equitable development and representations within development? One of the distinguishing features of these essays is that, although the contributors
self-consciously seek to theorize relations of gender, each thrust at
creating new knowledge is immediately tested by applying the new
framework to some aspect of Caribbean reality. Is this a generic phase of
theory-building, or will it be a characteristic of Caribbean feminist scholarship – that is, a determination that it will always stay grounded?
Barbara Christian cautions us to always stay grounded, reflective: "My
fear is that when Theory is not rooted in practice, it becomes prescriptive, exclusive, elitist" (Christian 1990, 340; in Stacey 2001, 99).

Theorizing from contrasting perspectives, Donna St Hill and I suggest that the relevance and viability of feminist scholarship in the region
are under threat. We undertake a healthy interrogation of the theoretical tools and conceptual frameworks that may have been employed
unproblematically. We display an intense desire to produce new meanings and to have these yield new revelations about women's and men's
lives.

In chapter 2 I confront the politics and power relations inherent in
creating new knowledges about women's lives. I do this by politicizing
and problematizing recent developments in Caribbean feminist discourse.
Citing Alcoff and Potter (1993), I theorize the intersection of gender politics with the production of feminist knowledge. I analyse the "unproblematized shift to the social relations of gender as an analytical
framework" as a means of exposing the everyday politics unleashed in
attempts to generate new understandings about women's lives and
Caribbean societies. I argue that Caribbean feminist scholarship has
taken an all too accommodating stance in the adoption of gender as its
main analytical framework. I state that nowhere did this adoption imply

that women's subjectivity was being replaced, but this has been one of the creeping tendencies. The chapter begins with theorizing and ends with questions that seek to disrupt the all too facile accommodation and dilution of the unexplored analytical worth that gender brings to feminism. My aim is to prevent women's subjectivity from disappearing from the discourses on gender.

In chapter 3 Donna St Hill questions the relevance and value of holding difference (especially as it relates to culture and nationality) central to feminist theorizing on gender equality in the contemporary Caribbean. Working somewhat within the vein of Martha Nussbaum (Quillen 2001), St Hill argues that we cannot jettison all the promises of universal human progress and emancipation contained in the modernist project in return for a mere deconstruction of society and what she terms a "value-absent post-modern focus on fragmentation and difference". I have used post-modernist feminist analysis to devise a way forward out of the theoretical and impractical impasse generated by the dominance of universalizing occlusions that are reproduced by the wholesale importation of liberal and socialist feminist theorizing in the Caribbean (Barriteau 1992, 1995a, 1995b).

St Hill's contribution is welcome and necessary because it signals future debates about the ongoing maturation of Caribbean feminist thought and its usefulness in helping to make sense of Caribbean societies. Her interest and intent in going against the trend of a post-modernist feminist analysis are, as she states, because "bad theory almost always leads to bad policy". That is a sound reason to offer a theoretical critique. The most recent policy initiative (marked by the rush to introduce gender mainstreaming), and its general failure to alter adversity in women's and men's lives, is not a product of post-modernist feminist analysis. It is instead an ongoing refined application of humanist feminism or liberal feminist theorizing (Barriteau 2001, 86).

Rosi Braidotti calls nihilistic the attempts to trivialize both the theoretical complexity and the subversive potential of post-structuralist philosophy by "replacing them with a generalized nostalgia for humanistic ideals" (Braidotti 1991a, 3). Donna St Hill cannot be accused of nihilism; she cares too deeply about what happens in Caribbean society. She wants to redeem humanistic ideals because she thinks their opposition in post-modernist discourse is dangerous for Caribbean society. Mridula

Udayagiri (1995) shares a similar concern. However, where Udayagiri rightly questions whether "postmodern analysis constitute(s) the only genre of critique that can contribute to political action because it engages and confronts difference" (Udayagiri 1995, 161), St Hill wants to minimize and contain any focus on difference. Citing Maynard (1994), she is concerned that a focus on women's differences is not sufficient to take into account dimensions of power such as patriarchal and racist oppression. Ultimately St Hill is concerned with revealing relations of power in poor women's lives and providing what she sees as the best theoretical prescriptions for doing so.

In chapter 4 Michelle Rowley raises two key questions for feminist pedagogy. The first examines what she terms the hegemonic immanence of the "virtue of development". According to Rowley it encourages a predetermined closure on the need to disrupt the hierarchies and power bases that have come to feminists via the dominant development paradigms. Her second theoretical question shares a strategy common to the three essays in this section. It undertakes an internal critique as it cautions us as feminist scholars to be always aware that immanent impulses are already at work in our critique of development.

Rowley is struck by attempts to mask the inherent power structures in development debates. In fact she engages with and effectively shows the relevance of the type of analysis that St Hill warns against. Yet, with St Hill, she critiques the "celebration of difference" within post-modern discourse on gender and development. Rowley's and St Hill's analyses complement and contradict each other. They apply a healthy scepticism about what they both see as the veneration of difference in feminist scholarship, yet they depart in terms of which theoretical approach is more useful. Rowley is not at all interested in the homogenizing effects of a monolithic, universalist humanist project, nor in seeing women in the South as vulnerable victims. Rowley uses the very post-modernist analytical techniques that St Hill decries to arrive at conclusions shared by both. This raises an epistemological question as to which is more useful in generating knowledge. Is it the application of a clearly demarcated conceptual frame, or an overt or subliminal political will driving the use of a particular theoretical frame for arriving at an overarching aim? Both scholars care deeply about a Caribbean feminist project and want similar ends. St Hill vests more in the methodology utilized, while Rowley sees methodology as a tool with which to advance a priori objectives for feminist scholarship in the region.

The critique of difference continues in the work of Patricia Mohammed in chapter 5, which also begins the second section, Theorizing Historiography, Historicizing Gender and Sexuality. The authors here either offer a sustained critique of the deficiencies of Caribbean historiography with respect to a feminist project or they theorize sexuality from a historical and contemporary perspective. Mohammed offers a rich, nuanced analysis of the intersectionality of feminist historiography with women's history and the project of engendering history. She notes that if the problem of gender for women was the struggle against patriarchy, then the problem of gender for men is the struggle to maintain patriarchal privilege.

Mohammed sets out to examine how history has benefited from the intervention of women's history and gender history and whether there is a difference between women's history and gender history. She defines gender history as a member of the family of feminist theory – a derivative. Mohammed's work underscores the contested heterogeneous grounding of feminist theorizing. She refers to gender as a range of different ideas and debates on which there is no consensus among either scholars or practitioners in the field of gender studies or policy formulation. In mapping out gender theory as a subset of feminist theory, Mohammed reminds us that "how we impose a feminist consciousness on the past must also be informed by a profound understanding of how gender is perceived and acted out during each historical period". She states that, in the last four decades, gender theory has shifted emphases from being equated with woman – with sex-role stereotyping, gender-role stereotyping, gender-role socialization and social constructionism – to extensive interdisciplinary debates drawing on anthropology, sociology, biology, psychology and psychoanalysis.

Mohammed demonstrates that history provides a space from which new ways of viewing gender may be continuously derived and from which new challenges to existing theory may emerge. She concludes by suggesting that feminist theory in the Caribbean began with a radical break from mainstream Western discourse because of the specific ways in which gender identities were constructed in the region.

In chapter 6 Richard Goodridge advances a very provocative and necessary diagnosis that a defect exists in Caribbean gender scholarship, particularly as it relates to historical analysis of gender. He argues that this condition exists because this scholarship is not grounded in African history and in a thorough understanding of gender regimes in African countries. As an outcome, the generalized discussion that arises results in some significant areas of omission. Goodridge charges that the arguments offered on female slave resistance by Beckles (1999), Mair (1987), Shepherd (1999) and others "do not appear to be grounded sufficiently in an exposition of African socio-economic and political practices".

To the extent that many popular references are made to African antecedents in shaping historical and contemporary Caribbean gender relations, this work makes a vital contribution to theorizing gender in the Caribbean. Goodridge offers a number of suggestions for further research in Caribbean gender studies. He points out that we need to study the masculinity of Muslim men in the Caribbean, and to examine the role Amerindian women played in pre-Columbian and pre-colonial Caribbean society.

In chapter 7 Hilary Beckles contributes a reconstruction of the world inhabited by enslaved women. His exposition spans pregnancy, lactation, fieldwork, housework and work as urban labourers. He argues that it was a world dominated by racist, patriarchal ideologies where, according to Beckles, to "extract two streams of return from female 'property' . . . [w]hite masculinity understood and practised the culture of accumulation". He observes that a notable feature of gender systems within slavery was the defeminization of enslaved women as a strategy to extract maximum labour and to perpetuate physical and psychological brutality.

However, Beckles shows how the shifting character of gender ideologies in the last quarter of the eighteenth century changed in response to developments in West Indian political economy. This necessitated a shift in focus from the slave ship to the womb of the enslaved woman as a means of guaranteeing a cheaper labour force. This development generated a new set of policies within the region to stimulate fertility, increase the birth rate and reduce infant mortality rates as a means of enhancing the reproduction of the enslaved labour force. These new strategies hinged on reconstructing the role of enslaved black women as fertile and maternal, and introducing structural features to ameliorate conditions for them.

In chapter 8 Kamala Kempadoo asserts that the reduction of sexual relations to a gendered dynamic is inadequate to theorize the various histories, experiences and everyday realities of the organization and exploitation of sexuality around the world. She furthers her argument by examining the construction of prostitution in colonial and post-colonial Caribbean societies. Her analysis is an attempt to complicate the existing theorizing of prostitution rather than an offering of an alternative theoretical framework.

Kempadoo also addresses the theme of Caribbean masculinity, a focus that becomes increasingly stronger in the following chapters. She critiques the fact that little has been done to examine policies that encouraged the construction of the black male stud, and how this informed ideas about black male sexuality. What emerges in this section is an indictment of Caribbean historiography for its failure to fully explore the power dimensions of gender by asking new questions about old historical data and assumptions.

Goodridge laments the failure of historical and contemporary research in Caribbean historiography and gender studies to acknowledge, investigate and grapple with African antecedents to the construction and expression of gender relations in the Caribbean. Kempadoo questions the lacunae in Caribbean historiography on black male sexuality and white women's sexual agency that maintain a void in our understanding of colonial sexualities. The authors' cumulative restlessness with the state of existing scholarship on gender indicates the future of interdisciplinary research on gender in the Caribbean. The gaps they identify are the gaps to be plugged by collaborative interdisciplinary research.

Kempadoo declares that the exoticization of the cultural "other" and the brown woman (with insufficient attention paid to black men's and white women's sexuality) was infused into new relations of power and privilege. These in turn were structured through anti-colonial and nationalist struggles for political independence. In analysing contemporary expressions of the racialized, exoticized sexualities of Caribbean women, Kempadoo notes that male sex-tourists believe that women in their respective home countries enjoy excessive power through which additional male authority is undermined. She continues that, as sex-tourists in the Caribbean, they are able to fully reaffirm their masculinity through sexual relations based on their racialized/cultural economic power. Similarly, European and North American female tourists experiment with and expand their gender identities through exercising economic control over men while retaining a sexualized femininity.

Again we observe the attention paid to repeating patterns and prevalence of power: the power of sex, the power of particular constructions of sexuality, the power of race, of economics, of gender identities, of knowledge. The analyses show that, in every sphere of life, relations of power undercut relations of gender.

Gender, genre and cultural/literary discourse are the themes of part 3. In chapter 9 Jane Bryce begins this section by reading two texts, from two diasporic popular cultural forms, against each other. She interrogates these texts to discover what they reveal "about form and identity, about the creative choices being made by a new generation of cultural practitioners and the way they negotiate questions of race, gender and cultural multiplicity". Bryce maintains that both works, one a film and the other a novel, revolve around the themes of gender, sexuality and power. She dissects the construction of black masculinity in diasporan identity as counter to identity, oppositional, authoritarian, homocentric, highly sexualized and dangerous. She argues that the film dwells on an explicit, violent, disenfranchised black masculinity that reveals the feminine as escape to "Africa" and as an alternative to disenfranchised black men. On the other hand, in the novel feminine power is openly expressed, not as an alternative escapist fantasy. It becomes a natural part of the search for a solution that involves a dialogue with the past towards reconfiguring the present. Bryce throws up the contradiction between Africa as homeland and the criticism levelled by Goodridge that insufficient scholarly attention is paid to African history in examining the extent to which the antecedents of gender in Africa influence contemporary Caribbean gender systems.

In chapter 10 Margaret Gill reads key literary statements and models that George Lamming proposes in two of his novels. She does this to demonstrate that some traditional West Indian literary texts and critical writings, produced mainly by men, hold remarkably similar questions and interests in common with feminist literary theory. She maintains that, unlike texts produced by Euro-American canonical writers, West

Indian texts often investigate women's conditions and account for their experiences with complexity. Gill revisits the theme of Caribbean masculinity from an unusual perspective. Through a rereading of these two texts, she attempts to redeem traditional literary texts written by men. Gill is careful to emphasize that she makes no claim that Lamming's theories and models are feminist. Instead she wants to reveal how a shared concern about challenging hegemonic oppressions (of which she states colonialism and patriarchy are only two) may also share strategies and goals common to feminist literary theories. She views these common strands as holding possibilities for new alliances, such as mining (male) West Indian fictional texts for theoretical insights, and using Euro-American feminist ideas to interrogate West Indian thought.

In parts 4 and 5 the contributors confront the operations of the power dimensions of gender in the post-colonial, post-independent Caribbean. They explore the confluences of gender and power in the public domain of the state. Part 4 focuses on a feminist theorizing of citizenship in terms of how constitutions construct women's citizenship or how the state conceptualizes women's economic agency.

Tracy Robinson begins theorizing women's citizenship in this section by immediately problematizing the often-repeated statement that the Caribbean woman is born to equal rights because Caribbean constitutions guarantee fundamental rights and freedoms to all individuals – regardless of gender. Her entry point is therefore to take issue with the view that women's citizenship is uncontroversial and has been resolved by the pre-independence enfranchisement of women and by independence and post-independence constitutional provisions. Her greater concern is the fact that women's citizenship has often been seen as irrelevant to the pressing issues facing women in the Caribbean.

Robinson reflects the feminist theoretical restlessness and dissatisfaction with the status quo in Caribbean feminist scholarship that is so evident in part 1. She seeks to reinvigorate debate and force new questions on the intersections of gender and citizenship as a way of recovering women's citizenship. She is very much aware that the idea and meaning of citizenship hold no final, foundational truth for women. Yet the whole thrust of her theorizing is not only to demonstrate the complications for contemporary understanding of woman the citizen that are embedded in the law, but to call Caribbean feminists to task for failing to interrogate the law in order to expose its deeply problematic and contrary conceptualization of women. Robinson turns a feminist lens on law and seeks to remove it from its omniscient, omnipotent vantage point in Caribbean societies. Robinson's feminist project is to interrogate the law on its relationship with woman the citizen, to expose its patriarchal genealogy and embedded asymmetrical gendered dynamics of power and practice.

She locates her analysis in the texts, interpretations and processes of transforming the constitutions of the Commonwealth Caribbean. Her larger context is the relationship between life and law. Robinson maintains that "the renewal of a meaningful discourse about citizenship in the Caribbean will show that, notwithstanding the gender neutrality of many citizenship laws in the Caribbean and the language of equality implied in Caribbean constitutions, men remain the paradigm of a citizen and, in significant measure, women are included as citizens through their relationship to men".

Ann Denis theorizes a gendered examination of work in the Commonwealth Caribbean. Her chapter supplies a strong feminist theoretical framework for assessing women's work. Denis critically reviews liberal, Marxist/socialist, neo-Weberian, materialist and post-modernist feminist theories in assessing what exactly constitutes women's work. She then evaluates the adequacy of these theoretical frames for conceptualizing women's work in Caribbean societies. Denis undertakes a detailed investigation of the theoretical literature and empirical studies on work in the Caribbean. She then creates a definition of work that encompasses "intentionality or obligation, including activities both paid and unpaid (revenue generating or not) done in both the public and private spheres, and including the possibility of multiple concurrent activities of work". Denis demonstrates that a gendered analysis of work challenges Western feminisms, a challenge she views as potentially strengthening for feminist theory.

Elsa Leo-Rhynie offers us an area of engagement fraught with ambiguity and ambivalence. This area is the confluence of gender, power and leadership. In this instance she explores the intersection of gender and power in electoral contests for student government at the Mona campus of the University of the West Indies. She observes that the continued absence of women in the top leadership positions of the Guild of Students is puzzling, given two facts often dragged out to support assumptions about male marginalization in tertiary education. First, since 1983 women have outnumbered men on the campus, and second, young women would be expected to be more assertive in seeking leadership, unlike women of previous generations, who were assumed to be more traditional about issues of power and politics. This work reminds us of the question Barry Chevannes poses and answers in the following: "Are males being marginalized? Certainly not, if the main factor being considered is power. Despite the increasing percentage of women at the University of the West Indies, it is the men who are elected to the seat of student power" (Chevannes 1999, 33). The study centres on themes emerging from the experiences of eight female members of student government in the late 1990s. Leo-Rhynie notes that while these narratives cover a small sample, they do have explanatory power. She concludes this study by noting that the influence of women on the campus is being controlled through blatant as well as subtle use of power to deny them access to certain leadership positions.

The final section interrogates the contemporary discourse on masculinity by approaching it as another manifestation of gender and power in the public domain. Aviston Downes and I engage with the thesis of the marginalization of the black Caribbean male from two complementary but differing disciplinary entry points. Aviston Downes uses Caribbean historiography to cross-examine Errol Miller's thesis. He amply illustrates the nineteenth-century genesis of gender ideologies informing hegemonic masculinity, as played out in the Barbadian colonial teaching service. I locate my analysis and critique of the thesis in changes in the political economy of gender in the late-twentieth-century Caribbean.

In reviewing research on the feminization of the teaching profession, Downes states, "The preoccupation of this scholarship with numerical ratios too often obscures the more fundamental issues of how gender ideologies were and are mobilized to justify the inequitable allocation of power, authority, resources and rewards within formal education structures." Downes dismisses the concept, as developed so far, in attempting to provide analytical insights into gender issues in education. He asserts that, apart from its crude descriptive value and its capacity to capture the perception and prejudices of female encroachment on previously male-dominated spheres, the concept cannot provide adequate theoretical insights.

Downes's research demonstrates that concerns about the feminization of teaching coexisted with policies to give women responsibility for delivery of the primary education product, while men continued to dominate the administrative and senior levels of the system. He concludes that the emergence of coeducation did not change the ideological perspective that viewed women principally as nurturers and held that they should be confined to the lowest salary scale.

In the final chapter I add a contemporary critique to the historical analysis of the male-marginalization thesis that Downes supplies. I argue that Miller's thesis of male marginalization is flawed in its construct, thus rendering its core assumptions more political than epistemological. Three of the several weaknesses I identify in Miller's thesis are that it places too much emphasis on coeducation, which is not universal in the region; it overemphasizes changes in material and ideological gender relations affecting Caribbean women; and it fails to examine men's gender identities and the construct and content of Caribbean masculinities. Rather than produce an epistemological breakthrough offering new knowledge about Caribbean men, I maintain that Miller's thesis simply posits men as having a priori rights to the resources of the post-independent Caribbean state. As necessary as research on Caribbean men and masculinity is, the thesis does not advance an understanding of what is ontologically different in the lives of Caribbean men. Instead an explanatory model is offered based primarily on external factors and a seeming desire to preserve a pristine, mythologized past, rather than being an analysis of the juncture where Caribbean men interact with a changing political economy. I conclude that the weaknesses of the current thesis underscore the need for a rigorous examination of the issues shaping Caribbean masculinity.

In conclusion, I move against the grain of issuing a standard stock of recommendations and offer instead a set of questions for reflection and strategizing. Stimulated by Elizabeth Grosz's examination of theories of power and subjectivity, these questions are meant to indicate the new practices that should emerge as we seek to discover these answers. Caribbean feminist theory must serve our societies in general and women in particular. Our work here cannot go beyond the social realities experienced by women and men in our societies. I am partial to Barbara

Christian's caution to stay rooted, to have our theorizing engage in continuous dialogue with both feminist and patriarchal practices.

In that vein I ask, Have we offered mechanisms for developing a strategy? Do we recognize the competing realities and alignments of power within and against which our theorizing operates? Are we offering a set of strategic interventions into patriarchal, social and theoretical paradigms and practice? Have we developed or suggested a versatile and wide-ranging set of conceptual tools and methodological procedures (Grosz 1990, 59)?

⚜Part II⚜

Epistemological Inquiries, Feminist Restlessness

Chapter 2

Theorizing the Shift from "Woman" to "Gender" in Caribbean Feminist Discourse

The Power Relations of Creating Knowledge

EUDINE BARRITEAU

Where have all the women gone?
Long time passing,
Where have all the women gone?
Long, long time ago?
Where have all the women gone?
Gone to Gender every one
When will we ever learn?
When will we ever learn?[1]

This lack of intellectual clarity is inextricably bound up with the political contradictions produced by our desire as women to escape domination on the one hand, and our fear that we might lose what seem to be fundamental social categories on the other. (Delphy 1991, 1)

Introduction: Where Have All the Women Gone?

In this analysis I interrogate the conceptual confusion, policy dilemmas and politics of deception and fragmentation that arise from and in feminist investigations from the unproblematized shift to the social relations of gender[2] as an analytical framework. Feminists and others now use gender as the primary and often sole analytical frame to examine the multiple, contradictory and often harsh realities of Caribbean women's lives. In the process of making the transition to gender we ignored or wished away some fundamental epistemological and ontological questions that are now threatening the relevance and viability of feminist scholarship and the women's movement in the Caribbean region. Using a feminist perspective, I begin a process of addressing these questions as a way of making explicit many of the grey areas that now cloud the use of the social relations of gender as the main analytical framework for investigating chronic conditions of inequality in women's lives. I argue that to leave these ambiguities unexamined leads to questioning of a feminist agenda to promote justice and fairness.

Some of the questions that arise are the following: What do the social relations of gender bring to an understanding of women's lives in the Caribbean? What do feminist scholarship and women gain by moving to gender? What have we lost? Why is there so much confusion? What were the structures and issues of other frames of analysis? What are the different ontological premises of the earlier approaches? I do not think we have done enough to establish the continuities between earlier feminist frames of analysis and the social relations of gender. We have not set out clearly what "gender" can do and cannot do. We have not addressed whether we need to continue to deploy earlier or other methodologies, and if not, why not? Because as Caribbean feminists we have not sought to answer these questions, we are unprepared for the hijacking of the explanatory powers of the social relations of gender and the deliberately and increasingly successful moves to divorce it from its feminist roots. So far we are unable to prevent the distortions of how it is now used.

This work is therefore an epistemological project. It begins in theorizing and ends with questions that seek to disrupt this all too facile accommodation and dilution of the analytical worth that the social relations of gender bring to feminism. Ultimately I want Caribbean feminists to confront the politics and power relations inherent in creating new knowledges about women's lives. In the process I attempt to both politicize and problematize recent developments in Caribbean feminist discourse and simultaneously to isolate features for comparative analysis with other countries.

In formulating extensive critiques of society, feminists investigated the public and private domains, the state and the economy, sexuality, mothering and other institutions and relations of society; feminists created and applied analytical tools to every dimension of women's lives. The methodologies and concepts of gender analysis joined a long and distinguished list of feminist explanatory tools that include *biology is destiny, the personal is political, dual systems analysis, sexual division of labour, capitalist patriarchy,* the *sex/gender system,* the *public/private dichotomy, multiple consciousness, multiple jeopardies, africana womanism,* the *contours of a black feminist epistemology,* and *identity politics.*[3] The social relations of gender enabled many feminists "to distinguish culturally specific characteristics associated with masculinity and femininity from biological features" (Hawkesworth 1997, 650). From their investigations feminists defined the social relations of gender to refer to a complex system of power played out in the different and often unequal experiences of women and men.

Its introduction to feminist discourse was not unproblematic. It was and is resisted, especially by radical feminists (Bell and Klein 1996),[4] but in spite of their warnings "gender" now demarcates the creation of knowledge about women, even though in the Caribbean it is becoming increasingly difficult to use gender to do so. The fact that the analytical strengths of gender analysis are being eroded has to do with very deliberate efforts within societies to nurture the resiliency of patriarchal relations, and not with any internal flaw in its theorizing. The social relations of gender advanced our understanding of the systemic character of women's experiences of material and ideological subordination and ongoing attempts to maintain these.

Joan Scott delineated four integral aspects of the social relations of gender, as well as defining it as a constitutive element of social relationships based on perceived differences between the sexes, and a primary way of signalling relationships of power (Scott 1986, 1067). The four elements she identifies (p. 1068) are

- culturally available symbols that evoke multiple (and often contradictory) representations;
- normative interpretations that set forth meanings of the symbols;
- a notion of politics as well as reference to social institutions and organizations; and subjectivity.

I define gender to refer to "complex systems of personal and social relations of power through which women and men are socially created and maintained and through which they gain access to, or are allocated status, power and material resources within society" (Barriteau 1998c, 188; 1994).

> Gender relations constitute the continuous social, political, economic, cultural, and psychological expressions of the material and ideological aspects of a gender system. Gender relations encode and sometimes mask unequal power relations between women and men and between women and the state. The extent to which the material and ideological dimensions of gender relations reinforce each other is frequently ignored. The extent to which prevailing ideologies affect or effect women's access to status, power and resources is rarely examined. (Barriteau 1998c, 189)

In the region there is no common understanding or shared concept of what we mean by gender. The foundational ideal of gender justice is a very contested one and has always been so from the time it entered Caribbean feminist discourse. Currently there are at least ten competing meanings of gender:

1. A more sophisticated concept for sex[5] (Miller 1994, 127)
2. Behavioural traits mapped onto biological differences or markers (Phillips 2002)
3. A synonym for women and men (Wilkie 1999)
4. Programmes and policies to introduce and maintain a focus on men (*Trinidad Guardian* 2000)
5. Women
6. Benign socialization that reproduces males and females as men and women (Trinidad and Tobago 1999)
7. Relations of power created and maintained in the hierarchies and values placed on masculine and feminine identities as well as access to and distribution of material and non-material resources such as status and power (Hawkesworth 1997; Barriteau 1994, 2000b, 1998c, 2001)
8. New, slick feminist strategies for dominating and emasculating men (*Sunday Advocate* 2000)
9. New, slick, sexist strategies for maintaining patriarchy (Taitt 2000)
10. Anti-religious, anti-family, anarchist anti-social beliefs (Wilkie 1997)

Tracking Gender, Losing Women

There is a relatively long trajectory in feminist theorizing on the social relations of gender. Yet, in feminist analysis and the gender and development discourse, four major periods and contributions marked the development of the concept as we know it. These periods are

- 1920 to 1935: an early breakthrough
- 1949 to 1975: the specific character of gender oppression
- 1970 to 1975: sex/gender systems; gender difference due to male dominance
- 1975 to present: relations of power in relations of gender.

The earliest proto-feminist awareness of the concept is found in the work of anthropologist Margaret Mead (1935). In identifying the key distinguishing features of the concept, Mead takes the view that sex is a biological fact, while gender behaviour is a social construction (Humm 1990, 84). Mead arrived at this conclusion by investigating the ways different societies treated motherhood in order to demonstrate the socially constructed origins of women's roles (gender) and how these operate in society. She revealed that "[t]he behaviour, attitudes and feelings different cultures attribute to, or expect from, motherhood change with different social conditions (Humm 1990, 142; Mead 1949). Accordingly, if mothering was natural, that is, innate to women, it would not be possible to change women's experiences of mothering, their approaches to it or their desire to be mothers. Neither would society place differing values on mothering over different time periods.

Mead's pioneering analysis contributed a breakthrough in feminist investigations of women's experiences in society and it demonstrates how ideologies of gender influence how society perceives and places different and hierarchical values on women's and men's roles. She indicates how these perceptions change and are manipulated to satisfy other societal objectives.

In *The Second Sex* Simone de Beauvoir contributed the next significant thrust in theorizing the analytical framework of gender. In 1949 she paved the way for abandoning a historical materialist explanation of women's subordination. "We must look beyond the historical materialism that perceives men and women as no more than economic units to comprehend the women's situation" (1949, 91). She argues that Engels tries unsuccessfully to reduce the antagonisms of the sexes to class conflict, but insists that the division of labour by sex and the division of society into classes cannot be confused. For one, there is no biological basis for the separation of class. For another, women – or men, for that matter – cannot be regarded simply as workers. A woman's reproductive functions are as important as her productive capacity. De Beauvoir's greatest insight in this piece is her statement that to "do away with family is not necessarily to emancipate women" (1949, 89). De Beauvoir's analysis of women's situation in 1949 contains a rudimentary recognition of the specificity of oppressive gender relations (Barriteau 1995b, 36). Rosemary Tong contends that, anticipating later feminist analysis, de Beauvoir "specified social roles as the primary mechanisms the self, or subject, uses to control the other, the object" (Tong 1992, 206). This is a substantial input. Margaret Mead isolated the social origins of women's and men's roles and destabilized the belief that these differentiated roles arise in biology. De Beauvoir identified the differently valued and hierarchical structures built into these roles. She showed how the social roles men perform were used to objectify women and generate control over women's social roles. According to de Beauvoir, women were not born – they were constructed and turned into the other, an object.

In 1975 American anthropologist Gayle Rubin supplied the third major plank in theorizing the social relations of gender. Rubin theorized the *sex/gender system* as the source of women's subordination. She used the concept to define how women in different societies experience similar processes of gender identity formation that oppress women and limit their lives (Humm 1990, 195). Rubin states that there is a universal system of sexual and reproductive relations in which all societies organize the biological differences between women and men (sex) into the specific arrangements (gender) that always place women at a disadvantage with men and therefore institutionalize women's oppression.

Rubin's insights constituted another significant breakthrough for feminist analysis and the evolution of the concept of the social relations of gender. Before Rubin's analysis, feminists theorized that what was wrong for women arose in exclusion from the public sphere, in biology or in the capitalist relations of production. The "biology is destiny" argument stated that women experienced oppression because our bodies were physically different and regarded as inferior. Accordingly, to be born woman meant to be born to suffer oppression. The *biological determinism* of this analysis was fatalistic, rigid and limiting. It froze women as victims and men as oppressors.

Jane Flax considers Rubin's concept of the sex/gender system as offering one of the first contemporary accounts of gender relations (Flax 1990b, 143–44). Flax asserts that Rubin challenges the predominant beliefs about sexuality and introduces the relations of gender as different from sex but rooted in it. Rubin locates the origin of gender systems and male dominance in the way that society takes biological sex and transforms it into gender. It does this through the way that family and kinship structures operate and through the *sexual division of labour* arising from those operations. Rubin contributes the following to the feminist concept of gender. She establishes a distinction between biology and the existence of the family, *and* between the existence of the family and the particular forms of organization of family functions and family structures. She states that the subordination of women can be seen as a product or outcome of the relationships by which sex and gender are organized and produced (Flax 1990b, 144).

Kate Millet and Shulamith Firestone further radicalized contemporary thinking about relations of gender. Firestone argues that gender distinctions structure every aspect of our lives by creating the unquestioned framework within which society views women and men (Firestone 1970; Humm 1990, 84). She concludes that gender difference is an elaborate system of male dominance (Humm 1990, 84).

Detractors want to keep as subjugated knowledge the fact that using gender as an analytical framework is a feminist contribution. The desire to contain feminist contributions within epistemology arises in the power relations and politics of creating knowledge.[6] More determined attempts are now being made to curb feminist advancement and, ironically, one of its most powerful tools is being deployed against it. For example, it is very common to hear women and men at conferences and workshops say, "I don't want to hear anything about feminism or feminists; I just want to deal with gender."[7] This situation is made worse by the fact that in everyday usage gender can mean almost anything. This strategy of denying the analytical weight of gender neuters the concept and makes it acceptable. This practice removes the analytical worth and significant insights that feminist research has revealed about women's unequal and subordinate positions. Practically, it retards the development of policies and programmes intended to assist women with the disproportionate responsibilities they bear for maintaining families and their right to be treated as autonomous citizens.

Gone to Gender Every One

> What relationship feminist understandings of gender have to dominant gender models and ideologies; can the former ever be entirely free of the latter; is this what we are striving for? This is a matter of subjectivity and self-identity, as well as a matter of politics. (Moore 1994, 15)

Henrietta Moore is not arguing for a universal feminist objectivity. The questions she raises remind us to consider the interconnections of our subjectivity, the political spaces we occupy and our political practices. Feminist understandings of gender cannot and should not try to be free of dominant gender models and ideologies. The searches we engage in should create new appreciation of the complex systems of gender that exist. They should enable us to introduce new models and to analyse and interpret competing gender ideologies.

As it stands now the concept of gender is in danger of becoming barren. Soon it may be unable to reproduce or give birth to new feminist investigations. What about this framework has been overlooked? Why is gender in danger of becoming sterile? Gender makes a very fundamental contribution to feminist theorizing that has been widely overlooked, or at best misunderstood. Before feminists used the social relations of gender, women's ontology was always examined, explained or approached in relation to that of men. Epistemologically, women were always comprehended through an androcentric lens and seen as deficient men. Jane Flax observes that that particular explanation of women's being is a recurring, consistent construct of western political philosophy (1992, 453). The construct of woman-the-deformed-or-incomplete-male is seen in the works of Aristotle, St Augustine, Machiavelli, Hobbes, Locke, Rousseau, Kant, Hegel and Freud, just some of the patriarchs of the Western political/philosophical tradition (Agonito 1977).

Yet the social relations of gender introduced two powerful ontological points of departure for women and men. First, the social relations of gender disrupted the linear continuity between biology and being, and destabilized the concept of biology as destiny. Second, the concept freed women's subjectivity from androcentric interpretations. The social relations of gender reinforced what de Beauvoir introduced to feminist theory – an existentialist understanding of the category "woman" which cannot be reduced "downward" to biology or "upward" to cultural constructions of gender (Lovell 2003, 94).

We have run with the changes this concept introduced as it relates to feminist analyses of male being and behaviour, and ignored or minimized what it tells us about women's ontology. As for women, the social relations of gender freed men from being prisoners of biology. It was demonstrated that men, like women, are recreated by the gendered power relations in societies. These relations are asymmetric and value male behaviour and roles more than those of females. But they destabilized the argument that men are intrinsically evil and exist to conquer women.

If the social relations of gender freed men from genetic programming to be oppressors, for women they went beyond being freed from their eternal status as victims. By showing that both women and men are socially constituted beings subject to asymmetrical power relations, the social relations of gender freed women from being understood, ontologically and epistemologically, from androcentric perspectives. The social relations of gender demonstrate that yes, women are different from men, but that difference is not within the recurring traditional frame that situates women in opposition to men.

That old Cartesian frame is binary and hierarchical. It argues that what men are, women are not, and vice versa. Since early liberal feminists like Mary Wollestonecraft, considerable intellectual energy has been consumed resisting the concept of woman as an empty category, the deformed sperm or mutilated male (Ross 1912). The practical intent of these works was to insist on a focus upon women. However, the theoretical baggage of their analyses remained grounded in redeeming women's ontology from male-defined categories. Many well-meaning feminists have struggled to overturn these binary categories and prove that, given the right opportunities, women are not different to men. From a post-modernist feminist perspective there is no need to explain women in relation to men. "Both women and men are equally implicated as the subjects of gendered constructs. Both are located in gendered societies. The recognition that men are equally gendered does not alter the reality that social relations predominantly benefit men" (Barriteau 1992, 16).

Recent developments in the uses of gender in the anglophone Caribbean underscore Elizabeth Potter's points that gender politics intersect with the production of knowledge and that the production of knowledge is a social or communal affair (Alcoff and Potter 1993, 9; Potter 1993, 165). The scenario in the Caribbean goes further. The politics of creating knowledge around gender expose attempts both to subvert the analytical strengths that the social relations of gender offer to understanding the subjectivity of women and to argue that women do not constitute legitimate subjects for gender analysis.

As a result, a vexing tension currently plagues several dimensions of Caribbean feminist scholarship and the women's movement. It paralyses analysis and activism. Women as subjects are rapidly disappearing from the discourses of gender. Gender is now not thought of as part of a feminist discourse. Ironically, the multiple openings of the categories that "women" made possible by gender analysis are now being occluded and closed off by insisting that "gender" is a synonym for women-and-men, or that doing gender means a simultaneous focus on women and men. The rich contributions made by differing schools of feminist thought have taken us to the point where the subjectivity of women as embodied beings has gained an epistemological significance and has finally transcended the empty ontological category of not-man. Paradoxically, at this very juncture we see the viability of feminist activism on the verge of regressing to a simplistic understanding of the way forward.

It is difficult to identify any recent publication of Caribbean feminist scholarship in which the word "women" predominates when compared to the word "gender". We are all enamoured of the latter term. In volume 59 (summer 1998) of the journal *Feminist Review* ("Rethinking Caribbean Difference"), of twelve articles by Caribbean feminist scholars, including mine, only four name the subject "women".[8] In *Caribbean Portraits: Essays on Gender Ideologies and Identities* (Barrow 1998b), the authors of seven chapters use the words "woman" or "women" in their titles, of a total of twenty-four chapters in the book. Contrast this with the 1986 two-volume collection of essays from the Women in the Caribbean Project (WICP), published in the journal *Social and Economic Studies*. The word "gender" is not used in the titles of any of the four-teen articles. Nine mention women explicitly in the titles, three discuss the methodology or research agenda flowing from the project, and the other two are about women.

As a focus of international development assistance and national governmental policies and machineries, women as subjects are being effaced. In Barbados the Bureau of Women's Affairs has been renamed the Bureau of Gender Affairs, with a mandate to look after the interests of boys and men (*Sun on Saturday* 1999, 5). In St Vincent and the Grenadines the Bureau of Women's Affairs will be renamed the Bureau of Gender Equality,[9] and in Trinidad and Tobago there has been a Division of Gender Affairs since 1997. In St Lucia on International Women's Day, Prime Minister Dr Kenny Anthony commented on the status of gender relations in that country. Shortly after that St Lucia's Bureau of Women's Affairs was renamed the Bureau of Gender Relations. Antigua and Barbuda now has a Directorate of Gender Affairs (Taitt 1998) but has never had an elected woman sit in Parliament (Emmanuel 1992; Barriteau 1998a). In Dominica the then newly elected minister with responsibility for women's affairs stated that Dominican men are marginalized and suffering in society, and the Bureau of Women's Affairs would be renamed the Bureau of Gender Affairs in order to focus on Dominican men (*Trinidad Guardian* 2000, 7). To cap off all these changes, in an executive management meeting in January 1999 the Women and Development Programme of the Caribbean Community (CARICOM) Secretariat was renamed the Gender and Development Programme. The women's affairs officer – the person in charge of executing the programme – learned of the change from the minutes of the meeting. There were no prior discussions or any indication that the name would be changed.[10]

The Canadian International Development Agency's (CIDA) Caribbean office invited comments on the male-marginalization thesis since, in planning a programme on gender equity, local staff had informed CIDA that in the Caribbean men are the ones who are disadvantaged on the basis of gender.[11] The Commonwealth Secretariat commissioned a background paper, "Re-examining Issues of 'Male Marginalisation' and

'Masculinity' in the Caribbean: The Need for a New Policy Approach"
(Barriteau 2000c), to address similar concerns.[12]

At the level where these developments affect feminist politics or
activism we are aware that something fundamental has changed. Yet we
are not quite sure what it is or how to respond. At the level where these
modifications are beginning to reconfigure feminist investigations of
social life, we recognize their existence but we have not problematized
what this means to feminist politics and research.

In 1987 Caribbean feminist scholar Lucille Mair began the process
of documenting and marking out the contours of this quandary. She
detected the power relations inherent in creating new knowledges about
women's lives. I use the questions she raises and contemporary occur-
rences as points of departure to explore what these changes are, what
they mean in the pursuit of gender justice and what is required if
Caribbean feminist scholarship and activism are to survive this challenge.

In the anglophone Caribbean two interrelated developments marked
the change in the conceptual framework and terminology used to examine the issues surrounding women's lives. In 1986 the University of the
West Indies (UWI) acknowledged the preparatory work undertaken by
campus-based women's studies groups to introduce the discipline of
women's studies into the academy. The UWI entered into a four-year
programme of Cooperation, Teaching and Research in Women and
Development Studies with the Institute of Social Studies in the Hague,
thus strengthening the embryonic project-based women's studies programme started in 1982. Caribbean feminists had begun to create and
disseminate knowledge about women's lives in the formal context of an
academic discipline. Their work enhanced the credibility and legitimacy
of feminist activism both within the academy and in the wider society.

In reviewing the establishment of the discipline of women's studies at
the UWI in the mid-1980s Lucille Mair (1988) confronts the emerging
power relations and politics of knowledge creation inherent in Caribbean
women's studies. She detected the coming struggle over feminist knowledge as a source of power for Caribbean women. She recognized the
reservations about and even resistance to efforts to institutionalize
women's studies that existed within the academy. She states that questions being asked included "Should it be called women's studies or

gender studies?"and "How feminist should such studies be?" Mair mentions that feminist academics were debating whether there is a place for men in women's studies and, if so, where (1988, 7) ?

The fact that feminists and other academics were debating whether there should be a feminist content to these new studies exposes the first stage of confusing the creation of feminist knowledge about women with its applications. It also exposes the latest attempts at the politics of containment. Feminists paid insufficient attention to "the suppression of feminist informed epistemologies as an exercise of power" and containment (Barriteau 1992, 6). While most of us collectively adopted the concept of gender as an analytical panacea for all our research and activist concerns, in our desire to continue to expose the adverse power relations in women's lives we did not bother to explore the genealogy of the concept or what it offered to feminist analysis. We did not investigate why suggestions were being made to do research on women uninformed by feminist perspectives, when it was feminist activism and analysis that had created the discipline of women's studies in the first place. Drawing on Foucault's analysis of power, I noted in 1992 that "control over what constitutes knowledge is the practice of power in areas not traditionally regarded as sources of power" (Foucault 1981; Barriteau 1992, 6).

Building on Lucille Mair's earlier questioning, I ask why gender studies and women's studies are posed in opposition, rather than gender studies being considered a particular methodology of women's studies. Why are they not seen as complementing each other? In 1986 we sowed the seeds of dilution when we allowed women as subjects to be confused with an analytical framework used to investigate the subjectivity of women. We began the process of watering down the need to investigate circumstances in women's lives when we allowed women as a focus to be confused with a particular way of revealing challenges in women's lives. Some contributors to that debate implied that gender studies were less threatening. Why would reducing or containing the feminist content of women's studies be a major concern? What is being protected by doing so? What is the knowledge created by feminist studies that must be suppressed or denied?

Mary Evans detected the appeal of the implied neutrality of gender and stated, "It is now socially convenient to abandon the uncompromising polarity of woman/man in favour of a more neutral term, a term which suggests that the interests of the sexes have now converged and that the differences in life chances between women and men are a matter of choice" (1990, 461). Similarly, in applying the concept in the development field, Eva Rathgeber also admits that "gender" is accepted as a more neutral term than "woman" (1995, 204).

Simultaneous with the debate surrounding the introduction of women's studies at the UWI was the ferment in feminist analytical frameworks. Many researchers and practitioners began to abandon earlier analytical frames as inadequate for revealing the complexities in women's lives. They shifted to gender both as an explanatory framework for women's experience of subordination and as a means of rethinking the naming of the discipline. In this regard the cautionary attitudes and emerging power struggles that Lucille Mair identifies were an additional dynamic for consideration and strategic positioning.

Long Time Passing . . .

> Firstly, what is gender? It is somewhat ironic that the term "gender," which was first coined by psychologists and then used by feminists to get away from the biologistic referent of the word sex, is now virtually synonymous with the latter word. Yet by using gender we are using a shorthand term which encodes a very crucial point: that our basic social identities as men and women are socially constructed rather than based on fixed biological characteristics. (Young 1988a, 98)

Caribbean feminists' shift to gender as an explanatory framework reflected successive streams of theorizing in feminist scholarship. These originated in feminist investigations into women's persistent experiences with a complex and punitive system of power differentials in everyday life. Feminists devoted considerable intellectual effort to searching for explanations for women's chronic and continuing experiences of subordination and adverse conditions in all dimensions of their lives.

Caribbean feminists' shift to "gender" occurred precisely when the academic structure for the discipline of women's studies was being strengthened and the environment for further feminist investigations enhanced by the programme of cooperation between the UWI and the Institute of Social Studies. This represented a critical moment. The point at which women's studies entered the academy was exactly the moment in which gender as an analytical framework gained ascendancy. Yet what emerged in popular discourse was not the analytical sophistication of the conceptual tools of gender, but rather a descriptive interpretation of gender to mean women and men. Feminist academics were engaged in conscious attempts to deepen the search for explanations for women's profoundly different and unequal experiences of political, economic and social life. The research thrust of that period became explicitly feminist in that it consciously sought to expose "oppression", "subordination" and "exploitation" in women's lives.

What should have been immediately explored by feminists, but was not engaged or perhaps adequately dealt with, is the diverse sentiments and opinions of the women and feminists interested in women's studies. Many of us had not resolved or even located some of the larger political implications and tensions of the new discipline. By its very content, women's studies is intellectually confrontational, challenging and subversive. It forces those directly involved in its teaching, research and dissemination to consider the profoundly patriarchal organization of Caribbean societies. Of course one may choose to sidestep these aspects and opt for a compensatory "we are just adding women's perspectives" approach. The irony of that location is that it does not alter the view of those who recognize the subversive character of a discipline that addresses how one-half of humanity has had to experience denial and exclusion.

Other women and men observing the development of the discipline will assume that what we are doing is questioning the fundamental unequal relations of power that is organized on the basis of gender – whether we do this or not – *and we should be doing this*. We may and should satisfy all the stringent rules of academia, but that by itself will not create or guarantee a ready welcome in the academy. We cannot afford to be naive about this, because the cautionary observers understand the long-term implications of research on women. For example, attorney-at-law Angus Wilkie argues that women and men are not meant to be equal and should not be treated like equals. He states that to do so will make men jealous of women and they will become violent against women. As a result women will be in a worse crisis than men. He concludes by insisting that women should be kept in their God-ordained subordinate roles (Wilkie 1999).

It is not accurate to say that psychologists were the first to coin the term gender, but the substantive point that Kate Young makes still stands. Some (but not much) of the current confusion arises from the fact that the term gender was not originally a feminist concept. Rosi Braidotti reminds us that "gender has a previous identity, derived from research in biology, linguistics, and psychology" (1991b, 8). Before the late 1960s the concept was used primarily to refer to the differences between feminine and masculine forms within language (Nicholson 1994, 80). But as it relates to feminist investigations of women's experiences of domination, gender has a precise meaning and a genealogy that predates its use in feminist discourses (Baron 1986; Braidotti 1991b; Hawkesworth 1997). It is the feminist insights that are being de-politicized and deliberately ignored in the rush to neutralize "gender".

Conclusion: When Will We Ever Learn?

Epistemologically the social relations of gender established women as social beings in their own right, requiring their own frames of analysis. They contribute to feminist knowledges about women's lives by deploying new methodologies. The reconceptualization of women thus introduced requires a different methodological approach in studying women's lives. Because they do not explain women in relation to men, the social relations of gender require new methodological approaches to studying the lives of women. This should be an exciting time for feminist scholarship in the Caribbean. In relation to theorizing Caribbean women's realities I demonstrated that, with the social relations of gender, research questions can no longer be posed as woman-in-relation-to-man; instead it is gendered woman interacting with and being acted upon by her social environment. The conceptual frame has shifted (Barriteau 1992, 20).

Practically, what this should mean is even more research on women and the need to devise new methodologies to re-examine all those fields that would have used an androcentric perspective. Instead, what seems to be happening is that the politics of knowledge creation are seeking to erase that aspect of the social relations of gender. All that is now promoted is the select aspect that men are also affected by relations of gender. We have not explored the fundamental shift from gaining an understanding of women's lives through androcentric lenses (or rejecting what those lenses reveal) to reconceptualizing women and men as subjects of asymmetrical relations of gender.

Yet many scholars and practitioners are deploying the notion that a shift to gender means a change from analysing relations of domination in women's lives to a simultaneous focus on women and men in all aspects of social investigations. A World Bank official argued in 1998 for reducing the focus on women because it has not worked effectively (Clarke 1998). We must first ask why interventions on behalf of women have not worked. Is it because policy-makers and researchers have not focused equally on men? Or is it because gendered notions of power coalesce to refuse to accommodate or accept women as equals? Are the two related? When we focus equally on men, as national machineries are now being mandated to do, will we see women accepted as equals or will we see attempts to contain the long-overdue gains that women have made? Are men the new victims? Are we so locked into binary, dichotomous thinking that we must always have oppressors and victims? From what set of practices and ideologies do problems for men arise? Do the legitimate problems that men experience arise from legislation, policies and practices that exist in the state and civil society?

Using insights from the social relations of gender means that men no longer occupy a transcendental, epistemological position. Like women, they are also constructed through relations of gender. This means that women and men exist in a gendered environment, but relations of gender have vastly differing outcomes for them. Shifting to gender certainly does not mean that women cease to experience relations of domination, even though it does demonstrate that these can be changed, since they are a product of social relations and not biology or nature.

Shifting to gender as an analytical frame certainly does not mean that the study of women is abandoned or that one cannot maintain an exclusive focus on women in research. Neither does it mean that gender studies must automatically include men. In research informed by gender the subject can be men alone, women alone or women and men. These constitute the subject of analysis, and the social relations of gender indicate the analytical frame that would be applied to the subject. One can have gender studies in which the subject is always men, and there is nothing wrong with the decision to investigate how men experience life; neither is it incorrect to examine women and men in gender analysis. However, the politics of containing knowledge about women's lives are saying that the shift to gender means that women are no longer legitimate subjects. This is wrong.

I do believe that men as gendered subjects should be studied and I support research and teaching on Caribbean masculinities. What I am challenging and in fact am interested in debunking is the position that to use gender analytically inherently means abandoning a focus on women's subjectivity and instead replacing it with a simultaneous focus on women and men. Even more perverse is the belief that research on women should cease and policies focusing on women should be abandoned. Feminist analyses of the social relations of gender underscored the dignity and humanity of man the social being, in spite of widespread and institutionalized violations of this, to the detriment of women. The social relations of gender must not now be used to erase women epistemologically or to serve as an excuse for abandoning meaningful social action on behalf of women.

Notes

1. To be sung to the tune of "Where Have All the Flowers Gone?" Lyrics and music by Pete Seeger, who was inspired by a passage from *And Quiet Flows the Don*, a novel by Mikhail Sholokhov; additional verse by Joe Hickerson. Copyright 1961–62, Falls River Music Inc., New York.

2. I use "gender" and "the social relations of gender" interchangeably. I use both to mean a feminist analytical category that brings to feminist theorizing its own set of conceptual tools and methodologies in order to yield additional insights into women's persistent but differing experiences of asymmetrical power relations in societies. In my critique of abuse of the concept, I make distinctions between the sophisticated feminist analytical category indicated by the concept of social relations of gender, and the pedestrian, but powerful, reductionist rendering of the term that bleaches it of its feminist roots and of any relevance to ongoing feminist investigations.

3. These are just representative of some feminist conceptual tools. For greater depth, see Maggie Humm, *The Dictionary of Feminist Theory* (1990), and similar works.

4. Radical feminists are opposed to using "gender" because they see it as decentring the subject "woman".
5. Voice of Barbados (radio station), 1996.
6. Dr Ikael Tafari, deputy chair of the Pan-African Commission, felt comfortable enough to call the centre in March 1999 and complain that we did not have sufficient male academics as presenters in a one-day conference, Theoretical Approaches to Gender in the Caribbean, and to name male academics who should be involved in any future work by the centre on gender, if our research efforts are to have legitimacy. The government-appointed Pan-African Commission has fourteen members, one of whom is a woman. I would like a graduate student of any sex to explore the epistemological and political dynamics of this situation.
7. This comment was made to me by a participant from a regional development institution at a Commonwealth workshop on gender-sensitive national budgets, Barbados, 23 April 1999.
8. Mohammed and Perkins 1999 may be the exception as a recent publication centring "woman". I do not mean to suggest that the more recent works do not examine women's subjectivity – they do. The work is more theoretically grounded and advances the WICP research. However, the perception hovers that to do gender means that one cannot examine women's lives.
9. Jeanie Ollivierre, coordinator of the Women's Affairs Department, Government of St Vincent and the Grenadines, telephone interview by Eudine Barriteau, 26 May 1999.
10. Gemma Tang Nain, women's affairs officer, CARICOM Secretariat, interview by Eudine Barriteau, 22 May 1999.
11. Ellen Hagerman, "Information Request on Male Marginalisation", e-mail message to Centre for Gender and Development Studies, University of the West Indies (Cave Hill, Barbados), 14 January 2000.
12. I do not suggest that Caribbean men do not experience problems with the material or ideological dimensions of gender or that gender analysis is not applicable to them. In fact I wrote the Commonwealth Secretariat background paper on men and masculinity in the region. I am focusing on the arguments given for no longer wanting to examine the effects of relations of gender on women's lives.

Chapter 3

Women and Difference in Caribbean Gender Theory

Notes towards a Strategic Universalist Feminism

DONNA ST HILL

Introduction

A prominent concern of gender and development theory has been to consider what empowerment for women would mean in different social contexts. This concern is an important one if female advancement is not to
continue to be out of reach for all but an elite stratum of women for
whom fortunate configurations of nation, class, race and sexuality have
allowed them to secure some individual levels of empowerment. If state-
of-the-art feminist theories of female empowerment are to apply to all
women, and not just a few women for fleeting moments in time, then it
is important that these philosophies are able to transcend the usual limitations of the cosmopolitan–communitarian impasse in political deliberations on universalizing human good. Feminists from both sides of the
philosophical divide have gone some considerable distance towards gendering the debate, but without resolving the central conflict. The post-
modern critique of social sciences has had a marked influence on feminist
theorizing of political justice across international boundaries, nuancing
the debate but at the same time leading to a theoretical cul-de-sac. To this
end, the purpose of this chapter is to question the relevance and value of

holding "difference", especially as it relates to culture and nationality, central to feminist theorizing on gender inequality in the contemporary Caribbean.

In theorizing gender inequality in the Caribbean, a long line of Caribbean gender specialists has been calling for respect for indigenous women's differences (Barriteau 1992, 1995a; Hart 1989a; Mohammed 1998; Wiltshire-Brodber 1988). These claims echo those by other women of the South and women of colour in the North that feminist theory frequently excludes women of colour because it is based on the experiences of white, Western, usually middle-class women, and in so doing excludes Southern women and women of colour. The region's theorists have not been left out of a global trend in which feminist discourse has turned to the local, the contextual and the particular, while repudiating past modernist excesses that are said to succumb to all-encompassing grand narratives and falsely universalizing assumptions about the human condition. This perspective views with suspicion and hostility those theories whose aim is to create formulations such as human progress, economic and social development, and sex equality. In this chapter I agree that we can no longer return to reliance on a single grand theory of feminism, or any social theory for that matter, for they have notoriously excluded women, people of colour and the powerless, with serious consequences. But I suggest that feminism cannot jettison all the promises of universal human progress and emancipation that are contained in the modernist project if all we get in return is a deconstruction of society and a value-absent post-modern focus on fragmentation and difference.

The reason that I want to go against this trend is that I am interested in theory's relevance for policy. Bad theory almost always leads to bad policy. I am particularly concerned with the impact of theory-linked policy because bad theory usually has the most severe consequences for the most vulnerable groups in society – the poor, the majority of whom are women and children. Therefore I begin with a theoretical focus that will relate foremost to the interests of that group of Caribbean women who suffer most under existing capitalist, patriarchal, white-supremacist social relations – low-income women of colour – and ask what a universal theory of gender justice could have to do with their lives. I start with the needs and priorities of poor women because in them we generally find the most complex and seemingly intractable cases of the reality of social inequalities in real people's lives. This is where my analysis begins, where Caribbean women's lived realities converge, because at the point where they enter society as equals, the whole race, class, gender and nation to which they belong will too be liberated. Therefore, as Peggy Antrobus, Barbadian feminist and member of the Third World feminist organization Development Alternatives for Women in a New Era (DAWN), puts it, "the strongest case for the focus on the poor Third World woman is that in her we find the conjecture of race, class, gender and nationality which symbolises underdevelopment" (1989, 202). This should not be taken to justify a single-minded focus on poor women to the neglect of non-poor women. Analysing the lives of middle-class and otherwise elite women under gender-unequal social systems is instructive, not only as a means for deducing the various forms that gender oppression can take, but also in paying attention to the possibilities and limitations of women's class privilege and economic emergence for gender justice. Their higher income and social privilege do not grant elite women freedom, but only pockets of reprieve from gender injustice, the universal intention and effect of female subordination. Rather, I stress poor women in poor countries not as a theoretical exclusion but to assert that, without a structural transformation of the lives of the poorest, most oppressed sections of all societies, there could be neither development nor gender equity (Kabeer 1992, 108).

In the critical humanist, universalist feminist analysis I propose, I hold that only a small stratum of elite women are exceptions to the often-discredited universalist claims of feminist theorizing. I argue that when we fail to universalize certain basic features of human life, poor women in poor countries have the most to lose. Yes, it is a question of politically defined interests. But it is also an issue when, through the process of their own marginalization, the weak do not challenge inequality and injustice, but adapt themselves in socially approved ways and become thankful for small mercies. Hence, perhaps a non-relativized notion of justice can offer women a more highly developed account of a flourishing human life. A focus on difference in the pursuit of gender justice is counter-productive, since differences of gender, race, class or nationality can be freely elaborated only on the basis that these differences are socially symmetrical in their constitution. Difference, as we shall see, is always connected to power in social life. Because these differences exist only to stratify and subordinate, to reify them as if the outcomes they generate were socially equal, positive or benign is to remove critical analysis from feminist theory and to limit progressive theory-linked public policy.

Feminism and the Tradition of Critical Theory

Marx's 1843 definition of critical theory as "the self clarification of the struggles and wishes of the age" is yet to be surpassed for its precision and continuing relevance to social science. Indeed, feminism does help to clarify the struggles of men and women in contemporary society, but while gender oppression is universal, feminist consciousness – the comprehension of a blatantly unjust system of male privilege based on sex-role differentiation, coupled with apprehension of the possibility of liberation from this alien force – is not. Hence, feminism shares with critical theory the view that society is in need of radical transformation, not just reform, that theory should be independent of existing forms of social consciousness and that the ideal of the objective, disinterested, independent theorist has no place in theories of the social world (Hoffman 1987, 234). Unlike typical problem-solving theory, feminist theory occupies the realm of critical theory as it too reflects on the process of theorizing itself, is aware of different theoretical options and is open to the possibility of developing a new perspective from which the problem becomes one of creating an alternative world. Above all, feminist theory is prescriptive theory.

The central problem of critical theory is the development of reason and rationality directly concerned with the quality of human life. Just as feminism itself has set about to do from the start, critical theory entails a change in the criteria of theory and the functions to which theory is to be put, according to the needs of contemporary society (Hoffman 1987, 234). It entails the view that humanity has potentialities other than those currently observable in society, and, as such, critical theory requires normative choices to be made in favour of meeting its transformative objectives (Cox 1981, 130). This means that it must limit the range of choice to alternative orders that will feasibly transform the existing world. A principal objective of critical theory would be to clarify this range of objectives in order to rank their usefulness. A feminist critical theory would seek not only to explain society by more accurately describing it, but also to change it.

Feminist theory then, at its best and most complete, is necessarily a critical theory, because its proponents, although they are part of society, must stand outside the existing social order and question how that order came about. It does not take existing institutions and relations of power for granted and concerns itself not only with the origins of those patterns but, most importantly, how patterns of social relations maintain and reproduce disadvantage and also which patterns interrupt processes of learning and internalized norms of subordination. Theory is the output of the systematic organization of knowledge. Critical feminist theory must know and understand gender relations, not to tolerate them, but to change them.

Humanist Feminism

I start from the understanding that, wherever they live, human beings have common resources and challenges, and that their special crises arise out of particular circumstances rather than out of any unique nature or cultural identity unlike that of any other group of human beings. In this vein I follow the Ghanaian philosopher Kwame Anthony Appiah, who proposes that "[w]e will only solve our problems if we see them as human problems arising out of a special situation, and we shall not solve them if we see them as African problems generated by our somehow being unlike others" (1993, 136).

All of humanity is faced with scarce resources to meet myriad ends, competition for these resources, avoidance of premature death, and the battle to sustain a life that flourishes. While collective or individual strategies to cope with these challenges or meet these objectives must, to some extent, be grounded in particular circumstances for them to succeed, a feminist concern must be with the process and normative content of people's living conditions and strategies. This vigilance is required if we are to prevent a concern about fostering relevant solutions from entering a debilitating slide into relativism, according to which the ultimate arbiter of what is good or right for human prospering must derive from a group's internal culture. A feminist reflectivity to theory applied in this way helps avoid a false either/or scenario between local and universal, as well as an apolitical live-and-let-live attitude to the suffering of the "other". Post-modernist notions of difference have been rightly critiqued because of their alarming similarity to the position of liberal pluralism, which sees the world simply in terms of differing groups of individuals (Allen 1972; Okin 1998; Fraser 1997, 97). The useful post-modernist critique of the exclusionary modernist underpinnings of polit-ical theory begins to lose its appeal for feminism when it reveals its reluctance to adjudicate among competing truth claims, because it teaches that value-based claims can never be truly or objectively known.

There are many examples of the limits to post-modernist theory for human, and especially women's, liberation. Development theorists influ-enced by post-modern thinking and cultural relativism have defended practices such as widow-burning in India (Spivak 1994), death from pre-ventable disease (Marglin 1990), hunger and malnutrition (Escobar 1995, 106) and female genital mutilation (Tamir 1996); they have regarded feminist concerns such as autonomy, dignity and independence as culturally and historically relevant to the value system of the West, and their opposites, manifested in the practices cited above, as cultural expressions of different rather than inferior value systems.

Some Third World feminists have also enthusiastically joined in the turn towards culture in feminism, where "social sciences have lost their purchase by comparison to the arts and humanities and where the great-est interest is now in symbolism, representation, subjectivity and the self" (Barrett 1992). The result is an attempt to deduce a normative politics of culture from an ontological conception of identity and difference. The consequences for the poor and powerless are that such thinking divorces all questions of difference from material inequality, power differentials among groups and systematic relations of dominance and subordination (Fraser 1997, 185).

But decomposing meaning is not an adequate substitute for justice for suffering or dying people. Deconstruction is an indispensable tool for any intellectual effort aimed at criticizing existing power relations and structures. Deconstruction of categories such as gender and race has made visible the contradictions, mystifications, silences and hidden meanings of which they are made up. However, the preoccupation in current writing tends to discuss and deconstruct categories such as gender and race as though they have no links to patriarchal or racist oppression. A focus on women's differences is not sufficient to take account of these latter dimensions of power (Maynard 1994, 1), because deconstruction tends not to illuminate the significant role that gender and race play in social stratification on a world scale. Poor women of colour are not likely to be the main beneficiaries of discourse that concludes that they are not the "most powerless" or "poorest of the poor", when for the majority of Third World women these are precise descriptors of their existence.

In the new preoccupation with words over things, materiality has taken a backstage role. The poverty of the most severely disadvantaged is being constructed discursively as a justification for development activity, an experience that now becomes largely a state of mind rather than a state of mind and body, as previous work up to this time might suggest (Jackson 1997, 147). As a result, localism has been put forward as an alternative to imperialist, essentialist interventions and to get around the seeming impossibility of adjudging good or bad except by a grounding in local concepts and the self-perceptions of those who are the targets of development.

A Feminist Strategic Universalism

Among the crucial problems with an overemphasis on culture as difference is that it sees culture as hermetically sealed off from "outsiders" (Benhabib 1995), and that it views difference as intrinsically positive and inherently cultural (Fraser 1997, 183). This is an example of where postmodernism's usual sophisticated and persuasive criticism of foundationalism and essentialism becomes anaemic when it comes to social criticism (Fraser and Nicholson 1990, 20). In a rapidly globalizing world, culture and communities cannot be viewed as bounded wholes without internal politics, contradictions and debates, if they ever could be. The fact that cultures are systems of meaning, values and interpretation, which are reproduced over time by individuals under the constraints of a material way of life, is elided by a certain idealism that is resolute in arguing for the radical incommensurability of conceptual frameworks and the untranslatability of language (Benhabib 1995, 245). Benhabib suggests that we need to distinguish between communities of conversation and culturally specific ethnic communities in which what determines who belongs to the former shifts with the conversation and the problem at hand (1995, 247).

With the current prominence that cultural dissimilarity has achieved in contemporary debates on international politics, it has become urgent that reflections on the role of culture in social justice differentiate between human universals and absolutes. Herskovits's explication is valuable enough to merit detailed elaboration here:

> Absolutes are fixed, and in so far as convention is concerned, are not admitted to have variation, to differ from culture to culture, from epoch to epoch. Universals are those least common denominators to be extracted inductively from comprehension of the natural or cultural world manifest ... To say that there is no absolute criteria of value or morals ... does not mean that such criteria in differing forms, do not comprise universals in human nature ... Certain values in human life are everywhere accorded recognition, even though the institutions of no two cultures are identical in form. Morality is a universal, so is the enjoyment of beauty, even some standards of truth. (1948, 477–78)

In an increasingly globalized world, which makes communities of conversation about humanist ethics both possible and necessary, twentieth-century developments have dissolved much of the cultural distance of the past, for better or worse. It is common human problems that today present the most urgent moral issues on the world stage. Addressing the moral problem of international racism, African-American cultural feminist bell hooks concedes that not being analytical and critical of a different experience, because it is supposedly different from one's own, can be as much a perpetuation of racism as the cultural imperialism she has so deservedly condemned (hooks 1989, 47). Notwithstanding the indisputable benefits of deconstructionism in social life, the fact that its proponents conclude by proposing a politics of difference as a remedy for social inequality shows that they have entirely missed the crux of the problem facing justice theorists today – which identity claims are rooted in the defence (or perpetuation) of social relations of inequality, and which are rooted in a challenge to such relations.

Relating to the moral problem of universal gender injustice, Chhachhi proposes that the basis of the charge that mainstream feminist theory is foreign to women of the South and women of colour arises from a failure to distinguish between the levels of feminist analysis at which theories are being constructed. There are three levels of analysis in most contemporary theories: basic concepts that are abstract and function as tools of analysis, such as relations of production or reproduction; intermediate concepts such as patriarchy or mode of production; and a third level involving historically specific analysis of concrete social phenomenon, such as slavery in the nineteenth-century Caribbean and bride-price in modern Africa (Chhachhi 1988, 79). Most often the limits of European theorizing on universal values have pertained to the second and third levels of analysis, where a historically and culturally specific analysis is often lacking and where a charge of regressive essentialism would be most appropriate.

If feminist theory is to be linked to gender-relevant public policy, it is of the highest importance that feminist theorizing sort out and encompass concepts of women's *practical gender needs,* which are system-conforming, and women's *strategic gender interests,* which transform systems of gender inequality and liberate women. Gender interests refer to those historically and culturally constituted constructions that arise out of women's social relations and their positioning in the gender hierarchy (Molyneux 1995, 1988). In Molyneux's original definition, examples of women's practical gender interests are access to clean water, shelter and a basic income. Strategic gender interests would include abolition of the sexual division of labour, outlawing of physical and sexualized violence against women, pay equity and political rights. Molyneux's distinction between practical gender interests and strategic gender interests differentiates theoretically defined interests (those in the strategic realm) from those empirically verifiable wants and needs that are practical requirements. Caroline Moser has substituted "needs" for "interests", arguing for a separation that focuses on the process whereby an interest is translated into a need (1989, 1819).

However, I prefer Kate Young's (1988a) finer distinction between strategic and practical gender interests. In addition to extending practical gender needs to include men's needs, thus avoiding the conflation of gender and women, it recognizes that in a patriarchal system it is entirely possible that men may benefit disproportionately when women's practical needs are met. This will not challenge the basis of gender injustice. However, it is women's struggle to achieve strategic interests that is met by conflict and contestation from men, because issues of male power and control are being directly challenged in ways that the achievement of practical needs does not always allow to women. While mobilizing around strategic interests almost always means that women are challenging the ideological legitimation of their subordinate position, having practical needs met often does little more than allow women to survive in a patriarchal order, or to perform more efficiently their patriarchy-assigned roles. The world's women have made tremendous strides in achieving practical outcomes, but for-midable checks on gender justice remain in the highly resistant, mainly ideological, barriers that prevent the widespread achievement of strate-gic goals. How well women survive to function within different patri-archal gender systems depends on how well their practical gender needs are met. Women's success in moving from basic survival to higher-order capabilities, such as to exercise power and control, depends on how well practical needs have been transformed into movement politics for securing strategic interests.

Therefore, in elaborating this proposal of strategic universalism, my feminist intent is to be essentialist. This is because I believe that women's strategic gender interests are essentially the same the world over while, depending on social contexts, it is practical gender needs that differ for men and women. My theoretical mission, then, is to challenge difference feminists to show, by argument and evidence, how poor women in poor countries are missing from a theory on strategic universal feminism, and to prove how, if these women are indeed excluded from theory, their being taken into account now would affect the theory. The essentialism I rely on refers to an understanding that human life has certain central defining features, below which level a person's existence is hardly a human life at all. I defend this deployment of essentialism especially in light of accusations by relativist, post-structuralist and post-modernist claims that an essential, non-relative account of human good implies an ignorance of history and culture and a lack of sensitivity to the voices of women and the subaltern. Like Fraser and Nicholson (1990), I support a weak version of post-modernist theorizing because I think it leaves room for a qualified version of feminist essentialism that is urgently needed in political life.

I propose that employing a strategic universalist approach to gender analysis would help us to solve the seemingly ineluctable problem of determining how much a theory of difference could add value to feminist theory and practice in the Caribbean. To do this, I will now embark on a critical assessment of two aspects of the difference question: female difference from males, which might imply two different ethical approaches, and differences among women, which could call for asking individual women themselves, in culturally, historically relevant social groups, about their well-being. After discussing the need for an internal/external policy alternative, I conclude by proposing what I believe is an appropriate state policy for operationalizing strategic universalism in the interest of gender justice.

Male and Female Difference: Ethic of Care or Justice?

The idea of difference has played an enduring and important role in feminist theorizing and activism. During feminism's first wave, women were thought to be fundamentally different from men, a distance borne out in women's roles, rights and potentials in nineteenth-century society (Gordon 1991). Second-wave feminists employed the concept of difference in a much more political way, by bringing out the fact that although in principle men's and women's biological sex differences were equal to each other's, sex differences as socially constructed were hierarchical. Women's "inferior" differences were revealed by feminists as subordinated to men's "superior" differences and all that was associated with maleness. This reconceptualization of gender difference also called attention to the way in which feminine attributes were derided, in time leading to re-exploration of such female traits as women's language styles, intuition and caring nature. The main outcome of this reinterpretation was a liberal conclusion that precipitated an ensuing search for gender equality. But since sexual equality in law and public policy is based on sameness, and gender characteristics are socially understood as difference, gender equality is actually a contradiction in terms, which may suggest why we have been having such a hard time getting it (MacKinnon 1987, 32).

The dilemma that feminists face here is a persistent one that perfectly illustrates the perils of theory that is irrelevant to practice.

Insisting that men's differences are equal to women's differences, this argument fails to pay sufficient attention to the fact that men and women are not social equals. Gender difference is based on hierarchical notions of difference, and those differentials in power in turn produce the real and imagined female differences that feminists have come to recognize as signifiers of gender inequality. What "women's differences" really describes is the experience that results from the systematic relegation of half of humanity to a condition of inferiority, which has then been attributed to their female nature. Nonetheless, an appeal to women's traditions, ways and discourse continues to provide an escape for some feminist theorists. Carol Gilligan's very influential research (1982) suggests that women's moral reasoning is often based on an ethic of responsibility and care, which flows from an emotional connection between self and others. By contrast, men's moral reasoning is said to stem from an ethic of principled non-coercion, which assumes and honours separateness.

The first part of Gilligan's analysis is a particular empirical assertion of a gender difference in moral behaviour. The second is the claim that we should value women's connective ethic of care over the separative ethics of men's justice. Her relativized analysis of human good is faulty, as it omits power and prejudice. It seeks to value positively those features that actually do distinguish women from men but obliterates the context in which feminine attributes are formed, by treating them as if they were not outcomes demanded by male dominance for its own ends, as if equality of differences already exists. Thus, for feminists to affirm difference when difference means dominance, as it does with gender, is to affirm the qualities and characteristics of powerlessness (MacKinnon 1987, 39). More than a hundred years ago, the nineteenth-century economist and philosopher John Stuart Mill, himself the husband of one of the earliest known feminists, Harriet Taylor, was quick to reject this false notion of women's naturally caring nature. He suggests that to call women's sexual personalities natural is about as plausible as to plant a tree with one half in a vapour bath and the other half in snow and then, seeing that one half withered and the other half grew luxuriously, to declare that it is the nature of the tree to grow that way (Mill 1995). To Gilligan's claim that women speak in a different voice, I join the unfairly much-maligned essentialist Katherine MacKinnon in her scepticism: "if you would take

your foot off our necks, then you will hear in what voice women speak"
(1987, 45).

Like these critical analysts, this chapter argues that feminist theory
must be concerned with the social shaping of preferences and desire, and
must refuse to accept uncritically the proposition of women's emotions
as a justification for women's inferior circumstances. As the deconstruc-
tionists would no doubt remind us, emotions are comprised of socially
learned beliefs, which for women are formed under conditions of injustice and, therefore, for women's sake, cannot be taken as the way things
ought to be. A calculation that ignores the social construction of women's
nature sets up a false dichotomy between care and justice and then asks
us to choose one, each being viewed as an intact moral sphere. This is
wrong. What care and justice actually reflect are two different aspects of
a prudentially valuable human life. Justice is no more natural to men's
possibilities than care is to women's. Justice is concerned with institutions; care and other virtues belong to the realm of character. They call
for reasoning in a different way (O'Neill 1989, 14). Removing gender
inequality is going to require more than revaluing women's differences
and caring ways. For poor women in poor countries, women's socially
caused vulnerability means that they cannot often refuse certain arrangements in which they are required to show an inordinate amount of concern for others, to the neglect of their own well-being and interests. Their
consent to these arrangements, often by virtue of caring attitudes and
practices, reflects injustice. As impoverished providers, poor Caribbean
women's capacities to act are constrained both by a lack of resources
and by commitments to others.

Oppressive institutional arrangements disable agency both by limiting
women's capacity to reason and act independently, and by increasing
demands to meet the needs and satisfy the desires of others. Therefore,
the principles of justice that are worth defending where women are concerned would seem to be, not the arrangements to which women currently consent within the bounds of their dependent or oppressive
relations, but the arrangements they would accept in institutional situations in which they had the option of refusal. Nor can we accept as just
situations in which women are made vulnerable by relations of structural dependency in which they rely on the strong not to exercise the
advantages that proximity and relations of dependence give them. As

Onora O'Neill points out, even when the powerful reliably exercise this restraint there is still potential injustice, because women in such circumstances depend for their well-being on the goodwill of others, and this is bound to affect their ability to question or thwart injustice:

> Whether the proposals of the strong are economic or sexual, whether they rely on ignorance or isolation of the weak to deceive them, or on their diminished opportunities for independent action, or on the habits of deference and appeasement which become second nature for the weak, they ride on unjust social practice. (O'Neill 1989, 32)

Genuine, legitimate consent is undermined by the very institutions that best present the appearance of consent, but in practice, the family as a basic structure of society is among those culturally and legally shaped institutions that most pervasively curtail women's capacity for flourishing. The role of theory-linked policy here is for institutions to be reformed so that the relatively powerless can secure the option of refusal or negotiation of variable parameters in the interests of those whose capacities are most diminished within them. To truly value women's differences requires distinguishing between which patterns of behaviour have been warped by strategies of resistance and compliance with patriarchy, and which behaviours that are socially required of women, but not of men, ought to be promoted throughout the whole human community.

Basis of Legitimation: Particular versus Universal Truths

There has been no shortage of writers on and analysis of Caribbean gender relations that draw attention to the differences of local women's experiences from a supposedly generic, but in actuality alien, white, Western, middle-class norm (Hart 1989a; Massiah 1986b; "Rethinking Caribbean Difference" 1998), even though these writers have themselves been criticized for not practising what they preach (Barriteau 1995a). Since it is believed that there is no one authoritative arbiter, we are told we must listen to voices in each developing country or regional context, giving the poor the opportunity to decide on developmental priorities, with well-being grounded in local concepts and the self-perceptions of the poor (Chambers 1988; Beck 1994). But this reveals an inconsistency in post-modernist theorizing, as it refuses to subject the local to the same deconstruction as globalism. This flaw highlights the continuing entrapment of post-modernism in dualistic divisions in which "if global equals bad, then local equals good" (Jackson 1997, 152). Since local cultures and communities are nearly always divided along gender lines (even in the unlikely event that there are no other major social cleavages), there are likely to be opposing conceptions of well-being and power differentials embodied in differences, and this results in some voices being given more legitimacy than others. These local, culturally relevant hierarchies will exclude and marginalize the voices of the poor and powerless as effectively as any "alien Western conception" of human well-being or development.

In the literature on gender and development, we hear more and more that solutions lie in the articulated priorities voiced by women themselves, without reference to how the voices of women are often muted and distorted by oppressive power relations. This now popular dictum – that theory-linked policies and political conclusions must start from women's experience – does not seem an appropriately critical feminist stance, especially when we consider the reality of Caribbean women's lives. The inferior social status of women relative to men in society is borne out in the statistical and descriptive accounts of women throughout the countries. When compared to women's condition around the world, Third World women's problems in gender-structured society bear out Susan Moller Okin's (1995) theory of outcomes that are "similar to those of white western women but more so".

In Antigua and Barbados 30 per cent of adult women have been abused by an intimate partner at some time in their lives, 30 per cent of married women report being battered by male intimates and 50 per cent of these reported seeing their own mothers being beaten by men (UN 1995, 160). In Jamaica, where the incidence of gender violence is acknowledged to be grave, reports of domestic violence have risen more than tenfold between 1985 and 1993 (UNICEF/PIJ 1997). An average of 35 per cent of all households in the Caribbean are headed by women, and the number is rising (UN 1995, 30). Most of these households are poor and are found mainly among the working class, where poor women are doubly oppressed by the unequal sexual division of labour in the household and in the labour market. Despite high educational attainment levels – even in countries such as Barbados, where female university graduation ratios are in excess of men's – women's unemployment rates remain stubbornly at about twice those of men, and employed women are still penalized by gender stereotyping in workplace allocation, wage differentials, promotion and salary (Freeman 1998; Albuquerque and Ruark 1998). As a result of these overlapping patterns of segregation and relegation in labour markets, women's share of national income in terms of real gross domestic product per capita is substantially less than men's, even in countries with the highest rankings of gender empowerment. In Jamaica, real per capita income at purchasing-power parity for males and females is $4,138 and $2,756; in Trinidad and Tobago, $9,600 compared with $2,756; and in Barbados, $14,946 compared with $9,252 for women (UNDP 1999). Yet neither gaining bodily autonomy nor ending the sexual division of labour are demands that are high on the agenda of the average woman in the region. Conversely, many women defend some minimum level of male dominance in their lives, in accordance with how they validate their own feminine gender identity. What this suggests to me is that feminist theorizing must indeed include the concrete experiences of people, but the complex phenomena being studied are much better understood if the theories of social justice and human well-being that we have managed to craft are, until then, brought to research sites to make sense of the empirical realities we find.

Some feminist development theorists are concerned that what seems to require defence in a post-modern ambience is the assertion that beyond women's voices are legitimate representations of "objective" gender interests, and that it is possible to speak for some subaltern interests identified in this way (Jackson 1997, 151). Jackson views attempts to construct theories of objective gender relations not as a substitute for self-perceptions, but as a legitimate dimension through which to engage with and understand these perceptions. Many Western feminists studying the Third World have become so overly sensitive to passing value judgements from their privileged position that they are undiscriminating of the difference between a critique of ethnocentrism and a cultural relativism, which leaves oppressive relations undisturbed, just because they occur in a different language or geographical area from theirs. When Third World feminists replicate this omission, it is even harder to justify. For example, analyst after analyst in the landmark Women in the

Caribbean Project (WICP) study was at pains to avoid entering the study with "a prior theoretical commitment" (Anderson 1986, 291), but avowed a determination to "let women speak for themselves" (Barrow 1986c, 133) and to avoid at all costs the inference of "false consciousness" on the part of the study's respondents (Clarke 1986). No wonder then that at the end of the study researchers expressed such analytical confusion over the contradictions they had unearthed (Barriteau 1992). Feminism begins from the lives of real women, and the lives of women are highly varied and highly contradictory. These variations and contradictions should be expected, given the diffuse modes of gender power and their equally diverse and fluid impacts upon women. A feminist theory should be expected to account for and to theorize across these variations. If not, the exercise is purely descriptive – and not feminist.

For Whom Theory, Victims or Agents?

One explanation for such restraint in local analysis is that Caribbean feminists are very concerned not to have women appear as victims. But this insistence would seem to invalidate the whole reason behind applying a feminist lens to gender relations in the Caribbean. Gender injustice is not a victimless crime. But even so, an absolute opposition of the terms "victimhood" and "agency" is an oversimplification and does not take into account the true complexity of women's experience of subordination and their continuous negotiation of what Kandiyoti (1988) terms "patriarchal bargains". A feminist consciousness not only involves the realization of gender-specific injury, but it is the very mechanism by which urgency, dedication and empathy become engaged with the utopian project of contemplating its transformation. Feminist consciousness of victimization is therefore a divided consciousness. When women perceive themselves as victims, they know that they have already sustained an injury, remain exposed to further harm and have at worst been mutilated, at best diminished in their being. But at the same time, "feminist consciousness is a joyous awareness of one's own power, of the possibility of unprecedented personal growth and the release of energy long suppressed" (Bartky 1975, 431). Only with a highly developed sense of victimization will women also be able to fully express their agency. Caribbean women are well aware of the special burdens that only women bear in their societies, whether they relate to unemployment, domestic responsibility or violence (Massiah 1986a). But, for millennia, women the world over have complained of their condition without a large-scale move away from seeing their situation as natural, inevitable and unchanging, no matter how completely they can list their catalogue of insults and markers of inferiority. To consider these complaints as indicating a low level of political consciousness would be to pre-empt gender justice and inadequate for a feminist theory and practice. As Young argues, while women are clearly active in trying to cope with their life situations as best they can, it cannot be assumed that they have perfect knowledge or understanding of the economic, political and social context of their lives: "Women as individuals may be well aware of their subordinate position and powerlessness, but the force of ideology may render this 'natural' or 'God-given'. Equally, when it is recognised as social, the structural roots of discrimination and inequality are not always easily identified" (1993, 143).

The overwhelming universal function and effect of gender subordination is to victimize women, and to deny that women are effectively victimized is to deny them the possibilities of their agency.

A focus on victimization under gender-unequal social systems does not imply that men and women are equally disadvantaged, as it is sometimes taken to mean. An examination of how racism diminishes white people's lives does not shift the focus from its real victims – people of colour. Neo-Nazi youth no doubt feel estranged from their communities at large because their extreme views and violent practices render them unable to feel welcome in mainstream white society. Yet the repercussions of racism for the real victims of neo-Nazi terrorism and hate-speech far outweigh any diminishment of the perpetrators' quality of life caused by patterns of living and beliefs that they have chosen to meet their own deformed interests. Similarly, we recognize that tutelage in male dominance interferes with the moral possibilities, identity formation and some freedoms of men. For example, the fact that women fear men and must organize their lives to some degree to minimize this threat (for example, exercise caution in walking alone at night or communicating with male strangers) imposes certain restrictions on the spontaneity of perhaps innocent men encountering women who live their lives in this state of alertness and suspicion. But the male and female consequences of women's fear of men are not symmetrical. Resentment or regret is not the same as disabling dread, and women's fear does not affect men's capacity to engage with the public sphere at times or in ways that are convenient or in places where most women fear to tread.

Thus cognizance of the extent to which various groups are victimized by gender hierarchy is not to claim that men suffer the pain of gender discrimination equally, nor is it to disparage women as its principal victims. Laws that protect all of us from theft and fraud do not turn us into pathetic victims rather than agents. Treating women with equal respect and dignity requires of public policy the recognition of how gender hierarchies disproportionately affect them, and that protections be put in place to eliminate these. Some women do survive against all odds, but we cannot conclude from this that the way to respect people as agents is to create and maintain for them an unequal, uphill struggle throughout their entire existence (Nussbaum 1999). An appropriate feminist acknowledgement of women's victim/agent status would necessarily acknowledge their resourcefulness under injustice while at the same time arguing for transformative change in male–female possibilities that would relieve women of the excessive burdens that gender bestows upon them.

A particularly thorny issue around discussions of women and agency is the problem of distinguishing between what women are currently allowed to do in gender-unequal societies and what choices women would exercise if equality did indeed exist. As a result of this overemphasis, an alarming trend in development practice has come about through linking women's agency with an expression of women's preferences. In development policy, for instance, where more emphasis is being placed on what women themselves say, an objective appraisal of women's condition has been eclipsed by the principle of consent as the basis of legitimacy (Fierlbeck 1995, 24). The social relations that influence women's choices, actions and even words are placed beyond critique by a concept of consent. Many gains are made from moral conformity and observation of the patriarchal bargain, but it is important to ascertain the unintended as well as the intended consequences of such choices for women, in both the short and long term. While post-modernism would seem to require that we conform normative standards to existing reality, a more strategic universal feminist approach would consider it negligent to characterize women's articulated perceptions as necessarily complete truths.

The conflation of enforced submission with women's consent is starkly personified in liberal theoretical approaches to rape, especially in marriage and by rapists known to the victim. Astonishingly, Caribbean feminists who criticize liberal theory for its gender blindness in such realms fail to distinguish free commitment and agreement by equals in everyday male–female relations from choices made under domination, subordination and relations of inequality. Contemporary consent theory presents institutions as if they were actually as consent demands – constituted through the free agreement of equals – and it is this conventional use of consent that helps to reinforce old beliefs about the natural characteristics of the sexes and the sex/gender double standard (Pateman 1995, 85). Sometimes this analytical tangle leads to a misinterpretion of whose interests are being met by women's expressed preferences and whether those outcomes are indeed manifestations of women's choices or, instead, a lowering of expectations and rationalizing downwards of preferences for accomplishments they feel they cannot achieve. Caribbean feminists who "let women speak for themselves" as a guide to women's condition and public policy inadvertently fall into this trap.

Take, for example, researchers' popular conclusion that historically high rates of out-of-wedlock births and low and declining marriage rates, leading to high percentages of female-headed households, reflect women's preferences and, consequently, high levels of female empowerment and equality in the Caribbean. It is true that many women will point to their recognition that a man in the house is not an unqualified good and that his absence may sometimes afford them more control over their labour and leisure, as well as a chance to escape physical violence and sexual coercion. However, most heterosexual women seem to prefer durable, stable, mutually caring relationships with men, and view their lives as lacking something significant when this is missing – as well they should. Thus it would appear that it is bad marriages that women hope to escape, rather than the institution of marriage (rightly or wrongly) that women strongly desire. Therefore, to conclude from women's testimony that women "choose" single lives and single motherhood is erroneous in the face of facts and the same cultural reading of these facts that Caribbean feminists insist upon. It is well documented that, however successful, a single woman in the Caribbean (as elsewhere) remains a class below her married counterpart (Barrow 1986b, 57). Women know this, and most importantly for the point I am making, men know that women know this. This knowledge would be especially useful to leverage male power over women who depend on men, not for financial provisioning, but for the social "protection" and mobility that marriage can provide, thereby undermining the equalizing effect of women's class privilege. It would not be unreasonable to infer, in light of women's overwhelming acceptance of the pain of male infidelity as a "fact of life" (Barrow 1986c, 58; Senior 1991), that women's desire for marriage, for the social standing and financial security it is supposed to offer, is a feature of their subordination to male intimates, whether legally married, cohabiting or in visiting relationships.

Consequently, the more accurate test of women's marriage "choice" would be an analysis that asks whether women themselves are in a position to propose and press for marriage once they so decide. If not, what is the relevance of their saying that they choose or prefer not to be married, when they do not themselves exercise this option? While this last question has not been adequately addressed in Caribbean gender studies, some African research on female-headed households suggests that it is only relatively wealthy women, if divorced, widowed or abandoned, who choose to reject the material and ideological pressures to marry (del Ninno 1993, 6, cited in Shaffer 1998). Throughout the countries in the Caribbean, never-married women with children predominate among the most economically and socially disadvantaged sectors. Bringing the dynamic of power back into gender relations as a social relation could point us in other, more fruitful directions in determining the extent to which ambiguous indicators such as women's single status or female headship of households reflect women's choice, rather than would a reliance on women's articulations alone.

Subjective and empirical realities, read with the awareness of cultural inscription, leads us from an original conclusion of autonomous choice to a phenomenon closer to adaptive preference formation, or what is well known as "sour grapes". Faced with real desires and imposing obstacles, women will often adapt their preferences to conform more closely to what is possible. Situations that develop out of social learning must always be evaluated according to informed preferences rather than just the given preferences. One should attach more weight to someone who knows both sides of the question than to someone who has only experienced one of them (Elster 1982, 220). It might be useful to add that, in evaluating women's preferences, we ought to give more weight not only to those who have experienced both sides of the question (for example, formerly married women), but also to those who have the power to enforce outcomes of either alternative scenario.

False Consciousness or External Constraints?

On the whole, utilitarian conceptions of gender justice are inadequate because they erroneously take the fulfilment of women's preferences as proof of justice. As a result, if it is based solely on women's articulated dissatisfactions or alternatives to the prevailing gender order, public policy based on a resurgent neo-liberal imposition of rational choice theory in matters of public life is destined to end up not delivering gender justice. Among contemporary theorists of inequality, Amartya Sen and Martha Nussbaum have perhaps elaborated most clearly and persuasively why the absence of protest or questioning of gender inequality must be received neither unproblematically nor as evidence of the absence of inequality (Sen 1995, 1992, 1990; Nussbaum 1999, 1998, 1995, 1993). They point out that the still fairly crude approach of polling people to find out their preferences and satisfactions does not do well enough, because people's satisfaction reports are frequently shaped by lack of information, lack of opportunities, intimidation and sheer habit. In explaining why the problems of perception and communication are so important, Sen highlights the difficult conundrum of women's lack of perceived personal welfare, which is often combined with a great concern for others (Sen 1990, 126), just the kind of attitude that helps sustain traditional inequalities. With their current low levels of informed and politically conscious awareness of gender injustice, Caribbean women can be expected to exhibit tremendous variation in their perception of individual welfare and that of women generally. These "differences" in local women's perceptions, which so confounded cogent analyses of the WICP data, appear to be differences in perceptions shared by women all over the world.

In household bargaining, for instance, women often attach much less value to their contribution to the family than men, whether women work outside the home or not (Sen 1990; Okin 1989; Waring 1989). Women's contribution to the family is universally underestimated, uncounted and devalued in relation to men's, despite the fact that women's inputs of money, household labour, time and emotional labour not only maintain the entire family but facilitate men's labour force participation and therefore men's earning power. This point of mutual but *asymmetrical* dependency is taken into account no more regularly by theorists of household bargaining than by women in inequitable families themselves. Many Caribbean women view fulfilment of these demands, exploitative and without commensurate reward though they may be, as part of what it means to be woman, wife, mother or daughter (Senior 1991). When your identity, social standing and sometimes physical well-being depend on it, who wouldn't want to be a good wife or mother? Despite these complexities, feminist theory must make an ethical distinction between rational wants and irrational wants – in other words, between wants and desires that are consistent with the full flourishing of human dignity and those that remove this prospect from women's lives. Sometimes women seem to have a preference for things that are clearly bad for them, like remaining in physically or mentally abusive relationships with men. Though often rationalized by a woman in terms of trade-offs in financial security for herself and especially for her children, staying in these types of relationships can result in a range of female disadvantages, from loss of self-esteem to loss of health, or even death. John Harsanyi explains how, by using an ethical calculation that includes an individual's personal preferences, we can maintain a distinction between a woman's rational and irrational preferences as the ultimate criteria to determining true preferences:

> All we have to do is distinguish between a person's manifest preferences and his true preferences. His manifest preferences are his actual preferences as manifested by his observed behaviour, including preferences possibly based on erroneous factual beliefs, or on careless logical analysis or on strong emotions that at the moment greatly hinder rational choice. In contrast, a person's true preferences are the preferences he would have had if he had all the relevant factual information, always reasoned with the greatest care possible and were in a state of mind most conducive to rational choice. (Harsanyi 1982, 55)

Given this distinction, a person's rational wants are those consistent with her true preferences, and therefore consistent with all the relevant factual information and with the best possible logical analysis of this information, whereas irrational wants are those that fail this test.

Although placing slightly less emphasis than Sen and Harsanyi on misperceptions of self-interests and more on external constraints on women's acting overtly in their best interests, Bina Agarwal's model shows how norms secured and accepted outside the immediate bargaining relationship may influence women's relative power in gendered negotiations. If the social legitimacy of a woman's claim to a share of the contested item is recognized, and only the size or proportion of the share claimed is in dispute, there is less complexity to the bargaining situation and greater opportunity for an unequal partner to press her claim (Agarwal 1997, 16). This ease may vary according to the item being contested. For example, the rights of women to access to paid employment is rarely in dispute in the Caribbean, but the legitimacy of women's right to demand that male partners share domestic and child care responsibilities equally is for most women still outside the arena of bargaining. Furthermore, when a goal is widely accepted, such as ending violence against women, which is now universally regarded as a human rights violation in international circles, organizations and collectives of women may press more securely for those rights. A reliance on women's differences reduces the important contribution that universal standards and best practices can have for women who are without the most basic of legal anti-violence provisions.

Today individual women in the Bahamas, Belize and Cuba may rely to varying degrees on the legitimacy created by international momentum, national laws and women's machineries as a determinant in bargaining over sexual harassment at work, to a greater degree than their counterparts in neighbouring countries, where such legislation is far from becoming a legal reality. For women who possess a fully formed concept of their true interests and preferences, but live in countries where anti-harassment laws are not in place, the bargaining still involves a dialectical relationship between the household and society, and could lead them to make "bad" choices and then to rationalize them. It would seem that both "false consciousness" and external constraints act against women's ranking preferences in their own best interests. Socio-historic circumstances of culture, race and nation do indeed influence the precise balance between the two. Yet this does not adequately explain why, for poor women in a variety of poor countries, apparently different social and historical conditions lead to more or less identical forms of subjectivity for women, which would seem to imply some consistent similarity in their material existence too (Berktay 1993, 126).

The job of truly relevant feminist theories of gender justice is to develop a thoroughgoing investigation of such fundamental concepts as preference, choice and desire in order to distinguish desire from intention, emotion and impulse, and other psychological items, asking questions about the relationship of each to belief, learning, ignorance and, most of all, to inequality. Feminist theory must be aware of how the experience of subordination warps people's preferences and thus their choices and rankings of these preferences. If not, our analysis of women's political consciousness will rest on not just a crude but also a highly questionable and unreliable foundation. As the experience of development, and especially structural adjustment, policy has shown, reliance on faulty theoretical constructs that fail to comprehend the consistent monotony of *structured* gender inequality – because they are blinded by the spectacular array of different *forms* of gender inequity – are particularly pernicious for the well-being of poor women in poor countries.

Conclusion: Women's Human Capabilities and Public Policy

If nothing else, post-modern theory has taught us that unchanging and universal truth-claims reflect the characteristics of the social settings from which they are derived. Hence, if we do not explicitly factor in and make critical judgements about the power relations arising from race, class, gender and national hierarchies, the knowledge gained from particular culturally and locally relevant research is distorted and likely to be of little progressive use to the most severely disadvantaged. To proceed without a normative evaluation or account of the human situation is to leave matters to rest on the wings of culturally structured social forces that, when applied to the lives of the poor in developing countries, are rarely ever benign (Nussbaum 1993).

Women are especially likely to be the losers when we defer uncritically to local traditions – which usually means the voices of powerful men and a few elite women, the ones who usually define what culture is. The perceived justice of existing inequalities, in the absence of a contrary sense of deep injustice, plays a major part in the operation and survival of these arrangements; the inequalities invariably depend for their perpetuation on making allies out of those who have the most to lose from them (Sen 1995, 260). As we have seen, women's preferences are distorted by absence of information, by intimidation, dependency and responsibility for others, and by long schooling in self-abnegation. The higher that social distinctions of race or class raise women's individual status, the more likely they are to be able to exercise autonomous choice. But two caveats are important here. One is that individual actions are not sufficient to challenge structured gender inequality. The other is that those women who go against societal gender norms often do so at tremendous personal cost, and even then, certain types of rejections of patriarchal cultural values may not bring women any closer to self-empowerment. For example, a rejection of female chastity in exchange for promiscuity or other high-risk sexual behaviours will diminish women's prospects for sexual autonomy, as well as for physical and psychological well-being.

This is why, even though feminist theory must include women's voices, it cannot start or end with women's differing expressions of satisfaction or happiness. When linked to politics, such a practice could create a public policy based on diseased preferences, which may cause women to suffer further political disabilities. Personal interest and welfare are not simply matters of self-perception; they are objective aspects that command attention even when self-perception would suggest otherwise. Sen suggests that we distinguish between the perception of interests and some objective notion of well-being (Sen 1990, 127). To achieve this, he has developed what is known as the Capabilities Approach.

In the informational basis of bargaining models of individual interest, the Capabilities Approach includes conceptions such as desert and legitimacy (Sen 1993, 30–53; 1990), which are usually ignored in efforts to move away from foundational concepts. Sen's approach claims that when we ask how people in Country A are doing, it is not enough to look at their satisfactions, as these can be deformed by a bad state of affairs as easily as they can be distorted by habits of luxury. Nor is an enquiry complete if it looks only at the presence or absence of resources, even when their distribution is taken into account, for human beings differ in their needs for different kinds of resources and also in their ability to convert these resources into valuable functionings. Above all, Sen's approach looks not only at actual functioning, as people in a relatively free society may choose not to carry out certain functions. The emphasis is rather on the opportunities or *capabilities* they have, and it is from these basic capabilities that they "choose" which functions they will carry out. The distinction between capabilities and functionings is of the greatest practical importance for theory-linked policy. A policy that aims at a single desired mode of functioning will often be quite different from one that tries to promote opportunities for citizens either to choose that function or not to choose it. For example, training in housekeeping skills produces a limited range of functionings in women, while a broad-based education gives women the capabilities to choose from a wider range of functions that they could perform. The securing of that wide range of choice for all human beings ought to be a goal of feminist theory-linked policy and of politics as a whole. Here the context and quality of choice are even more important than the quantity of choice. This approach takes difference into account by allowing various groups or individuals to express autonomous choice, but *only after* human life is raised to some basis of social equivalency. Aware of the possible objections from liberal pluralists, cultural relativists and post-modernists, Sen's formulation leaves plenty of room for plural specification of the major capabilities of men and women, which policy-makers can work out according to their own socio-cultural context and prioritized needs.

Nussbaum has further elaborated Sen's Capabilities Approach by outlining the role that public policy could play in raising women's human capabilities as a measure of the good life. It bears in mind the multiple ways in which public policy currently bypasses women's interests and the ways in which women's experience of sexual dominance in interpersonal bargaining also affects their participation outside of explicitly gendered structures such as the family. Against this background, raising women's capabilities would require the creation of internal prerequisites of functioning and the shaping of the surrounding material and social environment so that it is conducive to the exercise of choice in the relevant area. It would require that strategic interests and practical needs be targeted simultaneously: "A policy aimed at women's internal capabilities for employment outside the home would focus only on skills training and education. A policy aimed at combined capability would need to focus on non-discrimination in hiring, pay equity, sexual harassment and protecting women from threat and intimidation" (Nussbaum 1998, 776).

This protection from violence and intimidation would undoubtedly take public policy closer to home, where protection and relief of impoverished providers would mean relief from the exploitation and excessive burdens coming from women's own families. These domestic abuses of women are important, as they make women both vulnerable to domestic subordination and unable to participate fully in outside employment or other social structures that may be only implicitly gendered, such as the market and political life.

From past feminist research, we know that women's contribution to the household (of economic or caring labour) is not enough to offset the socially caused gender imbalance that is at the root of gender injustice. Kate Young and Susan Moller Okin argue that the more securely a woman's status is linked to status symbols valued by the outside world – principally ownership of private resources and possession of social resources such as advanced education and high salary and prestige of occupation (Young 1988a, 18–19; Okin 1989) – the stronger and more effective is her breakdown position in a bargaining scenario. Elite women all over the world are more likely to meet these criteria than are poor women in poor countries. The better a woman's breakdown position, the more likely she will be able to insist on bargains that reflect rather than distort her gender interests, and the more likely her choices are to indicate her true preferences. When women's external and internal capacities are unsuppressed, these are the conditions under which their autonomous preferences are reflected in decision making that facilitates their gender interests.

Sen's Capabilities Approach, even with its feminist elaboration by Nussbaum, may not be the perfect solution to current feminist dissatisfaction with modernist inadequacies nor to feminism's wariness of postmodernist hesitation to make moral judgements. But without an equivalent alternative formulation that at least addresses the major contradictions outlined here, Caribbean feminist theory will not have an adequate theoretical basis from which to petition governments for policy aimed at social justice and distribution. To reject a scheme such as the Capabilities Approach in favour of a theory that stresses difference only prolongs the feminist political gridlock at the level of theory and practice, while poor women continue to pay for this stagnation with their deteriorating well-being. On the other hand, a feasible improvement in how to execute a strategic universalist method in feminism can give us a well-reasoned theoretical account of gender justice, with clear directions for how we can put it into practice. Such an improved formulation would be an indispensable guide to more gender-equitable public policy, which poor women urgently need, but from which all Caribbean women, precisely because of what difference currently means in their lives, would benefit.

※ *Chapter 4* ※

A Feminist's Oxymoron
Globally Gender-Conscious Development

MICHELLE ROWLEY

Development is generally accepted to be a process that improves the living conditions of people. Most also agree that the improvement of living conditions relates to non-material wants as well as to physical requirements. Development goals that call for the increase of human welfare or the improvement of the quality of life reflect this agreement. (Bartelmus 1994, 1)

What does it mean to say that development started to function as a discourse, that is that it created a space in which only certain things could be said and even imagined? If discourse is the process through which social reality comes into being – if it is the articulation of knowledge and power, of the visible and the expressible – how can the development discourse be individualized and related to ongoing technical, political, and economic events? How did development become a space for the systematic creation of concepts, theories and practices? (Escobar 1995, 3)

Introduction

The dialogue that these two epigraphs generates, between the belief in "development" as a carte blanche paradigm of progress and a more critical plane of development as discourse, suggests that the civilizing mission of development has historically been an inherent exercise of power among disparate and hierarchically ordered subjects and locations. On one hand Bartelmus draws our attention to the "virtues" implicit in development projects. Escobar, on the other hand, draws the reader into a debate that is premised not on virtue, but on the realm of (im)possible signification within dominant paradigms of development. His inquiry is aimed at critiquing how we come to know what we know, and he questions why events and certain parameters of knowledge are accorded the power that they are. Escobar's epigraph encourages an interrogation of the hegemonic within the innocuous. For example, why do we imagine the need for development in the locations that we choose, requiring the actors who exist, and hierarchically positioned as they are?

The focus of this paper takes this debate farther and raises two theoretical questions that are of primary importance to feminist pedagogy. The first pertains to the hegemonic immanence of the "virtue of development" that encourages predetermined closure on the need to disrupt the hierarchies and power bases that have come to us via dominant development paradigms. We must bear in mind that both closure of what constitutes development and acceptance of dominant paradigms of development succeed because they are endorsed and supported by a number of varied yet resonant sites of construction and through a range of genres and media.

I approach the second theoretical question by way of an internal feminist critique, which warns that even when we are at our critical best as feminist scholars, we must always be cognizant of the fact that these immanent impulses are always already at work in our critique of development. I wish therefore to engage a discussion on the ways in which gender and development have interacted discursively within pedagogical sites to further construct inequities and pedagogic monopolies. My final aim is to outline a feminist pedagogical practice that will ensure that auto-critique becomes a constitutive component within our critique of dominant development paradigms.

The immanence of the hegemonic in the innocuous has been starkly impressed upon me by the plethora of ads that request the viewing audience to "sponsor a child". This new industry of "virtual adoption" across the divide appealed to my humanitarian spirit. I may even argue that the request touched on my feminist politics – a feminist politics that resists acts of social injustice, discrimination, inequity, poverty and violence. As a feminist of colour, I empathized with the appeal, and was cognizant that in this ad, all of the injustices listed above sat upon intersecting axes of race, class, location and the need for gender justice. This "face", this placeless child evoked a response, and well it should. I reminded myself that I must not become so jaded that a choice between the Disney Channel and an abandoned child – "cast upon the dung heap, forgotten by *the world*" – evokes a dilemma.

Yet this ad struck another chord in my feminist politics, and I questioned the inherent discourse. If "forgotten by the world", then where is this child? Where is this forgotten place? It should not go unnoted that there were no ostensible markers of location or even sex on the "model" child (unless we are privy to the ads that provide us with persuading biographical data). This appeal to the benign, in the supposed exercise of justice and fairness, made my structurally adjusted feminist politics cautious of this nameless, placeless ideology, and cautioned against this (im)moral sale of neutered, dislocated children and countries.

Why was I left to assume the geographical location of this face? Why must I only hazard a guess at the geopolitics involved in this apparent poverty? Why was there silence on the national politics that may either have fostered this neglect or be unable to assist or meet the needs of this child? Of course it must be the time and financial constraints involved in pulling together a thirty-second advertisement. Or is it?

I subsequently raised these questions with US-based undergraduates in an Introduction to Women's Studies course taught in November 1999. They were much more astute than I and confidently located this child as an orphan of "the Third World". I tried to explain to them that I was from "the Third World" and that I still did not wish to assume that I knew where the child belonged. Unfortunately they had difficulty understanding why a discussion on belonging and location would even be necessary within the context of women's studies, and a sense of closure had already been achieved on both the geographical location and the nobility of the project.

Yet it is the very nobility of the project that alerts me, for this ad represents a "noble project" that simultaneously requires gestures of conflation and dislocation to achieve "success". It succeeds because it appeals to our Western understanding that development, like all other "civilizing" quests, is noble.

To my mind the advertisement straddled a particular theoretical tension for feminists who are concerned about the "development debate". On one hand, there is the supposed nobility of the project. Yet on the other, the discursive unfolding of the project requires marginalization – if not elimination – of characters, events and subjectivities in favour of a placeless and nameless "other". Most disconcerting of all, and the focus of this essay, is the fact that interpolated in this concern are students and budding women's studies scholars who were unable to critique this tension, when the very foundation of women's studies has been to interrogate and challenge similar (mis)representations. This failure gave rise to the central concern of this work: In what ways has *feminism failed to critique itself* in its advocacy of "equitable" development and representations within development? How has feminism successfully critiqued traditional approaches to development while failing to simultaneously critique its own, possibly unwitting, support of discursive misrepresentations within its pedagogical sites of delivery? The evident tension that exists between the two opening epigraphs provides a useful analytical base on which we can begin to articulate a feminist autocritique of the pedagogical delivery of gender and development.

Development and Development as Discourse

First I draw attention to the excerpt from Peter Bartelmus, taken from *Environment, Growth and Development: The Concepts and Strategies of Sustainability* (1994). What strikes me about Bartelmus's statement is his immediate attempt to make the reader a confidant, an accomplice in a collectively and commonly held belief of what constitutes development. He writes, ". . . *it is generally accepted* . . .", ". . . *most also agree* . . ." and again, "Development goals . . . *reflect this agreement* . . ." As with our advertisement, I am struck by his attempt to mask any inherent power structures that may be present within development debates. How can we, driven by any humanitarian spirit, reject the need for *improved living conditions, increased concern for human welfare* and *quality of life* indicators? Easily establishing a good operational definition, the writer has begun to mark the parameters of his examination.

The need to mediate economic growth with concern for the welfare of human life permeates the documentation and proceedings of international organizations. The United Nations Development Programme *Human Development Report* is one example of such, having defined development as "the process of enlarging people's choices – increasing their opportunities for education, health care, income, and employment, and covering the full range of human choices from a sound physical environment to economic and political freedoms" (UNDP 1992, 2). Yet I find this point of departure equally as disconcerting as the need for nameless sponsorship of "Third World" children. These definitions and representations are disconcerting not for what is said, but rather for the silences that lie between the spaces and punctuation marks. Analytically and operationally, what types of processes and products would we encounter were we to explore these spaces with questions about agency and agents, were we to ask, "Development for whom, by whom, to what end? For whose gain?" and even, "Why development?" How would the *process* of finding possible responses radically alter Bartelmus's beginning?

In order to examine these possible processes, permit me to shift analytical emphases to Escobar's discussion of development as discourse. Escobar's development as discourse provides an analytical frame that allows us to critically interrogate the multiple influences and sites of power that have been brought to bear on shaping contemporary understandings of development.

As an analytical paradigm, development as discourse draws attention to a broad range of discursive formations that would not readily be considered part of a discussion on developmental paradigms. When Foucault (1972) refers to discursive formations, he points to a collectivity of rules, patterns of positioning and dialogue that exist across multiple spaces, which when dispersed, generate an appearance of regularity and unified representation. In this light he writes:

> If there is unity, its principle is not therefore a determined form of statements;
> it is not rather the group of rules which simultaneously or in turn, have made
> possible purely perceptual description, together with observation mediated
> through instruments, the procedures used in laboratory experiments, statisti-
> cal calculations, epidemiological or demographic observation, institutional
> regulations, and therapeutic practice? What one must characterize and indi-
> vidualize is the coexistence of these dispersed and heterogeneous statements;
> the system that governs their division, the degree to which they depend upon

one another, the way in which they interlock or exclude one another, the transformation that they undergo, and the play of the location, arrangement and replacement. (Foucault 1972, 34)

If there is unity regarding the content and constitution of development, it is certainly not as spontaneous as Bartelmus would have us believe. Discursive analyses, however, highlight the fact that the *appearance* of spontaneity and agreement is achieved only by concerted efforts. These efforts emanate from multiple and varied constructions of cultural, political and ideological unities within hierarchies of power, and can range from international policies on and approaches to development to thirty-second advertisement slots during the evening news.

Escobar therefore pays particular attention to the ways in which development debates arrive at their truths and falsities over time. He focuses on constructions of "normalized subject" and countries, thereby allowing for appropriation and correction of the "abnormal", as has historically occurred in the supposed relationship between imperialism and the "savage", between development and the underdeveloped native. Finally he concludes that the production of discourses and discursive practices works towards the consolidation of hierarchies of power.

Unlike Bartelmus's epigraph, Escobar's represents a healthy suspicion of developmental agendas. If we are to refer to development as a valid concept, then what are its underlying assumptions? Who are the agents of development? What are the genealogy and locus of its power?

In unmasking the innocuous, Escobar points to multiple, heterogeneous yet complementary sites that serve to build a coherent need for this phenomenon called development. In *Encountering Development* (1995) he observes that the genealogy of development includes a number of discursive events. Among these he highlights

- the designation of two-thirds of the world's population as underdeveloped after 1945 (p. 23);
- the construction of the North as the answer to this newly induced problem of poverty (p. 56);
- the professionalization and institutionalization of development, for example, development economics devoted to getting the figures right, and experts whose jobs required them to confront the abnormality of underdevelopment (pp. 57–101);

- the embodiment of poverty through iconic representations, for example, the images of the starving Sudanese child or the abandoned Latin-American child fulfilled, or the use of peasants, women and the environment as contemporary tropes whose survival hinges on the need for development (pp. 102–211).

Escobar notes that when these combined events are dispersed we are faced with a global scenario that makes it difficult to envision life without the need for development. He notes that it is not the presence of any one of these events that is significant, but rather the way these events are "able to form systematically the objects of which (they) speak, to group them and arrange them in certain ways, to give them a unity of their own" (1995, 386).

Underlying the claims of development has been an aura of truth and scientific knowledge that serves to consolidate loci of power in the development debate. For development to be seen as necessary and integral to life, Escobar argues, there had to be accompanying discourses on accuracy, need, efficiency, solutions and probability of success (as reflected, for example, in feasibility studies and cost-benefit analyses of many project-driven approaches). In this regard Escobar writes: "Development had to rely on the production of knowledge that could provide a scientific picture of a country's social and economic problems and resources. This entailed the establishment of institutions capable of generating such a knowledge" (1995, 37). Yet these power differentials, as discursive elements, are not superstructural. There are always counter-discourses, resistance and subversion. For example, alongside of, and occasionally within, the establishment of development-accrediting institutions there has been a strong feminist critique against the hegemonic assumptions and marginalizations of minority groups that are created by the pursuit of development.

A strong proviso needs to be inserted at this point. I am by no means attempting to overlook the very tangible evidence of world crises. The material dimension of discursive practices reflects military unrest, starvation, limited or negligible access to educational and health facilities, increasing marginalization with respect to technological advancements, environmental depletion and gender-based inequities. Yet the success of counter-hegemonic projects and acts of resistance is tied to an understanding of how power exercises itself and manifests geopolitical control.

Failure to recognize this inevitably undermines the aims and goals of any counter-movement and further makes those movements complicit with the very thing that they aim to de-centre (Escobar 1995, 381). It is therefore not surprising that we find the same hegemonic principles at work within the pedagogic sites of gender and development.

Nuancing Gender and Development

I want to draw attention here to some of the ways in which the field of gender and development, as an academic site of knowledge production, has served to perpetuate many of the inequities that plague traditional constructs of development. The field of gender and development has found itself lodged in a peculiar tension between its allegiances to a manifesto of feminism and a mantra of development. In many ways the field of gender and development has found itself complicit in perpetuating many of the assumptions rife in the construction of development as need.

Even at its most hopeful moment, when gender and development intersected with post-modernism in the vanguard of calling for a politics of inclusion, difference and contextual rather than a priori designation of problems, there were still concerns about the extent to which this academic rhetoric could adequately disrupt the hierarchies resonant in the politics of location.

Let us look briefly at excerpts from Marchand and Parpart's *Feminism/Postmodernism/Development* (1995). The bridge between post-modernism and development has emphasized destabilizing theories, questioning locations of power, construction of knowledges and forms of representation. It has also provided a long-needed space for dialogue between previously defined oppositional geopolitical voices. A post-modernist's deconstructive project of development has, according to Marchand and Parpart, provided "new ways of thinking about women's development. It welcomes diversity, acknowledges previously subjugated voices and knowledge(s) and encourages dialogue between development practitioners and their 'clients' " (1995, 17). A post-modernist approach to development rearticulates many of the issues previously raised by Third World women, such as diversity and inclusion as a transformative practice. As expected, the mood has been celebratory, as is evident in Marchand and Parpart's observation that "the celebration of difference and multiple identities has provided a welcome plurality and richness to feminist analysis" (1995, 18). Subjugated voices and acknowledgement of difference and multiple identities become signposts that signal intent to disrupt hierarchies, dislocate and challenge sites of power, and bring difference to the fore (for example, themes, representation, approaches).

Plurality has its underbelly though; it hints at undermining projects of solidarity, and again the authors ask, "If women's identities are constructed and fluid and the world is full of uncertainty and confusion how can women in both the South and North mobilize to defend their interests?" (1995, 18). One should simultaneously ask, In what ways do present hierarchies serve to tie these interests into a zero-sum relationship?

I take issue, however, with the celebration of difference within postmodern discourses on gender and development. By this objection I do not mean to suggest that discourses around the issues of diversity and inclusion have not posed the critical challenge that discourses of difference pose to omissions, silences and tensions of imperial and hegemonic metanarratives. It is, however, intended to bring to the foreground the idea that any exercise aimed at "exploding the canon" must ask why it is that, in this historical moment, the environment allows for acknowledgement of diversity while remaining startlingly unresponsive to the extreme Westernization of development or to the imbalance present in epistemological formation and institutionalized discourses on development.

These concerns have long been voiced by Third World organizations such as the Development Alternatives for Women in a New Era (DAWN) network and other organizations representing the interests of women in the South. Let us turn, for instance, to Peggy Antrobus's[1] opening comments at the Fifth International Forum of the Association for Women in Development (AWID). She observes:

> However, the association has certainly changed its complexion by becoming more international and, now, by inviting practitioners and grassroots activists to its meeting. Just notice what happens when academics allow such people into their forum – not to mention the heavy dose of women's culture and feminism! I recall my feeling of alienation at my first AWID meeting. I felt out of place; I didn't belong. I didn't think I would ever return. But now I am impressed at the progress of the association not only in inviting increasing

numbers of women from the South but also in making us all feel "comfortable". (1993, 9)

I find Antrobus's statements telling, and subtly reflective of the systemic problems in the gender and development debate. Her lived intersectionality as activist, academic, Third World woman of colour (as an ideological/ethnic configuration) and policy-maker highlights a number of these concerns. Take, for example, her identification of the divide between activism and academia, where the "field" and the "expert" exist contiguously, if not as mutually exclusive categories: "However, the association has certainly changed its complexion by becoming more international and, now, by inviting practitioners and grassroots activists to its meeting."

Also apparent in this geopolitical and ethnic divide is the manner in which this dichotomy influences the production and institutionalization of knowledge. Antrobus suggests that less dichotomized and hierarchical discourses possess the capacity to transform the *content* of development paradigms: "Just notice what happens when academics allow such people into their forum – not to mention the heavy dose of women's culture and feminism!" In so doing she raises significant theoretical connections between the importance of diversity, issues of identity and difference and their potential to disrupt the existing power differentials that obtain in centre–margin relationships.

In making this assertion, Antrobus points to the fact that nothing adequately compensates for the "structured absences" of previous paradigms as does a foundational critique of the power/knowledge base that holds these hierarchies, intellectual priorities and exclusions in place (Julien and Mercier, quoted in Giroux 1992, 118). The excerpt from Antrobus therefore suggests that feminist development practitioners need to critically examine the cultural, institutional, political and ideological formations that establish geopolitical dualisms such that the dominant discourses regarding power and knowledge continue to reside in the North.[2]

However, what I find particularly telling in the excerpt from Antrobus are the interpretative possibilities of her use of the word "comfortable". It reveals not only the extent to which normalized subjectivities are produced, but also the immanent and tenacious hold of power differentials among feminists within the global divide. While Antrobus lauds the *appearance* of inclusion, there is simultaneously the sense that as an activist Southern woman of colour, she is still *other*ed and must be "made comfortable" by those whose domain it remains.

This telling slippage raises questions around the power of the voice. Whose voices are heard in the production of knowledge within gender and development debates? Further, in what ways are these voices appropriated and deployed without subverting the power differentials of gender and development?

Despite, and because of, the inscription of the other in development discourses, notions of Northern centrality remain very much a part of the development debate. What appears as a project in participation and cross-cultural dialogue often becomes little more than diversity tokenism.

Further, paying homage to difference, issues of diversity and participation often provides development practitioners in the North with a red herring; it often absolves them of responding critically to their own positions of privilege as agents within locations and sites of structural inequities. The appropriation of the subaltern's voice as a native informant for first-world intellectuals resurfaces again and will continue to do so within the discourse of gender and development as long as these power structures remain unchallenged and undisrupted (Spivak 1999, 284).

The Historicity of Present Conceptualization

An overview of three of the more influential planning and policy approaches for women in development – Women in Development (WID), Women and Development (WAD) and Gender and Development (GAD) – also highlights the extent to which the field of gender and development has appropriated and deployed Southern women for development. Many of the projects, policies and policy formulations associated with these three approaches aimed to assist the needs of low-income women in the Third World (Moser 1993, 55). However, with this as their point of departure, they similarly adopted a myopic understanding of development as a problem of poverty and underdevelopment, in ways that are unrelated to broader geopolitical discourses of inequity and consumption. As such these policies perceived the "condition" of women as subject to the same economic pathologies and solution possibilities that had already been assigned to the nation-state.

Equity, anti-poverty and efficiency strategies of WID and WAD approaches have invariably highlighted the need to generate welfare-type support for women in the performance of their multiple roles. These strategies aimed to increase women's participation in, and benefits from, the possibilities of development approaches. Yet an assessment of the impact of incorporating women's "traditional" modes of production into national productivity schemes forces us to ask who really benefits from micro-enterprise systems. How is the exploitation of women's time and labour within national economic plans justified according to principles of optimum use and elasticity? Further, how often are women of the South trained in local development projects (often micro-enterprise) for the purpose of subordinated integration into an already uneven global market?

Admittedly, the field of gender and development has been instrumental in naming women's invisibility in the labour market, identifying the importance of their roles to social cohesion and economic production, and even highlighting how women have subverted dominant discourses on development through the disruption of many village/community-based projects.

Despite these political successes, two points drastically undermine the claims of gender and development to incorporate difference and provide alternative, more equitable means of constructing development. First, the field of gender and development is often prone to articulating its themes and concerns against existing lines of asymmetries, as opposed to in an innovative and self-critical manner. This presents a global scenario in which women in the North are rarely ever implicated in discourses of asymmetry, for even at the points where imperialism and neocolonialism are named, these political constructions wear a decidedly masculine face. The domain of gender and development has very much been constructed in essentialized terms, where the face of the North – home to the development practitioners and policies of adjustment – has been masculinized, while the face of the South – home to the clients of development – has been that of feminized poverty. Feminist practitioners of the North therefore remain dangerously benign, placeless and without ideology in this dichotomized representation.

In this light, I am reminded of a conference I attended entitled "Global Women's Studies in a Globalizing World", where I sat in on a panel discussion called "Women and Globalization: From Above/From Below". The panellists' inability to recognize their own culpability and connection to the poverty and exploitation of the transnational agencies, which their missionary spirit so enthusiastically decried, immediately outraged me and my graduate colleagues who were present. I not so calmly suggested that we could not afford to confine the macroeconomic questions of our research to discrete geographical locations, and "these women" work in factories and produce for a market: *Where is it?* Policies come from somewhere: *Where do they originate?* And someone or some categories of people are benefiting from this structure of production: *Who are they?* I was told in turn – according to some inexplicable and misdiagnosed assessment of my Caribbean accent and, I suspect, an attempt to make me feel included – that they had also done research on Jamaica.[3] Without the necessary auto-critique we continue to perpetuate erroneous dichotomized representations of development as a bad, masculinized paradigm, designed to do harm to poor women of the South. In this model too many actors go uncharted and unchecked.

Second, globally inserting women of the South as, first and foremost, vulnerable victims of these masculinized development paradigms results in (re)presentation of Southern women in the context of visibility without power. It becomes too easy therefore to see the squalor and not the agency exercised in the daily routines of life. The gaze, while turned southward, filters what is seen through the lens of privilege and othering, as discussed by a number of noted post-colonial feminists (Spivak 1999; John 1996; Visweswaran 1994; Mohanty 1991). Mohanty, for example, in her seminal piece "Under Western Eyes" rightly takes issue with the monolithic if not iconographic construction of the "Third World woman" in the development debate. She argues that "This mode of feminist analysis, by homogenizing and systematising the experiences of different groups of women in these countries, erases all marginal and resistant modes and experiences" (1991, 73). This type of scholarship, I argue, is particularly dangerous, on two grounds.

First, the iconographic representation of the poor, vulnerable Southern woman perpetuates the need for the world's gender experts to come from the North (Escobar 1995, 177). Equally as potent is the fact that the voices which do come from the South are muted by discourses of erasure, by virtue of the translation that occurs through the politics or representation by these same North-based "gender experts". If we as feminist practitioners are to redress this, then we must constantly recognize the power/knowledge impulses that fuel these constructions. It is useful here to pay attention to Escobar's admonition that

> The study of gender as difference (Trinh 1989) has to be told from a non-ethnocentric feminist perspective. The difficulties are clear enough, for this entails developing languages through which women's oppression can be made visible cross-culturally without reinforcing – actually disallowing – the thought that women have to be developed and traditions revamped along Western lines. (1995, 189)

While the latter is a broader and collective project that needs to be conducted within and from multiple sites and locations, I want here to focus on the ways in which gender and development within academia serves to perpetuate this ethnocentric feminist perspective on development.

Gender and Development as Discursive Pedagogical Constructions: Constructions of Difference and Subordination

The present discussion on gender and development unfolds in ways that are strongly reminiscent of a childhood game played in the Caribbean called "There's a Brown Girl in a Ring". The ditty that accompanied the antics in the ring was

1
There's a brown girl in a ring
sha la la la la
There's a brown girl in a ring
sha la la la la la la
There's a brown girl in a ring
sha la la la la
And she looks like a sugar an' a plum plum plum

2
Girl show me a motion
sha la la la
Come on, show me a motion

sha la la la
Show me a motion
sha la la la
And she looks like a sugar an' a plum plum plum

3
Come hug and kiss yuh partner
sha la la la
Come hug and kiss yuh partner
sha la la la
Come an' hug and kiss yuh partner
sha la la la
And she looks like a sugar an' a plum plum plum

Much of the discourse on gender and development, like this game, seems to be driven by ideas of performance ("show me your motion"), the pursuit of solidarity ("come hug and kiss your partner"), positionality and location (Where in the ring are you?) and stereotypical (mis)representations ("And she looks like a sugar an' a plum plum plum") between and among women. I use these components as an analytical base to discuss the ways in which these elements of the academic development debate combine to reproduce and perpetuate existing global asymmetries among women.

Show Me Your Motion: Gender Performance and Development

By highlighting gender performances I wish to engage in an examination of the ways in which Third World female academics in the field of gender and development are structurally called upon to perform stereotypes and typifications of their ethnic and gendered identities. By using the term "perform" I am referring to the fact that the gendered and racialized/ethnic body does not exist a priori or in abstraction, but rather via a multiplicity of meanings that are discursively applied with intent to produce coherent representations.

As part of this discourse, signs and symbols work within shifting orbits that comply with or subvert these representations. The idea of performance suggests that, while there is no core sense of identity, the shifting appellations and significations present visual unitaries that signal the existence of the identity. In this light Judith Butler writes:

> In other words, acts, gestures, and desire produce the effect of an internal core or substance, but produce this on the surface of the body, through the play of signifying absences that suggest, but never reveal, the organizing principle of identity as a cause. Such acts, gestures, enactments, generally construed, are performative in the sense that the essence of identity that they otherwise purport to express are fabrication manufactured and sustained through corporeal signs and other discursive means. That the gendered body is performative suggests that it has no ontological status apart from the various acts which constitute its reality. (1990, 136)

Geopolitically, the relationship between ontology and social meaning is reflected as part of a dialogue on dress, language, gender, race/ethnicity and other signifying elements. These components combine not only to construct a sense of identification/representation but also induce a performance of these identities. Therefore, while bodies exist materially, they have symbolic representations; further, regulatory expectations of how the material body – dressed, for instance, in a sari, or bearing a face characterized by tribal marks – ought to perform its ethnic and national identities.

The structural enactment of these performances is readily obvious at conferences on gender and development. To date I have yet to attend a conference on gender and development at which the polarity of North and South is not reflected in the structure of the panels. I have yet to attend a conference on gender and development at which the polarity of North and South is not reproduced both in the thematic focus and in the ways in which panellists are asked to speak on these themes. Global conferences appear to be characterized by formats that link themes such as *emerging capitalisms* and *teaching/theorizing/organizing* to practitioners from the North, while themes such as *stories from the field, theorizing action/acting on theory* and *mass movements and gender struggles* are invariably represented by scholars of colour from the Third World. Epistemologically, this creates false binary and polar relationships between theory and action, one of the major shortcomings of the discipline as a whole. Also perpetuated are identity constructions that cast practitioners in the North as the bearers of high theory and those of the South as the activists and fieldworkers.

This dichotomy was especially glaring at the conference "Which Way for Women and Development? Debating Concepts, Strategies and

Directions for the Twenty-first Century" (New York City, 15–17 October 1998). Discussant Eudine Barriteau, while summarizing the main points of a panel entitled "Stories from the Field: Theorizing Action? Acting on Theory", was prompted to ask, "If we, the women from the South, are considered the field, then where is the Great House?" – thereby invoking the powerful image of inequity present in the plantation relationship between slave and master.

A Vision of Solidarity: Unity in Diversity

The essays in *Feminism/Postmodernism/Development,* despite their analytical and thematic differences, collectively address the need to disrupt meta-narratives and engage in a valorizing of women's multiple voices. In an insightful essay Maria Nzomo (1995) questions the relevance of post-modernism to Kenya's political terrain. She observes that there is still some relevance to universal ideals as a means of strategizing for women's political advancement, and she highlights the need for unity in diversity. Similarly, Marchand and Parpart warn of the dangers attached to fervent adherence to difference; they write:

> Postmodern feminism, taken to its extreme, can stymie collective action among women, both within nations and on a world scale. The emphasis on difference and indeed on the often deep divisions between women in the South, minority women in the North and more privileged (often white) women in the North (and some in the South as well) offers both insights and dangers. (1995, 18)

The dangers they refer to are the inactivity and inertia that can result when points of difference undermine a sense of a "collective women's struggle" against patriarchy and gender hierarchy. However, if we take constructions of patriarchy and hierarchy as meta-narratives with multiple (therefore "patriarchies" and "hierarchies"), variable and culturally specific manifestations, then the extent to which women are able to unite around these amorphous and unnuanced phenomena remains doubtful.

At the point that patriarchal and gender hierarchies are translated into lived concepts – such as domestic violence; the feminization of poverty through structural adjustment policies or imposed embargoes;

unequal terms and conditions applied to scholarly research grants and projects in the South and North; starvation and hunger not because of the absence of food, but due to consumption and distribution – one can easily ask how and when women have collectively struggled against patriarchal and gender hierarchies.

In support of Nzomo's call for unity in diversity, I also think it useful to conceptualize solidarity in terms of scales.[4] Invariably one finds that the larger or more complex a system, the more vulnerable that system becomes. As expected, as the points of interaction shift from the household to the community to the nation, region or other geopolitical grouping, not only the number of actors increases, but so do the points of difference and dissonance, thereby making unity and solidarity a tenuous concept at best.

However, what is particularly striking about the rhetoric of inclusion and diversity in the field of gender and development is the language of appropriation, ownership and privilege that attends it. Assertions such as that post-modern feminism "acknowledges previously subjugated voices" (Marchand and Parpart 1995, 17), while simultaneously bemoaning the monopoly that "development experts have had on the field", belie the dilemma of inclusion without challenge to the embedded nature of power in the field of gender and development. At the risk of my being critiqued for over-reading, "to acknowledge" is no more than to admit to the existence of something. However, the mere recognition of presence does little to disrupt relations of power between "practitioners and their clients", neither does it signal a preparedness to engage structurally with the issues, themes and concerns that are foregrounded by these voices of diversity.

There's a Brown Girl in the Ring: Issues of Positionality and Location

Judith Butler observes that "language gains the power to create 'the socially real' " through the locutionary acts of speaking subjects (1990, 115). When applied to the field of gender and development this statement prompts a series of related questions such as: Who have been the speaking subjects? Where do they speak from? What is said? And further, what forms of "the socially real" are engendered by what is said? (Foucault 1972, 50–63).

Here I am concerned not so much with the verbal speech act as I am with its translation via the technologies of script and publication. The extent to which discourses of development derive their legitimacy is in no small part linked to the power of the interlocutor. This is not to suggest that the power of the discourse is reducible or equivalent to the authority of the interlocutors; it suggests rather that the power associated with language is very much determined by the sites from, and to which, articulation occurs. Academia, therefore, is not only one such site of legitimization and verification, but it is also mediated by supporting and interacting mechanisms and institutions such as conferences, classrooms and publishing houses, which serve to validate the spoken word by facilitating its documentation in written text.

This relationship between power and knowledge raises concerns about the ways in which the politics of publication further nuance a gender and development field that is characterized by a seemingly silent South and a speaking North. This is further concretized through curricula used in classrooms and other sites of knowledge construction and dissemination.

A quick overview of three of the more popular publishing houses for gender and development easily shows the imbalance between the published voices of the North and those of the South. Both Zed Books and Women, Ink self-identify as being among the few publishing houses that not only take a global view but in so doing hold a specific interest in the writings of "Southern women". Interestingly, despite this stated claim and the fact that many of the texts listed in their 1998 catalogues did make reference to issues and sites in the South, many of the academics and practitioners were identified as already having inserted themselves into the dominant discourse through their institutionalization in US universities. However, other publishing houses such as Routledge, while – and possibly by virtue of – being more mainstream, show a completely inverse relationship with texts, themes and authors from the South.

This scenario raises a range of issues that cannot be fully addressed here, but which are equally relevant to our discussion. Among these issues is the strategic potential of Third World academic practitioners of gender and development, as many operate in positions of privilege and power within academic institutions in the North. Notwithstanding this potential, there are very real problems of institutional signification,

signification that results in a tendency to dismiss the voice of these academics as either the "true and authentic native" who is representative of "her people" or the equally reprehensible corollary, as not being the true and authentic native, because she is several times removed (geographically, intellectually and occasionally in class) from the stereotypical poverty, need and vulnerability of the "true native". Both are often institutional responses to the need to fulfill requirements for faculty diversity, and both are gestures of conflation that eliminate the difficult moments involved in dealing with diversity, by reinscribing monolithic representations and concerns of women from the South. These gestures, however, are supported by classroom and curriculum choices that, in seemingly more benign ways, erase from the field of gender and development the multiple and complex realities of women in the South, through the use of case studies as a teaching mechanism.

The Politics of (Mis)representation

The increasing shift from meta-narratives of development to project-driven community-based approaches highlights and even centralizes the use of case studies as a teaching aid. While this tool has been useful for training practitioners who are conducting simulation and improvisation sessions, the approach runs the risk of again rendering "the South" and the experiences of the South as a monolith. The vast majority of these case-studies provide practitioners with examples from the South, again perpetuating the representation of development as a problem of "underdevelopment" housed in "the South".

In addition to the southward gaze of these cases, the use of certain set tropes has come to represent the circumscribed poverty and hardships of the South. Recurring images – of the poverty-stricken or acid-burnt Bangladeshi woman, the African female battling for survival and a sustainable livelihood as she gathers fuel-wood, the Thai prostitute – all become part of a singular representation of the "Third World woman". This, as we have explored, presents the *reality* of women in singular terms and by way of state-assigned pathologies. These combined representations not only propel any feasible notions of development into stasis but also deny women any acts or performance of agency, autonomy and self-representation.

The use of case-studies also responds to developmental approaches and strategies that are generated out of concerns for inclusion, participation and the position of less-disadvantaged groups. They respond to the underlying assumption that participation increases a sense of ownership and makes the solutions for problems more sustainable. Therefore, localized village solutions to developmental problems are more easily translated into the classroom for analysis. They become a prepackaged mode of presence within the classroom. Unfortunately they are often the only exposure that North-based students may ever encounter to the geopolitical location being examined. And while as practitioners we are prone to ask what the case-study presents, we may also glean fruitful discussion by asking our students to discuss what the case-study does *not* present.

Alternative Development or Alternatives to Development? Pedagogy as a Site of Construction

The classroom is a site of knowledge production, conferences, publications, images and forms of representation. All influence what is filtered into communities, policies, planning and the further definitions of women's lived-experience "problems and problem-solving" models. I am further concerned that an emerging cadre of "development practitioners", by virtue of being trained in the North, possesses limited and somewhat diminished skills in critically undermining the representations and marginalizations of self within academic circles. This weakness is due to the very institutional rules and regulations of conformity that exist within academia (for example, grades, recommendations, referrals and so on).

Nonetheless, a sense of critical pedagogy must pervade the field of gender and development if we are to disrupt hegemonic constructions of development, gross marginalizations and silences. I draw my use of the term "critical pedagogy" from Henry Giroux's work, which argues that pedagogy may be seen broadly as a pattern of learning that allows people to see themselves. He writes:

> Border pedagogy must provide the conditions for students to engage in cultural remapping as a form of resistance. Students should be given the

opportunity to engage in systematic analyses of the ways in which the dominant culture creates borders saturated in terror, inequality, and forced exclusions. Students need to analyze the conditions that have disabled others to speak in the places where those who have power exercise authority. (1992, 33)

With this in mind, how can we then construct pedagogical sites that allow the South to not merely find reflections of itself within academia, but rather to become central and strategic to discussions of issues, concerns and themes? I maintain that gender and development cannot be apolitical or assume positions of neutrality. A critical pedagogy of gender and development requires that the classroom become a transformatory site that challenges marginalizations, misrepresentations and the established boundaries and dualities. A critical pedagogy of gender and development must expose and disrupt discourses that have served to exclude the voices of subordinate groups, and must give precedence to those voices in the formulation of curricula, as both a theoretical and methodological pursuit.

Further, critical pedagogy must be governed by a language that allows for competing solidarities without reducing issues and themes to scripts of singularity. Most importantly, the task of critical pedagogy must harness its energies so that transformative intellectuals not only question their own positions of privilege, but by extension question, confront and challenge the multiple sites in which this privilege resides.

I have not asked that we dispense with the idea of development. I have, however, argued that as feminist practitioners from the South, we need to aggressively construct sites of critical pedagogy that challenge the structures of privilege and hegemony as they affect the representation and interpolation of women from the South in debates on gender and development. I maintain, nonetheless, that unless Northern practitioners respond transformatively to their own sites of privilege, as well as to the need to become developmental anthropologists in their *own space*, the voices of women from the South will continue to be marginalized from the potential benefits upon which our opening epigraphs assume we all agree.

Notes

1. These remarks were delivered on 21 November 1991, at which time Antrobus was the coordinator of DAWN.
2. The polymorphous exercise of power within development as discourse requires that we include policy-makers, technocrats, politicians, students, activists, academics, funding agencies and project managers under the heading of practitioners. It is also important that we not absolve local elites from their exercise of similar types of control over decision making and resources. Also important are the ways in which local elites become complicit with Northern development practitioners. However, this dimension lies marginally outside the scope of this work. Notwithstanding that, the same discursive frame of analysis can be applied to local power differentials.
3. It is significant to note that industrialized countries, which represent only 26 per cent of the world's population, nonetheless consume 81 per cent of the world's energy and produce 70 per cent of the world's chemical fertilizers and 87 per cent of world armaments. One US resident, for example, has been noted as using as much energy as 7 Mexicans, 55 Indians, 168 Tanzanians and 900 Nepalis (Escobar 1995, 212).
4. This idea of scale was brought home to me most insightfully by my graduate colleague Elora Chowdhury.

⁂Part III⁂

Theorizing Historiography, Historicizing Gender and Sexuality

⇥ Chapter 5 ⇤

A Symbiotic Visiting Relationship
Caribbean Feminist Historiography and
Caribbean Feminist Theory

PATRICIA MOHAMMED

All history is the history of thought. In so far as human actions are mere events, the historian cannot understand them; strictly, he cannot even ascertain that they have happened. They are only knowable to him as the outward expression of thoughts. (Collingwood [1946] 1994, 115)

For the feminist historian this is an especially appealing theoretical perspective. It makes critical analysis of the past and the present a continuing operation; the historian can interpret the world while trying to change it. It also insists on the need to examine gender concretely and in context and to consider it a historical phenomenon, produced, reproduced, and transformed in different situations and over time. (Scott 1988, 7)

Nor is theory in a position to "reflect" on anything. It can only tear concepts from their critical zone of reference and force them beyond a point of no-return, a process whereby it loses all "objective" validity but gains substantially in real affinity with the present system. (Baudrillard 1997, 40)

History and Feminist Theory: A Mutual Dependence

Gender is an order by which human society takes sexual difference and shapes it into recurrent cultural practices and social relations between men and women. The role of feminism in the latter half of the twentieth century has been largely that of refining "gender" as a conceptual tool for social and historical analysis and making more evident the myriad concerns brought on to social progress by sexual differentiation. From this perspective, Jane Flax defines feminism's role as follows:

> Confronted with such a bewildering set of questions, it is easy to overlook the fact that a fundamental transformation in social theory has occurred. The single most important advance in feminist theory is that the existence of gender relations has been problematized. Gender can no longer be treated as a simple natural fact. The assumption that gender relations are natural arose from two coinciding circumstances: the unexamined identification and confusion of (anatomical) sexual differences with gender relations, and the absence of active feminist movements. (Flax 1990a, 43–44)

The set of ideas developed in feminism and feminist theory thus far has withstood major attacks from its detractors both inside and outside the academy. On the contrary, feminist theory has gained greater precision from these critiques, as it should. In the evolution of feminist thought there is a genealogy of concepts and ideas that can be traced as far back as the fourteenth century, if not before.[1] There was, however, a noticeable acceleration of ideas and concepts in feminist thought and activism over the past forty years. From the 1960s onwards feminism entered university classrooms, marched on the streets and clattered the pots and pans in the kitchens of many households, rather than preoccupying only a limited group of conscious women and men, as had occurred in the previous centuries.

History – a history of ideas, as well as a history of events and practices – provides the backdrop against which the conceptual development of gender in feminist thought must be examined. This relationship between practice and the development of ideas and concepts is a symbiotic one in feminism, as it has also been for other disciplines. Ideas and concepts are born out of social practice. Such ideas are themselves further challenged by people's understanding and interpretation through their continued practice. History is the main discipline through which change in ideas and practices may be examined, measured and assessed over time to allow one to see patterns of thought and behaviour.

One example in feminism may serve to illustrate this symbiotic relationship between history and theory, particularly the application of concept in theory. Patriarchy was formally identified and acknowledged as an ideology, concept and practice evident in the relations between the sexes in Kate Millett's *Sexual Politics,* which was first published in 1970. By 1986, in *The Creation of Patriarchy,* Gerda Lerner extends and adds to the value of the concept of patriarchy by scrutinizing it through a historical lens. It is worth quoting her at length:

> A correct analysis of our situation and how it came to be what it is will help us to create an empowering theory. We must think about gender historically and specifically as it occurs in varied and changing societies . . . Our search, then, becomes a search for the history of the patriarchal system. To give the system of male dominance historicity and to assert that its functions and manifestations change over time is to break sharply with the handed down tradition. This tradition has mystified patriarchy by making it ahistoric, eternal, invisible, and unchanging. But it is precisely due to changes in the social and educational opportunities available to women that in the nineteenth and twentieth centuries large numbers of women finally became capable of critically evaluating the process by which we have helped to create the system and maintain it. We are only now able to conceptualize women's role in history and thereby to create a consciousness which can emancipate women. This consciousness can also liberate men from the unwanted and undesired consequences of the system of male dominance. (1986, 37)

Lerner sharpened a primary conceptual tool of feminism through her examination of its different forms over long spans of history. This allowed her to conclude on the continued relevance of patriarchy, if not crucial value, as a concept in feminist theory, even while its use was fluid and changeable in different and varied contexts.

Another fundamental concept in feminist thought is that of difference, at first referred to as "sexual difference" – how women and men are anatomically different, as well as the way in which women's identity is different from that of men. In the 1980s the concept of difference was hinged against equality – the "equality versus difference" debate – and presented the terms in opposition. It posed a serious dilemma to and limited the potential for feminist theory as a liberating theory for both women and men and, as Hermsen and van Lenning point out for Dutch feminism, divided thinkers into different camps: "equal rights feminism" and "ethical feminism" (1991, 19). If women were different from men, then how could equality ever be achieved between the sexes? Joan Scott's brilliant "deconstruction" of the terms through philosophy itself led to new and vastly richer ways in which the concepts of difference and equality could be interpreted. Rather than as an opposition, they could be viewed as mutually dependent on each other: "both concepts presuppose each other in the sense that they have no meaning without each other. Considering both equality and inequality is, of necessity, based on thinking about differences" (Hermsen and van Lenning 1991, 20).

This opening has also led to the concept of difference gaining more and more nuances with time, coinciding with the increased feminist activism and thought in other societies across the globe. The concept of difference expanded to include debates about equality and differences among women themselves by class and ethnicity within the same society, and to differences between women of developed and of developing societies. More than this, it overlapped with ideas in post-modern thought, for example, that of negating the hierarchical value system placed on cultural differences in favour of acknowledging the inevitability and necessity of cultural differences in the practices of human society. Such insights in feminist theory were again sharpened by the theoretical debates alongside the practical activity of feminism over the last few decades. Ideas need historical time and space. They incubate and hatch new ideas only when people test them against reality, whether consciously or inadvertently.

To underscore the importance of history as a discipline shaping feminist theory is not to presume that all feminist theory has been dependent on and determined first by knowledge in history. On the contrary, second-wave feminist theory has taken its cue more from the practice and activism of feminism and from insights revealed by other disciplines, particularly those of literature and psychology. Nonetheless, Lerner bemoaned the fact that until the 1980s, and persisting for several years, much of the theoretical work in modern feminism had been "ahistorical and negligent of feminist historical scholarship . . . The reasons for this lie in the conflict-ridden and highly problematic relationship of women to history" (1986, 3). Yet the most frequently employed concepts in feminist theory, such as *woman, patriarchy, femininity, masculinity* and *gender,* attain rigour in feminist thought precisely when they undergo historical scrutiny. The meaning and interpretation of words change in different historical contexts, but in the exchange between history and theory we can establish continuities and discontinuities in words, ideas and practices.

To exemplify this point, let us take the concept of femininity as applied in contemporary gender scholarship. The idea of femininity makes sense only as a recurring definition and description of womanhood relative to past constructions of femininity. "Femininity" at one point referred primarily to the state of being female. With conceptual development it was also defined more categorically, in relation to and against masculinity. In addition, feminist analyses have begun to investigate *process* – becoming woman, attaining womanhood. Becoming a woman from girlhood is a process that takes place from birth and is mediated by a host of deliberate strategies and consequences rooted in the historical moment into which one is born, as well as the events and the historical time in which one lives. The femininity expectations and roles of an Indo-Trinidadian female born in the nineteenth century in a Presbyterian household are different in some ways from those of an Indian girl born at the end of the twentieth century. Yet both exhibit features or qualities defined as Indian femininity. Some features are recurrent, others change. A specific case makes this clearer. Anna Mahase Sr was born in 1899 in Trinidad. She writes in her autobiography of her years in a Presbyterian mission orphanage:

> Apart from attending regular church services twice a day, Hindi service twice, Hindi service in the morning and English at night, we did quite a lot of religious studies at the Home . . . There were among forty girls in residence more or less, some going out after marriage, others coming in. A girl did not have to be an orphan to be sent there. They came from comfortable and Christian homes to be trained to be good housewives, who would and should be leaders and examples wherever they went. When the girls were fifteen years old and over, the parents found a suitor for them, came and took them away and married them. Miss Archibald (Canadian missionary) and our matron would assist. If on the other hand any one wished to marry one of the girls, he would write to Ms. Archibald and she would arrange. We graduated there by marriage, some were successful, others not. My own sister, Dorcas, was one of those unfortunate ones. A suitor was selected for her in Tunapuna and ended up in separation because the Morton's policy was that the Tunapuna girls must marry in the Tunapuna field. (Mahase 1992, 26–27)

The particular construct of nineteenth- and early-twentieth-century Christian – and more precisely Presbyterian Indian – femininity was carefully moulded by the circumstances at the time. The Presbyterian missionaries' goal was to convert what they perceived as a heathen population. They proceeded to educate the boys, converting them in the course of doing so, and to equip the girls to be suitable wives. Gender relations and concepts of gender identity were circumscribed by the possibilities allowed each sex at the time. Education of girls was considered unfeminine. Christianity had prescribed some boundaries for Indo-Trinidadian femininity outside of Hinduism and Islam. Arranged marriages and control by the church may have disappeared by the end of the twentieth century, but other cultural factors still mediate in the shaping of Indo-Trinidadian femininity today. These resonate with the past history of Indians, not only in the history of Indian migration and settlement within this society, but farther back to the expectations of femininity for women in India. Only thus can we seriously comprehend the constructions of femininity or different femininities that coexist in the same society at the same time, or be able to evaluate changes.

Gender may be more easily appreciated as this process of moulding and construction, blending possibilities along with constraints. Gender socialization is by no means fixed throughout the lifetime of the individual. Changes in social and economic conditions are very likely to shift cultural practices and expectations of each sex, adding to the complexity of how gender is constructed over time. Cultural practices that define gender sometimes undergo rapid shifts from one generation to the next. For instance, among certain groups of Ovambo peoples in northern Namibia, the mark of feminine beauty for a woman of the last generation was four light cuts on each cheek, leaving parallel scars about one inch long. Women were also expected to remove two middle teeth in the lower jaw. When boys attained manhood, they were to have their permanent teeth sharpened into points, with larger spaces between each tooth. For the present generation of men and women in the same groups, these alterations are unthinkable, although other notions specific to masculinity and femininity in these cultures still survive.[2]

Collectively, in the same way that one individual experiences a gendered history, so does a society. For instance, the policies and ideologies that permit or disallow female education within any society also affect the entry of women into various professions. The more the boundaries established for femininity become eroded, the more it is seen (generally at first) as an encroachment into masculine terrain, and therefore ideas of masculinity also undergo change. Thus the construction of femininity and masculinity, as these are constituted within any society at a particular time, is the sum total of a number of historical events and social practices.

Again, this point may be made more evident by examining the condition and concept of masculinity. In the Caribbean, colonization by the imperial Old World societies and African slavery laid the subterranean foundations for the definition of black masculinity in the New World. The resulting "problem of masculinity" has been that of male marginality in both the family and public power and a presumed emasculation of black men. More recent history reveals continued and similarly difficult periods for both men and women, and a persistent impact upon the development of familial and gender roles. Velma Newton in *The Silver Men* pointed out that migration to Panama (1850–1914) was predominantly male, and that for most of the nineteenth century the number of females in Barbados, Jamaica, and the Leeward and Windward islands exceeded the number of males, with a preponderance of females in the age groups between nineteen and forty-five – women of childbearing age. Newton observes:

> The large-scale emigration of men folk would have accentuated the matrifocal character of the West Indian family system . . . In the absence of legal ties, some fathers neglect their families, or leave most of the major decisions to the mother . . . What are the effects which the prolonged absence of fathers would have had on some children? . . . Apparently the returned migrant who had previously been an agricultural labourer hardly ever resumed such a lowly occupation immediately upon his repatriation. When his newly acquired wealth had been exhausted or after he realized that he could not survive on the income from his plot of land, or had failed to find some other type of employment, then he considered plantation labour, and probably experienced a loss of status in the eyes of his neighbors and friends. (1984, 107–8)

Gender identities are always created in relation to other identities and take shape over time. Gender systems are not static organizations of gender roles. A vertical understanding of gender across time supplies the

empirical basis for analysis and appreciation of the ongoing constructions of femininity and masculinity and of gender relations in a society.
Historical data, although selectively adapted as most history is, illustrate
the shifting status and conditions of men and women and allow the
analysis of power imbalances, where these exist, and knowledge of the
organization of sexual difference. In this sense history as the sum of
events and practices is best placed to "define an outlook within which
ideas develop, a theory in the original sense of the word, a conceptual
vision" (Kelly 1984, 66) of gender in any society.

The capacity of history as a linear progression of ideas and practices
that may help to shape or define an outlook and conceptual vision is
itself hotly debated in historiography. Post-modern history has posed a
severe challenge to these already contested notions with its incredulity of
the meta-narrative and revelation of many truths and positionalities
(Lyotard 1997), and a depiction of history as "events which follow one
upon another, canceling each other out in a state of indifference"
(Baudrillard 1997). I am wary of presenting a teleological view of history in the development of feminist thought, as I am also of throwing
away the real insights that may be gained from present schools of
thought that are still being sifted for intellectual value. I would like to
draw on my own sense of the strengths of both, and negate the more
obvious inherent weaknesses, to speculate on the contribution that feminist historiography may have made and may continue to bring to the
development of feminist thought in the Caribbean.

Gender and Feminist Theory: A Marriage of Convenience

Caribbean gender theory has borrowed generously from the global
expansion of feminist theory over the past three decades. There has been
a simultaneous sharpening of the conceptual vision and scholarship in
this area within the region. Developments in feminist theory took place
at a time when female access to education was growing in the Caribbean,
and furthermore when women's studies and gender studies had entered
its struggle to be formally included in the curriculum.[3] The editors of
Engendering History (1995), Verene Shepherd, Bridget Brereton and
Barbara Bailey, observe in their introduction to this book that "the establishment of gender studies as a legitimate area of academic

discourse has facilitated the engendering of mainstream acade
through more valid epistemologies. History is one of the disciplines
which has benefited from this illumination" (Shepherd, Brereton and
Bailey 1995, xiv). The questions that this raises are how history has actually benefited from the intervention of women's history and gender history,[4] and whether there is a difference between women's history and
gender history. The first question need not be resolved in this chapter; the
second I return to later.

The concept that is opaque at this time is that of gender and its derivative, gender theory. The word "gender" is used widely, popularly, very
loosely sometimes and, I have found, very often differently by different
groups of people. I want to constitute gender theory as a member of the
family of feminist theory. The two are often conflated because they are
interconnected and arguably inseparable. There would be no gender theory without its parent feminism and feminist theory. Social and historical analysis have required a concept within feminist theory that can be
delineated, even measured. Politically convenient, clearly rich in its linguistic nuances, the term "gender" developed as the category for social
analysis among writers, particularly in the English language. We need,
however, to appreciate the distinction between gender and feminist theory.

At present, when we use the term "gender" in an informed way, we
are referring to a range of different ideas and debates on which there is
no consensus among either scholars or practitioners in the fields of gender studies and policy formulation. Policy-makers argue that gender must
be derived from the lived ways in which communities experience gender
and that the academic usage of the word is irrelevant. In the academy,
biological determinists and essentialists maintain that biological and psychoanalytic sexual differences lead to gender oppression. Social constructivism, post-structuralisms and post-modernism place emphasis on
gender as a social category constructed with deliberate asymmetry to
benefit the male sex, and therefore possible to deconstruct in order to
relieve power imbalances. It is being argued that gender is neither biologically determined nor socially constructed, but a *rapprochement*
between the two (Wieringa 2002). "Gender" refers discursively to the
ongoing construction of masculinity and femininity, and politically to
the social organization of sexual difference.

Post-modernism added another dimension to understanding gender through the disciplines of psychoanalysis, philosophy, literary criticism and cultural studies. In her anxiety over what she calls "gender trouble", Judith Butler outlines the foundation of these interdisciplinary interventions and their contemplation of gender. Butler deconstructs the grand narrative of Freudian theory – that there is a coherent pattern of identification of the gendered self (*man, woman, masculinity* and *femininity*) derived from the father-mother-child triad. She suggests that fragmented and discontinuous gender identities are very possibly outcomes of early childhood and predicated on a wider range of identifications, beyond that of the linear and temporal Oedipal narrative. She challenges the idea of the primary role of parents in gender identification, and asserts the importance of secondary identifications such as relations with siblings, thus providing a major critique of the object relations theory proposed earlier by Chodorow (1978). For Butler gender is variously "a set of signs internalized, psychically imposed on the body, an act, a performance, . . . manipulated codes, rather than a core aspect of essential identity".[5] In de-essentializing gender, Butler disrupts the notion that woman is always the "other" of man, the victim of a superordinate patriarchy, the objectified sex – a central theme in phallogocentric Western discourse. The deconstruction of gender through psychoanalytic theory is a valuable one in that it allows us to perceive gender not only in terms of its measurable or tangible components. For gender and feminist theorists this is a valuable insight. Gender identities are married to psychological and sexual identities; they are not extricable elements in a chemical equation of the body. Nor are they fully described by measurable parts of economic, political and social factors. Post-modern explorations of gender inform much of contemporary feminist thought and have been debated in the Caribbean, providing a window through which writers such as Barriteau (1992, 1998b) and Mohammed (1996, 1998) have configured both man and woman as gendered subjects in the Caribbean past.

While post-modern theoretical explorations appear at first glance to offer limited scope for historical enquiry, the historian of gender must nonetheless be constantly influenced by the conceptual developments guiding us in how we think or do not think about gender at any time. For example, the way we collect data and what we determine to be the data of gender vary according to conceptual shifts in gender. Similarly, how we impose a feminist consciousness on the past must also be informed by a profound understanding of how gender is perceived and acted out during each historical period. An example may again serve to make this point clearer. In the history of Indian migration and settlement in the Caribbean during the nineteenth and early twentieth centuries, wife beating and wife murders preoccupied the colonial rulers, who dismissed the Indian population as immoral and heathen, and the early historians, who also interpreted this data with another kind of moral outrage.[6] Early feminist historiography tended to view women largely as passive victims of a disrupted Indian patriarchy that sought to regain its earlier control over women. Apart from the earliest colonial interpretations, the analyses of previous historians still provide partial truths on the subject of gender crimes among Indians. More contemporary analyses have attempted to extend such readings and look at the position of masculinity in relation to femininity and of post-migrant men in relation to women, at the spheres of power available to both sexes, at the imbalances caused by disruption of a shared gender-belief system and at the conditions in a new society that allowed a different, perhaps more violent negotiation between the sexes.[7] Such readings of gender will continue as long as gender as a theoretical construct also gets modified with time.

In general, however, the most popular and accessible debates in gender theory pertain to the ongoing conceptual shifts in ideas about biological sex and social gender, the pendulum swinging back and forth depending on what research findings are thrown up to support this or that case, what political issues are being contested between the sexes at the time and what mental and linguistic gymnastics are being played out in academic discussions. While gender theorists and academic feminists may be *au courant* with this discourse, for many outside this relatively small circle, gender is equated with woman and a quarrel with male power, as if men had no gender. The popular and public understanding of gender is that it refers to woman, and that to make something gender-sensitive, whether it is history or sociology, you simply "add women and stir". Yet in the space of the last four decades gender theory has shifted emphasis from being equated with woman, with sex-role stereotyping, gender-role socialization and social constructivism, to extensive interdisciplinary debates drawing on anthropology, sociology, biology and psychology and psychoanalysis, among others, about the ongoing and complex ways in which gender identities are constructed in society.

What separates or distinguishes feminist theory from gender theory is in my view *first,* the old fashioned distinction between levels of theory itself, and *second,* the distinction between levels of theory and concept – theory as ideas, and concepts as ideas or tools for analysis. Feminist theory contextualizes the problem of gender temporally and spatially, and establishes the politics of the researcher or the institution. At the same time we must conceive of feminist theory not as a monolithic ideology but, as Rosemary Tong describes it in the 1990s, "many theories or perspectives . . . that each feminist theory or perspective attempts to describe women's oppression, to explain its causes and consequences, and to prescribe strategies for women's liberation. The more skillfully a feminist theory can combine description, explanation, prescription, the better that theory is" (1992, 1). For instance, feminist theory that is influenced by Marxist thought locates women's nurturing and labour, particularly in the domestic sphere, as the dominant reason for their oppression as a sex. Radical feminist theory, on the other hand, sees the control of female sexuality and female reproductive capacity as the basis of women's subordination. As feminist theory and explanations in gender have progressed, it is now apparent that no one explanation is sufficient and that each perspective provides more grist for the theorist's mill.

Gender and what has now emerged as gender theory is a second generation of concepts within feminist theory, not to be undervalued because of its youthfulness, but still dependent on and derived from the broader framework of feminism and feminist theory. Gender theory arises from one overarching concern: how societies take the raw products of biological and anatomical sexual difference within their culture and materially and ideologically produce the following:

- the essence of gender – gender identity, masculinity and femininity, man and woman;
- the components of a sex/gender system – kinship, marriage and family, the sexual division of labour, control of female and male reproduction, and women's versus men's role in the economy;
- concepts of desire, romance and love;

- construction of male and female sexuality and sexual identity;
- the popular cultural processes of constructing masculinity and femininity, such as, for instance, how racial differences in femininity and masculinity were constituted during seventeenth-century slavery in the Caribbean;
- the institutionalized processes by which the dominant ideas of gender at any time are controlled or challenged, and by which group or groups in the society.

Whereas gender may be appropriated as a conceptual category and tool for social and historical analysis outside of the feminist framework, feminist theory commits the researcher or analyst more directly to "gender trouble". What therefore is feminist theory? Feminist theory is a groping towards a more universal reasoning of and for gender oppression, uniting theory and praxis in the materialism of the moment. There is a necessary contradiction here. If feminist theory as vision takes its cue from the material struggles within the society, then this undermines a fundamental premise and unifying concept in feminism, that of "woman" as the universal category and woman's oppression as the universal manifestation of gender oppression. This is a particularly crucial issue in feminism and feminist theory, as not one but several perspectives compete to explain the reasons for sexual subordination in society, and classes or groups of women have been included among the oppressors. For this reason, feminist theory can also be culturally located, moving from universalizing ideas about female subordination in general, to grounded explanations specific to a society. This latter progression in thinking about feminist theory can itself be historically traced.

We need history to understand shifts in feminist theorizing. Joan Kelly suggested that at its root the original *querelle des femmes* or feminist problematic emerged in Western discourse from the fifteenth century in France, through the work of Christine de Pisan, and was later continued by Mary Wollestonecraft in the eighteenth century. She suggested that theory was essentially oppositional to the dominant culture in three ways:

- The *querelle* was almost polemical . . . In all these writings women took a conscious dialectical stand in opposition to male defamation and subjection of women.

- In their opposition, the early feminists focused upon what we would now call gender. That is they had a sure sense that the sexes are culturally, not just biologically, formed.
- The immediate aim of these feminist theorists was to oppose the mistreatment of women. Their concern was for women, that they might have the knowledge and confidence to reject misogynist claims . . . By exposing ideology and opposing the prejudice and narrowness it fostered, they stood for a general conception of humanity (1984, 66–67).

We must admit, in scholarship at least, that these general ideas laid the groundwork for later feminist polemic. Theoretical contributions to feminism have been made largely by a class of literate women who had access to education and who were themselves oppressed by the domestic role-prescriptions idealized for them, leading to a decline in their power both inside and outside the home. Reddock demonstrates that this process also took place in the Caribbean, in her analysis of women's struggles with labour in Trinidad in the nineteenth century. She shows that the growing "housewifization" of women in the post-emancipation period undermined women's power in the workplace as well as in the home (1994), leading to a class of women who would react in different ways to their reduced power. Who constructs feminist theory and why, where they position themselves in the debate of who is the oppressor and who is the oppressed, are part of the dynamic of feminism itself. This in my view may be disentangled from the conceptual understanding of gender and its constituent parts.

Much of gender oppression or subordination recurs with remarkable similarity across societies so that *gender is possibly the more universal concept, as is patriarchy,*[8] even if linguistically they may not be similarly applied in another language. Feminist theory is today, at the beginning of the twenty-first century, far more grounded in the specific material history, conditions and struggles of a society or geographical space. It defines the vision that the people of a region share about the origins or creation of patriarchy, the causation of gender asymmetry or hierarchy, the configuration of gender identities, the status of women in relation to men, and the solutions proposed to correct imbalances in the system of gender relations.

History is one of the main disciplines through which these ideas can be debated. A knowledge of the past and changing practices provides us with the meat for analysis of gender phenomena over time. It is interesting that much of this historical material on gender may be found in anthropologists' notebooks rather than in those of the orthodox historians. Historical research in gender and in feminism are ultimately not extricable one from the other. The act of carrying out and writing a history of gender relations is, sometimes inadvertently, part of the process of feminism and of constructing feminist theory. In this I selectively draw on some of the work that has emerged in the feminist historiography of the region and read into these some gender debates and the shaping of an indigenous theoretical feminist discourse for the Caribbean.

A Genealogy of Caribbean Feminist Historiography

Caribbean feminist historiography has evolved as part of the project of feminist epistemology, developing around three major axes. These are

1. Recovering women – creating visibility
2. Theoretical perspectives in the writing of history – locating the problem of gender in Caribbean historiography
3. Methodologies and sources of history – empiricism and women as knowers

Recovering Women: Creating Visibility

In a first writing of women into the history of the region, the category "woman" was generally treated unproblematically. Women were viewed in relation to their ethnic group and as a racialized category representative of the class into which they were born. This approach revealed not only women as a generic category but also the differences that existed between women, as well as the differences between women in the various territories. Caribbean feminist historiography easily locates its origins in the work of Lucille Mathurin, who in 1974 completed the first historical study of women in Jamaica, entitled "A Historical Study of Women in Jamaica from 1655 to 1844", as a doctoral dissertation. While differentiating women in Jamaica as white, black or mulatto, Mathurin maintains a clear distinction between the different groups of women, consistent with the class and ethnic distances between groups at the time. The study is pioneering and deserves credit for legitimizing the writing of women's history within the academy.[9] Barry Higman's demographic studies of slave populations (1973, 1984) are not generally represented as gender historiography, but his research on family history provides a vast fount of data and insights that are continuously being tapped by gender historians. In a study of household structure and fertility in Jamaican slave plantations in the nineteenth century, Higman's evidence points to the existence of strong bonds of kinship and sense of family among the slaves. While literary sources had thus far been the dominant source of information on family and gender relations, historical data provided the substance on which to build more informed knowledge of gender relations in slave society and between black and white men and women.

Hilary Beckles's study of slave women in Barbados etches the role of black Barbadian women in history as "natural rebels". Beckles is a prolific writer in Caribbean feminist historiography. His major theme in the earlier work of the 1980s centres on the condition of black women in Barbadian society and their resistance to the control of the plantation, including the sexual exploitation to which they were subjected as enslaved and virtually powerless women (1989b). Similarly, Barbara Bush's study of slave women in Caribbean society also focused on the central role of black women in the gender historiography of the region. Like Mathurin and Beckles, Bush emphasizes the importance of black women's reproductive capacity and sexuality to configurations of gender relations in slave society (1990). Rhoda Reddock's study of women, labour and political struggle in Trinidad and Tobago from the nineteenth century onwards, first produced as a doctoral dissertation in 1984 and published in 1994, signalled another important recovery of women in the region. Reddock's analysis is not restricted to white or black women, nor to a distinctly polarized black working class and white upper and middle class. Here is the emergence of different groups of women and their co-optation into class and ethnic categories in the struggles of labour and politics in this society. Women are identified as sometimes unwitting, but not docile pawns in the trade-off between capital and labour.

While woman is the central subject of their historical investigation, the theme of resistance and strength among black women pervades these texts, thus placing the cornerstone of Caribbean feminist theorizing – the original polemic or *querelle* for the region – the African-descended Caribbean women as strong and unwilling subjects in their subjugation.

The question of differences among groups and races of women continued its evolution, and here the work of Rhoda Reddock (1986), Verene Shepherd (1993), Patricia Mohammed (1994b), and later Shaheeda Hosein (1996) and Halima Kassim (1999) begins another recovery of women – this time of women of East Indian descent. Interestingly enough, in these writings Indian women are not set in opposition either to black women or to white but in relation to the colonial script of indentured Indian femininity and against their own patriarchal struggles within the reconstituted Indian communities in Jamaica and Trinidad. The depiction of Indian women as bearers and preservers of the Indian patriarchal culture is a dominant theme. The subtext is similar to that of the recovery of black women. The texts attempt to remove the stereotypes of passivity that were attached to the role of the Indian woman in Caribbean society.

By 1999 Verene Shepherd's *Women in Caribbean History* had established a tendency that was evident in the historiography and here brought more into focus. This book illustrates that women's history had become by this time more embracing of all women rather than selectively focused on some groups. Written as a text for secondary-level students, its inclusion of all groups of women, including indigenous women in Caribbean history, signals the passage of historiography from selective recovery of women to investigating differences between them. There is a theoretical shift taking place here, from woman as undifferentiated to conceptualizing differences among women themselves, parallel with movements in feminist theory and feminist activism during the period from the 1970s to the 1990s.

The first contribution of historiography was to recover the visibility of women from obscurity. By consciously recognizing woman as a sex that had contributed to past history while making history, women's history also brought to the drawing-board the problem of gender in history. In other words, feminist theorizing benefits from historical recovery of data as it creates a polemic in history of the status and condition of one sex *vis-à-vis* the other. In identifying the presence of categories of women whose femininity may be differently shaped and between whom there are power imbalances, feminist theory also enters a dynamic frame, not simply the opposition or difference between masculinity and femininity, but situating as well variations by race, ethnicity, class. This is the basis in which feminist theorizing in the region must be grounded, as contemporary explanations of gender in each society can be safely measured only against past constructions of gender. The comparative study between different societies in the region that themselves have varied histories merely sharpens the theoretical focus. Recurrences allow one to make more informed theoretical statements, while variations allow for the qualification of theory.

More recent contributions by Linda Sturtz (2000), Mohammed (1994a, 2000a),[10] Brana-Shute (2000) and Beckles in *Centering Woman* (1999) continue this tendency of differentiating womanhood. Rather than accepting a static definition of white womanhood, Sturtz builds her methodology on Mathurin's racialized gender identities and investigates how whiteness and femininity became constructed in Jamaican society over time. Mohammed, also building on Mathurin's study, explores the emergence of the "mulatto woman" as the desired from the eighteenth to the nineteenth century, while Shute looks at female slaves who were liberated to females in Suriname who liberated slaves, investing women with the economic power that some did possess during slavery. Beckles places the slave woman at the centre of the slave order and identifies her sexual and economic roles as central to the slave mode of production. He illustrates that the power imbalances between women due to race and class differences were manifestly more apparent at the time. In the process of recovering women and creating visibility, the problem of gender differences between women again surfaces through the findings of history.

Theoretical Perspectives in the Writing of History: Problematizing Gender in Caribbean Historiography

The debate that concerns us here is whether feminist historiography refers to women's history or to engendering history. The latter refers to the treatment of gender as a conceptual category of historical analysis, the former to the recovery and addition of women to the historical narrative. This is a superfluous distinction in the sense that both approaches were and still are necessary and are constantly undergoing transformation. The problem of viewing the category "woman" as the underdog of history, because of her femaleness, keeps oppression based on sexual difference as a natural rather than social phenomenon. Conceptual developments in gender as a category of historical analysis (Scott 1988) allow new ways in which we may think about female and male gender roles in history and how gender works in history. As suggested by Mohammed, "to write gender into history, the historical construction of masculinity and femininity or the construction of gender identities must itself be posed as the problem" (1995, 20).

The superfluity of a distinction between women's history and gender history becomes more obvious when further scrutinized. "Woman" as a category is hardly or rarely interrogated as a singular subject in any study. Women are generally depicted in relation to men and their status in relation to patriarchy. They are also invariably discussed in the context of other categories of social analysis, particularly those of race and class. Rather than the problem of gender in history being primarily the recovery of women from obscurity and invisibility in the past (whether to depict the sex as victims or as heroines in the historical process), history becomes the space in which we can see gender and the construction or performance of gender roles as an active agent or by-product of the historical past. A few examples may serve to illustrate this point. Lucille Mathurin points out in her dissertation of 1974 and her Elsa Goveia Lecture of 1986 (Mair 1986) that "motherhood, with its biological and customary social implications, is frequently perceived as a conservative force which imposes constraints on female activism". She argued that in the later years of slavery in Jamaica, motherhood became a catalyst for much of women's subversive and aggressive strategies directed against the might of the plantation. Women withheld their labour, and that of their children. They induced abortions to counter the pro-natalist policies of slavery. Was this a feminist act on the part of women, or a response which as a sex they surely could have made, employing a means of control that they could exert?

In a second example Brereton examines family strategies undertaken by women in the post-emancipation period, and the role of gender in the shift to wage labour in the British Caribbean (1999). Mohammed (1994b, 2001) demonstrated that masculinity is itself a contested factor in the gendered past. If the problem of gender for women was the struggle against patriarchy, then the problem of gender for men is the struggle to maintain patriarchal privilege. Among post-indenture Indians in Trinidad, gender relations were constituted largely around the reclamation of patriarchal power that Indian males had lost during indentureship and which could now be revalidated with the constitution of an Indian community. Women colluded as well as rebelled in the recreation of an Indian patriarchy, setting the pace for changes in the gender system brought from India. History provides a space from which new ways of viewing gender may be continuously derived, and from which new challenges to existing theory may emerge.

Methodologies and Sources of History: Empiricism and Women as Knowers

The validation of voice and knowledge through history is another major contribution that gender historiography has made to feminist theory in the region. Here the work of Bridget Brereton (1988, 1994, 1998), among others, is valuable in situating the authenticity of new sources of data. In "Gendered Testimonies", Brereton summarizes this contribution:

> Over the last quarter of a century, historians have been engaged in the effort to rescue women of the past from their invisibility in the traditional record. This work of recovery and retrieval has made possible the redefinition of "history" to include aspects of life previously seen as non-historical; they were seen as "natural" and therefore timeless and unchanging, especially family relations, domesticity and sexuality. It has made it possible – indeed, imperative – for us to insert gender and gender relations into our work as historians, to "engender history". (1998, 143)

Acknowledging that the presumed sphere of "natural" gender needed to be deconstructed, and that new sources of data were required to do this, diaries, letters and autobiographies – "sources which speak to women's experiences in past societies" – have been important to the construction of knowledge in the region (Brereton 1994). The reconfiguration of historical knowledge and the use of different sources provide a key challenge to the basis of history itself, to the ways in which we have begun to think about and dispute existing knowledge and the ways in which these partial knowledges have assumed the mantle of truth (Hall 1995). This is true not only of gender or feminist historiography, but equally applicable to the historiography emerging in post-colonial Caribbean society by scholars from within the region. As part of the feminist epistemological project, this validation of another voice seems to me a valuable component in the construction of feminist theory and key to the self-assured development of theory as both ideas and vision.

Polemics in Contemporary History: The Shaping of Indigenous Feminist Theory

Historical research presented us with the subject matter and data to situate gendered categories in the region. We have begun to understand the conditions of women and men under slavery and indentureship, and under the successive systems of labour that followed these. We have only just begun to challenge this material with the insights that gender and feminist theory may bring. Much remains to be done. Not only do we need to continuously recover lives, voices and categories of information but we also need to revisit some of the findings of past historians and scrutinize them with a gendered lens. Gender/feminist historiography has produced a sense of the specificity of gender construction of the region and the origins of the gender problematic. Debates in feminist historiography seem to have shifted from its origins in the region three decades ago of recovering women in history to a clear challenge to feminist theoreticians to define the politics of feminism itself, continuing the long tradition of feminist theory identified by Joan Kelly as a polemic and opposition to dominant culture and to patriarchy.

In his book *Centering Woman: Gender Discourses in Caribbean Slave Society* (1999), Hilary Beckles challenges feminist scholarship in the region to mine the data that gender historiography has produced and the new issues raised in relation to the ongoing construction of feminist theory. He notes that historians and social anthropologists, inspired by considerations of systemic decolonization and nation-building, targeted the black woman's history in search of general explanations for social and cultural processes. Black women are represented essentially as "culture carriers" and "morality bearers" of a disenfranchised people seeking cohesion and upliftment (p. xiii). From this point of view, issues such as instability in gender relations, matrifocality of the black family and the status of the black woman emerge as the primary problematic of feminism in the post-colonial project.

In *Centering Woman* Beckles locates the problem of "woman" from another vantage point. He argues that the ideological formation of the modern Caribbean is in some way best explained in terms of a central paradigm that juxtaposes the white male and the black female as binary signifiers. What he is identifying here is another *querelle* of Caribbean feminist theory, another vantage point from which we may locate theory. As Beckles has redefined it, the problematic of "woman" and feminism in the Caribbean begins with a primary opposition between the black female and white male, rather than the customary male–female or sexual difference opposition of white male and female in mainstream Western discourse. The parallels between the Caribbean and the black feminist perspective of the United States are therefore more apparent. In other words, Caribbean feminist theory from its inception is not reducible to a simple formula of sexual difference or to the constituted gender differences between male and female/masculinity and femininity, but must incorporate simultaneous considerations of race and class hierarchies and sexual politics that affect both black and white women and black and white men. While demographically there were more black men and women in Caribbean societies than there were white men or women, in the creation of the nation-state and the evolution of patriarchal control, the imposition of the dominant white male patriarchy, rules, regulations and doctrines imposed by white colonialism, set the boundaries of black masculinity as it did for all femininity. The emergence of the nuclear family and women's domestication created the setting for primarily black and working-class female oppression, with the domestication of white women viewed as an accepted ideal. Thus white upper- and middle-class women, and men of varying ethnicities, colours and hues, are situated either in the ranks of the oppressors of one sort or another or on the margins of any feminist consciousness. The basis of feminism and feminist theory in the Caribbean is therefore a Marxist-like deterministic script, contesting the Western feminist discourse that although all women are reproduced in relation to a dominant patriarchal system that subordinates femininity, enslaved black women and free white women comprise a bipolar context for womanhood and femininity. Black and white femininities are at odds with each other from the inception. Black women are sexually desired yet outside the realm of a desired femininity; white women suffer as undesirable, yet are constituted as feminine. Interestingly, a parallel discourse is inscribed for black masculinity, which finds itself as a physically and sexually endowed masculinity with little or no power in society. There is no middle ground of differentiation and nuancing of femininities or masculinities. By centring women in this off-centred way, Beckles destabilizes a concept of woman that is fundamental to feminist theory, that of biological sameness. This tendency to separate by race and class serves to weaken the analytical value of the concept of woman, which, although problematic, has united and supported feminism across several centuries.

Beckles argues that there was no politicization of women's gender identity within the mission of enlightenment's democratization for civil equality and social justice. The overall result then is a textual representation of women as victims in historiography, in diverse ways and to varying degrees controlled by the masculinist enterprise of colonialism. He employs the word "radical" in relation to Caribbean women in an unorthodox way compared to its use in mainstream Western radical feminist theory, where female sexuality and reproduction are the source of their subordination. Conflating radical with Marxist feminism he produces a socialist/anti-colonial perspective as the prescription for feminist theory and intervention: "The first radical opposition and movement of Caribbean women emerged within the politics of the bloody wars against colonialism and slavery, by the Kalinago (Caribs), Taino (Arawak) and Ciboney women" (1999, 178). Radical or root causes of female oppression and resistance are thus primarily anti-colonial from inception. Amerindian womanhood is also written into the anti-colonial script as resistant and rebellious. That women themselves were principal participants in the contests over the definitions and characteristics of womanhood and femininity is evident both in this text and in recoveries by other scholars of women in history. That women allowed themselves or were naturally configured as subsidiary actresses in the anti-colonial and nationalist struggles in the region is not fully appreciated. Gender consciousness and identity cannot be itemized under a priority checklist of identities. The elements of gender and sexual identity compete with notions of nationhood and race/ethnicity in culture, and at different times one may take pre-eminence over the other. In "Towards Indigenous Feminist Theorizing in the Caribbean" I argue that there is a seeming eclecticism of the feminist movement and feminist theory in the Caribbean, because women have "responded at the same time to issues of class, race/ethnicity, nationhood and (*to other concerns with sexual and*) gender identity" (1998, 17).

This debate and polemic of history, that the original binary opposition in gender was not that between men and women, suggests that feminist theory in the Caribbean begins with a radical break from the mainstream Western feminist discourse, resulting from specific ways in which gender identities were constructed in this region. There is no doubt that we need to extend our understanding of the many kinds of struggles that women and men have continuously forged in the past. At the same time we need to recognize the selective ways in which historians work and present ideas. The task of the feminist theorist is to constantly decode the subject matter and ideas presented by the historian into explanations for gender subordination in society, and into a vision for humanitarian politics for the society, regardless of sex and difference. Essentially I am proposing that gendered history in the Caribbean has already provided us with a basis for constituting an indigenous feminist theory that departs from mainstream Western feminist theory, and has already responded to Eudine Barriteau's call for "historical research that would promote the task of producing a locally grounded post modern feminist theory" (Beckles 1999, 191). What we need to guard against is overplaying those ideas that invite major chasms among women of different groups, and between women and men, in the ongoing project of feminist epistemology.

Notes

1. The French school of feminism traces its origins back to Christine de Pisan in the fourteenth century, whose work formed the basis for the *querelle des femmes* (Kelly 1984).

2. This information was gained from actual ethnographic fieldwork experience of the author in a community in northern Namibia, in the area of

Ehangano, between the towns of Ondangwa and Oshakati, in summer 2000.

3. This pace has been consistent with the breakdown of a universalistic set of concepts and ideas about gender that has characterized the postmodern discourse.

4. How the discipline of history itself has benefited from the intervention of women's history and gender history is an important question to the discipline of history and the methods of historiography, and a digression from the main emphasis of this essay.

5. Source: <http://www.colorado.edu/ . . . butler.html>.

6. Having said that, this is not true of all historians' reading of gender crimes, one major exception being Bridget Brereton's *Race Relations in Colonial Trinidad* (1979), which anticipates feminist interpretations.

7. These ideas were first documented in the PhD thesis "A Social History of Post-Migrant Indians in Trinidad 1917–1947: A Gender Perspective" (1994b), and further developed in the publication *Gender Negotiations among Indians in Trinidad 1917–1947* (2001).

8. I am more convinced about this now, even though it may be awkwardly developed at this stage of my thinking, particularly after my third summer of teaching gender research methodology to groups of mature students in Namibia, where ideas of feminism and feminist theory are seen as Western importations, while the concepts of gender and patriarchy are largely understood and accepted as tools for social analysis and research.

9. The vast data and findings uncovered by Lucille Mathurin in this body of work carried out for a PhD dissertation remains unpublished and only available in West Indian reference sections of the three libraries of the University of the West Indies.

10. "But Most of All Mi Love Me Browning", published in *Feminist Review* (2000a); original conference presentation published in *Differentiating Caribbean Womanhood* (2000b).

Chapter 6

"How Our Lives Would Be Affected by the Custom of Having Several Wives"

*The Intersection between African History
and Gender Studies in the Caribbean*

RICHARD A. GOODRIDGE

Gender has long been central to Caribbean life, although this centrality has not been adequately recognized in regional scholarship. This work is partially inspired by some of the comments made by students during an undergraduate course on women in twentieth-century Africa – comments that dominate popular thinking in Barbados on male–female relations in Africa. These comments betrayed the fact that most students had no more than a nodding acquaintance with the regime of gender relations in Africa and the manifold influences that had shaped those relations. Indeed, while Caribbean gender scholarship has made passing reference to the influence of the African past, it is suggested that this scholarship is not sufficiently grounded in African history.

It is my contention that enlightened discussions on gender relations in Africa are a necessary precondition for analysis of gender developments in the Caribbean, especially during the period of slavery. Yet the literature on the Caribbean has thus far been defective in two main ways. First, the thrust has been towards generalized discussion of the gender division in Africa, which has resulted in some significant errors of omission. Thus, for example, it has been asserted that women were responsible for agriculture in Africa, an assertion that is not true in the case of some major ethnic groups, nor does it take into account major modifications to the principle asserted. Second, Caribbean literature has not sufficiently addressed issues that were important to the formulation of male–female relationships in Africa before transatlantic slave trade was terminated, and which ought to inform the discussion and analysis of African behaviour in the Caribbean. Islam stands out as a major example in this regard.

I suggest that African history offers to gender scholarship significant intellectual support in the quest for greater understanding of the Caribbean experience. This support is provided in terms of increased knowledge of the African background as a result of greater research and theorizing about Africa, as well as inducing students of the Caribbean past to pay more attention to those themes that have been neglected in the Caribbean but which are central to African history.

Five years ago, in the midst of the public debate surrounding whether black/African history should be taught in Barbadian schools, the institution of polygamy – seemingly poorly understood, if comprehended at all – sometimes influenced the discussion. Among the opponents of the introduction of black/African history into the curriculum were those possessed of the misconceived notion that mere teaching about the African past would lead to the adoption of "harmful" socio-economic practices from the continent. The concerns of the opposition group were reflected in a letter to – of all places – a "Matters of the Heart" column in a local newspaper.

The letter writer, "Maureen", while insisting that it was "a great idea" to let Barbadian children know about life and conditions in Africa where the slaves came from, simultaneously indicated her anxiety "as a woman" over the possible fate of women in Barbados should African history be introduced into the school curriculum. However, and this is the crux of the letter writer's dilemma,

> the problem I have is how our lives would be affected by the African custom of having several wives. I think it would be a retrograde step to adopt polygamy in Barbados, but I am certain that this practice would appeal to some of the same people that [*sic*] are pushing African studies in our schools. We already have too many men having multiple affairs in and out of marriage.

It is to the credit of the columnist that she unambiguously replied to Maureen, "Your fears are unfounded."[1]

The views of the letter writer, while disregarding the laws of logic and casting aspersions on the morals of those involved in a fight to broaden the curriculum, were consistent with widely held sentiment about the alleged promiscuity of the black (or African) male in the Caribbean, which dates from the slavery period. This position was articulated towards the end of the eighteenth century by Thomas Atwood of Dominica, who found that, with reference to blacks,

> so little are the sexes attached to each other or constant in connubial connections, that it is common for the men to have several wives at a time besides transient mistresses; . . . and the women to leave their husbands for others, and to submit to the embraces of white men for money and clothes. (quoted in Shepherd 1999, 58)

The compiler of a recent text on women in the anglophone Caribbean was, in response to the position articulated by Atwood, at pains to demonstrate that enslaved African/black men were capable of remaining in stable unions, that nuclear family units existed in various territories and that contemporaries of Atwood rejected his claims about the widespread promiscuity of enslaved African/black women. Yet some of the evidence cited in support of the latter point seems to buttress the racist image of morally depraved blacks[2] and the promiscuous black male, for it was found that "the really respectable female negro has generally only one husband; and in this particular only is the respectable female negro more moral than the male" (Shepherd 1999, 58). Perhaps one may ask at what point did one become "respectable".

The issue of the untrustworthy black (male) has figured in Caribbean gender studies. It is my view that the work produced on gender issues in the Caribbean has not been *sufficiently* grounded in African developments and influences. I seek to make a contribution by pointing a way towards which male–female concerns in our region might be usefully addressed through a greater reliance on the African historical record. This comes at a time when gender issues are deservedly being highlighted through several media, including introduction of the subject matter in university-level courses that cover the Caribbean and Africa as well as Europe. This analysis has been influenced by an earlier work on women in Africa and the diaspora (Terborg-Penn, Harley and Benton Rushing 1989) and by the somewhat superficial treatment in Caribbean historiographical writing of matters that have been important in African history and historiography. I contend that greater appreciation of these ought to illuminate our knowledge and conception of gender roles in Caribbean history.

The sentiments expressed by Maureen, quoted earlier, represent a simplistic and distorted but popular misrepresentation of socio-economic organization and gender-role differentiation in the African past. Further, Shepherd's valuable compilation on Caribbean women, which first appeared in 1999, does not properly address the African background. Similarly, Beckles argued in a recent work that – with reference to the differences between analysis of experience and the theorizing of constructed representation, and between history and politics in the context of women versus gender studies – "only an integrative discursive practice can adequately tackle epistemological questions arising from the notion of meaning" (Beckles 1999, xxiii). Yet it seems unlikely that mere experience in the Caribbean or theorizing about that experience can be sufficient if it lacks a clear reference to developments in the area of male–female relationships in Africa, particularly during the period of Caribbean slavery from the seventeenth to the nineteenth centuries. At the same time, however, my analysis is informed by common features of the existence of African and Caribbean women in the twentieth century, particularly the way in which colonialism and neocolonialism affected the lives of women in Africa and the Caribbean.

I divide the work into two major sections. Initially I attempt to survey some of the critical ideas raised in discussions of gender/women's issues in which the emphasis is placed on the errors of omission. I then suggest how studies of gender might benefit from an "incorporatist" approach, that is, one that seeks to incorporate not only gender theory but also a greater appreciation of the actual developments in African history. I suggest that the overall study of Caribbean history would benefit from such an approach.

Verene Shepherd, the compiler of the *Women in Caribbean History,* identified enslaved black women's roles in the Caribbean in the following main areas:

(a) production (for owners or selves);
(b) domestic service for owners;
(c) reproduction of the labour supply;
(d) family life;
(e) resistance.

These are all topics over which there has been some discussion about the African influence, although in terms of (a), Shepherd makes no mention of the African influence or background in her initial discussion. Her comments on the organization of field labour are, however, useful and worth outlining here:

> Field work was generally undertaken by three gangs. The first gang, which comprised males and females usually 16- to 50-years-old, did the heavy work. The traditional view that first gang workers were adult males who did the heavy work is, therefore, not supported by the historical data. Lighter work was done by the second gang, which was made up of younger slaves between 12- and 16-years-old. In the French-colonised territories, the second gang included those recently arrived from Africa and new mothers; while in the Danish-colonised territories, workers deemed "weak" (young or old), were also in that gang. The third or children's gang was responsible for weeding and clearing the fields of twigs and debris . . . Typically the women worked a 12-hour day in these gangs with breaks for lunch and sometimes breakfast six days a week weeding, cane holing, carrying and planting. (1999, 53)

Shepherd does not sufficiently confront the issue of whether the old school had been wrong in asserting that adult males did the hard agricultural tasks, in keeping with African practices. Happily, however, she does mention African influence when discussing independent production and marketing, thus:

> The enslaved were allowed to sell a variety of goods and marketing was dominated by women. This practice *seemed* [my emphasis] to have followed the African custom in which they took care of farming and household economy, while the men engaged in hunting and the like. In the Caribbean the men sometimes worked the provision grounds with women, but the latter attended the Sunday market. (1999, 54)

Taken together, the two extracts raise critical concerns: What was the nature of the division of labour in Africa, not only between economic sectors but also within a single sector? Was this division affected by the level of political sophistication achieved by the societies? A discussion of this subject is critical on account of its relevance to a wide range of topics such as slave resistance, familial roles and black masculinity in the Caribbean.

In terms of slave resistance, Shepherd attempts to highlight women's participation and, while she acknowledges that resistance took many forms that could be described as gender-specific, she does not seek to delve into causes of resistance, preferring instead to treat them in a gender-neutral way (1999, 60–63). This raises the question of the extent to which Shepherd is dealing with a gender division of labour, especially given Beckles's claim that enslaved men in the Caribbean might have resisted because they found themselves doing "women's work", that is, agricultural labour (Beckles 1997). Yet Beckles's argument itself stands in need of modification, for he, like Shepherd, may be guilty of generalizing or simplifying the division of labour and failing to examine the fundamental practical differences across (West) African communities.

It is true, for the most part, that women were responsible for agricultural production in Africa (Boserup 1970). Further, men did perform the physically demanding tasks such as first acquiring and then clearing the land to render it suitable for cultivation, and both adult males and children joined women in harvesting the product. Yet there were significant exceptions to the rule that women were the primary agricultural producers in Africa. In many parts of Ethiopia and among the Hausa of northern Nigeria, men were responsible for agricultural production. While none of these areas is thought to have provided a large body of slaves for Caribbean plantations, the same cannot be said of the Yoruba, among whom males, not females, were allotted primary responsibility for agriculture. In addition, men normally had control over tree crops such as the oil palm, which would help them to achieve greater economic advances than women under colonialism; among the Igbo, cultivation of yams – the staple food crop – was restricted to men. In light of these important modifications to the belief that women were responsible for agriculture in Africa, especially given the significant numbers of Caribbean slaves of Yoruba and Igbo origin, one would have to review any hypothesis on the relationship between resistance and gendered forms of work. One preliminary test of this reassessment would be to focus on slave resistance in nineteenth-century Cuba, which imported large numbers of Yoruba slaves during that period.[3]

Resistance by women has been a major theme in Caribbean studies. Even before Shepherd's recent summary of the field, which was primarily undertaken for Caribbean history teachers, both male and female scholars had been hard at work highlighting and seeking explanations for resistance activities and tactics by black women. Lucille Mathurin Mair, one of the pioneers of Caribbean women's studies, paid attention to the activism of the female agricultural worker in Jamaica. For Mair the "subversive and aggressive strategies" pursued by female agricultural workers formed an integral part of Jamaican history. When the need arose these women withheld their labour and that of their children from the plantation and participated in major uprisings (including the epochal Morant Bay Rebellion of 1865) and in the twentieth-century popular protest of the largely female urban proletariat, itself a product of the Morant Bay Rebellion.[4] Similarly, the quest has been on to find the female heroine, the "rebel woman" and the "natural rebel".

It has been suggested that the search for the natural rebel begins with Brathwaite's assertion that the slavery system had a deeper impact on the black female than on the black male (1984). According to this argument, the slave mode of production in the Caribbean placed the woman's most personal and essential female characteristics – her fertility, sexuality and maternity – on the market, and this produced in her a "*natural* propensity to resist and to refuse as part of a basic self protective and survival response" (Beckles 1999, xxii). There is some support for this position in Mair's comment that "[m]otherhood with its biological and customary social implications is frequently perceived as a conservative force which imposes constraints on female activism. It became, however, in this instance, a catalyst for much of women's subversive and aggressive strategies directed against the might of the plantation" (1987, 11). Although space does not permit me to outline the arguments in great detail, some comments are in order.

The claim that the slave system affected black women in more profound ways than it did black males is certainly open to debate, both in the context of the slavery period and in the face of modern concerns about masculinity and male marginalization, a subject to which we shall return.[5] The arguments of Beckles, Brathwaite, Mair, Shepherd and others on female slave resistance do not appear to be grounded sufficiently in an exposition of African socio-economic and political practices, in spite of the admission that, in the words of Hilary Beckles, "the rebel woman" is essentially a cultural icon whose location within the slave community is derived from the ascribed matrifocality of the African social legacy. This admission by Beckles may be better understood in the light of his recent challenge to scholars to pay increased attention to intellectual forces, including the "patriarchal mobilisations of gender ideologies", in their explorations of Caribbean slavery.[6] More importantly, we think, any discussion of resistance by black female slaves ought to consider the African context.

Such discussions must take into account the existence of a regime of slavery in Africa, as well as its obverse: opportunities for women to participate in the political and economic process in Africa prior to enslavement in the Caribbean. In other words, the approach to understanding female slave resistance is not to exclusively or even primarily consider the enslaved women's reactive antithesis to the slave-master's abuse, but to privilege their pre-Caribbean traditions of autonomy, power and participation. This is not to suggest that the discourse on resistance by female slaves is unaware of the African influence. Rather, it is our contention that the comments are often too regional (usually West African) and general rather than local or specific in character. Perhaps the discourse has been primarily concerned with identifying the *collective* resistance (Beckles 1989b).

It has been found that in less well-developed societies such as hunting and gathering communities, the tendency was towards egalitarian relationships, an equality that emerged, it is believed, because men did not mobilize the labour of the young and women to produce a surplus product (Sacks 1979). While hunting and gathering communities were not prime suppliers of captives for the Atlantic trade, it must be stressed that the rights of women varied according to more or less advanced modes of production in Africa. Across pre-colonial West Africa, women had considerable latitude in such areas as farming, trading and "female rites of passage", and there existed organs or groups that formulated and enforced rules to maintain this latitude. Thus, for example, male and female secret societies were a feature of West Africa, particularly among the Yoruba and societies of the Upper Guinea Coast and the Ivory Coast, areas heavily involved in the process of meeting the labour demands of Caribbean plantations. Female secret societies served to create cohesion among women and something of a balance in the sphere of secular polit-ical power (Wipper 1995, 164–70). Some further, albeit limited, discus-sion of women's political role is necessary but is restricted to the Yoruba and Igbo systems, since relatively large numbers of Igbo and Yoruba are thought to have been enslaved in the Americas.

Political practice in the centralized kingdoms of the Yoruba was geared towards forestalling royal absolutism. The power of an *oba* (king) was checked in various ways, including by his need to consult with his council of lineage heads (*igbimo*), by the existence of taboos and by the constitutional provision, albeit unwritten, under which the council could remove the *oba*. Where constitutional provisions did not exist, it was understood that the council of chiefs, or *igbimo,* could ultimately organ-ize a general insurrection of the people to get rid of an oppressive ruler. Atanda was at pains to stress the participatory nature of pre-colonial Yoruba government, specifically citing the fact that the general popula-tion would join the council in toppling the monarch as evidence that government among the Yoruba was not just a matter for the chiefs (Atanda 1973, 1980). This practice may also be used to argue that Yoruba women had a tradition of resistance to oppressive or tyrannical rule and would, therefore, be reasonably expected to resist the arbitrary behaviour of a slave-master. Moreover, women held key formal posi-tions within the structure of Yoruba government, with the *iyalode* (Awe 1977, 144–95) being the best-studied institution.

The Igbo political system, on the other hand, is traditionally classified as lacking centralization and being essentially egalitarian (Nzimiro 1972). While Afigbo found that there were many types of Igbo political systems – if one used as the criterion the domination, or lack of it, of gov-ernment by the kinship system (Afigbo 1973, 13–23; Amadiume 1987) – their egalitarian nature has been upheld by the research, and this leads us to suggest that there had to be a clear role for women in political life. Indeed, among the Igbo there were several gatherings of women as well as female equivalents to male institutions, which formed the basis of women's political power. The gatherings that performed the major role in women's self-rule were the village-wide meetings of all adult women based on common residence, while Igbo women were (and still are) noted for their "insulting" and militant behaviour towards men as part of the effort to promote and protect their interests (van Allen 1972, 165–81; Ardener 1975). Amadiume found that Igbo women's protest against colonial rule partly stemmed from the British practice of privileging male leadership institutions or titles while disregarding their female equivalents.[7] Not surprisingly, therefore, given the existence of various women's political and social institutions in Africa and the culture of defence of women's rights, female slave resistance in the Caribbean had firm practical and ideological roots in Africa.

One area that has been of major interest to researchers in the last two decades is slavery within African societies. Central concerns of that research have included the questions of women, Islam and abolition. Generally there was an increase in slavery in Africa during the era of the transatlantic slave trade. "Slavery" covered a wide range of relationships involving dependency and loss of freedom, but it was hardly "benign".[8] While there is no agreement on the nature of slave systems in Africa, it has been clearly established that women formed the bulk of the enslaved population.[9] While women slaves were highly valued for their reproductive roles, they were still more highly appreciated for their manual labour. This is not surprising given the gender division of labour in which many of the economically important skilled tasks were performed by males. It is of some significance to my analysis that in Muslim areas, a female slave who gave birth to a child for the master was freed once the master admitted paternity (Lovejoy and Hogendorn 1993, ch. 4). However, we need to return to the argument that slavery in the Caribbean had a more profound impact upon the female slave.

Nothing useful would be gained by denying that serious offences were committed against the female, but it must be borne in mind that these would also have had a severe impact upon enslaved men who held the basic patriarchal values espoused by white slave-masters and who may have exercised domination over women in Africa. Although this work contains evidence to indicate that women in Africa had some measure of autonomy, participated in political life and organized themselves so as to articulate their own interests as distinct from those of men, it cannot be denied that (West) African societies were patriarchal. Indeed, Robertson points out that "the issue of matriarchy is problematic both conceptually and in its use of African evidence" (1996, 10).

In general, women were ranked at the bottom of the African social pyramid, which was regulated by both gender and age considerations. Women constituted the base, while a narrow band of elder males constituted the apex. Women were ranked with children and below both adult and junior males. We know from the nineteenth-century data that the bulk of agricultural and all pastoral – as distinct from hunting and gathering – communities were patrilineal, with pastoral societies also being patrifocal. The dominance of patrilineal and patrifocal practices was clearly established in those communities where Islamic values prevailed. Even where the matrilineal principle was dominant, as among the Akan of modern Ghana, uncles and nephews held power. In African societies, then, the most important kinship relations were traceable through the male line. Women's inheritance rights were for the most part meagre, as women were themselves inherited and children often belonged to their father's lineage (Goody and Buckley 1973, 108–21).

There is no agreement on the extent of the rights of women who were inherited when their husbands died. African inheritance systems have been influenced by European legal norms as a result of the colonial experience. Thus, for example, in the bilingual republic of Cameroon there now exist two conflicting extremes for widows: British law places the widow as the first beneficiary of her deceased husband's estate, while French law places her third in line to inherit, after the children and relatives (Morikang 1999). These clear-cut positions obtain where a will has been made, but in the absence of such a testamentary statement African law and custom prevail, and widows are in a seriously disadvantaged position. Similarly, the Zimbabwe Supreme Court made two rulings that led some to conclude that Zimbabwean women had no rights in their own country and should be considered virtual sex slaves. The unanimous position of the court in April 1999 was that women were not equal to men according to "the nature of African society" (Zulu 1999) – a view that was even more potently established across Africa in the precolonial era.

The point being illustrated by this brief outline of a complex socioeconomic and political system is the dominant position of the man, a superordinate position that was reflected in the existence of polygyny and the absence of polyandry in African households. Loss of control over women, especially over their sexuality, had to be a major shock to the enslaved male in the Caribbean. The literature on gender in the anglophone Caribbean is characterized by a paucity of material on black masculinity, but some attempt is being made to fill this void in Caribbean historiography.[10] However, even if such work addresses the dominant position of African men, it will remain incomplete as long as it continues to exclude the Islamic influence.

It must be recognized at the outset that since the 1970s there has been greater sensitivity to and study of gender issues in the Islamic world as part of the process through which gender studies have become firmly established in academic circles. However, the focus has been directed towards Islamic femininity rather than masculinity (Ahmed 1992). Scholarly scrutiny has been applied to such themes as the general oppression of Muslim women, as well as the more specific feminist issues of female circumcision and genital mutilation. However, no one subject has attracted as much attention from scholars and policy-makers as the issue of the Muslim woman and the veil (Engineer 1992; Mernissi 1991; Zuhur 1992). Yet Caribbean historical studies have not yet begun to effectively tackle even Islamic femininity.

Having pointed out some of the shortcomings in the literature on women in the Caribbean, especially during slavery, I intend to offer some tentative, brief suggestions on how scholars of the Caribbean experience might more meaningfully explore gender issues.

It should now be clear that I am arguing for a more systematic and rigorous incorporation of research on Africa into the intellectual enterprise that seeks to increase our understanding of male–female relationships and women's activities and roles in Caribbean history. Again this is not to suggest that African historical influences should be ascribed exclusive explanatory status. Rather, Caribbean gender studies will benefit from a comparative approach[11] in which the research findings on African historical and gender issues are applied to Caribbean gender studies.

One theme that suggests itself as suitable for application of the comparative approach is Islam. Across the anglophone Caribbean there are significant Muslim populations. Islam is traditionally associated with the Asian element of the Trinidad and Guyana populations, but there is a growing Black Muslim component in places like Barbados. We must be mindful of the fact that some of those enslaved in the Caribbean came from societies in Africa that were at least already nominally Muslim. We know of James Albert Ukasaw Gronniosaw, a Muslim from Borno (in present-day northern Nigeria), itself one of the strongest centres of early Islamic development in West Africa (Smith 1971, 158–201). Gronniosaw arrived in Barbados in the 1720s. Venture Smith was born around 1729 and was shipped from Guinea to Barbados via the Gold Coast (Handler 1998, 129–41). Islam was clearly established in Borno by 1700; in the Guinea region it underwent a phase of revival and renewal in the eighteenth century, with *jihad*s in Futa Jallon and Futa Toro (Rodney 1968, 269–84) that were forerunners of the great *jihad* movement of the nineteenth century.

Slave resistance on the part of Muslims may be explained at one level as carrying out the religious injunction incumbent upon Muslims to resist all forms of oppression and domination exercised over them by "unbelievers". At another level, we need to determine the extent to which religious rather than gender issues would have influenced Muslim slaves to resist; as well as how Islam influenced male–female relationships in the Caribbean during and after slavery. I am unaware of the existence of a large corpus of literature that deals with masculinity in the Muslim diaspora. Certainly the issue of Muslim masculinity, especially during slavery, has not been dealt with in reference to the Caribbean, and it is one area on which Caribbean gender scholarship might focus. Thus, for example, students of Caribbean history could pay renewed attention to the complaints addressed by indentured Indian workers[12] to the office of Protector of Indians in the nineteenth century, but utilizing the vista of religious-cum-gender analysis.

A focus on Islam and the related issues of Muslim masculinity/femininity is likely to have the beneficial effect of redressing the imbalance in Caribbean gender studies, which is heavily weighted in favour of the black (slave) woman. This imbalance particularly disadvantages the Amerindian woman, who remains largely absent from the general historiography of the Caribbean and from Caribbean gender discourse (Kerns 1982, 1983). The slave trade from Africa ended in the nineteenth century, and by that time Amerindian society had undergone major changes stemming from the presence of both Europeans and Africans. Perhaps the great interest in women's roles within African systems in the pre-colonial period that has so far informed (albeit insufficiently) gender analysis of Caribbean blacks ought to be extended to Amerindian soci-ety,[13] for it is more than likely that the pre-colonial African woman had more in common with her Amerindian counterpart than with the twen-tieth-century black woman in the Caribbean. It seems plausible to sug-gest that undeveloped African and Amerindian societies shared some characteristics in critical areas such as land tenure, which held enormous implications for women's rights and autonomy, or lack thereof.

The recommendations of this section are in line with the views re-cently articulated by Claire Robertson on the African factor in New World gender discourse. These views, it must be added, were made pos-sible only because of increased scholarly research into gender as well as slavery in Africa. These views are therefore worth quoting:

> Among the many forms of socio-economic deprivation, African slavery on both sides of the Atlantic has probably provoked the most historical debate, and recent contributions to it have focused on women slaves. Still there has been little cross-fertilization of ideas between Africanists and new world spe-cialists. It is time to remedy this situation. In the 1990s [and beyond] we need to look at our African heritage and the various sorts of issues that muddy these waters. The study of gender issues in particular provides an excellent lens for new analyses, while use of comparative method can clarify much about socio-economic structure. (1996, 3)

Robertson identified matrifocality – "especially as it pertains to pos-sible African retentions" – and the gender division of labour as among the priority issues. While these are critical issues, I suggest that we prob-ably need to pay greater attention to the difficult, almost impossible, task of locating the *sources* of the slaves from Africa. Some progress is being made in this direction as a result of the efforts of David Eltis and others to place the records of twenty-five thousand transatlantic slave-ship voyages between 1595 and 1866 in a new multimedia format, which permits a regional survey of the voyages (Eltis et al. 1999). It must be stressed that these records indicate the ports from which the slave ships departed, and not necessarily the areas from which the slaves were acquired, yet it is a beginning.

The importance of more closely determining the areas from which the slaves were obtained lies in the fact that research has already pointed out the existence of significant variations across Africa in the "status", roles and rights of women both within and between regions. A better idea of the regions that provided the enslaved populations of the Caribbean and of the social, economic and political organization in those areas would permit us to more reliably determine the level of women's participation in political and economic life prior to their arrival from Africa. This is a necessary precondition to offering more or less tentative conclusions about the importance of African practices to an under-standing of gender developments in the Caribbean, the legacy of European domination notwithstanding.

It is clear that Caribbean historical writing would benefit from a more rigorous incorporation of developments in African history, including the growing field of gender relations. Both historical research and writing would be enhanced by greater use of theoretical formulations about developments in Africa and the Caribbean. Yet we must also make greater use of comparative analysis to tackle those areas in Caribbean historical development that have been systematically understudied, such as gender relations among Muslims in the Caribbean. A more system-atic application of African historical knowledge to the study of the Caribbean past should help minimize the many misconceptions about the (black) male, including those articulated by undergraduate students and correspondents in the local newspaper.

Notes

1. See "Unfounded Fears about African History", in the "Dear Ila" column, *Barbados Advocate,* 10 December 1994, 13.
2. For an exposition of racist doctrine see, *inter alia,* Edwards 1966, Long 1970 and Brodber 1982.
3. On the ethnic composition of Caribbean slaves see, for example, Curtin 1969, Gemery and Hogendorn 1979, and Eltis and Richardson 1997.
4. See Mair 1987, especially pp. 11–12. For a general discussion of women and plantations, see Jain and Reddock 1998.
5. The educational system has figured prominently in the discussion on male marginalization; see, for example, Miller 1994 and Sewell 1997.

6. For a fuller discussion of the intellectual arguments see the introduction to Beckles 1999.
7. On equivalency among the Igbo see Amadiume 1987.
8. Miers and Roberts 1988 provide a general survey of the debate in chapter 1.
9. See the introduction to Robertson and Klein 1983a.
10. See, for example, Beckles 1996a and Downes 1997.
11. On the value of the comparative in history see Frederickson 1995.
12. See, for example, Shepherd 1994 and Look Lai 1993.
13. Irving Rouse (1964, 1992) has done some useful work on Amerindian societies.

⧏ Chapter 7 ⧐

Perfect Property
Enslaved Black Women in the Caribbean

HILARY McD. BECKLES

The nature of the enslavement of African people in Atlantic societies shortly before and after the Columbus era was informed as much by discernible gender ideas as by economic factors. Defining the place of the enslaved woman was a matter of considerable concern for Europeans who conceived and implemented the legal framework for slavery in all jurisdictions (Beckles 1989b, 1999, 2000).

Judicial supporters of Caribbean slave-owners are recognized as the critical pioneers in the achievement of this task. Their gender ideas shaped social planning and legal engineering about the socio-economic functions and legal locations of the enslaved woman as a special kind of slave. They ascribed to black womanhood as a social construct, a specific place, while promoting in a general way ideas about race, colour, class, culture and age as important social markers (Bush 1981, 1990; Bush-Slimani 1993; Burgess 1994; Gaspar and Clark Hine 1996).

The trade in enslaved Africans, both across the Atlantic to the Americas and through the Sahara to the Islamic and Christian Mediterranean worlds, was conducted within the context of such clearly defined and understood ideas about sex, gender and work. These ideas and understandings gave cultural shape to judicial and legislative policy that determined how private property rights in humans could facilitate the production and distribution of goods and services.

Within the trans-Saharan trade in enslaved blacks, women were in the vast majority. There was a specific market bias in favour of females, and the demand was effectively met by slave traders. Enslaved females were in demand primarily to work as domestics or concubines and in agriculture. Some 65 per cent of enslaved West Africans sold on these markets were female.[1]

The feminization of slave society in Islamic North Africa, the Middle East and the Christian Mediterranean also influenced the nature of judicial responses to property rights in slaves, and reflected the primary interests of slave-owners in the conversion of humans into chattels. The leisure and social services bias within this demand, however, engendered a flexible approach to slave management that facilitated access to freedom by both legal provision and social assimilation. Islamic law, for example, facilitated social processes that enabled enslaved females to experience in significant numbers their advancement into free society. Enslaved women, therefore, could normally look forward to attaining freedom for themselves and ultimately for their children, through manumission, marriage, concubinage or self-purchase. Islamic theology encouraged domestic and cultural assimilation through household membership, and the movement of enslaved domestics and their children into free society was not discouraged (Inikori 1982; Kopytoff 1979).

The sixteenth-century transatlantic slave trade, however, represented a significant rupture in and departure from this well-established tradition of slave-owning and management. Transatlanticism created a new, race-based civilization built around systems of commodity production and global trade. It enabled the Caribbean, as its primordial American site, to invent a system of African bondage that came to be known as chattel slavery.

Spanish settlers in post-Columbian Hispaniola were the pioneers; the system was later perfected by Portuguese colonists in Brazil. In Spanish Caribbean colonies the mining industry was the incubator, while in Brazil it was the sugar plantation. Slavery had taken this distinct form in the Caribbean by the 1590s. As developed by the Portuguese in Brazil it was applied by the English, French and Dutch in the Lesser Antilles during the early seventeenth century. In all these imperial jurisdictions the facilitating context was the same: a transforming upsurge in agricultural and mining activities.

By the mid-eighteenth century most of the Caribbean was held in the economic and cultural grip of "sugar and slavery". In territories that produced commodities other than sugar the development of the slave system was borrowed from the plantation sectors. Women constituted 35 per cent of the enslaved Africans imported into the Caribbean. Black women's minority status in the trade was reflected in the demographic structures of most colonies throughout the slavery period. Few colonies achieved a balanced sex structure, and only Barbados developed a female majority in the eighteenth century (Morrisey 1989; Schartz 1985; Fox-Genovese and Genovese 1983).

The legal architecture of the institution of chattel slavery was conceived by Europeans in order to meet a broad range of discernible objectives. There was nothing ad hoc about its design and implementation. Neither were the roles and functions of sex and gender representations fortuitous. Known core values and objectives had to be met; these called into consideration ways in which to think about gender and how to act with respect to measuring the comparative economic output of the sexes.

In the legal definition and social regulation of enslaved African women, primary emphasis was placed on the concept of unrestrictive property rights and its translation into the unlimited social authority of the slave-owners in all jurisdictions. The forms of constraints placed on slave-owners with respect to enslaved females were the same as those that applied to other forms of property such as animals, trees and buildings. For example, penalties could be imposed by government on property owners who felled certain kinds of trees or destroyed buildings without official approval. Enslaved women were entitled to protection under law in these regards, but no more.

The normal, well-understood right of the individual to enjoy private property applied in all circumstances. Laws promoted and assured the enforcement of the slave-owner's right to the full use of women's socio-economic capacities. Slave-owners could buy, sell, rent, hire, lease, sub-let, mortgage and exchange enslaved women without let or hindrance. These rights were applicable to enslaved women with or without children, though towards the end of the slavery period in most jurisdictions, laws were passed to prohibit the separation of children from their mothers in market transactions. This policy shift was part of a general effort to ameliorate the conditions of enslaved women in order to stimulate fertility and enhance natural reproduction.[2]

Enslaved women, then, did not experience any significant preferential mitigating treatment with respect to legal provisions. For most of the period there was no policy that distinguished enslaved women as deserving of a less harsh condition, partly because they were not conceptually represented, unlike white women, as a gentler, more delicate sex. No laws within English, French, Dutch, Spanish or Portuguese colonies fashioned a social or economic experience for enslaved women based on the idea of their physical or mental inferiority. Equality in work and under the whip was the operating principle. When adjustments were made by way of social reforms that targeted enslaved women there were always clear economic objectives in mind. This was very much the case when an effort was made after the 1770s to encourage a higher birth rate as it seemed clear to slave-owners that the slave trade from Africa would soon be abolished.

While, therefore, the political economy of gender determined the general nature of demand for labour and informed the experiences of the enslaved, the superordinate role of racism shaped colonial representations of Africans and defined them as culturally inferior and hence worthy of enslavement. The ideology of race, particularly its phenotypic expressions of colour and culture, was less flexible than gender in determining the experiences of enslaved Africans. Social and economic functions considered fit for Africans were not allocated on the basis of gender. An effect of this was that gender representations of blacks were unstable and changed drastically under specific socio-economic pressures within management policy. "Race" remained fixed as an ideology that structured the hierarchical culture of the slave system (Shepherd, Brereton and Bailey 1995).

For this reason Lucille Mair has argued the existence of a broad-based race typology of women in slave society while cognizant of significant internal variations based on the class relations endemic to unequal property ownership. She stated that in the Caribbean slave society the white woman consumed, the coloured woman served and the black woman worked. This "race" structure reflected a general perception of juxtaposed categories based on the production, distribution and consumption of goods and services. The white woman, in both her roles as wife and mother in the slave-owning household, and as principal slave-owner in her own right, did not enter the slave system as a marginalized outsider to masculine power, but as a critical co-creator and collaborator (Mair 1987; Beckles 1993).

Elite white women represented less than 10 per cent of all white women in the slave societies of the Caribbean. The demographic data on the enslaved collected in the form of registers by colonial governments during the 1810s indicate the extent to which white women owned slaves of their own and were financially independent of their husbands and sons. They owned 24 per cent of the slaves in St Lucia in 1815. In Barbados in 1817 they owned less than 5 per cent of the properties with fifty or more slaves, but owned 40 per cent of the properties with fewer than ten slaves. Furthermore, they comprised 50 per cent of slave-owners in Bridgetown with fewer than ten slaves, and about 52 per cent of the town's registered slave-owners (Beckles 1993).

More significant was that the majority of enslaved persons owned by white women were black women. White women owned more enslaved females in Bridgetown than did white men. In 1817 the sex ratio (males per hundred females) in Bridgetown of enslaved blacks belonging to males was more than double that for female slave-owners, though the majority of the enslaved in the town were owned by white men: the sex ratio of enslaved blacks belonging to white men was 111; for white women it was 53. In Berbice in 1819 enslaved blacks owned by males had a sex ratio of 132, while those owned by females had a ratio of 81 (Beckles 1993).

Elite white women who owned enslaved persons were generally urban and in possession of fewer than ten, most of whom were female. It is correct then to show that, in the urban context at least, white women were the principal owners of enslaved black women, while on the plantations a woman was more likely to derive her authority from her status as mother and wife. Most white women, however, lived in materially impoverished and insecure households with men who represented subordinate white masculinities, such as overseers, artisans, clerks, militiamen, sailors, police and unskilled workers. Few of them could afford to purchase or hire more than one enslaved African (Higman 1984).

The enslaved black woman emerged as the key component in reproduction of the slave system. In all jurisdictions, starting from the immediate post-Columbus dispensation, it was established in law and custom that all children at birth took the status of the mother. The matrilineal inheritance of slave status was designed by white slave-owning males who had discernible social objectives in mind. It was no coincidence that reproduction of the slave system was attached to the enslaved female. White conquistadores who conceived and fashioned this system wished first and foremost to reproduce themselves as a property-owning elite. The process of inheritance in this regard was critical; it was a well-understood social mechanism and had deep roots within European culture. As agro-commercial entrepreneurs, the colonial elite wished to pass on their accumulated property – slaves included – to their white sons. But blacks were a peculiar kind of property; they engaged in sexual relations with whites and produced offspring. Wherever slavery was established, blacks and whites, enslaved and free had sex with each other. As a benefit of property, the law invested slave-owners with a right to the sexuality of the enslaved. It did not recognize rape in this regard as a legal offence. Each year, hundreds of mixed-race children were born and simultaneously conceived by the legislators as disturbers of the colour codes that had been established as an instrument of social control.

As part of the package of property rights over humans in law and custom, whites secured permission to extract from black women a wide range of non-pecuniary socio-sexual benefits as a legitimate stream of return on capital, and an important part of the meaning of colonial mastery. In real terms slavery led to the legal recognition of sex with the enslaved as an intrinsic and discrete social and economic product. For the enslaved woman, production and reproduction oftentimes overlapped. The sexual violation of an enslaved woman, which was first and foremost an attack upon her as a human, was not recognizable, for the reason that under the slave-laws property could not be raped (Beckles 1999, chapter 2; 1996b).

The enslaved woman, therefore, was completely powerless before the law as far as her body was concerned. Legally she had no body of her own, and certainly no prior right to it. She could not legally deny her owner total access to it – anytime, anywhere, for whatever purpose. Sex was demanded as a physical act in much the same way that labour was expected. Also, just as her labour power could be rented or leased, a woman's sexuality could be socially alienated as a commodity. It was part of the entertainment culture of slave-owning males, for example, to finish a dinner function by providing enslaved girls to overnighting guests for sex.

According to Patterson, the legal non-recognition and powerlessness of enslaved women meant that more often than not they chose rape over other forms of brutality that followed acts of refusal and resistance. In reality the finest line imaginable existed between their compliance and violent subjugation. Oftentimes this cycle of sexual exploitation was accompanied by pregnancy, miscarriage in the workplaces or death in childbirth (Patterson 1967).

The question of defining the status of an infant born to an enslaved woman was of paramount concern to white men who wished to ignore or deny paternity. A principal issue was to ensure that their mixed-race children did not constitute an empowered group that could make a legal claim upon their property. For this reason they made statute provision that the child at birth acquired the status of the mother and was therefore unable to act as a legal party in any form of judicial contest. The protection of property from the "offspring of property" seems ironic, but points to the contradictory nature of slavery as both a legal institution and a form of social relation.

Equally ironic was the nature of the legal principle that established matrilineal inheritance of freedom. The children that white women produced with enslaved men were born free on account of their mothers' status. The 1715 census of Barbados, for example, contains cases of free-born "mulatto" children whose mothers were white. Such cases were considered unusual, and warranted special listing by the church wardens who recorded the data. No special mention was made of the thousands of "coloured" children in the colony who were born into slavery.

The white woman carried the status of freedom as a natal legal condition. This circumstance meant, however, that the white male, in order to limit access to freedom by blacks, had to devise ways and means to control her sexual freedom. She had to be denied legitimate sexual relations with enslaved men. As a result, public institutions and social convention did not sanction multiracial domesticity for the white woman.

The white male, on the other hand, established this culture for himself and sanctioned it as an expression of his property rights and social authority. Social exclusion, and sometimes death, awaited the white woman who broke free of these constraints (Beckles 1993).

But even in the most oppressive of social conditions, convention was sometimes subverted by the triumph of human compassion articulated in complex forms of rationalization. Many enslaved mixed-race children were manumitted by their white fathers and entered free society, though with a restricted liberty. When manumission was not available, the very act of paternal recognition was sometimes enough to ameliorate their social lives. Coloured women especially were favoured as lovers, and in most societies they were the majority among those freed or kept in "privileged" slave relations. The roles of mistress and prostitute often overlapped, and there was no easy way to untangle the complications of socio-sexual and economic functions.

The enslaved offspring of black women constituted first and foremost a capital addition to the inventory of assets. In the records the child's human identity was subordinate to the financial statement of the capitalization process. The financial value of the child was listed in the inventory of assets in a column that included "animals, stocks, and machinery". The child's value was also listed annually, reflecting appreciation that oftentimes corresponded proportionately to the mother's depreciation. A common expectation was that the child's market value would increase significantly after the weaning exercise – usually between two and four years of age – to exceed the value of the mother by its mid-teens. In this way an enslaved woman could easily replace several times the capital outlay involved in her purchase.

The slave-owner, therefore, could convert his social and sexual exploitation of the enslaved woman through impregnation and child-rearing into a process of wealth accumulation. That is, he could extract two streams of returns from his female "property": one social and the other economic. This was the multiple expectation associated with investments in enslaved females. White masculinity understood and practised the culture of accumulation in this way and protected interests in slavery for the power relations it represented and the wealth it generated.

Rape and other forms of sexual exploitation experienced by enslaved women were, then, also mechanisms for producing a labour force and capitalizing properties. Enslaved women suffered the double indignity of knowing that their "coloured" daughters were likely to be selected for prostitution and concubinage. Most "coloured" girls, though, languished in the fields with their enslaved black mothers, sisters and aunts. Furthermore, it is often stated that white men sexually abused coloured girls more than their black sisters. Reference is made in the literature to the greater terror associated with "serving" in the household as opposed to labouring in the fields, and to the notion that women readily chose the former when given the opportunity. The few cases in which enslaved women told their own story suggest that such dichotomous experiences did not exist. Rather, they detailed a narrative of physical and mental abuse that involved field gangs and white households – sexual violation and psychological terrorism intersected by moments of compassion and consideration.

Enslaved mothers wished that some good could come of it all, and indeed many were able to gain freedom because of cash raised by their daughters from their multiple work activities. But the overt violence and grief that characterized their daughters' worlds overshadowed the possibility of conceiving any strategy of escape to freedom. The majority of enslaved women, whether represented as black, white or coloured (mixed-race), were field hands on sugar plantations. Unskilled work was their primary occupation. Less than 10 per cent of them found non-agricultural work as housekeepers, domestic labourers (washerwomen, cooks, cleaners), wet-nurses or sugar factory operators (Bush 1990).

Outside the role of principal housekeeper, women had few prestigious professions, particularly in the artisan craft sector. The carpenters, masons, coopers, boilers, distillers and first-gang field drivers were men. Women did find employment as second-gang drivers, but managing the first gang was the job that offered social and material high status within the slave village and among whites. In the production system, then, women occupied the lowest categories, as life-serving menials.

Many enslaved women found an escape from plantation bondage in the towns, a flight that was in some ways not a sweet alternative to making sugar. The washerwomen, prostitutes, tavern attendants, hucksters and construction labourers were physically challenged in order to meet the work expectations of owners. Greater intimacy with whites generated its own kinds of terror. Less-developed kinship systems in towns meant that psychological support mechanisms were not readily available. It was common to see enslaved women abandoned when they were sick, infirm or aged, and forced to subsist as street beggars. The poor-relief facilities in most colonies were unable to accommodate large numbers of such persons, who in this degenerate state were still vulnerable to the ravages of unjust slave relations.

The rapidly changing demographics of enslaved communities between the mid-seventeenth century, when most colonies developed an export-driven plantation sector, and the early nineteenth century, when serious general emancipation discourses were taking place on both sides of the Atlantic, is the critical context within which to discuss transformations in enslaved women's social experiences as workers. It is possible to discern distinct stages in the evolution of their engagement with production and reproduction. Each stage connects them to representations about work and social relations.

It is important to keep in mind, though, that the critical single development in each colony was when the sugar plantation system was established. This eruptive process took place at different moments across imperial jurisdictions. The first sugar revolution is usually associated with Barbados and the Leewards in 1645–70; the experience was repeated in Jamaica (1680–1740), the Windwards (1763–1800), and Trinidad and Guiana (1800–30). The discernible trend in each of these staggered processes was that enslaved males were preferred in the formative period and enslaved females in the developed years. In general terms this translated into a political economy of gender in which male muscle mass was desired in the phase of infrastructure development and females were preferred for the enhancement of productivity levels.

Sex ratios within slave societies over time and across the regions indicated the extent to which the black community could reproduce itself naturally within this changing political economy. Given the male majority in most colonies for the better part of the time, the overall trend was natural decline. All societies up to the late eighteenth century experienced disastrous growth performance.

The genocidal reality lived by enslaved Africans in those years represented a demographic continuum from the Arawak/Carib experience. Slave-owners had no interest, until the last quarter of the eighteenth century, in the natural growth performance of the enslaved. Pregnant and lactating mothers were seen by plantation management as a drain and a drag upon efficiency and output. The costs of raising a child, expressed in loss of productivity during and after childbirth, were computed as considerably greater than the price of purchasing a "fresh" African. In classical economic theory such calculations served to mark slave-owners as rational, profit-maximizing entrepreneurs.

The low and negative emphasis on child-rearing and maternity resulted in horrendous mortality rates among women in childbirth and among infants. Up to 70 per cent of babies born during the eighteenth century died before their third birthday. Slave-owners were more concerned about the frequent loss of mothers in childbirth than with the death of infants. These demographic experiences, when placed within the context of low fertility and birth rates, guaranteed the natural decline of the black population (Beckles 1989b).

If the typical enslaved woman could reasonably expect to survive childbirth, she could have no such expectation about her child surviving the weaning period. There was no widespread empathy among whites for black women as mothers and nurturers. They were represented in pro-slavery discourse as brutes without maternal instincts or sense of care for family values. In effect they were "defeminized" within discursive representations and persistently described in masculinist terms. References were frequently made to their alleged ability to "drop" babies while in the field and to continue working after a short break.

Defeminization, as a discursive strategy by slave-owners to extract maximum labour and perpetuate physical brutality, was linked also to a conceptual disassociation of black women from notions of beauty. The black skin was represented within pro-slavery imagery in a way that conjured receptiveness to punishment, moral denigration and social non-recognition. When linked to the enslaved woman, the black skin implied she was ugly, rough and harsh. She was de-sexualized on account of her blackness; that is, she was not to be seduced by loving tenderness but rather to be raped and physically plundered.

The concept of "black and ugly" emerged as the social device that sealed the black woman's sexual identity within colonial discourse. Meanwhile, the "brown woman" was idealized by the white male as a sexual icon that spoke to masculine lust and unrestricted mastery. The brown woman was to be domestically kept, seduced by privileges and serenaded in ballads that spoke of her beauty and voluptuous sexuality. Few white men, it was said, could resist the lure of these "mulatresses" (Beckles 1989b).

The black woman, then, was conceptually defeminized and desexualized within pro-slavery discourse in ways that exposed her to the violent sexuality of white males for whom she was primarily a form of property. The creation of a social world that attached nothing positive in terms of human value to the black skin kept her prisoner as a life-server; furthermore, it eroded important aspects of her sense of beauty and inner worth. Because she was unable to socially legitimize her beauty within the dominant culture, the "black and ugly" narrative had a telling effect upon her decision making and ultimately shaped much of the aesthetic of the black community. Resistance to this colour representation was, however, relentless. A counter-aesthetic emerged as a site of resistance that was as important as the battlefields of violent self-liberation.

During the last quarter of the eighteenth century, shifting economic and political circumstances in the slave trade coalesced to impact upon slave-owners' policy with respect to enslaved women within the labour force. Even on estates where enslaved men marginally outnumbered enslaved women it was normal for field gangs to carry female majorities, since black men occupied a greater share of the supervisory and artisan professions. Rapidly rising prices on the African slave market, the effective ending of the period of attractive profits in the sugar industry, and the loss of the US market following the independence revolution produced a management "rethink" that focused on cost-cutting and financial rationalization. Emerging from the realignment of new market forces and management ideology was a policy position that targeted the enslaved woman as the key to future dispensation.

The core concept of the revised slave-management strategy was that it was now cheaper to "breed" than to import slaves. This constituted a reversal of tradition. It enabled slave-owners, nonetheless, to claim commitment to a new moral order that featured the structural amelioration of enslaved women's conditions. Calculations of the relative costs of "buying" and "breeding" depended upon the availability of females within slave communities. Enslaved women had to be available, both locally and in West Africa, in order to enable slave-owners to benefit from the new policy, the logic of which was that the slave market was responsive (Craton 1979; Higman 1979).

Across the region, slave-owners implemented a "woman" policy. In Jamaica, where a black female shortage was reported, measures were taken to purchase from the slave ships more females than males. Elsewhere, in the search for a cheaper labour force the shift from the slave ship to the slave womb was aggressively pursued. Slave-owners understood that policy effectiveness would be measured in three areas: (1) stimulating the fertility of the slave community, (2) increasing the birth rate and (3) reducing the infant mortality rate.

The first of these objectives was considered the most difficult to achieve. The opinion was that enslaved women had turned their backs against the culture of maternity, and were critical of family development and kinship formation within the hostile environment of slave relations. Slave-owners indicated that enslaved women were practising gynaecological resistance and that they were possessed of a mentality that had to be turned around as far as child-rearing was concerned. They knew that this entailed "normalizing" the social and maternal conditions of slave women by introducing prenatal and postnatal policies. The initiative was devised and implemented to unlock and enhance the fertility of black women as the first step in pursuing a positive growth performance in the slave population. A natal programme was set out. An effort was made to soften the work regime of pregnant and lactating women, improve their nutrition and allow for the emergence of a supportive domestic environment for motherhood.

Less astute managers were provided with a body of pro-natal literature that presented the content and context of the policy in a clear and coherent manner. Pregnant women were to be removed from gang work after the sixth or seventh month and put to light tasks. Improved nutrition was ordered during this period and a system of supervision put in place in case of miscarriage or attempted abortion. In addition, a broad-based approach to improving the material and social environment was recommended. The objective was to encourage fertile women to perceive maternity and motherhood in a positive light, and to create within them a desire for child-rearing. Social and financial packages were offered to women. Detailed arrangements varied from colony to colony over time, but were built around the following provisions:

- Monetary and material awards for the delivery of healthy children. Incentives were progressive and sometimes carried the boon of freedom after six or more children. Midwives were also offered cash rewards for their effectiveness.
- Material support for children and mothers, including better nutrition, housing and health care, and the provision of a crib, cash and animals as gifts.
- Permission to marry and cohabit in a household. Christian baptism and marriage were also offered towards the end of the slavery period.
- Assurance that children would not be sold nor families separated, and domestic unions would be recognized and respected (Beckles 1989b).

These initiatives were designed in order to make the culture of maternity and domesticity as attractive as possible for enslaved women. Enslaved men were not targeted directly by these provisions. Slave-owners reported varying degrees of success by 1800, but were clear that a systematic approach was needed. Most spoke of the general responsiveness of enslaved women to the incentives, but reported negative results in terms of inherent gynaecological complications, the prevalence of venereal disease, and medical ignorance on the part of mothers and slave midwives.

By 1806, when the British anti–slave trade law was passed, only the Barbadian blacks, who since 1700 had experienced a balanced sex ratio, could claim a positive growth performance that was discernible and sustainable. Slave-owners there claimed a demographic breakthrough and explained it in terms of significantly reduced infant mortality and increased birth rate. When the importation of Africans was made illegal the following year, they boasted that the colony was well stocked with labour and that they might very well be adversely affected by a surplus. The evidence of the accuracy of their judgement resides in the fact that Barbados after 1807 was a net exporter of slaves, supplying Trinidad, Guiana and the Windwards in an increasingly important internal (inter-colonial) slave trade.

In general, then, only the Barbados slave-owners could counter the charge of the anti-slavery lobby that slave conditions were genocidal and evidence of their vicious inhumanity. The Jamaican slave-owners who owned over 50 per cent of the enslaved women in the British Caribbean were entirely vulnerable to the charge. In this largest slave society, the continuing natural decline of the black population could not be interpreted in any other way. The brutalization of enslaved women was everywhere documented by the physical, social and domestic evidence. Anti-slavery campaigners collected such evidence on Jamaica, as the principal colony, and made the following accusations:

- the majority of enslaved women who worked in field gangs were treated more like beasts of burden than human beings;
- that the daily circumstances of work and punishment subverted enslaved women's interest in domesticity, maternity and femininity;
- that slavery was destructive of the black family and the Christian moral values that surround monogamous family life;
- that the slave plantation system, with its seasonal fluctuations in economic activity, encouraged and promoted slave prostitution during the non-harvest time, and the rape and sexual plunder of women generally;
- that slavery had produced a genocidal effect on the black population that was not reversible.

Slave-owners everywhere wasted no time in formulating responses to these charges. It was an important challenge for them to illustrate that the enslaved woman was "well treated" within her enslavement. The conceptual relationship between "good treatment" and enslavement was not considered contradictory in pro-slavery thought, since freedom was not recognized as a state that was natural or morally available to blacks. Rather it was argued that the issues were about diet, punishment, natal considerations, health and domestic life. The effect of the dialogue was to centre the enslaved woman within the slavery discourse, a location that was not only conceptual but rooted within the managerialism of the institution.

Anti-slavery campaigners in England were satisfied that they had found, finally, the moral Achilles heel of slave-owners. No matter how they tried, slave-owners could not get around the argument that the enslaved woman was subject to daily sexual exploitation, physical brutality at work and general social abuse within an extreme tyrannical, masculinist culture. The evidence was all around to be seen: children on auction blocks, paternally denied and abandoned mulattos, black husbands powerless within domestic unions and female bodies lacerated by the whip. Such evidence was also witnessed and reported by visitors to the colonies, many of whom – though pro-slavery in their politics – were forced to admit that the conditions under which enslaved women lived were a disgrace to civilized human conduct. It was here that slave societies and slave-owners were indicted by majority metropolitan opinion that preferred to imagine the enslaved woman as mother, wife and family maker.

The projection of the importance of mastery within pro-slavery discourse highlighted the centred location of the enslaved woman. According to Elsa Goveia, slave-owners' unrestricted masculinity constituted a psychological force that inhibited their rational approach to the anti-slavery challenge. Had they been rational, she suggests, that is, driven purely by the best-case options the market economy could offer, they would have seen the considerable economic opportunities involved in transforming the social relations of slavery. For example, they could have developed a fully fledged wage economy within slavery that socially empowered slaves with real, attractive options for freedom, by self-purchase or as a productivity benefit. But the fear of losing social control over the enslaved – women especially – got in the way of significant reform possibilities. At emancipation, not being able to command as a right the sexuality of enslaved women was considered a devastating loss to white masculinity. This loss was reflected in a sudden drop in the mulatto population in the immediate post-slavery period (Goveia 1965; Gautier 1983).

While it is clear that enslaved women were centrally located and collectively victimized and exploited at a superordinate level by the logic and culture of the slave system, there is quite substantial evidence of the experiences of many individuals who, through strength of character and strategic vision, transcended these constraints and achieved considerable social autonomy. These narratives of personal voyages are recorded in texts that include advertisements for runaways, trial transcripts, manumission papers, self-purchase invoices, and dictated and written letters and memoirs, as well as the "software" of community memory. They transmit orally, through the folk tradition, echoes of liberated souls that ring out but also conceal the feelings of immeasurable misery and untold anguish.

The litany of minor refusals has gone unnoticed, but they were major decisions for enslaved women who had no law or empowered love on their side. Grand refusals have found the way into the record and stand as monuments to ultimate sacrifices. Enslaved women swung on the gallows in protection of an inner world that cried freedom; they also slept in the white man's bed in search of love, property and privileges, as well as freedom for themselves and their kith and kin. At times the militancy of minorities gave meaning to an existence that typified the malaise of majorities. Moments were also recorded when treacherous minorities subverted the grand missions of majorities. Slavery was more about death than life and cannot be understood outside the concept of genocide, invoking high rates of mortality and the notion of survival. The reign of terror was etched deepest in their souls in codes as yet undeciphered. These and such like perspectives can direct us to explorations of the interior existence of enslaved women who were held by the legal provisions of the market economy as perfect property.

Notes

1. See Eltis 2000, chapter 4, "Gender and Slavery in the Early Modern Atlantic World"; Greene 1996; Robertson and Klein 1983b; and Inikori 1992.
2. See Beckles 1989c, Blackburn 1997, Cohen 1980, Curtin 1990 and Davis 1966.

☩ *Chapter 8* ☩

Theorizing Sexual Relations in the Caribbean
Prostitution and the Problem of the "Exotic"

KAMALA KEMPADOO

Introduction

In social, historical and anthropological studies, prostitution stands as a prism through which the social organization of sexuality can be viewed. Since the 1970s such studies have been profoundly shaped by radical feminist theorizing in which prostitution has been theoretically located as a universal expression of violence to women and as the quintessence of patriarchal dominance and female sexual subordination.[1] Nevertheless, other feminist approaches have indicated that there is no straightforward correlation between patriarchy and prostitution (Truong 1990; Shrage 1994; Kempadoo 1996; Lim 1998). Rather, it is argued, entrance into prostitution or other forms of sexual relations, and the contexts and conditions in which these sexual activities take place, vary according to local, regional and international relations of power along gendered, economic, national and ethnic divides.[2] The reduction of sexual relations to a gendered dynamic is thus seen to be inadequate to theorize the various histories, experiences and everyday realities of the organization and exploitation of sexuality around the world.

In this chapter I further this argument through an examination of the construction of prostitution in Caribbean colonial and post-colonial societies. Central here is an exploration of how the exoticization of the cultural "other" through Caribbean history has contributed to the construction of the prostitute and to the shaping of sexual relations. Prostitution can be seen through this history not simply as a way in which women's bodies, sexuality and labour were acted upon, exploited or strategically employed under patriarchal domination, but also as an articulation of racialized relations of power and resistance[3] at both local and global levels. Some of this complexity is illustrated here through historical and anthropological studies of the colonial Caribbean. In the second part of this paper I investigate the articulation of exoticism in the post-colonial tourism industry, drawing on an analysis of postings to an Internet website by sex tourists to the Caribbean in the 1990s.

The tracing of a history of prostitution through the discourse of exoticism is not an attempt to dismiss the relevance of masculine control of female sexuality as a crucial factor in the construction of prostitution and other sexual relations. Rather, this analysis seeks to emphasize the ways in which colonial and global relations of power and ruling have contributed to the process. As Parker, Barbarosa and Aggleton summarize the state of the study of sexuality at the turn of the twenty-first century, "One key challenge confronting sexuality research has thus emerged as the urgent need to rethink the effects of colonialism and neo-colonialism" (2000, 9). In this way, this essay can best be read as an attempt to *complicate* existing feminist theorizing of prostitution, rather than to offer an alternative framework.

Historicizing Colonial Sexuality

The Caribbean region has been richly studied, interpreted and reread for the ways in which notions of race and ethnicity have constituted the cultural, social and political identity of its peoples and nations, and the elaboration of this focus with a critical gender analysis has produced a substantial body of work that describes and theorizes Caribbean women's lives and experiences.[4] To more fully apprehend the intersectionality of racialized, sexualized processes and relations of power in the Caribbean, the theoretical notion of exoticism is of interest, for it captures the simultaneous romanticization and oppression and exploitation of the racial, ethnic or cultural other, and has been defined as part of the practice and ideology of earlier colonial and imperialist projects (Said

1979; Alloula 1986; Kabbani 1988; Rousseau and Porter 1990a; Hentsch 1992; Lewis 1996; Yeğenoğlu 1998; di Leonardo 1998).

Exoticism has been most commonly identified in the context of orientalism – the broader lens through which Europe viewed "the East" during the eighteenth and nineteenth centuries – although is not confined to the western European cultural response to that part of the world nor to that historical period only. As an approach to the non-Western world, it is associated with the legitimation of European conquest, control and domination, as well as with escapist fantasies and vicarious enjoyment of sex and violence by European literary intellectuals and artists. In a contemporary reflection on this particular period in Europe, Rousseau and Porter write:

> The invention of the "exotic" evidently satisfied needs amongst a European and, later, an Atlantic, civilization which, as it progressively explored and dominated the entire globe with its guns and sails, increasingly assumed the right to define human values and conduct in their highest expression. Other cultures, other creeds, were not merely different, not even merely lower, but positively – even objectively – strange. It was not merely the remoteness of geographical distance in a world where miles counted for much, but the ineluctable sense that all their mental processes and logical deductions were equally as alien. Labeling the anthropological Other as exotic legitimated treating the peoples of the "third world" as fit to be despised – destroyed even, or at least doomed, like the Tasmanian aborigines, to extinction – while concurrently also constituting them as projections of Western fantasies. (1990a, 6–7)

Exoticism valorized peoples and cultures that were different and remote, concomitantly imposing a status of inferiority upon them. "The Orient" was captured as the epitome of the exotic: a strange and unfamiliar world, both fascinating and terrifying, inviting to the curious explorer yet threatening to all the standards of civilization upheld in Europe, seductive in its paradise-like, unblemished "virgin" state, yet bestial in its perceived barbaric, cannibalistic moments. The eroticization of women of these different cultures was integral to this movement, whereby their sexuality was defined as highly attractive and fascinating, yet related to the natural primitiveness and lower order of the other cultural group. According to Porter, exotic lands and peoples provided

Europeans with "paradigms of the erotic". Away from the repressive sexual mores of western Europe, strange cultures, and particularly the women in them, became sites where sex "was neither penalized, nor pathologized nor exclusively procreative" (Rousseau and Porter 1990b, 118). Womanhood among the colonized came to represent uninhibited, unbridled sensuality and sexual pleasure for the colonizer. Asian female sexuality signified temptation, eroticism, pleasure and danger – veiled mysteries to be possessed and controlled within western Europe's expansionist project – and theorists of orientalism have pointed out that it was the harem of Persia, courtesan arrangements in India and Japan, *devadasis* (temple girls) of India, *ronggeng* (dancing girls) of Indonesia and polygamous lifestyles that were seized upon by Western travellers, traders, photographers and crusaders to illustrate and perpetuate myths of the exotic other (Alloula 1986; Kabbani 1988; Yeğenoğlu 1998). Exoticism in its various expressions brought legitimacy to Western rule; it is distinguished from other racisms by fostering the illusion of an admiration for and attraction to the other while simultaneously enacting murder, rape, genocide and enslavement.

Di Leonardo's elaborate study of American exoticism points out that the discourse was not tied simply to direct colonial rule that proceeded from western Europe, but also to those imperial projects through which the United States began to assert its dominance in world affairs. Exoticism, she notes, appeared most prominently at the end of the eighteenth and turn of the nineteenth centuries, bringing "a sense of psychic healing and therapeutic personal integration" to the elite at a time also marked by "recurrent crises of masculinity and American state actions against 'primitives' both at home and abroad" (di Leonardo 1998, 159–60). It was

> a period of the consolidation of capitalist industrialization, of a bloody war against a significantly European immigrant labor force, and of federal abandonment of reconstruction in the South and the establishment there of a white reign of terror against black Americans . . . It was as well the end of the war of expropriation against Native Americans . . . the heyday of American imperialist expansion into the Caribbean, Latin America, and the Pacific; and the period of an ongoing Victorian woman movement still twenty-seven years short of the achievement of female voting rights and tinged by racist and classist response to short-lived post–Civil War black male suffrage. (di Leonardo 1998, 4)

While exoticism is most often identified as a white masculine dis-course, it has been pointed out that it was also mediated through the white imperial feminine imagination, although the subjectivities, posi-tions and roles of white women have not been much explored in studies of colonial or post-colonial societies (Hall 1995). Nevertheless, we are reminded that women cannot be overlooked in the production of an ori-entalist or exoticist discourse. In Reina Lewis's study of nineteenth-century feminist writings she argues that it is necessary to examine all the contradictory positions inherent in imperialism, to " 'disentangle' the ways in which representations of an orientalized Other simultaneously undercut and contribute to Orientalist ideas and policies" (1996, 26). Regarding women writers during the nineteenth century she notes:

> As agents socialized in an age of everyday imperialism it would have been impossible for the subjects of this study to be unaware of, or influenced by, imperial discourse – even if they couched their relationship to it as opposi-tional. That some of the key writers of the twentieth-century feminist literary canon, like Brontë and Eliot, couched their demands for female emancipation precisely through the Orientalizing of a structural other requires even more our willingness to include the conditions and discourses of imperial difference in our analysis of the work. (1996, 29)

Writers such as Lewis open the door to thinking about how white/ European women participated in the construction of the gendered other – feminine and masculine – in imperialist and colonial projects. The analyses suggest that it is not simply overt "racist" white women's behav-iour and ideologies that can be seen to reproduce the imperial gaze and conditions, but that many women were complexly located in relations of domination and ruling.

The Caribbean has not escaped exoticization. Colonialism, with its attendant systems of slavery and indentured labour, also produced ide-ologies of the exotic, and few women in the colonies were not subject to an eroticizing, sexualizing gaze. While black African women were defined by Europeans as "slaves by nature" and as passive, downtrod-den, subservient, resigned workers, they were also perceived as sexually promiscuous, "cruel and negligent as a mother, fickle as a wife" and immoral (Bush 1990). A prevailing view of black women under Caribbean slavery as naturally "hot constitution'd" and sensuous in an animal-like way, lacking all the qualities that defined "decent" woman-hood or women of "purity of blood", has been consistently noted by various scholars (Morrissey 1989; Bush 1990; Kutzinski 1993; Reddock 1994). The sexual imagery, leaning on associations between black wom-anhood and natural earthy instincts, licentiousness, immorality and pathology, was often painted to arouse disgust and abhorrence for pur-poses of maintaining slavery by the plantocracy or, alternatively, to illus-trate the abolitionists' cause by pointing out how slavery degraded the lives of Africans. It did not, however, deter European male pursuit of sexual intercourse with black women or their fascination, delight and pleasure with the black female body. Henriques concludes that the planters "became adept at attributing their own promiscuity to the inherent licentiousness of the Negro" and to the "debauchery" of slave women (1965, 195). The region came to be represented in Euro-pean imaginations "as a land of sexual opportunity for young European males", and black women – enslaved or free – were defined as the sex-ual property of white men (Morrissey 1989, 147).

Perceptions of black women as sexual and erotic objects were con-solidated in various ways. Researchers on slave-trade activities in the seventeenth century, for example, have noted the predominance of young girls and boys in the slave-ship crews' "property", as well as emotional attachments of slave-ship captains and officers to young African women during the middle-passage voyage, leading them to conclude that par-ticular women, girls and boys were targeted as sexual slaves or servants (Bush 1990; Postma 1990). Thus even before arrival in the colonies, African women were objectified as sexualized beings in the eyes and minds of the traders. Romanticized descriptions of African women as "ebony queens" and "sable beauties" can also be found in documents of European travellers, traders and plantation owners, and were later echoed in nineteenth-century art, poetry and literature (Bush 1990, 17).[5] This specific appreciation of black femininity, while popular among Europeans, was not parallelled to the same extent in the United States, yet had a profound impact on notions of eroticism and beauty in Europe and Europeanized Caribbean colonies.[6] Nevertheless, throughout the Americas women of mixed descent were in general perceived more favourably by the European elite than "pure" African women, a view that has barely diminished in post-colonial societies. If white womanhood represented the pinnacle of femininity, couched in assumptions of fairness, purity, frailty and domesticity, and black womanhood the total opposite because of its presumed closeness to nature, dark skin, masculine physique and unbridled sexuality, the combination of western Europe and Africa produced notions of the "light-skinned" woman who could almost pass for white yet retained a tinge of colour, as well as a hint of the wantonness and uninhibited sexuality of exotic cultures. The "coloured" woman was then often described as possessing "a great physical attraction for the European" (Henriques 1965, 110), and observations such as the following echoed this sentiment:

> Physically, the typical fille de couleur may certainly be classed, as white creole writers have not hesitated to class her, with the "most beautiful women of the human race". She has inherited not only the finer bodily characteristics of either parent race, but a something else belonging originally to neither, and created by special climatic and physical conditions – a grace, a suppleness of form, a delicacy of extremities . . . a satiny smoothness and fruit-tint of skin – solely West Indian. (Henriques 1974, 110)

Rogers's three-volume study of race and sex also documents in rich detail various views of the colonial elite and European male travellers during the eighteenth and nineteenth centuries in the Dutch, Spanish, English and French Caribbean, illustrating the trend of exoticization of "mixed-race" women in the region. Remarked a surgeon in the Dominican Republic, for example:

> When among the populations of the Antilles we first notice these remarkable metis, whose olive skins, elegant and slender figures, fine straight profiles and regular features remind us of the inhabitants of Madras or Pondicherry (India) we ask ourselves in wonder while looking at their long eyes, full of strange and gentle melancholy and at the black rich silky gleaming hair, curling in abundance over the temples and falling in profusion over the neck – to what human race can belong this singular variety . . . (Rogers 1972, 146)

Interestingly, a commonality in the perceptions, desires and passions of European men for women in the East and West is lodged in this particular image. The mixed-race woman in the West Indies is likened to mixed-race women from "the East" – in this instance, India. Women from both parts of the globe, in the eyes of the surgeon, constituted a particular "race" – remarkable and decidedly different, other, strange – constituted by a brown complexion, silky, loose-curling hair and facial features and a physical build that approximated the European ideal. The surgeon's comments reflect not only a fascination with slim, "olive"-skinned women but also elements of an orientalist ideology through its equation of Indian women with exotica – not simply a racialization of non-Western peoples, but again a delight in European male minds with foreign, "exotic" others. Historical records left by men living in or visiting the colonies confirm descriptions of these women as frequent objects of sexual desires and passions, enacted far away from the everyday confines and repressions of European society and the dominant sexual morality (Bush 1990). The "high brown", "mulatto", "morena", "metis" or light-skinned Caribbean woman remained highly desirable and attractive to European men.

Much post-colonial theory has designated orientalism and exoticism as a Western approach or "textual attitude" that includes dreams, images and vocabularies about the "other". "Orientalism," writes Yeğenoğlu, "refers to the production of a systematic knowledge and to the site of the unconscious – desires and fantasies" (1998, 23). This discourse is not, however, without material and embodied dimensions, and thus is defined not only as authorizing colonial and imperial domination for economic and political purposes, but as articulations of social relations, institutions and everyday practices. Exoticism thus is visible not only in ideologies and perceptions, but also in embodied relations, and in the Caribbean under colonialism was most evidently lodged in, and visible through, prostitution and other non-romantic sexual arrangements.

Sex in Caribbean history is inextricably tied to the power and control exerted by European colonizers over a black population, at a time when western European nations sought to find new resources for the accumulation of capital and new sites upon which to establish empire, and the enslavement of Africans was integral to the consolidation of racial power in the Americas. Beckles points out that slavery meant "not only the compulsory extraction of labor from the Blacks but also, in theory at least, slave owners' right to total sexual access to slaves" (1989b, 141). White slave-owners made ample use of this "right": rape and sexual abuse were commonplace, and concubinage and prostitution quickly became an institutional part of Caribbean societies. "In time," writes

Henriques, "no European male in the Caribbean, who could afford it, was without his colored mistress, either a freedwoman or slave" (1965, 195). Bush (1990), Morrissey (1989) and Henriques (1965) also point out that this power was exerted not only by the colonial elite and planter class but, because of the existing racial hegemony of white over black, extended to include white men of lower classes. Even European bond-servants, who stood at the margins of white society in a position almost comparable to that of slave, were seen to have "augmented the process of their masters" through engaging in clandestine sexual affairs with slave women as a result of the privilege that their whiteness conferred upon them (Henriques 1965, 201).

Racialized dimensions of sexuality under slavery were, however, not uniform, with the category of women "of mixed race" – the mulatto, "mustee" or "coloured" woman – being considered particularly exotic. This social category, which itself arose from the exercise of power over black slave women, was, however, legally and ideologically placed out-side of white society, representing to Europeans racial impurity and moral, racial and social degradation, constituting an "unnatural trans-gression of the rules of social propriety" (Kutzinski 1993, 75). The mulatto woman (*la mulata*) represented the erotic and sexually desir-able yet was outcast and pathologized and emerged during slavery as the symbol of the prostitute – the sexually available yet socially despised body – the eroticized other, the trope of the exotic.

Within the context of slavery, prostitution was lodged at the nexus of at least two areas of women's existence: as an extension of sexual rela-tions (forced or otherwise) with white men and as an income-generating activity for both slave and "free coloured" women. Beckles notes about Barbadian society in the early 1800s that slave women were frequently hired out by white and free coloured families as "nannies, nurses, cooks, washerwomen, hucksters, seamstresses" yet "the general expectation of individuals who hired female labor under whatever pretense, was that sexual benefits were included" (1989b, 143). Concubines often served as both mistresses and housekeepers and were sometimes hired out by their owners to sexually service other men "as a convenient way of obtaining cash" (p. 142). Furthermore, in times of economic slump on plantations (particularly in British colonies), when blacks, both men and women, were expected to provide for themselves or to bring in wages through work outside the plantation, "the number of slave women placed on the urban market as prostitutes by sugar planters would rapidly increase", and in the towns "masters and mistresses would frequently send out female slaves as prostitutes for ships' crew" (pp. 142–43). Reddock reports that in Trinidad, "For the most part women were hired out as domestic slaves, field labourers, as concubines, to temporary male European settlers, or were made to work as petty traders or prostitutes handing over most of their earning to their masters" (1994, 20). Black women's manual and sexual labour was, in effect, "pimped" by the slave-holders. Beckles suggests that white women were not exempt from this position of pimp, as they "may have owned and managed as much as 25 percent of Caribbean slaves, with a greater concentration of ownership in towns" and many "made a thriving business from the rental of black and colored women for sexual services in the port towns" (1999, 168, 65). Geggus (1996) furthermore remarks upon the numerous cases mentioned in historical records of slave women in the French Caribbean who, besides their marketing activities, were able to profit financially from selling their own or their daughters' sexual labour. Morrissey (1989) concludes that in the early nineteenth century in the British Caribbean, domestics who worked in taverns and inns in the towns also served as prostitutes.

Colonial sexual relations – forced or otherwise – often produced children, yet in the absence of marriage and formal recognition of the child by the white father, the child took on the condition of the mother and was defined as part of either the slave population or the free coloured class. Sex during slavery thus was a way in which the labouring classes and slaves were reproduced. Abraham-Van der Mark points out that "concubinage gave them [Jewish men in nineteenth-century Curaçao] the benefits of a category of children which, if necessary, provided labor but could not make any legal demands and were excluded from inheritance" (1993, 46). Moreover, mulattos were more highly valued in slave markets, and children of black slave women and white slave-owners could bring in a higher income than children of black parents. Beckles argues that in this respect, the sexual servant or prostitute was particularly valuable to the slave-owner, for "unlike other female slaves, she could generate three income flows: from labor, prostitution and reproduction" (1989b, 144).

The period immediately following slavery in the Caribbean has been characterized as a time when women established autonomy of work away from the plantations and where gendered relations were transformed under changing relations of production.[7] Waged labour for women took on greater importance, with European middle-class patriarchal family ideologies gaining primacy, yet many areas of "women's work" that had been established under slavery continued. Domestic service, marketing and prostitution continued to be constituted as black and "coloured" women's activities. Henriques also notes that "emancipation did not fundamentally alter the patterns of sexuality which had been established under slavery. Women might no longer be bound to masters but the 'white bias' in the society still facilitated illicit sexual relations between white and colored" (1965, 203). While there is a paucity of research from which to draw from for this period in Caribbean history about black and brown women's lives, Kerr's study on female housekeepers of lodgings in Jamaica concurs with Henriques's observations. She notes that the women – who were predominantly mulatto – "turned their weaknesses into strength by capitalizing upon white men's sexual desire for them. Their lodging houses became places 'flocked to' mainly by white males who sought sexual services from women of color. The housekeepers diversified their services so that they not only increased their incomes but eventually became women of importance" (1995, 210). However, the significance of racialized hierarchies and identities within the sex trade, the new constraints and possibilities for women in the labour markets, and the changes in demand for sex work remain underexplored and require far more attention than has been given by historians.

Almost completely hidden from view is the story of sexual relations between white or European women and black men. Apart from conventional understandings that white women were positioned as the symbols of moral purity and ideal domesticity in Caribbean colonial society and required protection by white men, Beckles proposes that during slavery, because children took on the condition of the mother and the male planters' interest was to reproduce the slave population and not the group of free people of colour, black male sexual access to white women had to be blocked so that "the progeny of black males were not lost to the slave gangs" (1999, 69). Black men, he states, "faced punishments such as castration, dismemberment, and execution for having sexual relations with white women, who in turn were socially disgraced and ostracized" (p. 68). Nevertheless, he indicates that sexual relations between white women and black men "were not as uncommon as generally suggested" (p. 62).

Such claims, while perhaps hinting at some dimensions of the sexual relations between white women and black men and emphasizing the ways in which white male patriarchy and the plantation economy shaped white women's behaviour and roles, nevertheless seem overly deterministic and fail to allow for explorations into the constructions of white female or black male sexuality and sexual agency under colonial relations. So while in this history much emphasis has been placed upon the ways in which black women were considered important by the planter class for "breeding" slave populations, little has been done to examine the ways in which the flip side of such policies encouraged the construction of the black male "stud" as an important impregnator of women, and how this informed ideas about black male sexuality in the Caribbean.

Alternatively, the characterization of European women as morally corrupt and degraded through interactions with black men and women has left little space for the interrogation of white women's sexual agency and desire in the context of colonial relations of ruling, although some recent attention has been given to the more general construction of white womanhood in Caribbean colonial societies (Hall 1995; Beckles 1999; Campbell 2001). These lacunae in Caribbean historiography leave a void in our understandings of colonial sexualities.

Despite this paucity of historical studies about the significance of racialized, sexualized subjects in the post-slavery context, the introduction of indentured workers from India in countries such as Trinidad, Guyana, Suriname and Jamaica signals another social group that was subject to an eroticizing gaze. While stereotypes of a "docile, insipid, tractable shadow of a being with no mind, personality or significance of her own" has dominated Caribbean understandings of Indian womanhood (Cumber Dance 1993, 21; Poynting 1987; Espinet 1993; Moore 1999), an orientalist representation of her – as a highly sexual being and a temptress – follows close behind. Reddock (1985a), Mangru (1987) and Shepherd (1995) observe that in discussions about the recruitment of female labour from India in the indentureship programme, British colonial government officials held that many of the female immigrants were prostitutes, social outcasts and women who had abandoned marriage and domesticity, all of whom were considered to "have gone astray", to be "prone to immoral conduct", to exercise a "corrupting influence" on "respectable" women, or liable to be tempted into "abnormal sexual behavior by single men with money". In the eyes of officialdom then, the women were highly sexual, of dubious character and well outside the boundaries of "decent" colonial womanhood. Reddock notes that the skewed perception of Indian womanhood held by the British reinforced patriarchal tendencies within the Indian community, locating the women not only as immoral, but as corrupted sexual servants to non-Indian men.[8] Often labelled and categorized as lewd and lascivious, working-class Indian women were cast as evil, corrupting elements who disrupted dominant notions of decency and proper family values. Indian men were complicitous in upholding certain sexualized notions of Indo-Caribbean womanhood. However, while Indian men may have deplored and vilified working women, an exoticist discourse that celebrated non-white female sexuality – while inscribing it with racial and gender inferiority – was performed through black male lyrics in the post-indentureship period.[9] Gordon Rohlehr's analysis of Trinidadian calypsos in the 1930s to 1950s (1988) notes that among the various racialized and gendered images, Indian women gained attention as exotic temptresses but were also classified as "unattainable" – of being guarded and hidden away from men – as the classic trope of Oriental mystique. Equally pervasive was the image of Indo-Trinidadian women as "street girls" working for "Yankee dollars" that emerged through these popular songs. Shalini Puri's analysis of texts of two black male calypso singers – Mighty Killer and Lord Superior, popular in 1952 and 1958 respectively – indicates that the songs vividly conjured up an image of Indian women as exclusively sexual actors – prostitutes – who worked for the American military troops stationed in Trinidad during the Second World War (Puri 1993; Reddock 1998a).

Exoticism was thus both an attitude and a set of practices visited upon the Caribbean by Europeans during slavery and in its aftermath, constituting the "brown-skinned" colonized and enslaved woman, as well as the lands she inhabited, as sites for sexual pleasure and fantasy as well as exploitation, enslavement and violence. Constructed through the domination of the Caribbean by western Europe and consolidated through slavery, it can be argued that this history has had profound implications, both within the Caribbean itself and between the region and neocolonial centres of power. In the remaining part of this essay I explore dimensions of the continued legacy of exoticism, in which tourism plays an increasingly important role.

Exoticism in the Twentieth Century

The shift from a discourse that was primarily articulated through the white European, masculine, colonial consciousness to one that is embedded in the imaginations and desires of the colonized man has been a subject of interrogation and discussion by anti-colonial Third World intellectuals. This discourse has been explored through black American perspectives (hooks 1993; West 1993) and lightly touched upon in Caribbean gender analyses (Mohammed 1998; Lewis 1998). It is my argument here that besides the profound influence that colonialism has had on notions of the superiority of whiteness (including white femininity) among the colonized, it has also imparted a legacy of exoticization of the cultural other and the brown woman. Both were infused into new relations of power and privilege structured through anti-colonial and nationalist struggles for political independence that appeared on the Caribbean landscape in the twentieth century. One encounters attitudes and ideas within the Caribbean itself that reflect both a racialization of sexual desire as well as an exoticization of cultural difference, much of which revolve around the brown female body and identity. In Cuba, for example, the *mulata* was considered exotic not only by foreign men, but by male Cuban writers, artists and poets, who also "enshrined the erotic image of Cuba's *mulatas*" during the nineteenth and early twentieth centuries (Schwartz 1997, 86; Kutzinski 1993). In Curaçao, sex with a light-skinned women from the Spanish-speaking Caribbean or Latin America has been considered highly attractive and desirable among local men. A popular image that dominated on the island during the twentieth century identified women from the Dominican Republic as specially trained and groomed to provide sexual pleasure to men, and thus particularly suited to sex work. Haitian women, however, were located by this population as "too black" and "unhygienic" for sexual encounters (Lagro and Plotkin 1990). The exotic "Sandom" image in the minds of Curaçaoan men in this particular instance combined with colonial state policies during the 1930s and 1940s to attract large numbers of migrant workers from surrounding countries – for work in the oil-refining industry, to provide a base for the US and Dutch naval fleets, and simultaneously to protect local womanhood from the "coarse" sexualities of the sailors and other migrant workers. Foreign, culturally other women in this scenario were legalized to work on the island as prostitutes and domestics. The national, cultural and ethnic differences of foreign women were coded as sexually desirable but inferior to notions of proper femininity, and those who provided erotic, sexual services became relegated to marginalized, informal – and heavily policed – sectors of society.

Similar notions of the exotic, erotic other have been recorded in research on prostitution in Suriname and Guyana, where "light-skinned" Latin American, Brazilian and Spanish-speaking Caribbean women have been positioned as migrant workers in the sex trade, and thus highly exploitable and highly vulnerable in relationship to the resident population, yet defined as "hyper-sexual" by local dominant gender ideologies (Kane 1993; Antonius-Smits et al. 1999; Red Thread 1999). In Haiti male sexual preference for the lighter-skinned, silky-haired Dominicans is cited as part of a "culture of exoticism" that includes beliefs that Spanish is "the language of love" and that women from the Dominican Republic are more "professional" and attractive in sex work and preferable over Haitian women (Chanel 1994, 14). Equations of the cultural other with notions of the erotic can be seen to continue beyond the Western male imagination, and also to dominate contemporary Caribbean male perceptions and appreciations of sensuality and sexuality.[10]

Expressions of exoticism run through Caribbean history, constructed under slavery and Europan colonialism, pulsing though American constructions of nation and coursing through masculinist national ideologies and practices in the post-colonial societies. This view reasserts itself through the new forms of Western economic and cultural imperialism, inscribed in the tourism industry. Promoted by the United Nations since the 1960s as a strategy to participate in the global economy, tourism was adopted by Caribbean governments at different times as a way to diversify their economies, to overcome economic crises that threatened to cripple the small nation-states and to acquire foreign exchange. The largest tourism market in the 1990s was North America, and in second place was Europe, with France, the United Kingdom and Germany taking the lead. The industry accounts for approximately 25 per cent of all formal employment in the region and is generally seen to be one of the fastest-growing sectors in the twenty-first century. Tourism represents one of the few ways in which small island nations can compete in the global economy. Using the estimate that for every person in formal employment in tourism there is at least one other engaged in informal activities in the industry, it is predicted that tourism in the Caribbean will continue to be an important source of livelihood for its working peoples (*Travel Industry* 1997; Patullo 1996).

Caribbean tourism hinges on the exploitation of a number of the region's resources, particularly its year-round sunny conditions and beaches, but also its tropical rainforests and coral reefs, as well as its music, such as reggae and calypso, its cuisine and other cultural symbols such as carnival. It offers a variety of packages, including golf vacations, weddings and honeymoons, dive trips and eco-tours, its sole *raison d'être* to provide pleasure to the visitor. Caribbean women and men in this sector work for meagre wages in jobs such as barman, waitress, cook, cleaner, maid, gardener and entertainer. Male and female labour and energies constitute a part of the package that is paid for and consumed by the tourist during the period in which she or he seeks to relax and enjoy – in the leisure time the tourist has set aside to recuperate and restore the mind and body in order to maintain a healthy and productive working life on return home (Crick 1989; Walvin 1992; Kinnaird and Hall 1994). Caribbean sexuality also constitutes a critical resource within this panorama, and it is in arrangements and representations of this aspect of the tourism industry that new articulations of exoticism are evident. An examination of Internet representations of sex in the Caribbean, drawn from a website that allows people to exchange experiences and views about commercial and other types of sex around the world, illustrates some dimensions of contemporary exoticism.

Exoticism and Tourism

In the eighty-three letters written about the Caribbean that were publicly posted on a "World Sex Guide" website between November 1994 and July 1999, over one-third explicitly related racial and cultural difference to sexual desirability.[11] For the authors of these letters, a hierarchy of attractiveness associated with notions of race and culture emerged. Comments about Puerto Rican Latinas, Cubanas, Dominican "mulattos" and "light-skinned" Caribbean women tended to prevail and to be highly positive.[12] Some of the recurring ideas about the erotic, hypersexual "nature" of the Caribbean and its women were represented as follows:

> I decided I wanted to go on vacation, but with that decision, there were two things I had to consider: first, that I didn't have a lot of money to spend on such things, two, that availability of sex was VERY important!! . . . the Caribbean made sense.[13]

> A guy with enough hard currency can have the time of his life in what is probably the most romantic city in the world with, in my humble opinion, the most dropdead gorgeous sultry tanned beauties in the hemisphere.[14] [Written about Havana, Cuba.]

> The DR has wonderful possibilities. Prostitution jives fairly well with the culture, Dominican women are beautiful, prices are excellent, and you have a fair chance of being treated well . . . I find that watching a fine brown-sugar Dominican teenager take off her clothes and shake her ass like only Dominican chics can does wonders for clearing your mind and getting up your guts (not to mention you [*sic*] cock) for the bargaining process.[15]

> The whole island is a brothel, possibly the cheapest one in the world.[16] [Written about Cuba.]

> You can live like a king, complete with harem, on less than $500/week. I did.[17] [Written about Cuba.]

Latinized, Spanish-speaking Caribbean cultures and "brown" femininities are often represented in the letters as sexually attractive and available to the men. As one tourist clearly described this,

> Since I prefer Latinas and brunettes, for me Cuba is the closest thing to paradise I think I'll ever see. It's heavenly because many of these young Cubanas are "available".[14]

Or as others write,

> Aruba is the place where you go to get the knockout of your life. The Ladies are all from Colombia and Venezuela.[18]

> For $100 per night . . . one can find a gorgeous, light skinned and young latina to spend the night with.[19] [Written about the Dominican Republic.]

Promotional materials for tourism to the Caribbean have appropriated the image of the brown-skinned sexy Caribbean woman to seduce and entice potential clients. As Dagenais points out, popular representations of Caribbean women "portray them as sexual objects and publicity drops; the tourist industry presents them as sensual mulattoes with endless free time to enjoy the beaches and, of course, the (male) visitors" (1993, 83). There are, however, some exceptions to this generalized pattern, with a few authors on the sex-tourist website expressing a specific appreciation for black women.

> By far the best place for sex in Jamaica is Negril. Sex is available and cheap, and for those of us who prefer black women, I can't think of anywhere that comes close.[20]

There are also comments that denigrate blackness (sometimes associated with Haitian nationality):

> I know beauty is in the eye of the beholder, but most of these women are truly not great lookers . . . This is not to say that there were not some attractive women available – but they are in the minority. In terms of race, most are black – about 70% – while the rest are more Latino looking – There were actually a number of nights that I went back to my hotel room alone because none of the women appealed to me (this would never happen in Brazil or Thailand!) . . . these are without a doubt some of the butt ugliest women I have ever come across. Unbelievably ugly. Most are Haitian and are old (at least in hooker years) and heavy.[21] [Written about the Dominican Republic.]

These patterns that position the brown-skinned woman as more desirable than the black woman in the contemporary tourism industry do not seem to contradict the earlier-described European-American and Caribbean notions of the exotic. However, they are reinforced by a comparison with sexual relations in the North (the United States in particular) and the sensuality of the white (female) body, where a delight in *sexy, mixed-race, mulata, sultry, tanned, Latin, brown-sugar* Caribbean women contrasts with representations of white femininity and sexuality as staid, cold, impersonal or mundane:

> Let's start out with a pleasant introduction to Latin sex . . . Unlike [massage] places in the US of this nature, it is not a rip-off: they aim to please.[22] [Written about the Dominican Republic.]

> I went in and noticed that most of the girls were not Puerto Rican. Most looked like rejects out of an American (NY, LA, Dallas) strip bar. The show was pathetic . . . Immediately some lady from New York came up. She was too ugly . . . As soon as she left a hot Puerto Rican girl came up with large breasts and a nice body . . .[23] [Written about Puerto Rico.]

> Another very noticeable thing was how friendly all the girls were. There was none of that "hard ass" attitude so commonly seen here in the States . . . Being with these girls was a thoroughly pleasant experience.[13] [Written about the Dominican Republic.]

> I love it here the table's [sic] are turned and the women were chasing me around. New York women are cold as fish, in comparison.[24] [Written about Cuba.]

> Be warned: eurochicks will want a real romance from you, with all the related mind trips, they consider intercourse a mere byproduct of that . . . As usual, you will have to pay for their drinks and stay up late speaking about psychology and their childhood to get some, the day before you leave, once.[18] [Written about Aruba.]

Cabezas notes that "Dominican women reported that foreigners construct them, both sexually and racially, in opposition to European women . . . White skin is devalued because it is connected to civility, or feminist discourse, and is thus less sexual" (1999, 111). The exotic is sexier than femininity or sex in white post-industrial "developed" societies, and is thought to be found in the still natural backwards, untamed world. The contemporary tourist industry enables the men to dabble in their exoticizing sexual fantasies while away from home.

In addition, many of the men described the women in the Caribbean as "non-professional". They write that many, most or all of the sex workers are "not real hookers" but that they participate in prostitution because of financial need and lack of other economic opportunities. However, even though the authors stated that the women are in sex work because of financial need, the letters indicate that the men believe the women genuinely enjoy all types of sex with them, and that the women are particularly good at what they do:

> None of these are real hookers – most are part time girls who like sex and want to make some money for clothes and . . .[25] [Written about Cuba.]

> Just how good are they sexually speaking? Pretty damn good for the most part . . . No dead fish here . . . They really are very uninhibited . . .[21] [Written about the Dominican Republic.]

> Basically Marcia (not her real name) is not a real hooker, but a very attractive and horny girl who likes to make a bit of extra money (much needed in Jamaica). In return, if you treat her right, she'll give you a great time with no hassle. There's plenty of village girls like this around Negril and Montego Bays these days.[20] [Written about Jamaica.]

> You never get the feeling that they are after your money, and they don't have a [sic] attitude of a whore . . . These chics have so much class its hard to believe they are prostitutes.[26] [Written about the Dominican Republic.]

The highly sexualized image of Caribbean women held by sex-tourists about Caribbean women, explain O'Connell Davidson and Sanchez Taylor, rests on assumptions "that local girls 'are really hot for it' " and the women's "highest ambition is to be the object of a Western man's desire" – that, after all, the women "are doing what just comes naturally" to them (1999, 47). They are not, in the minds of the men, prostitutes who are having sex for money, but are perceived to be poor women who genuinely enjoy the sex. The idea that the women are naturally sexy and desire to have sex with much older men for pleasure enables the tourists to deny any exploitative aspects of their relationship with the Caribbean. Indeed many tourists rationalize their visits to the Caribbean for sex as a way to benefit poor, oppressed women; twenty-two letters in our sample presented some aspect of this idea. As one writer put it,

> I much rather sponsor a Cuban family by renting a room in their house than giving the money directly to the Cuban government . . . I much rather give my money to a suffering Cuban . . .[27]

Furthermore, the idea that women in the Caribbean are hyper-sexual creatures who are not professional prostitutes often results in the tourists presenting their encounters with the women as "romances" or "love":

> These women are not whores by choice, nor are they doing it just to buy jewelry. Because they are average women caught in circumstances beyond their control it is all that much easier to fall for them.[14] [Written about Cuba.]

> We spent the day together, Life was good! My American buddy just about married the girl he was with . . . Pamela took me to the airport early in the morning . . . She cried . . . I felt like shit. I wish I could have brought her home with me . . . If you are going to Santa Domingo be prepared to fall in love with these women. I'm going back again . . .[26] [Written about the Dominican Republic.]

> Girls are incredibly sexy and behave like real girlfriends.[28] [Written about Cuba.]

> Is she ever hot though! They just don't come that way back home . . . I'm in love. I'm pretty convinced she is too . . .[17] [Written about Cuba.]

Constructing prostitution in poor countries as something that comes naturally to the local inhabitants, as romance or as a way to "help" women and their families masks the inequalities of power that are involved, and allows the sex-tourist to perceive of himself as benevolent and desirable. Tourism in the Caribbean at the end of the twentieth century appears to confirm exoticizing tendencies present in the region since the sixteenth century. However, new global hegemonies, which rest upon an increasing economic gap between post-industrial capitalist centres and peripheral areas that provide cheap labour, natural resources and playgrounds for the rich, can been seen to extend its scope. Western European and North American women are increasingly participants in a form of tourism that involves exoticization of the local population. As a male tourist explains:

> There are tons of beautiful German (80%), Italian, and French women from 18 to 50 who are willing to pay for sex and affection!!! believe it or not. I saw many 9 and 10 [good-looking] twenty year old girls paying for it!! One had to see it to believe it. There seems to be a fantasy thing with German (both men and women) to find the darkest (and sometimes no [sic] so pretty) locals and pay to be with them. There was a German girl next door to me that had

about 10 guys in a week. She lookes [*sic*] like Demi (Bruce Willis' wife, but younger) . . .[29] [Written about the Dominican Republic.]

Such observations are not widely found on sex-tourist websites that traffic in fantasies and tales by men about women. Nevertheless, female sex tourism in the Caribbean has been noticed, researched and commented upon since the 1960s and is a growing spectacle in countries such as Barbados, Jamaica, the Dominican Republic, the Dutch Antilles and Belize. O'Connell Davidson and Sanchez Taylor note about this trend, "As Others, local men are viewed as beings possessed of a powerful and indiscriminate sexuality that they cannot control, and this explains their eagerness for sex with tourist women" (1999, 40). Specific to this trend is not brown sensuality and feminine eroticism, but an image that secures the young Caribbean man as the "Black stud" (Phillips 1999). The darker the man is, the more sexually attractive he is considered, with some being explicitly rejected for not being "black enough". Blackness is equated with "well-defined muscles", dreadlocked hair and "skin darkened almost blue-black" – characteristics that signal an African ancestry brimming with "an untamed, primitive nature and exotic appeal" (Phillips 1999, 187). It is an image that harks back to older notions in both European and US culture of the black African man as an embodiment of insatiable sexual appetite and uncontrollable lust, with a penis size to match. Albuquerque remarks that this image of black male sexuality and body also stirs the passions of some female tourists to the Caribbean, causing them to "literally get off the plane single mindedly embarked on the holy grail (the search for the big bamboo)" (1998, 88).

Similar to the ways in which some male tourists perceive sex in the Caribbean to be "not really prostitution", so too do tourist women often define their sexual encounters with black men as "romance".[30] In their study of sexual relationships between female tourists and Jamaican men, Pruitt and La Font (1995) define many of the sexual relationships as such. Likewise Ragsdale and Anders (1998) describe the relationship between some women tourists to Ambergris Cay, in Belize, and Belizean men as a form of *makoibi* – a "love sickness" in Belizean Creole – which the authors compare in intensity to a first love. Nevertheless, it has been pointed out that while "romance relationships between tourist women and local men serve to transform traditional gender roles across cultural boundaries" and may contribute to "[b]reaking taboos and challenging tradition", it has been acknowledged that the relationships end up "recapitulating the patriarchal structure of tourism" or "reproducing much of what is challenged" (Pruitt and La Font 1995, 436–38). The relationships can also be seen to be reproducing long-standing racist stereotypes of black male sexuality. O'Connell Davidson furthermore points out that the ambiguities inscribed in informal tourism-related prostitution allow for a form of self-deception, "so that even when the women tell themselves that they can only have sex in the context of romantic intimacy, they are not disbarred from sexually exploiting local men and boys in poor countries they visit" (1998, 183).

Many male sex-tourists express the view that in their home countries women enjoy excessive power, through which traditional male authority is undermined (O'Connell Davidson and Sanchez Taylor 1999; Cabezas 1999). In the Caribbean they are able to fully reaffirm their masculinity through sexual relations based on their racialized and cultural economic power. Simultaneously, black Caribbean masculinity becomes the ground upon which European and North American women experiment with or expand their gender identities. While they retain a sexualized femininity, it is commonplace among women tourists to exercise control over (local) men. The black man is required to be the sexually aggressive and dominant partner, allowing the tourist woman to combine economic power and authority with traditional Western notions of femininity as sexually submissive and subordinate. It would appear that in such scenarios, exoticized Caribbean masculinity and femininity and male and female bodies become a platform for reshaping and redefining Western identity and power – "a stage for First World gendered performances" (Kempadoo 1999a). O'Connell Davidson and Sanchez Taylor (1999) also note that the sexual encounter enables the tourist to attain a sense of control over her or his sexuality while reassuring himself or herself of racial and/or cultural privilege. Caribbean men and women alike are constructed in tourist imaginations as racialized sexual subjects/objects – the hyper-sexual black male "stud" and the "hot" mulatto or black woman – whose main roles are to service and please the visitor. Taking into account both racializing and gendered structures of power and domination reveals some of the contradictory positions that women and men from post-industrial centres hold in relation to the eroticized, exoticized other – both female and male.

Conclusion

Sexuality – the ways in which it is organized, expressed, enjoyed and exploited – has not been a focus for many Caribbean scholars, for while the region has a long-standing international reputation for being a sex haven, and Caribbean women and men have both been the objects as well as the subjects in writing the sexual script in the Caribbean, it remains an undervalued area within social research. Nevertheless, drawing from the few studies available, I have argued here that the subject of Caribbean sexuality requires investigations that address the intersectionality and simultaneity of gendered and racialized relations of power. Privileging one axis of power serves to elide other important social relations and dynamics. The notion of exoticism as a discourse that romanticizes and eroticizes black and brown bodies and subjectivities in the Caribbean, yet also reinforces exploitative and oppressive regimes, offers a possibility. Prostitution becomes one of the prisms through which we can witness the naked performance of exoticism – its lusts and desires as well as its violence and oppressions. In tracing exoticism through the history of prostitution in the Caribbean, this essay offers a glimpse at the configurations and reconfigurations that have taken place over time around sexuality. However, it also makes visible areas that could use further exploration. In particular this essay points to a broader need for Caribbean scholarship to uncover histories of black male sexuality as well as the construction of white Caribbean women's identities, desires and sexualities in relationship to histories of empire. It also points to some of the other silences that have shaped sexualities, raising questions about how relations of domination and power around not just gender but also race and ethnicity have in the past infused sexual relations – and continue to today. Most importantly for a post-colonial society, it poses the question of how we can proceed with theorizing our own sexual heritages and desires. Sex, it would seem, still requires much thought.

Notes

1. For classical radical feminist definitions of prostitution, see Barry 1984, Jeffreys 1997.
2. For an overview of these studies, see Kempadoo 2001.
3. Because of the scope of this work, the element of resistance is not explored in this essay. However, resistances of racially sexualized subjects have been noted elsewhere. See, for example, Kempadoo 1996, 1999b and Barnes 2000. Nevertheless, it remains an area for further investigation in both historical and contemporary contexts.
4. See for example, Mathurin 1974, Beckles 1989b, Bush 1990, Reddock 1994, and Peake and Trotz 1999, and essays in the edited volumes on women and gender in the Caribbean by Mohammed and Shepherd (1988), Shepherd, Brereton and Bailey (1995), López Springfield (1997), Barrow (1998b), and Kanhai (1999). Far less attention, however, has been paid to the experiences and lives of men in the Caribbean from a critical race/gender framework, although the works of Frantz Fanon, Errol Miller, Barrington Chevannes and Linden Lewis have provided invaluable insights into the social and psychological constitution of racialized Caribbean masculinity.
5. Baudelaire's "Black Venus" and other poetry inspired by his mistress of colour, the bust *Venus Africaine* sculpted by Cordier in 1851 and Picasso's *Olympia* of 1901 all belong to the tradition of Europe's exoticization of African women (Nederveen Pieterse 1990, 182).
6. In di Leonardo's account of exoticism in the United States, the Chicago World's Columbian Exposition in 1893 exemplifies how nineteenth-century "America" viewed and defined the "other", with certain groups of women marked as particularly exotic. "In the common orientalist parlance, Asian and Middle Eastern women were largely apprehended as embodiments of exotic beauty and sexuality . . . Black women, however, were frequently portrayed as offensively ugly and frighteningly savage" 1998, 7. White women, on the other hand, though coming "close to slipping into the category of 'otherness' reserved for 'savages' and 'exotics' " in the perceptions of the exposition's male architects, were redeemed from this category "through their capacity to serve as mothers of civilization" (p. 8). In the Caribbean, both black and brown women were sexualized through the eyes of the colonizer.
7. See, for example, Brereton 1999, Shepherd 1995 and Reddock 1994.
8. Mohammed Orfry, CO 571/4 WI22518 (1916), quoted in Reddock (1985a, 84).

9. Although most of the studies on the period after indentureship concern Trinidad, it is reasonable to assume that similar images were constructed in other parts of the region, given the parallels in histories of Indians in the Caribbean.

10. The complexity of colour and sexual desirability in the post-colonial Caribbean societies remains a contested subject. Noting the shift around beauty ideals in the Caribbean during the 1960s, Henriques, citing research by Errol Miller, points out that attractiveness was no longer seen as constituted by white femininity, but rather "the beautiful girl has Caucasian features and is Fair or Clear in color", but that "the paradox of the situation is that even the most vehement of Black Power leaders in both the Caribbean and the United States tend to have white wives" (1974, 113). This is not unlike trends I encountered in my earlier research in Curaçao (Kempadoo 1996). Barnes (1997) and Mohammed (2000a, 2000b) have also both grappled with this complexity, exploring aspects of the ideologies of "whitening-up" and "browning" that cohabit with notions of sexual desirability.

11. <http://www.paranoia.com/faq/prostitution>; <http://www.worldsexguide.com/world/cuba/index.htm>. These letters described tourist experiences in the Caribbean countries of Aruba, Cuba, Curaçao, Dominican Republic, Jamaica, Puerto Rico and Suriname. In most cases the authors did not identify their home countries, but several authors indicated that they lived in Chicago, Los Angeles, Miami, New York, Nevada, Texas, Canada, Germany, England, the Netherlands or the United States in general.

12. It should be kept in mind that these images combine with actual prostitution activities in which the women's sexual labour is criminalized and their lives are subject to intense harassment by police and government authorities, coercion and force by men seeking to make a monetary profit from their exoticized bodies and exploitation for the satisfaction of tourist's desires. See Kempadoo 1999b for case studies and rich descriptions of the conditions of the sex trade in various Caribbean locations.

13. 11 February 1996, <http://www.paranoia.com/faq/prostitution/Boca-Chica.txt.html>.

14. 11 June 1997, <http://www.paranoia.com/faq/prostitution/Havana.txt.html>.

15. 20 October 1997, <http://www.paranoia.com/faq/prostitution/dr_expert.txt.html>.

16. 4 March 1996, <http://www.paranoia.com/faq/prostitution/cuba_bits.txt.html>.

17. 16 April 1996, <http://www.paranoia.com/faq/prostitution/ dr_travel.txt.html>.

18. October 1996, <http://www.paranoia.com/faq/prostitution/aruba_ general.txt.html>.

19. 20 January 1997, <http://www.paranoia.com/faq/prostitution/ dr_travel.txt.html>.

20. 6 May 1997, <http://www.paranoia.com/faq/prostitution/ Negril.txt.html>.

21. 5 September 1996, <http://www.paranoia.com/faq/prostitution/dr_ travel2.txt.html>.

22. 11 March 1997, <http://www.paranoia.com/faq/prostitution/ Santo-Domingo.txt.html>.

23. 7 March 1997, <http://www.paranoia.com/faq/prostitution/ Puerto-Rico.txt.html>.

24. n.d., <http://www.paranoia.com/faq/prostitution/Guanabo.txt.html>.

25. 28 March 1997, <http://www.paranoia.com/faq/prostitution/ Havana.txt.html>.

26. 27 June 1995, <http://www.paranoia.com/faq/prostitution/ dr_travel.txt.html>.

27. 2 July 1995, <http://www.paranoia.com/faq/prostitution/ cuba_faq.txt.html>.

28. 26 July 1998, <http://www.worldsexguide.com/world/cuba/index.htm>.

29. 19 March 1997, <http://www.paranoia.com/faq/prostitution/drbits.txt.html>.

30. Perhaps the best-known illustration of the eroticized relationship between North American women travellers and Caribbean men can be found in Terry MacMillan's novel *How Stella Got Her Groove Back*. MacMillan's account has also spurred the notion that "love" can be found by women vacationers to the Caribbean. As one young woman writes under the heading "Want What Stella Had!": "My girlfriend and I are planning a JAMAICAN getaway in July/August, but don't know where to go. We want a place that's suitable for two 25 year-old (single) best friends . . . We're looking for our groove with the hope of getting it back like Stella did!" (22 December 1999, <http://www.jamaicatravel.com/cgi-bin/ mboard/jamaica/thread.cgi?361,0>). In a more reflective mode, Gearing (1995) – a white American woman – offers one of the more honest accounts of doing anthropological fieldwork as a doctoral student and marrying one of her "native" informants.

⚜Part IV⚜
Gender, Genre and Cultural/ Literary Discourse

Chapter 9

"What Have We to Celebrate?"

Gender, Genre and Diaspora Identities in Two Popular Cultural Texts

JANE BRYCE

In this work I attempt to read two texts from two diasporic popular cultural forms against each other in the light of a series of questions suggested by the comparison. The forms in question are a novel set in Toronto that could be described as futuristic fantasy or "speculative fiction", written by Nalo Hopkinson, a young Trinidadian-Canadian woman, and published by Warner Aspect, a company "committed to finding science fiction's voices of the future"; and a rap movie set in New York, directed by Hype Williams, a male artist whose name is well-known in the world of the music video. I am interested in what these two texts, *Brown Girl in the Ring* (1998) and *Belly* (1998), have to tell us about form and identity, about the creative choices being made by a new generation of cultural practitioners and the way they negotiate key questions of race, gender and cultural multiplicity.

To begin with, there are several notable correspondences between the film and the novel: both are young, in terms of both author/director and audience, black, diasporic, urban and futuristic. Beyond that, they diverge widely. The provenance of *Belly* is hip-hop culture, with all its stylistic signifiers – the clothes, the body language, the talk and above all, the music – characterized by an aggressive masculinity and featuring in the central roles well-known rap artists (Nas, DMX, T-Boz and Method Man). The concerns of the film are with the power of this culture to shape the identities and life choices of young black men whose imperative is survival in the harshly competitive environment of the New York streets. As an adjunct to this essentially African-American narrative, there is also the Jamaican presence in New York, with two important sequences that actually take place in Kingston, so that embedded in a movie whose style is familiar from music videos is an intriguing representation of the Caribbean. The project of the novel, on the other hand, is to offer a representation of femininity that quite deliberately distances itself from macho posturing and violent crime, aligning itself instead with Caribbean/African–derived forms of spirituality as an alternative source of power. Both, however, explore the problematics of identity and its construction in an urban diasporic context, and it is in this frame that I want to view them.[1]

What connects the novel most closely to the film is the representation of the city as the site of crisis for the notion of a diaspora identity. Like New York, Toronto is shown at the moment of inner-city breakdown, when the streets have been left to their remaining (subculture) inhabitants, while everyone who is able to has moved to the suburbs. We are asked to

> Imagine a cartwheel half-mired in muddy water, its hub just clearing the surface. The spokes are the satellite cities that form Metropolitan Toronto . . . the Toronto city core is the hub . . . rusted through and through. When Toronto's economic base collapsed, investors, commerce, and government withdrew into the suburb cities, leaving the rotten core to decay. Those who stayed were the ones who couldn't or wouldn't leave. The street people. The poor people. (Hopkinson 1998, 4)

This nightmare cityscape is familiar from recent film representations such as Kathryn Bigelow's New York in *Strange Days* or Cronenberg's Chicago in *Crash,* and anticipated by earlier ones such as Stanley Kubrick's surreal British urban wasteland in *A Clockwork Orange* and Derek Jarman's London in *Jubilee.* As in those films, the city takes on a malign personality of its own, becoming an actor in the drama for which it is also the stage.

This is equally true of *Belly,* which plays two cityscapes against each other, New York against Kingston, demonstrating in the process the shallowness of tourist stereotypes of the Caribbean. Tommy, the character who boasts that he is so in control of his environment in New York that he can flaunt his law-breaking activities – shooting a red light while smoking weed – in front of the police and they cannot touch him, is unsettled by Kingston, where everything – the violence, the drugs, the sexuality – is rougher and more dangerous than what even he is accustomed to. Like *Strange Days, Belly* traces the last moments of the year preceding the new millennium, concluding, exactly like *Strange Days,* with a climactic scene on New Year's Eve, at the threshold of the transition to the next century. *Brown Girl* too offers us a futuristic scenario already being realized in the inner-urban conditions of the present moment. In this respect, both these works participate in the generalized sense of momentous and impending change dismissed by sceptics as millennarial hysteria. What marks them as different, however, is their concern with and focus on a diaspora identity that is seen to be in crisis in very specific ways, which I will elaborate.

The question of what constitutes a diaspora identity, cultural practice and politics, as it has been shaped in recent years by the interventions of Stuart Hall, Paul Gilroy, Cornel West, Michelle Wallace and bell hooks, among others, places the emphasis firmly on two key elements: a loosening of the restrictive bonds of essentialism, with its fetishization of race and gender, and the centrality of popular culture. The term "diaspora" emerges as a kind of signifying on "post-modern", with certain key differences. If "post-modern" is the generic term denoting the cultural and temporal space at which we have all now arrived at the start of a new millennium, "diaspora" recognizes and insists on the specificities of history, culture and experience that inflect that space. For Stuart Hall, addressing the issue of cultural identity and diaspora as it relates to the Caribbean, the New World presence connotes above all displacement, movement and migration:

> It stands for the endless ways in which Caribbean people have been destined to "migrate"; it is the signifier of migration itself – of travelling, voyaging and return as fate, as destiny; of the Antillean as the prototype of the modern or postmodern New World nomad . . . it is one of our defining themes, and it is destined to cross the narrative of every film script or cinematic image. (1994, 401)

For Hall, diaspora is coterminous with heterogeneity and diversity, and the whole concept of a diaspora identity is necessarily therefore a "production" – as he puts it – that is always in process, never complete, not a fixed essence or origin, but "always constructed through memory, fantasy, narrative and myth" (1994, 395). For him, then, the function of contemporary cultural forms such as music and film is "allowing us to see and recognise the different parts and histories of ourselves, to construct those points of identification, those positionalities we call in retrospect our 'cultural identities' " (p. 402).

Film is indeed an important reference point for a reading of *Brown Girl*, as much as it is for *Belly*. Nalo Hopkinson's book and Hype Williams's film, both firmly embedded in urban-based popular youth culture with its reference points in crime, drugs, sexuality and survival, quote extensively from the repertoire of images contained in film representations of that culture. An interesting point of divergence between them, however, is the way each is manipulated in the cause of separate but related projects, and the way the medium – film or literary text – to an extent defines and predetermines the outcome. It is generally recognized that fiction is a key instrument in the hands of Caribbean women writers, in exactly the same way as the music video and its spin-off, the rap film, is for young black male directors such as Ice Cube (*The Players' Club*) or, as here, Hype Williams.

Stewart Brown, in his introduction to the *Oxford Book of Caribbean Short Stories* (1999), points to the plethora of women writers who have emerged in the period since independence, to the extent that they now constitute the majority. While he attributes this to increased educational opportunities for women in the Caribbean and to social change brought about by feminist activism, in terms of my work it begs another question: Why are more black/Caribbean/diaspora women not making films as a result of these developments? Here I would like to refer again to Stuart Hall and his article "What Is This 'Black' in Black Popular Culture?" Hall proposes that the three essential ingredients of black/diaspora popular culture are style as an end in itself; music, as what he calls "the deep structure of their cultural life", as opposed to a logocentric tradition from which diaspora blacks have been largely excluded; and the body as "cultural capital . . . We have worked on ourselves as the canvases of representation" (1997, 129). Hall speaks of the commodification of popular culture, its appropriation by "the circuits of power and capital" via "the circuits of a dominant technology" (p. 127) as being necessary and inevitable, and emphasizes that black popular culture is no different from any other kind in being impure, contradictory and contested. He cautions, however, that its very plurality of interests may generate internal conflict. For instance, he suggests,

> certain ways in which black men continue to live out their counteridentities as black masculinities in the theaters of popular culture are, when viewed from along other axes of difference, the very masculine identities that are oppressive to women, that claim visibility for their hardness only at the expense of the vulnerability of black women and the feminization of gay black men. (1997, 132)

Similarly, Jeffrey Louis Decker, in an essay on hip-hop, comments on the "unabashedly patriarchal" nature of hip-hop nationalism, the relegation of women performers to the status of quasi-mythical Afrocentric icons like Cleopatra or Nefertiti, Mother Africa and Isis, while "Black nationalism's primary focus is the actualization of black men's political agency in the struggle for liberation . . . It is the principle cause for action" (1994, 109). In the case of hip-hop, says Decker, "black men control black women's messages by framing their voices and images" (p. 110), and this is done in the interests of promoting an idea of Africa as homeland, projected by way of black women's bodies and femininity. This idea of Africa as homeland is indeed one of the central messages of *Belly,* one of two alternatives the movie offers to the endless cycle of crime and violence, and it is the narrator's girlfriend, the most positive female figure in the film, who articulates it.

To compare *Belly* with *Brown Girl* is to be made aware that *Belly* is centrally concerned with the crisis in black masculinity, one aspect of which is typified as follows in an essay, "Masculinities in Transition", by Keith Nurse:

> From a revolutionary standpoint the traditional myth of male privilege, power and status blinds men to their own gender oppression and therefore limits the possibilities for an emancipatory transition from within the boundaries of masculinism. This illustrates that the prospects for a preferred future in gender relations are dependent on the continued unmasking and deconstructing of the core components of hegemonic masculinism. (1996, 23)

Brown Girl also deals with masculinity, but demonstrates its bankruptcy and need for another way of seeing, another source of power, which is identified in the novel with the feminine. In this respect it participates in the process of unmasking and deconstructing towards which the quotation above gestures, while suggesting a possible alternative to "hegemonic masculinism", albeit from a feminine perspective. In what may well be a future trend in fiction by a new generation of Caribbean woman writers, the novel ends with Ti-Jeanne allowing her baby-father, Tony, into the thanksgiving at the balmyard, but retaining her autonomy by remaining outside with her child. "Ti-Jeanne looked into his eyes, feeling none of the desperate obsession she used to have for Tony, none of the longing for him to make her life right, either. And, to her surprise, no hatred, not really. Just pity. Her heart was free" (Hopkinson 1998, 246).

The pleasure of the novel lies not only in its imaginative and original use of urban space as the arena for an archetypal battle between good and evil, envisioned as good and bad forms of obeah, but in the way it uses an individual relationship to speculate about the whole structure of power relations – racial/cultural as well as sexual – as the root cause of contemporary alienation. In this respect the film and the novel, while fuelled by the same sense of urgency, nonetheless differ widely in their ideological and aesthetic responses to a lived material reality. While *Belly* overtly questions the relegating of black men to an underclass characterized by crime and violence, the popular cultural nexus of the rap music video format dictates conventions of gender representation that ultimately reinscribe the sexual status quo. The construction of black masculinity that emerges is, in Hall's formulation, a "counteridentity" – oppositional, authoritarian and homocentric, with women represented either as highly sexualized and dangerous or, as Nurse puts it, "providing a *refuge* from the dangers and stresses of relating to other males" (1996, 17).

The following analysis by Washington and Shaver in their essay "The Language Culture of Rap Music Videos" is a useful summary of the politics of representation underpinning *Belly*:

> Rap is the music of the dispossessed freed by the civil rights legislation of the 1960s . . . During this second Reconstruction, there was a massive migration of middle-class and upper-income African Americans from the central city to the suburbs . . . The working class and the poor were concentrated in the central cities in deteriorating housing, in areas plagued by high unemployment

rates for young African American males and escalating crime rates as the government lost both its war on poverty and its war against drugs. (1997, 169)

As a result, say the authors,

> gangs were engaged in full-scale war for the increasingly lucrative drug-trade
> that changed neighbourhoods in the central cities into a postapocalyptic land-
> scape with vacant lots, abandoned buildings, homeless people, crack houses,
> and deteriorating government-subsidized housing . . . [T]he culture of hip-hop
> [was linked] to these economic conditions, increased violence in the inner
> city, social alienation, polarization of social units, and spiritual deprivation.
> (1997, 169)

This description applies equally to the cityscapes of both *Belly* and *Brown Girl,* just as drugs provide the motor for the action of both texts. In *Brown Girl* the drug of choice is called "buff", made from the bufo toad in Haiti, which induces a state approximating the initial stages of zombification. In *Belly* it is called Brown Sugar, can be assimilated through the skin without puncturing and comes from Asia via Jamaica. Significantly, the Caribbean connection is shown to be of central importance in the global drug trade in both texts, which present parallel figures in the Posse leader, Rudy, in *Brown Girl* and the Jamaican drug lord in *Belly.* The use of this figure as a signifier for diasporan identity, power and masculinity is what I want to explore next.

One of the most striking features of *Belly* is its location sequences in Kingston, which raise the issue of what the Jamaican connection means within the larger framework of the film. The difficulty of getting a Caribbean film industry off the ground has meant that representations of the region in film from elsewhere have largely been as stereotypes already circulating in the United States, such as the view of Jamaica as a site of sexual fantasy and spiritual regeneration that we get from a movie like *How Stella Got Her Groove Back.* However, music commentators have repeatedly linked hip-hop and dancehall as post-modern urban musical forms that speak to an alienated black identity. Louis Chude-Sokei, tracing the evolution of Jamaican sound systems, describes how music/sound becomes the means for a black underclass to define itself in opposition to other groups:

This process of inventing authenticity applies widely, from the intimate rituals of Rastafarian "groundings" to contemporary dancehall and hip-hop subcultures, where belonging requires that each subject be fluent in the "vocabulary of national possibilities" as expressed in style, language, gestures, demeanour, and (of course) knowledge of and specific response to communal sound. (1997, 187)

The first third of *Belly* establishes New York as a domain over which the young black men – the narrator, Sincere (played by rap artist Nas), and Tommy (played by DMX) – have total control. In successive sequences we see them enclosed inside an expensive car, always driven by Tommy, the streets outside refracted through the windows as they glide through them, planning their next move. When the narrator remonstrates with Tommy for shooting a red light, Tommy replies that the police cannot catch him, he does what he likes, he breaks the law and remains untouchable. *Belly* then takes us to Kingston to show how, rather than being a site of idyllic escapism and sexual regeneration, it is a place where the rules of the urban underclass are even more savagely applied. Tommy, who accompanies the drug don to his homeland, far from being welcomed back to his roots, finds himself discomfited and out of his depth in the sequence I am now going to describe.

This section of the film has been preceded by Tommy's visit to the drug don at his home, an impossibly splendid mansion in the district of New York known as Jamaica, where right away the hierarchy is established. Tommy is allowed to enter through the kitchen and conducted through a series of hallways to a private room where the don is watching the Jamaican football team on television. His first response to Tommy's reference to Brown Sugar is refusal. "I don't want to touch you, you too hot." As Tommy starts to defend himself, he inadvertently throws out a challenge: "You scared?" he asks the don, who silences him with a gesture. The speech that follows establishes the parameters of their future interaction: "You come in my house . . . don't you ever bring scared business to me. You looking at the toughest rassclaat Jamaican in the United States of America. I run shit, I kill for nothing . . . Don't bring that shit to me."

He agrees to give Tommy the access he wants to the new drug, but, "You owe me a big pussyclaat favour." The next time we see the don, he is seated at one end of a highly polished conference table, speaking to Tommy by phone. The subtitle informs us it is July 1999. The don is smiling, relaxed, while Tommy is reduced to semi-audible responses through the earpiece. The camera pans slowly up the length of the table as, with deceptive friendliness, the don asks, "So what's going on down there? . . . We're going on a vacation. I have a ticket waiting for you at the airport. You owe me one, nigger. Remember that I tell that you owe me one? Well, listen this, hear what happen now, the big vacation is what you owe me." Cut to a plane landing, cut to a car; subtitle: Kingston, Jamaica. The soundtrack, which has until now been dominated by rap, switches to a dancehall track featuring DMX and Jamaican DJs Sean Paul and Mr Vegas, both of whom appear in the subsequent dancehall sequence.

As in New York, we are inside the car, in an enclosed, hermetic space, the world outside revealed to us in a series of flashes or as a point-of-view shot from the perspective of Tommy, the spectator. Tommy and the don are sitting in the back seat, Tommy in tropical floral-print shirt and shades. The don, naked to the waist and adorned with an outsize gold chain and medallion, smoking an enormous spliff, effortlessly dominates the entire scene. His voice provides the commentary to glimpses of graffitied walls, broken-down cars and slum houses, while Tommy simply nods in acknowledgement. "This is the ghetto . . . true sufferation . . . you know, rude bwai, this is the slums, seen? You have to pick up the gun here to survive, seen?"

Cut to a shot of street children running alongside the car, reflected in its contours, hammering on the bodywork. Tommy turns to look and what he sees is a gun being held against the widow by one of the boys, also naked to the waist. His consternation is evident, but the don fails to notice. "You have to be the quickest of the quickest to survive." He passes Tommy the spliff. "You see I-man live like king in America. This is where I come from." Tommy appears uncomfortable with the spliff, but the don is oblivious. "I feel 'urting for the youth down here yah-so, I feel 'urting. I try my best but things cyaan change . . . But anyway, don' worry about it. We come to Jamaica to celebrate the rebirth of Kingston's finest . . . Don Gorgon." From now on his words are interspersed with Tommy's coughing and spluttering as he chokes on the joint. "We're going to make you fuck a phat [or *fat*: the play on words is presumably deliberate here] Jamaican pussy tonight . . . you can handle it?" Tommy's response is inarticulate. "Make you get 'ard like Rottweiler, seen? See wha me a deal with?" The don's face hovers close to Tommy's, half-obscured and semi-distorted by the clouds of ganja smoke. His presence in this scene is that of a powerful, dangerous, possibly evil tribal chief-tain in territory where Tommy is an alien. The fade at the end of the scene leaves his teeth till last: rotten, discoloured, threatening. The absence of explanatory subtitles for the Jamaican patois, so raw as to be almost indecipherable to the uninitiated, heightens the sense of otherness and alienation projected through the otherwise streetwise Tommy.

To revert to my earlier question about the meaning of the relationship between Jamaica and an urban black American identity, Louis Chude-Sokei points to the central importance of Marcus Garvey and West Indian immigration in the development of a modern and, in the case of hip-hop and dancehall, post-modern black culture in New York. This provides a clue to the significance of the Jamaican presence in *Belly,* in that it suggests that a discussion of black diasporan identity would sim-ply not make sense without it; but there is a further possible reading of Jamaica as contrapuntal to Africa in relation to black American culture. In this reading, Jamaica (as in *How Stella Got Her Groove Back*) is con-structed as a site of black authenticity and a source of alternative iden-tity. The difference in *Belly* is that black authenticity means bigger, badder, harder, more macho, more dangerous.

Turning now to *Brown Girl,* I want to suggest that it is as understand-able culturally for Nalo Hopkinson's revisionary view of the future of black diaspora identity to realize itself in the particular form of the novel as it is for Hype Williams to be drawn to the media of film and rap music. Though *Brown Girl* does not conform to any pre-existing pattern set by the tradition of Caribbean fiction, it is clearly marked by it. If it is a first, a new kind of writing, it achieves this by combining familiar ele-ments in an unfamiliar way, in response to the urgency of a new set of questions. The writer's revisionary view is projected, moreover, by means of another Afrocentric mythology, that of the Yoruba *orisha*s, which, far from being a set of archetypes frozen in time, are shown to be mis-chievous individuals who need to be propitiated in order for their power to be harnessed by the novel's protagonist. She is not therefore simply identified with a romanticized and masculine-defined version of feminine power, as Decker suggests is the case with hip-hop. She in fact starts by resisting any initiation into the spiritual realm inhabited by her grandmother, and only gradually comes to accept her own relationship with it. She learns to be a woman in a new kind of way, and the power she assumes by the end speaks to the need for more than survival in the treacherous diasporic waters she navigates. If both she and her creator draw this power from a previous generation, they also radically reshape it to answer the exigencies of the present.

Despite its post-modern urban context, the novel's tropes and images are familiar from earlier Caribbean texts, by no means exclusively by women. These include Erna Brodber's treatment of spirit thievery in *Myal* and the struggle with conventions of femininity in the work of Jamaica Kincaid or Merle Collins. Even the title of Hopkinson's novel recalls Paule Marshall's seminal treatment of a diaspora childhood, *Brown Girl, Brownstones*. To a greater extent, however, it takes its place alongside works by other contemporary diasporic writers: Leone Ross's *Orange Laughter* (1999), Shani Mootoo's *Cereus Blooms at Night* (1998), Robert Antoni's *Divina Trace* (1991) and *Blessed Is the Fruit* (1997) and Lawrence Scott's *Aelred's Sin* (1998). All of these manifest a concern with transcending gender boundaries, with the non-rational as an alternative source of power and with exploring the way the past manifests itself in the present. And indeed, despite the well-rehearsed problems for black/diasporan/women writers of getting published, reviewed, promoted and distributed, Hopkinson spells out her debt to a sustaining literary tradition in her intertextual references to oral and written Caribbean texts. Starting with her title, these include ring games, traditional sayings – "When horse dead, cow get fat" (p. 37) – songs, call-and-response chants and popular mythology. Most significantly, however, she points to Derek Walcott's play *Ti-Jean and His Brothers* and a work by her father, Slade Hopkinson, *The Madwoman of Papine*, as being seminal influences on her as a writer. She suggests that her choice of the novel form, especially in its "speculative", metaphysical manifestation, may arise as much from a cultural as a gendered predisposition.

Walcott's play in fact provides the novel with both its structure and one strand of its imagery. In the novel a (Trinidadian-Canadian) black woman rescues the city from the overlordship of Posse chief (Jamaican-

Canadian) Rudy, pitting her spiritual power and knowledge acquired from her grandmother against his spirit thievery and subversion of her grandmother's magic. Walcott's play follows the folk-tale motif of three brothers, each of whom challenges the devil. The first two, Gros-Jean and Mi-Jean, lose and the devil devours them. The third and youngest, Ti-Jean, wins and conquers the devil. As in the play, Ti-Jeanne, the heroine, is the third in a line of women seers and healers, following her grandmother and mother, whose lot it is to contest for power with the evil patriarchal figure of Rudy, and she is the first to succeed in overcoming him. Like the youngest brother of Walcott's play, she relies on instinct and common sense and the help of other, powerless people whose respect she has gained. A recurrent motif of the novel is the incantation from Walcott, "Give the Devil a child for dinner / One, two, three little children . . .", referring to the fact that Rudy gains his power by feeding his daughter's duppy with human blood, necessitating an unending stream of victims. Like the play, the novel is populated by figures from popular West Indian mythology – the Jab-Jab, the Soucouyant, the Bolom, the Diablesse – as much as by the *orisha*s in their diasporan versions – Papa Legba, Osain, Shakpana, Emanjah, as well as Osun, Shango, Ogun, Oya and Eshu. Walcott's chorus of Frog, Bird and Cricket is mirrored by Hopkinson's trio of hoodlums, Crack Monkey, Crapaud and Jay. Ti-Jeanne's unnamed baby is referred to as Bolom, and like Walcott's, it attains human life and identity through Ti-Jeanne's efforts.

The setting of the novel is Toronto, but the centres of power are the balmyard, presided over by Gros-Jeanne, the grandmother; the palais, or Necropolis, where she performs her ceremonies of invocation of the spirits; and the CN Tower, the tallest structure in Toronto, where the Posse leader, Rudy, performs his grisly rituals in a horrible parody of the grandmother's. A post-modern narrative of an urban diaspora is played out entirely in terms of a Caribbean spiritual belief system and iconography, which, in making the transition from the islands to the metropolis, redefines that space through the power of its own metaphors. But as always the result is a new form of hybridity, in which the diverse signifiers play with and against one another. Equally important to the novel therefore is what it owes to its setting and to North American popular cultural forms. They combine with the folk-tale elements in such a way as to transform them into something peculiar and contemporary. One of

Walcott's figures in *Ti-Jean* is the Bolom, an unborn child, which "may be a ball of moving fire / A white horse in the leaves, or a clothful of skin, / Found under a tree . . ." (1970a, 98) that "rolls in a blue light towards the hut" (p. 99) where Ti-Jean and his brothers live, evoking the many supernatural terrors of West Indian folk-tales. Nalo Hopkinson's duppy, equally terrifying, is nonetheless pure Disney, recalling Casper the Friendly Ghost and other such cartoon visualizations of the supernatural. In the following passage from the novel, Rudy is terrorizing Tony, Ti-Jeanne's baby-father, into obedience by demonstrating the full extent of his sadism. It begins with a horrifying description of him skinning a woman alive (*pace Silence of the Lambs*) before he slits her throat and feeds her blood to the duppy he keeps trapped in a magic bowl:

> With a quick slash, Rudy slit the woman's jugular vein. Bright arterial blood gouted into the bowl. An appalling sound came from it, like someone guzzling great amounts of liquid as fast as they could. Melba's body relaxed into death . . . The slurping noises from the bowl stopped. In its ring of cloth it rocked around and around, fast, then was still. A red mist seeped out of it and hovered in the air. Shapes coalesced from the mist, then melted back again: grasping, clutching hands; a rictus of a mouth, lips pulled back into a snarl; deranged eyes that appraised Tony like so much meat on a hook. Petrified, Tony was the monkey transfixed in the tiger's frozen stare. Nothing in his world had prepared him for this creature from another reality. He was looking at a thing that must have died and never stopped dying, a thing that Rudy would not allow its natural rest, that he kept barely appeased with the blood of the living. Tony's heart clammered in his chest. He could not endure another moment of that gaze . . . Rudy wiped his gory hand on the leg of his pants. He'd need a new suit. He said to the duppy, "Never mind what I tell you before. Once he give the heart to the hospital, I want you to kill all of them: Ti-Jeanne, Tony, everybody." It did not make a noise exactly. More something like the remembered sound of a wail of agony. Then it sharpened into an arc and poured itself at speed right through the wall to the street outside. (Hopkinson 1998, 138–40)

The reference to the heart is important here: Rudy has been offered a large sum of money to acquire a human heart as a transplant for the ailing Canadian prime minister. Tony is a doctor who became involved with the Posse through his addiction to buff, and Rudy needs his medical expertise to help him choose an appropriate victim as heart donor.

Tony has already tried to escape once by appealing to Ti-Jeanne and her grandmother, who called down the spirits to make him invisible, but Rudy forestalled him by invoking the greater power of the enslaved duppy. Having caught him, Rudy designs the scene above to impress on Tony the futility of attempting to escape. Body parts are a central metaphor, therefore, for both the novel and the film, recalling Stuart Hall's images of the black body as "cultural capital" and "canvas of representation".

The word "belly" carries multilayered connotations: from George Orwell and others' description of the United States as "the belly of the beast", picked up by Stuart Hall when he describes himself as "living all his adult life in England, in the shadow of the black diaspora, in the belly of the beast", to rap parlance in New York, in which "beast" connotes the police. "Belly" also carries a deeper layer of meaning, signifying literal incorporation by a larger entity, a wholesale swallowing by an all-encompassing body/imperialist machine. In the movie it is also the underbelly, the underworld or underclass of the New York–Jamaican drug culture in which the characters are immersed. In *Brown Girl,* the body-part trope is the heart: Tony kills Gros-Jeanne, the grandmother, and her heart is transplanted into the Canadian prime minister, who thereby has both literally and metaphorically a change of heart, and decides to institute a programme of regeneration for the dispossessed of the inner city. *Belly* similarly ends with a change of heart. The protagonist, Tommy, is hired by the FBI to assassinate a black religious leader who approximates Martin Luther King, Malcolm X and Louis Farrakhan, and who is due to give a public exhortation at the moment of transition to the twenty-first century. Confronted by his murderer, the black churchman makes an appeal for life over death, light over darkness, offering an escape from the belly of the beast through cessation of crime and violence.

The oppositions are clear: *Belly,* which ends with an embrace between the two men, is about black masculinity, and the means proposed for the transformation and decriminalization of African-American identity and culture is, on the one hand, acceptance of a higher spiritual power and authority, represented by the black churchman. On the other hand we have the back-to-Africa option exercised by Sincere, the character played by Nas and identified with femininity via the character of his girlfriend (played by T-Boz). This option, needless to say, represents an opting out of contemporary urban reality, there being no suggestion that twenty-first-century problems have any place in Africa. *Brown Girl*, in contrast, is about the necessity for an alternative here and now to the patriarchal structures that produce competition and conflict and have led to dereliction and the victimization of black people, and it is a black woman's heart in a white woman's body that provides the conduit for this alternative, figured in terms of an African/Caribbean iconography. It is therefore not surprising that Nalo Hopkinson celebrates Walcott in the acknowledgements that follow the story, where she thanks him "for writing the play *Ti-Jean and His Brothers,* one of the first examples of Caribbean magic realism I ever read" (1998, 249).

But her debt to him and her other precursors goes further than form, to the roots of identity construction within a Caribbean cultural aesthetic, affirming a genealogy of ideas and forms even while testing these out in a new context. Derek Walcott too addresses this issue in an essay introducing a collection of his plays that also contains *Ti-Jean*: "What the Twilight Says: an Overture". Echoing Fanon and Sartre, he refers to the "nervous condition" of the native, and goes on to ask this question, "Slaves, the children of slaves, colonials, then pathetic, unpunctual nationalists [and, he might have added, migrants and emigres], what have we to celebrate?" (1970b, 20). In common with Walcott himself and with younger writers from Antoni to Ross, Nalo Hopkinson's novel, despite its elements of horror, sadism and urban alienation, shows very clearly what there is to celebrate in a diaspora heritage of Caribbean origin. For Walcott, the liberating force that would deliver the slave from servitude "was the forging of a language that went beyond mimicry" (1970b, 17). According to him, it was not enough simply to identify with the old gods, the African pantheon, since for New World blacks their power was no longer accessible. "Ogun," he says, "was an exotic for us, not a force . . . our invocations were not prayer but devices" (p. 8). Hopkinson's novel shows that his prescription of thirty years ago is as relevant now as ever: "what is needed is not new names for old things, or old names for old things, but the faith of using the old names anew . . . baptising this neither proud nor ashamed bastard, this hybrid, this West Indian" (Walcott 1970b, 10). As opposed to a simplistic faith in transferring the old gods wholesale and unchanged across time and space, Hopkinson's invocation of the Yoruba *orisha*s meets Walcott's definition of "using old names anew". In the same way, she and her contemporaries are replacing the "anxiety of influence" with an intertextual dialogue with her father's generation.

By bringing together these two texts, I have attempted to raise questions about the new meanings that come into play as a result of the meeting of gender and an inherited cultural predisposition with the effects of diaspora, displacement, exile and/or urban alienation. Without wishing to generalize from the particular, I find in *Belly* a conspicuous absence of the tropes of black folk culture that inform the work of, for example, Toni Morrison and Alice Walker and are a central motif in Leone Ross's *Orange Laughter,* which is set in the underworld of the New York subway. In speculating as to the reasons for this, I have been led to an examination of how race, gender, class and culture interact to produce forms that, while addressing many of the same issues, remain quite distinct. And yet, despite its explicitly masculinist code, it appears as though the West Indian irruption into *Belly* could be construed as the return of the repressed in the movie's unconscious, with Jamaica standing in for the absent folk-culture so freely celebrated in *Brown Girl.* I would further venture that the film carries a latent message of repressed anxiety about gender, sexuality and power, in the threat to the protagonist embodied by the Jamaican drug lord. The heightened strangeness and otherness of the Kingston sequences, with the devilish don at their centre, call to mind the evil Rudy in his CN Tower; in both cases their power is based on control over a mind-altering drug and wielded with extreme violence and ruthlessness. *Belly*'s solution to the problem this poses for disenfranchised black men is either an alternative patriarchal structure (black church leadership) or escape to Africa, which is associated with the feminine. For *Brown Girl,* it consists in a reordering of reality and a transcendence of gender through another order of power altogether, brought about by turning the weapons of evil against itself. In this construction, Africa is alive and present in Toronto, not a distant destination offering escape. It suggests furthermore that feminine power, repressed in *Belly,* finds expression in *Brown Girl* as a natural part of its dialogue with the past and its reconfiguring of the present.

Note

1. I want to make clear from the outset that my concern here is less with the specificities of hip-hop culture, vital though these are to the style and message of the movie *Belly,* than with its portrayal of the Jamaican drug baron and its intriguing shift to Kingston for one sequence. I want to acknowledge up front that hip-hop is a culture to which I have access only as an onlooker, but even so, I claim the right to read the movie as a cultural artefact in the general context I have outlined.

⊰ Chapter 10 ⊱

Feminist Literary Theories and Literary Discourse in Two George Lamming Texts

MARGARET GILL

Introduction

What are the theoretical challenges, issues and concerns raised when the discipline of literature is approached from the perspective of gender? Do these challenges differ when approached from different standpoints? What are the implications for our understanding of Caribbean realities? Taking an oblique angle on these questions, I propose to read some key literary statements and literary models proposed by George Lamming, West Indian novelist and critic, in light of critical statements and observations made by dominant feminist literary theories. I will concentrate on Lamming's novel *In the Castle of My Skin* (1953) and his non-fiction text *The Pleasures of Exile* (1960). I chose these texts deliberately, as they are less likely to be utilizing any of the insights that we have come to know as gender analysis. My thesis is that some West Indian literary texts, and traditional critiques of them that utilize mainly class and race as critical analytical concepts and do not undertake gender analysis as we know it, will show significant overlap with features of dominant feminist literary theories. It may in fact be that in the face of hegemonic oppressions (of which colonialism and patriarchy are only two), crucial concerns and strategies raised by peoples whose lives are severely circumscribed may be more similar than we give credit for.[1]

I do not claim that Lamming's theories and models are all feminist. Nor do I claim that feminist literary theories of the dominant writers are universal. Significant differences do exist between dominant feminist literary theories and Lamming's writings. There are in fact key points of specific interest and strategy where the two clash, as I shall show. There is also the fact that the concept of gender foregrounds women's roles and positions in a way that analyses specifically targeting race and class do not. However, what I do suggest is that some traditional West Indian literary texts and critical writings, produced mainly by men, hold remarkably similar questions and interests in common with feminist literary theory.[2] Further, contrary to the Euro-American male canonical writings that dominant feminist literary theories interrogate, these West Indian texts and critical statements are often seen to investigate women's condition and account for their experiences with complexity.

The early West Indian literary statements to be examined here appear not to invest in the same hegemonic masculinist ideology as the Euro-American canon. My argument is that they do so because these works deal necessarily with reader resistance and radical challenge. Resistance and challenge against hegemonic forces, after all, are the values that must wrest a nationalist literature from a colonial history. It would therefore be erroneous to take for granted that West Indian male-authored texts and criticisms generally constitute a local masculine canon in the way that the male European canon has existed. For example, it seems to me that George Lamming's *In the Castle of My Skin* is seen as one of these classic canonical nationalist West Indian texts, having stereotypical images of the few women characters who fit in the margins of that text. I suggest that there is a need to re-examine this assumption. Women in this text do not passively endure their circumstances or limit their interests to narrowly defined domestic issues, nor are they treated in rigidly circumscribed ways. Furthermore, in this text there is also a concern – which is very familiar to feminists – with reconstituting a shrouded and debased culture and tradition.

I will proceed in this analysis by first identifying the particular feminist statement or model and then examining what I perceive as a corollary in the Lamming texts identified. No attempt will be made to examine Lamming's texts in any detail in light of the criticisms made by black and post-colonial feminist theories. Such observations will be included only where they are critical to an argument being made, as my focus is on the statements made by dominant Anglo-American and French literary theorists, that is, feminists whose work has sometimes been cited as imperialist by black and post-colonial writers.

The Historicity of Literature

Before proceeding further it is necessary to underline that the contours of feminist literary theorizing have been shaped by several perspectives and at different historical moments. Thus its output has sometimes been more contentious than unanimous. However, there are two principal values to which all feminist literary theories suscribe:

1. No account, as Toril Moi states (1985, xiii), is ever neutral.
2. The subordination/oppression/suppression of women is not natural, not a necessity of their biology that dooms them to inferiority, as Aristotle supposed, but is historically explainable by patriarchy.

The first of these values that I shall examine is the question of the neutrality of the critical project and, by extension, of the text that was presumed to precede it. Feminist literary theorists recognize and take as their starting point the existence of inequality in literary representation and portrayal. These theorists, whose work began to surface around the second decade of the twentieth century, noted that the literature that had been established as a canon of excellence was silent on women's literary contributions and represented their condition in ways that consistently disabled and disempowered women relative to men. Assuming that a social rather than a natural reason produces these distortions, feminist literary theories sought to expose and account for the presuppositions, choices and constructions that constitute texts, their production and the practice of criticism.

Historiographies of feminist theorizing claim Virginia Woolf and Simone de Beauvoir as important foremothers who began asking critical questions of the canon, about women's representation in it and about what constituted this category "woman". Woolf observed, in *A Room of One's Own,* that the men who were the writers of the texts and who established the canon were themselves the ones who determined what values were being applied to categorize good literature. Men, she perceived, also controlled the application of those values, as they controlled the publication process and academia (1989, 50–56). Woolf further pointed to the way in which many of these men stereotyped women as intellectually and otherwise inferior, and never in their writings problematized the relationship between their beliefs about women and women's apportionment in literature (p. 54). According to Woolf, the canon apportioned women as either "the angel in the house . . . the aesthetic ideal through which [women] have been killed into art, or the angel's necessary opposite and double, the 'monster' whose medusa-face also kills female creativity" (p. 17). De Beauvoir reasoned that woman was a construct and, unlike man, was not a "fully constituting subject" (Dietz 1998, 83). Both she and Woolf argued, therefore, that the ideological, which language, literature and other symbolic or representational systems express, has vast explanatory power and was a fertile ground for the transformation of particular social relations – in this case relations that define and position women in ways inferior to men.

Already we can see fundamental points raised above that a nationalist literature and nationalist critical tradition might share: basic assumptions about exclusion, the constructedness and devaluation of colonized people, the co-joining of private and public political concerns, and the basic objective of transformation. George Lamming well articulated on behalf of West Indians the transgressive stance that West Indian writing took against problematic assumptions and positions of colonial literature; he argued in *The Pleasures of Exile* that it is in the West Indian novel that, "For the first time, the West Indian peasant becomes other than a cheap source of labour. He [*sic*] became through the novelist's eye a living existence . . . It is the West Indian novel that has restored the West Indian peasant to his [*sic*] true and original status of personality" (1960, 38–39).[3]

Kamau Brathwaite, a contemporary of Lamming's and a fellow Barbadian writer, similarly had no doubt that literature functioned politically. He was quite forthright in what he reckoned the responsibility of West Indian fiction to be: "an exploration and mapping of the physical, social, moral and emotional territory that is ours" (1984, 8). And critic Sandra Pouchet Paquet tells us:

As [Brathwaite and Lamming] wished, the literature of the fifties is demonstrably sensitive to the general social condition. More often than not, the

exploration of the private self or of the individual experience is tied to
an exploration of the interdependence of private and public worlds; to an
exploration of the individual's relationship to the inherited structure of values that dominates his [*sic*] society. (1995, 53)

These works and critiques all formulate the same problematics as feminist literary theory. They emphasize the historicity of literature and its
embodiment of ideology. Feminist critics Catherine Belsey and Jane
Moore explain the grounding of literature and critical work in ideology
thus:

All interpretation [that theory facilitates] is political . . . [Feminists] perceive
that [a] text invites its readers, as members of a specific culture, to understand what it means to be a woman or a man, and so encourages them to reaffirm or to challenge existing cultural norms . . . Fiction it seem[s] both
manifest[s] and influence[s] the ways in which societies under[stand] themselves. Literature [is] in this sense profoundly historical. (1989, 1–3)

Patriarchy

Feminists theorized as patriarchy the ideology that governed women's
relationship to literature. The term traditionally derived from Greek and
Roman law and meant the rule of the father, whereby the male household
head held ultimate legal and economic power over young males and all
females. The basis of this law was the belief that women are not only different from men, who are taken as the standard, they are inferior on the
basis of their biology. Women are generally physically weaker than men,
and on this basis were thought incapable of rationality and had therefore
to be ruled and subordinated. Aristotle argued in *Politics* that women are
in fact "mutilated males", devoid of principles of the human soul and
with an undeveloped mental faculty. Feminists argue that these beliefs or
variants of them have come to undergird the unequal way in which
women are perceived and treated in society and culture.

Exposing the roots of this absolutist claim about women's difference
in *The Second Sex*, Simone de Beauvoir made the famous assertion that
has now become almost a rallying cry of feminist theorizing: "one is not
born but rather *becomes* a woman". To express what she perceived as

women's immanence and men's transcendence, de Beauvoir coined the concept of woman as "other":

> Thus humanity is male and man defines woman not in herself but as relative to him; she is not regarded as an autonomous being . . . she is defined and differentiated with reference to man and not he with reference to her; she is the inessential as opposed to the essential. He is the Subject, he is the Absolute. She is the Other. (1949, 16)

Virginia Woolf advanced another idea that is also important here. In her text *A Room of One's Own,* she embraced the idea of androgynous writing as women's response to their textual oppression. This is the presentation in a single text of an elusive multiplicity of perspectives that refuses to be tied to any singular meaning, as a strategy that women could bring to representation. This is a position from which the woman as author could gain more individual autonomy and freedom because of the claim it establishes to the power of defining. Woolf reinforced this case in her own discursive practice in *Room,* when she warns her audience that " 'I' is only a convenient term for somebody who has no real being. Lies will flow from my lips, but there may be perhaps some truth mixed up with them" (1989, 4). Through this position Woolf pointed to the constructed nature of truth/reality, and hence to the constructed nature of woman and consequently to possibilities for change.

Subsequent theories espouse different perceptions from those of Woolf and de Beauvoir about the weight of the effect of patriarchal ideology. However, all tend to accept the fundamental thesis they proposed: that patriarchal ideology mediates women's subjectivity in language, both within texts as well as in their capacity to define themselves through self-inscription.

The Caliban/Prospero Model

The parallel to the concept of patriarchy in West Indian (and certainly Lamming's) literary theorizing is, to my mind, the Caliban/Prospero complex proposed by Lamming, among others (Lamming 1960). Prospero, protagonist of Shakespeare's play *The Tempest,* fits neatly into the role of patriarch, and Caliban, the native of the island that Prospero "discovers", is the dependant. Not only is his rule over Caliban legalized, according to Prospero's own law of capture, but it is also paternalistic. Prospero adopts the pose of one who *rescues* Caliban from his natural (read mentally undeveloped) "savage" state by adopting him and becoming his parent and teacher in a civilizing project. Elaborating on Prospero's perspective, Lamming states, "Only the application of the Word to the darkness of Caliban's world could harness the beast which resides within this cannibal" (1960, 109).

Prospero is guilty, Lamming asserts, of manufacturing a way of seeing/interpreting that is rooted in a "background of opposites". In this way of seeing, the terms "virtue, nobility, chastity and beauty" are associated with the world of him and his daughter, Miranda, and are set in "antithesis" to those of "degeneracy, bestiality, lust and physical deformity", associated with Caliban (1960, 105). What Lamming and many other West Indian critics after him emphasize, however, is Caliban's perspective.

Fuelled by their own critique of and resistance to the colonizer, they are able to reread and reorganize the Shakespeare play, giving Caliban, a character who is important but not critical, more scope. The aspect of the play much quoted by these West Indian critics is Caliban's statement to Prospero that, because Prospero has taught him language, Caliban can now use that language to curse him. Caliban's curse becomes the West Indian theorist's trope for transgression and revision.

In the revision referred to above, Caliban is able to offer an alternative way of reading his own actions in relation to his cursing of Prospero, and his actions with respect to Miranda. Whereas Caliban is presented in Prospero's version as bestial and incapable of rationality or proper "human" gratitude and morality, in Caliban's version his own rationality is impeccable. He has in mind that he has extended vital knowledge to Prospero as his invaluable guide when he arrived on the island, but that Prospero returns this favour by claiming the island and confining Caliban's movement within it. Caliban is well aware that no equal exchange is perceived in Prospero's teaching of him. He also understands that no matter how much he accedes to Propero's civilizing plan for him, Prospero will never see him as human enough to be a son-in-law. And so, on Prospero's word, we hear that Caliban, the "beast", has tried to "seduce" Miranda. Caliban knows, in essence, that he is expected always to be Prospero's inferior "other", and therefore he feels justified in cursing this self-appointed master.

It should be noted that several persons have pointed to the limitations in Caliban's linguistic strategy. They claim that the using of the master's language only ultimately confirms the master's power.[4] However, my argument is that, as he yet retains his original sign system that he shared with his mother, Sycorax, and can now also claim Prospero's language as his own, he has both established a necessary counter-discourse and increased his potential for creative action. He is now, in fact, able to see from several perspectives. This multiplicity of perspectives is much like the advantage that Woolf suggested women writing could claim. It is the benefit that creolization offers to the West Indian writer, which I will discuss in more detail later.

Identity Politics and Democratizing the Canon

The next development I want to examine in this comparison between dominant feminist literary theories and the Lamming texts concerns the issue of identity politics. Following the initial dominant models of feminist examination of literature, the so-called second wave of Anglo-American feminist theorizing, arising in the 1960s, moved in two basic directions (Moi 1985, 75):

1. work aimed at identifying how patriarchy inscribes women, which came to be called "images of women" criticism; and
2. work aimed at accounting for women's writing, termed "gynocritics" by Elaine Showalter. (Moi 1985, 75)

The concern of these feminists seemed to be democratization of the canon by correcting its exclusion and cultural impoverishment of women. Very influential with respect to this concern were the black American civil rights movement of the 1960s and the struggle for political independence in the developing world in the late 1950s and through the 1960s (Moi 1985, 22). Apart from the larger black struggles of the civil rights movements, models for feminist literary theory strategies were also available through Afro-American women's writing.[5]

The essence of these struggles was about identity and self-definition. For persons of African descent in the United States, their struggle was for a self-determining, fully acknowledged personhood *vis-à-vis* the state and the dominating white race whose interests it served. For those in the colonized world, their struggles sought to assert national identity in the face of imperialist domination.

Influenced by these developments, feminist literary theory undertook a parallel project for women – the validation of their beleaguered humanity in the face of sex-identified domination. Furthermore, the challenge to authority posed by feminist literary theory during this phase was not only to the validity of representational claims but also to the hierarchy implied between author and reader. Toril Moi, speaking of Kate Millett's work *Sexual Politics,* the most acclaimed treatise of the strand of theorizing aimed at gender analysis of male texts, says: "Her approach destroys the prevailing image of the reader/critic as passive/feminine recipient of authoritarian discourse and as such is exactly suited to feminism's political purposes" (1985, 25).

Images of Women

Kate Millett (1970), Mary Ellmann (1968) and Germaine Greer (1970), proponents of the "images of women" trend, proposed a radical rereading of canonical texts that revealed the latter's fetishization of the word and of the phallus as representations of "the rule of the father". Ellmann exposed the phenomenon of sexual analogy: "All forms are subsumed by our concepts of male and female temperament . . . the hunter is always male, the prey female . . . all butterflies are taken to be frivolous and effeminate creatures . . . Thanks to Melville, all whales are more or less males simply because they are big enough to scare men" (1968, 8–9). Ellman argued that male writers, with their analyses grounded in biology, construct women within stereotypes connoting passivity, immanence, the magical and ultimately the lack of authority (Moi 1985, 34). As Moi underscores, Ellman further demonstrates how these stereotypes are self-destructive, encapsulating as they do extremes of the ideal at one end and total anathema at the other. For example, Ellman deconstructs the stereotype of the mother, who can be described as both a "venerated idol" and a "castrating bitch" (Moi 1985, 37).

Millett argued that male writers disseminate the "sexual politics" of male domination of women through the word/the stereotype, which comes to have the force of creation. She went on to reveal the covert or open sexism in the works of D.H. Lawrence, Norman Mailer, Henry Miller and Jean Genet. In the latter's work in particular, she was able to show the "arbitrariness" of sex-role allocation, as it is "revealed as the category, *even the function of a nakedly oppressive social system*" (Millett 1970, 343; emphasis added). As sex roles are enacted among Genet's homosexual community, masculine and feminine "stand out as terms of praise and blame, authority and servitude, high and low, master and slave" (p. 343).

Images of women theorists pointed to Freud and psychoanalytic theory as prime agents of patriarchy. The main culprits they exposed were Freud's misogynistic theories of penis envy and female masochism, which hold men up as the desired standard and being and see woman's as a position of inferiority (Belsey and Moore 1989, 5).

Lamming's constructions of the woman in his text challenge the patriarchal representations identified by the images theorists so far, but they also challenge the theorists themselves. Take, for example, the case of the figure of the mother. Just as Ellman (and Woolf and de Beauvoir before her) does, Lamming locates the mother as an important site of social control. However, while the three feminists see mothering as a source of women's oppression, a critical site of their subordination, Lamming interrogates it as a source of power, and in this he is not far from the position taken by some black women novelists and theorists. The stereotype of the mother targeted so quickly by feminist literary theory is also one of the stereotypes of black women against which black female author-theorists first inveighed, though for somewhat different reasons. In the southern United States and the Caribbean, as a strategy of slavery the black woman was the one perceived as the mother, the "mammy". Black theorists such as Barbara Christian (1985) and Hazel Carby (1987) argue that stereotyping black women as the mammy allowed white women to participate in the congruent stereotype of the pure, innocent, fragile, ornamental romantic figure (Christian 1985, 2). The stereotype that was promulgated by both white and early black writers presents the mammy figure as grossly fat, nurturing, fanatically religious, kind and strong, in the sense that she herself needs or demands little (Christian 1985, 2).[6]

On the other hand, Lamming marks mothering as a space where women can achieve personal power even when they appear as a foil to a main character. Although we never get the name of "the Mother" in *Castle,* she, like other women in the text, stands as a figure of strength and agency. The story in *Castle* is the boy G's, but the Mother is right there at the beginning of the story. Through her control of memory, she is the one holding the important key to the boy's past and his connections to family and community. Like "Pa", the old man who in his dream travels holds the key to the African past, the Mother has the capacity to provide meaning to the self through her control of memory of the past. And in her recounting of the family history in response to the boy's queries, it is significant that she states that the grandmother has gone to Panama to work on construction of the canal. Formal historiographies have yet to document the history of the women who went to Panama during the great West Indian migrations to the Canal Zone. It is also not accidental that the person who gives the boys the true story about Barbados's slave past is an old woman, a mother type. She is held in stark contrast to the teachers of authorized history at that site of imperial control the school, who would have the boys forget their true past; a forgetting that leaves them with no authentic sense of the self.

Mothers, then, exist in the officially unsanctioned oral culture, one that many West Indian writers see as a realm of being and knowing that has great counter-discursive possibility. Women, particularly mothers, are linked with the culture as transmitters of orality, and male and female West Indian writers exploit the oral culture as a site where a distinctive counter-culture against colonialism is upheld and celebrated.[7] But the trope of the mother works in a complex way. Male and female protagonists are forced to see the mother in a dual fashion. She must be defined as in some ways collaborating in her own oppression (as her apparent acceptance of colonial religion and her problematic relation to the child-father[8] testify), in which case the protagonist separates from her as a necessary loss to enable maturation. But then the mother, or the culture she represents and which represents her, must be re-envisioned and reintegrated into the psyche to be carried forward as a strategy of counter-discourse. In *Castle* the boy G goes through such a parting at the end of the novel. However, his interior monologue in the very last lines of the novel and Lamming's formal presentation of it are testimony to the other vision of the reintegrated mother, which G holds: "The village / my mother / a boy among the boys / a man who knew his people won't feel alone / to be a different kind of creature" (1953, 303).

But apart from how he uses the mother figure, Lamming undermines the colonial and patriarchal complex by further widening the roles women perform. Mrs Foster goes to the Landlord to get him to undertake his custodial role of fixing things after the flood. True, when she is so uncritical of the Landlord's definition of their relative status, she enacts the role of the colonized who has internalized self-abasement. However, she takes as a right his responsibility for reparation after the flood, and so quite boldly makes the positive step to go to him and invoke his responsibility rather than passively await his decision to act. We again see this agency in the case of the drunken old woman who goes to the city during the riots and returns to report to the villagers. It is true that her son's death at the hands of the riot police weighs heavily, but she sharply criticizes Mr Foster and the village men for not participating in the riots. "I jus from the city . . . while you a big stinkin' nigger man wrap up in yuh blasted bed I been in the city an 'tis men like you they want" (p. 197). The role of organizer that she takes in this speech is all the more significant in that she represents a figure that is so at odds with what is considered proper, in terms not only of colonial manners, but also the way that patriarchy would have women behave.

Another woman who plays a role that is self-directed and self-authorized is Ma. In reading her role it is important to understand that the community sees her, along with her husband, as a leader. In her interaction with the villagers who go to buy bread at the bread cart, they give way to her, leaving her a clear pathway ahead of them. More importantly, Ma is the only one who voices concern when Pa and the villagers would equate Mr Slime, the ex-schoolteacher with his seemingly radical plans, with Moses, who delivers his people from their oppressors. She recommends that the village take a more sagacious look at Mr Slime. He in fact betrays the whole village by literally selling them out, and Ma's caution proves prophetic.

The argument may be made that Lamming sets out to correct images of the colonized or of women – a criticism offered to the images of women theorists. The criticism is that in seeking to state what the "real" woman is like, these theorists fail to consider that the real is a contested construct, that literature is not simply a reflection of reality but a site of competing "truths" (Moi 1985, 45–46). In other words, there could be no one "real" woman. However, despite the strong roles that Lamming gives his female characters, he does not leave women or mothers unproblematized. Mothers can be unreasonable or domineering, as sometimes are the Mother and Mrs Foster. Mothers' relationship to fathers or to sexual partners may also be perceived in terms of their weakness and the men's strength, at least according to the boys in their discussion of the relative merits of absentee fathers. And often through their internalization of colonial values, as is the case of Ma's defence of the Landlord, women can be the staunchest defenders of critical aspects of the status quo.

A related criticism may also be that in pursuit of authentic representations, theorists thus concerned with truth dig themselves into a hole of reifying realism as a literary strategy. However, although Lamming is very interested in issues of representation, he does not hold to the novel as a strictly mimetic device, nor does he hold to realism as his sole literary strategy. It is true that in *Castle* a realist vein can be perceived, but Lamming also flouts many of the principles of realism. He draws heavily on the practices of orality and its consequent heterogeneous, and sometimes contradictory, voices. He stresses storytelling and changes of narrator, with consequent fragmentation. The narrator is sometimes G, sometimes an omniscient third person and sometimes the boys in their own voices. He includes popular sayings and songs such as the ones taught to the children in school to help them memorize information:

Thirty days hath September,
April, June and November;
All the rest have thirty-one
Except February, which hath but twenty-eight and
    twenty-nine in a Leap Year

(p. 41)

And

a	b	ab	catch a crab
g	o	go	let it go
a	b	ab	catch a crab
g	o	go	let it go

(p. 40)

He does not follow neatly the Aristotelian narrative structure of a chronologically ordered text with a beginning, middle and end, and he uses parables to convey principles of right acting. Two of the stories are the Bots, Bambi and Bambina saga and the story of Jon, the character who gets caught between two women waiting at two different churches at the same time to marry him. Jon hides in a tree in the cemetery to see what will happen, rather than act one way or the other. He is caught between belief and action, much like how the villagers are caught between an emotional loyalty to a landlord they know and the need to support the rioting that promises to deliver them from an exploitative system that mortgages their lives to the plantation (p. 131). In the saga of Bots, Bambi and Bambina, peril comes to the trio when they allow the colonizer, in the form of a visiting white anthropologist, to dictate what should constitute a valid conjugal relationship (p. 133). In terms of structure, Lamming breaks up his text with a dream sequence, a whole chapter (chapter 4) and parts of others he presents as the dialogue for a play, and he even includes a detailed recipe for making the Bajan national dish, coocoo (p. 274).

The advantages to orality as counter-discourse are several. It enables multi-vocality through shifts in linguistic registers, and consequently opens out the power of authorizing or taking authority. This offers the possibility of seeing how the oppressed accept some responsibility for their state and consequently how they control some degree of freedom to change their circumstances. In other words, they are not portrayed statically as victims. Orality also enables the inscription of certain strategies common to itself but outside the form of the novel, such as strategies described above and the use of the trickster figure. This figure has subversive potential in its continuous efforts to contravene authority and draws attention to the importance of the storytelling mode as a method of asserting selfhood. I argue that the local politician (in this case Mr Slime),[9] who springs from among the people and represents their dreams for collective freedom, but who succumbs to personal greed, is such a figure.

In adopting these strategies it could be argued that Lamming is self-consciously challenging the received novel form and exposing manipulation of the word – and hence ideological manipulation – for what it is, a process dedicated to maintaining skewed power relations. It could also be argued that he is doing this in order to promote challenges to the process of mystification and exploitation. In this sense, he is showing the cracks and opportunities in domination.

Gynocritics

"Gynocriticism", the second stream of document feminist literary theories, offers two positions that are important here for my argument on counter-discourse. One position holds that writing by women is itself a subversive act. The other is that women writers use madness as a textual strategy. Feminists of this second theoretical trend, rather than totally condemning psychoanalytic theory, rehabilitate it by drawing on Freud's two major contributions: the creation of the unconscious and the existence in the infant of undifferentiated desire. Freud argued that as the infant comes to acquire language so the unconscious is created. The unconscious is the site in the psyche where unsanctioned desires, such as desire for the mother and same-sex desire, are repressed. Jacques Lacan, who extended Freud's theory, offered the thesis – which feminist literary theories support – that language, the symbolic order, was the law of the father, of patriarchy, and it was this law that required suppression of desire for the mother. Patriarchy therefore marked and controlled the subject's entrance into the social order.

Uncomfortable with the absolute power of patriarchy to define and control women in the earlier theories, feminists of the second theoretical trend sought to explain how it could be that some women were writing in the presence of such power and control. Consequently they concentrate on women's writing and on the ways in which it may be different from men's. Feminist literary theorists of this school argue that the unconscious or the imaginary is the site that ideology does not cover, and it is from there that alternatives or challenges to patriarchy arise. They see writing by women as a subversive act getting its motive force from within the alternative spaces of the unconscious and of undifferentiated desire. This form of theorizing is called "gynocritics" by Elaine Showalter, the most acclaimed of the early gynocritics.

Showalter's argument, in her publication *A Literature of Their Own: British Women Novelists from Brontë to Lessing* (1977), is that women's writing constitutes a "literary sub-culture". This writing remains a subculture because it is deprived of a means of consolidating itself by the disruption that occurs every time each generation has to start anew, as no known tradition exists. Showalter's documentation of women's writing from the 1840s to the 1980s uncovers such a female tradition.[10]

Two other major contributors to gynocriticism, Sandra Gilbert and Susan Gubar, examined a range of Victorian women's writing and identified the "madwoman" as a textual strategy used by these writers. The writers used this strategy, Gilbert and Gubar argue, to inscribe the "tension, self-doubt, renunciation and above all, rage against the society which confines them" (Belsey and Moore 1989, 8). This construction, they propose, comes of the woman's refusal to be silenced. The woman writer perceives that she cannot without serious distortion of herself fulfil the limited and limiting roles that have been ascribed her. For her then, "madness" becomes an escape. Its value as a textual and political strategy is enormous, since madness is perceived to represent a protean state in which the disintegrated "othered" self can be reassembled according to a more autonomous, wholesome image. What this state offers politically is the discovery that the self is multitudinous, and that the creation of subjectivity is a political process involving the power of selection, as the Freudian theorization of the unconscious and undifferentiated sexuality of the infant demonstrated. Furthermore, the value of this trope is that if this subjectivity can be disassembled, then an alternative assembly that is subversive of patriarchy must be possible (Gilbert and Gubar 1979, 77).

Lamming's focus on debased knowledges and practices as noted earlier seems resonant here, as is the trope of Caliban's curse. The subculture of orality, with its emphasis on the vernacular – the coocoo recipe, Pa's visions and memories of Africa as unsanctioned history, the boy's song when the fowl-cock is made, not quite accidentally, to mess on the Landlord's clothes – provides textual strategies that erupt into the space of ideology. If gynocriticism argues that the imaginary/unconscious is the site where ideology does not overwhelm and that out of it alternatives arise, then Lamming locates this site in the oral culture, and it is significant that women are the spiritual guides in this realm.

One cannot help but notice also the connections between gynocritics' use of the potential for subversion offered by Freudian analysis and

Lamming's use of the allegory of Caliban's curse. In a quite remarkably similar way to how gynocritics appropriate Freud, Lamming perceives his possibilities for appropriating Shakespeare at the point of Caliban's insertion into Prospero's symbolic order, when his capacity to curse Prospero is created. So the availability of his creole culture, created when the English text meets African/Caribbean oral structures, enables Lamming to disrupt the traditional Anglo-American novel form.

Some criticisms have been launched against gynocriticism, but difficulty occurs in applying them across the board to Lamming. First, the criticism that gynocritics reinstate the author as the transcendental signified and the reader as subordinate cannot be laid at Lamming's feet. Certainly, although the text is partly autobiographical, he disperses meanings with his use of several narrators and perspectives, including that of the Landlord. Such dispersal, as well as his frequently used open-ended strategy at the end of his novels, allows the reader some power while retaining the author as an important contributor to meaning. Black feminists in fact support Lamming's authorial presence in that they argue for race identity to be retained as a classificatory code in explicating meaning. For them, like Lamming, being subordinated by their history raises in them the need to consider issues such as authenticity of voice and representation (Belsey and Moore 1989, 18).

Psychoanalytic approaches rooted in French psychoanalytic theory offer a second critique to gynocriticism; Lamming's work would have to be examined against them in respect of the points where he and gynocritics overlap. The criticism is that gynocriticism is marred by a kind of biological essentialism in its invocation of "female creativity" and in its presentation of patriarchy as homogeneous and all-embracing. Psychoanalytic critics Hélène Cixous and Luce Irigaray understand that insertion into the symbolic order of language and culture is never complete and that identity is therefore a continually unstable process. Cixous's work turns on a rejection of the binary logic that poses men and women in sexual opposition, that demands passivity and object status from women while activity and subjectivity are accorded to men. She believes instead in the bisexual nature of all human beings and in a kind of writing that, as Moi nicely puts it, "split[s] open the closure of the binary opposition and revel[s] in the pleasure of open-ended textuality" (1985, 108). Cixous also argues that this feminine writing can be done by either men or women, although given women's place in history and culture, they can come more easily to this type of writing.

Cixous urges that woman must write herself into history, as writing is the very possibility for change. This strategy, which she identifies as *écriture féminine* – a feminine discourse – would bring women back to their bodies, that is, to subject positions that are constituted not by lack of what the man has, defining woman as simply non-man, but by total otherness to men. Writing "will not only 'realise' the decensored relation of woman to her sexuality, . . . giving her access to her native strength; . . . it will tear her away from the superegoized structure in which she has always occupied the place reserved for the guilty" (1981, 250). Social change for Cixous is possible and women's writing can evoke the utopian vision of a non-oppressive and non-sexist society necessary to inspire revolt against present oppression.

Luce Irrigaray makes a case somewhat similar to that of Cixous in her concept of "womanspeak". This female language arises from women's libido, their imaginary (in Lacanian terms), only in the presence of other women and serves to declare woman as "multiple, decentered and undefinable" (Moi 1985, 147). For Irrigaray, this female desire, "inscribed in writing, is a force capable of rupturing the patriarchal symbolic order" (Belsey and Moore 1989, 14).

Cixous and Irrigaray can be seen to offer no critique to Lamming's position, given his investment in similar destruction of the binary and his adherence to the principle of multi-vocality. He directly addresses this concept of binary logic in his critique that we discussed earlier of the antithesis proposed by Prospero for interpreting the world. Furthermore, a strategy that he uses to model this multi-vocality is his use of dialect. West Indian critic Kenneth Ramchand's statement about West Indian writing in general is especially relevant here:

> West Indian literature would seem to be the only substantial literature in which the dialect-speaking character is the central character . . . This characteristic feature of West Indian writing reflects the more obviously new event – the centrality of the Black or Coloured character and the articulation of this hitherto obscure and stereotyped person. (1970, 96)

Furthermore, because of the writer's command of a wide linguistic range from Standard English to dialect, he is able, as Ramchand says, to bridge the distance between the voice of narration and the voice of the character (1970, 95). In fact the narrative voice can also be made to adopt the language of the character. Ramchand continues: "To understand the certainty with which West Indian writers have turned the dialect to such literary account . . . we must remember that co-existing with the new literary growth in the West Indies, and pre-dating it is a long oral tradition of story-telling and folk poetry in dialect" (p. 114).

Through this mechanism that draws on a creole heritage, Lamming therefore stands in agreement with several aspects of psychoanalytic feminist arguments. Where he parts company with them is his refusal to privilege an essential voice. The dilemma facing Cixous and Irrigaray in their attempts to define the feminine is not his, claiming as he does linguistic range. Neither is theorist Mary Jacobus's attempt to resolve the dilemma when she advocates with Roland Barthes the "death of the author". For Lamming, the speaker/author cannot be summarily dismissed because the concept of author/ity and the language the author chooses are themselves historicized, as part of the problem under consideration, by the black, lesbian and post-colonial text. As we have seen, Lamming's *Castle* problematizes these issues of authority and language.

Julia Kristeva is a psychoanalytic critic, part of whose position is, I think, very similar to Lamming's. She posits another analysis: that political and power interests meet in the sign/word (Moi 1985, 158). This means in her formulation that struggle – the coming to voice of the victimized – is accorded the same value as oppression. Kristeva also deconstructs the binary opposition operating in the symbolic order (for example, masculine/feminine, nature/nurture) and thus discourages any politics based on identity. She recommends strengthening of the semiotic or pre-Oedipal (the imaginary phase) "to allow the jouissance [pleasure] of semiotic motility to disrupt the strict symbolic order" (Moi 1985, 170).

However, Kristeva's lack of sufficient attention to history attracts criticism. Her post-modernist concern with discourse "precludes a grasp of the objective conditions of women's lives", one critic reasons (Kruks 1992, 90). Kruks further argues that a notion of the self as more than an effect of discourse, as having a degree of autonomy (the primary thesis of identity politics), is necessary for political action, and this is constantly deferred in discourse politics. Kristeva's emphasis on subversion arising from disruptions from the unconscious or the semiotic precludes questions of organization and collectivity that could move struggle from solely at the margins to also operate at the centre, and thus be more likely to effect significant social transformation. In other words, in Kristeva's logic, the only challenge to the oppression of the symbolic order would be that provided by the individual, arising out of spontaneous disruptions emerging from contradictions in the individual's unconscious. Such disruptions may spell instances of freedom for the individual, but they are incapable of effecting real change for oppressed women as a whole.

Conclusion

As has been demonstrated, feminist literary theories have made significant contributions to the study of literature. Several of these contributions are similar to those made by West Indian novelist and critic George Lamming. Images of women theories, as well as later theories, have established literature as an important site of struggle, given the way that language is mediated by patriarchal ideology. The initial theories, by their explication of patriarchy and how it functions, have added to the understanding of underlying structures of investigations of texts that already act to structure the realities they purport to explain. In respect of literature, this has meant the revelation of literature as literature. In the latter sense, feminist literary theory has also contributed to and been necessary for revelation of the exclusionary nature of the discourse of literature. Since women as subjects have been absent, then the discourse that continually shows them to be objectified must be implicated in that presentation.

The latter point paves the way for identification of the contributions of gynocriticism in particular. This brand of theorizing has widened the scope of knowledge and knowledge creation in respect of what constitutes "great" literature. By validating women's experiences as a legitimate basis for creating knowledge it both politicized and contextualized literature and its effect, critical practice. These arguments, I have shown, parallel concerns and issues raised by Lamming in the two texts examined.

Subsequent feminist theories that stress the importance of discourses in structuring consciousness have added to the understanding of the nature of identity and its fictionality or createdness. Such understandings have thereby pointed to possibilities for change through exposure of the political process involved in the creation of identity, and the knowledge that a greater plenitude of being is possible. Importantly, discourse theories have also contributed to the knowledge that the margin – that is, the spaces away from the centres of power (the individual's unconscious, for example) – is an important site of struggle. They have also identified that feminist theorizing can appropriate dominant paradigms towards a transformative practice. Even more critically, these theories have all demonstrated the possibility of alliances among different struggles towards more liberating social practices and conditions.

In teasing out the links between these forms of feminist literary theorizing and Lamming's practice in *Castle* and *The Pleasures of Exile,* I have pointed to such a possibility for alliances. I hope to have shown that it is possible that West Indian fictional texts can be usefully mined for theoretical insights, and that feminist ideas of the Anglo-American tradition can usefully be interrogated by West Indian thought. Further, there is considerable scope still in utilizing categories such as creolization and orality to read Caribbean literature.

Notes

1. My hypothesis is similar to that made by Julia Kristeva, feminist psychoanalytic critic, when she proposes that "insofar as women are defined as marginalised by patriarchy, their struggles can be theorised as any other struggle against a centralised power structure" (Moi, 164).
2. Space limitations preclude discussion of these hypotheses here, but I think that they can be fruitfully tested in works by Kamau Brathwaite, V.S. Reid, Samuel Selvon and others.
3. Lamming here is historically unable to see that parts of his argument need to be purged of its exclusion of West Indian women and middle-class urban blacks, for example. However, as far as women are concerned, we have the contradictory evidence of his conscious and complex treatment of them in his fiction.
4. See Savory 1995, 211–30.

5. Many black American women writers writing since the late nineteenth century (although their work would have had very limited readership) were concerned in their novels, sometimes explicitly, with correcting the stereotypical images of black women held by contemporary racist ideology. These included Frances Harper (published in 1890), Pauline Hopkins (1900), Nella Larsen (1928), Jessie Fauset (1931), Ann Petry (1946) and Dorothy West (1948) (Christian 1985).

6. This figure stands in opposition to the mothers being created by black women writers of the 1970s and on. For one thing, the writers create mothers who rebel against being stereotypes. Toni Morrison's mother in *Beloved* interprets her mother role as bringing freedom to her children, and refuses to let them live in slavery by taking the harsh measure of killing them. Mothers are not hesitant when they perceive the time is right to promote individual identity-formation in their offspring; they may even initiate it. At the same time they also foster a mother–child bond that enables firm connections to others and to home county, as does the mother Annie in *Annie John,* by Jamaica Kincaid.

7. Renu Junega notes that "the women are transmitters of the oral tradition which keeps alive knowledge derived from the African past" (1996, 38).

8. Women are seldom defined only in terms of themselves, but rather in terms of the relationship with a partner. This is not straightforward, however. In those relationships, West Indian women are likely to participate in negotiating positions that are favourable to themselves, as we see with the two women and the single man in the stories of Bots, Bambi and Bambina and Susie, Jen and Jon.

9. Mr Slime is given the role of flouter of authority from as far back as his days as a schoolteacher, when it is suggested that he was having an affair with the schoolmaster's wife. He later becomes the one who introduces the radical idea of the penny bank and campaigns for the villagers to join and save towards buying their house-spots.

10. Again it is significant to note that Afro-American novelist and scholar Toni Cade had seven years earlier, in 1970, edited a book called *The Black Woman* (see Christian 1985) in which she recovered a collection of neglected black women's fiction, but which receives little recognition in Anglo-American historiographies of feminist literature. While it is certainly not as extensive as Showalter's, the existence of this work and especially the sentiment that gave it impetus are a real critique of dominant feminist literary theory.

⁎Part V⁎

Gender and Power in the Public Domain: Feminist Theorizing of Citizenship

ৰ Chapter 11 ৯

Beyond the Bill of Rights
Sexing the Citizen

TRACY ROBINSON

Introduction

The unspoken, and sometimes explicit, starting point of analyses on the status of women is "the fact that the Caribbean woman is born to equal rights, since each country's Constitution, the supreme law of the land, guarantees fundamental rights and freedoms to all individuals – regardless of gender" (Senior 1991, 3). Underlying this constitutional guarantee is the concept of a citizen who transcends gender, but this question of women and citizenship has never been much more than an entry to Caribbean feminist thinking. Having identified a gap between the rhetoric of equal rights to women as citizens and women's reality, Caribbean feminists have often adopted a pragmatic response, more concerned with addressing Caribbean women's specific social and economic issues than with challenging how citizenship is constructed. One result is that we have tended to view the question of women's citizenship as uncontroversial, by which I mean as having been resolved by the pre-independence enfranchisement of women and by independence and post-independence constitutional provisions. Equally, and more critical, that question has also been seen as irrelevant to the pressing issues facing women in the Caribbean. To the extent that women and citizenship have remained a live issue in regional and national discourse, it is the wide-scale migration of Caribbean women within and outside of the region that has shaped public conversations.[1]

I want to urge that the debate about gender and citizenship, which has until now been transfixed in *time* by the earlier period of nationalist struggles and the transition to independence, and in *place* on the borders of the nation and the people moving across it, be reinvigorated. Like Ruth Lister (1997, 195), I believe that citizenship provides both an invaluable theoretical concept for the analysis of women's subordination as well as a potentially powerful political weapon in the struggle against it. Here I am using "citizenship" to connote both a status with a notion of personhood in the legal and bureaucratic sense and carrying a set of rights with it, and as a practice implying participation in public institutions broadly defined (Lister 1997, 196; Berkovitch 1999, 10).

Taking notional rights in a constitutional text to be conclusive of citizenship has not been very productive. The abstractness of the exercise simply causes us to abandon citizenship as a way of understanding life in the nation. The renewal of a meaningful discourse about citizenship in the Caribbean will show that, notwithstanding the gender neutrality of many citizenship laws in the Caribbean and the language of equality implied in Caribbean constitutions, men remain the paradigm of a citizen and, in significant measure, women are included as citizens through their relationship to men. At another level, an exploration of citizenship demonstrates how law and life are not polarities and that law is cultural practice and gender discourse as well. Feminist theorizing on the question of citizenship also offers new possibilities for critical feminist practice. Theorizing citizenship in the Caribbean today, seeing what roles we expect men and women to play in the life of the nation, provides a way of understanding the contentious front lines of gender politics, where the "woman question" has become so controversial that it can hardly be discussed, and the contradictory moments of public engagement where it looks like the "woman question" is being discussed, but where women's bodies, objectified and given meaning by others, form the centre of a debate that is not necessarily committed to discovering women's humanity, totality and embodied selves. Ultimately I believe that using citizenship as everyday discourse can provide a unique opportunity to preserve women as "active and intentional subjects" (Grbich

1991, 75) and maintain the legitimacy of women as the subject of analysis and activism.

The constitutions of the Commonwealth Caribbean – their texts, interpretation and the process of reforming them – are my site of analysis. As the highest law in the land, each constitution establishes the powers of the state, defines the citizenry and explicates the relationship between the two. For my discussion, as important as what a constitution does is what it represents: "it is a document of immense dimensions, portraying, as it does, the vision of the people's future".[2] Constitutional law is a conversation in which fundamental questions about the organization of social and political life are self-consciously and explicitly dealt with (Macklem 1988, 118). Consequently, constitutional language, discourse and process must be understood as valuable elements of gender discourse, ideology and cultural practice.

I will confess that I am trying to do many things at once in this chapter and I am aware that the result is a measure of incompleteness – that some themes raised cannot be adequately addressed here. Interpolated with my inquiries about citizenship is a larger conversation about the relation between *life* and *law,* one I began elsewhere (Robinson 2000). When compared with the humanities and social sciences, there has been an even more noticeable dearth of feminist theorizing in law in the Caribbean, but notwithstanding this, law continues to be heavily employed by Caribbean feminists as a tool of empowerment and liberation. The under-theorization of law is not dissonant with the centring of law; it is itself the product of the way in which law has been foregrounded through mystique. Caribbean people express cynicism about those who are involved in the administration of law, but they still to a large degree believe in law. This is a type of faith, by which I mean a belief premised on some notion of a truth that people feel they will never fully understand. The enthusiasm for law is often born out of a perception that law is somehow bigger than life and beyond human comprehension. Nowhere is this truer than with the constitution, whose supremacy as law lends to slippage into feeling that it was authored by omnipotent beings and, for many, a good life comprises contemplating its meaning and trying to understand the intent of its framers.

As a feminist lawyer I am anxious to challenge this notion that law stands apart from, even above, life. I want to further explore the dichotomous picture of law as the embodiment of truth and rationality and life as full of subjectivities. When I speak of "life" here I am in part speaking about the nature of things, "a reflection of how things are, those things we cannot change and must simply accept, best summed up in the expression, 'That's life' " (Robinson 2000, 3). In this chapter I move through denser and thinner layers of law's abstraction and life's unchallenged assumptions, using the construction of citizenship for women to allegorize the relation between law and life. I start in the eye of law – the text of the constitution – where there is an unnatural calm disconnected from the turbulence all around, and the capacity for vision and understanding truth looks clearest here. In this exalted world, only tiny specks of life appear, but I see them as the salt – flavouring and giving meaning to the words in the text. Shifting gears after the first two sections, I step out of the dense calm of legal doctrine and text to a more animated law, this time of legal processes and personnel enacted in legal spaces such as the courtroom. Here it is possible to do more than identify from the text a *viewpoint* of women in law; one can catch a *view* of women in law. In the last two sections I emerge most fully into the visceral elements of life, where we see the most materialized images of women and feel the fiery politics of gender. Law seems distant but it contours our sense of the way things are – our conviction about the natural order of things. Whatever the vantage point of looking at citizenship for women, the relation between law and life is not one of dissociation or polarity, as it often appears, but of complex constituting and reconstitutings of each other (see Maurer 1997). Each angle of viewing the construction of citizenship reveals different layers of what are often mutually reinforcing insights about gender ideologies and practice in the Caribbean.

Defining "We the People"

The constitutional history of the region predates independence; contrary to common perception, written constitutions in the Caribbean were not an innovation of independence. Likewise the enfranchisement of women in the Commonwealth Caribbean, generally through universal adult suffrage, preceded dates of independence. Nonetheless the texts designed to give effect to independence signified the defining moment in the formation of the modern nation-state in the Caribbean and offer a useful entry point to the question of women and citizenship.

The early independence constitutions in the Caribbean explicitly created classes of citizenship for men and women.[3] Men were given rights – not afforded to women – to pass on citizenship to their foreign spouses and children born outside the jurisdiction.[4] Only unwed mothers of children born outside the jurisdiction automatically passed on citizenship to those children. Here citizenship passing through the maternal line was entirely by default because, under the common law, that child was *filius nullius,* belonging to no one. The patriarchal family therefore was the constitutional foundation, and the male head of household was the paradigm of a citizen. Women and children were cast as dependants of men and obtained their rights to participate in civil society through men. During the second wave of independence, from the 1970s onwards, and through later reforms of the early constitutions,[5] Caribbean countries abandoned most of the discriminatory language of the early texts, and today we find almost everywhere in the region gender-neutral language in the citizenship provisions of the constitutions. The Bahamas and Barbados are the only two independent Caribbean countries that still contain these patently discriminatory provisions, and it is fairly certain that the latter will remove them.[6]

Women's full incorporation into the nation as citizens is often assumed from those provisions in the constitutions that imply that men and women are entitled to equal rights, as well as those that grant men and women equal rights to transmit citizenship to their spouses and children. In fact, there is no inevitability about full citizenship for women arising from such constitutional provisions. Guyana, the Caribbean country with the most wide-ranging human rights protection in its constitution, makes this clear quite dramatically. The Constitution of the Co-operative Republic of Guyana (1980) has in article 29 the most definitive language guaranteeing gender equality that can be found in a Commonwealth Caribbean constitution. This article speaks not just to civil and political rights, but to some key social and economic rights for women. It states that men and women have equal rights and the same legal status in all spheres of political, economic and social life. It outlaws all forms of discrimination against women on the basis of their sex. It goes further to ensure the exercise of women's rights, by according women equal access with men to academic, vocational and professional training, equal opportunities in employment, remuneration and promotion, and in social, political and cultural activity, by special labour and health protection measures for women, by providing conditions enabling mothers to work, and by legal protection and material and moral support for mothers and children, including paid leave and other benefits for mothers and expectant mothers. (Guyana 1980)

In 1982 the Guyana Court of Appeal in *Nielsen v. Barker*[7] considered the meaning of equality in article 29. It was examining an immigration law that established who qualified as a "belonger" in Guyana. The foreign wife of a Guyanese male citizen had belonger status under the legislation because she was deemed to be a dependant of her husband, but the foreign husband of Guyanese female citizen was excluded from the definition of "dependant" and therefore could not qualify as a belonger. The judges of the Court of Appeal concluded that "what is said in [article 29, the equality clause] has in no way altered and is in no way inconsistent with the concept of 'dependency' for the purposes of the Immigration Act".[8] In effect they held that this law, which failed to give Guyanese women equal rights as citizens to confer status on their foreign spouses to reside in the country, did not conflict with the guarantee in article 29 of equal rights for men and women and the same legal status in all spheres of political, economic and social life.

This remarkable conclusion was partly explained by one of the judges, Massiah JA, in this way:

In order to have a proper apprehension of article 29 of the Constitution there is a need to understand the conceptual framework within which that provision was formulated. This can only be done if there is a true understanding of and regard for the historical evolution of feminine emancipation. Central to it all is the desire to achieve equality of the sexes; *it has nothing to do with the elevation of the man.*[9] (Emphasis in the text.)

The Court of Appeal was manifestly anxious that the applicant, Mr Nielsen, an escaped convicted criminal from Denmark, should not benefit from belonger status under the immigration legislation. At times this looks like the whole point of the case, but it is not. Mr Nielsen's wilfulness and wiliness, in overcoming the boundaries of prison, travelling far across the Atlantic into South America, finding a wife and settling in the land, presented flashes of the quintessential pioneering citizen (albeit misdirecting his energies). His dishonesty lay not just in his pretending to be a *bona fide* immigrant and turning out to be a serious criminal, but in his invocation of subordinate status when his mettle epitomized citizenship. The missive was: "You are a man; stop pretending to be a woman by trying to belong. Maintain your dignity as a man; go back to the land of your citizenship; a man's cell can be his castle."

There is another context in which the judges were worried about the "elevation of the man". They had a concern that a gender-neutral definition of dependency could impose on a wife the responsibility for financial support of her husband. In circumstances where women still experience economic vulnerability, there is always a legitimate query about the application of "identical treatment" of men and women in family law, but the judges did not explore this. In fact their insistence on the congruity between *equality for women* and *dependency status of women* resonates more powerfully in the social and political registers than in the economic one they were asserting. This is because Caribbean women have always been expected to achieve a certain degree of economic independence. There is no illusion that women's commitment to the family should preclude paid work or other income-generating activities. Carla Freeman (2000, 109, 112) observes that even idealized prescriptions for femininity treat economic independence and work as integral to womanhood and also that this work is interpreted as an expression of familial obligation. The same article 29 of the Guyana Constitution articulates much the same when it says that equality means, among other things, that mothers must be facilitated in the economic support of their families with the provision of "conditions enabling mothers to work and by legal protection and material and moral support for mothers and children, including paid leave and other benefits for mothers and expectant mothers" (Guyana 1980).

What we are then left with, though the judges of the Court of Appeal hardly said so, is a description of women as socially and politically less than men. Dependency in this context imports most strongly status inferiority and subordination. It is the antithesis of citizenship, especially in the post-colonial age, when the developing concept of citizenship has been so firmly linked to independence (Fraser and Gordon 1997, 28–30).

At a fundamental level, I think it was the idea that men could be characterized as dependants (not *the* citizen, but *a* citizen) that was truly unimaginable. If we look at the opening words of the Guyana constitution, the preamble, we can see that, despite the impressive language guaranteeing equal rights to women and men and the official commitment to advancing the position of women, men remain the paradigmatic citizens in Guyana. It reads, "We the People of the Co-operative Republic of Guyana" are "the proud *heirs* of the indomitable spirit and unconquerable will of our *forefathers* who by their sacrifices, their blood and their labour made rich and fertile and bequeathed to us our inalienable *patrimony* for all time this green land of Guyana" (Guyana 1980; emphasis added).

On reading these opening words, instinctively we understand "We the People" to be men, but immediately deny that this could be so. We tell ourselves that women must be included, because we know that to be the mandate of gender equality that the same constitution so vigorously asserts. The problem is to get women to fit into "We the People"; they do not readily, except tangentially as the mothers, sisters and daughters of the men. Men remain the centre of constitutional concern. As a Women in the Caribbean Project (WICP) respondent said, "You see a woman because you see a man; you say so and so and his wife" (Barrow 1986a, 51). Women are not excluded from citizenship, but that citizenship is conceived first in terms of women's relationship to the paradigmatic citizens, men (Robinson 2000).

Shades of Equality and the Hierarchy of Rights

Most of us read the reasoning of the Guyanese Court of Appeal in *Nielsen* with a measure of surprise. We might be prepared to acknowledge the patriarchal foundations of the nationalist project that produced Caribbean constitutions. We might also readily admit, as Belinda Edmondson (1999b, 8) urges, that the idea of the nation was inseparable from the issue of defining West Indian manhood. She observes that Victorian debates on whether or not the Caribbean region was deserving of independence often revolved around the issue of black West Indian masculinity: could Caribbean men prove themselves to be the masculine equals of Englishmen? Still, we tend to conceive equality, once articulated even in its most general sense, as having the force of inevitability. At the very least at an emotional level, especially given our still intimate connection in the contemporary Caribbean to the nationalist struggles, many of us want to say that the race-centred nationalism "*incorporated women freely* with an *understated and unarticulated concept of equality* . . . that has worked in favour of women . . . in the postcolonial era into the present . . ." (Mohammed 1997, 25; emphasis added). The element of surprise in the *Nielsen* case is partly related to how willing we are to acknowledge the extent to which the nationalist project manifested and reproduced male forms of domination that formed a continuum from colonial times to the construction of a post-colonial society (Lewis 2000, 270). We are sometimes least able to come to terms with our fear that perhaps, as Natasha Barnes puts it, "nationalist commitments, rather than simply delaying the development of feminist identity politics, made its male and female ideologues downright hostile to the epistemological revisioning that a feminist intellectual and political agenda would demand" (1999, 38).

What I am pointing to here is how we construct an image of equality's certainty and indisputability while qualifying it by pitch – describing it as having the capacity to be "understated" and "unarticulated" and, I suppose, also "overstated" and "clearly articulated". What do such qualifications mean for the very idea of equality? In this section I plan to explore the contradictions that inhere in equality when we listen to tone and pitch, not to suggest abandoning it as a theoretical construct or strategic device for women, but in order to encourage a more sophisticated appreciation of how it works and its strengths and limitations (Lacey 1998, 180). Here, through the constitutions, I step into the centre of law – what I will call the eye of law. There might be instability all around and within it, yet the eye of this system (for me, constitutional texts and jurisprudence) maintains the appearance of calm and coherence. My aim is to show the disruptions we experience once we ask broader questions about constitutional meaning.

The words on the parchment on which constitutional texts are inscribed tell only part of the story. Constitutional meaning derives from the tone and rhythm of the conversation about the organization of social and political life that constitutional law fundamentally is. The eloquence and rhetoric, even the hesitation, in that discourse are what enliven the words brought together in the text. Recently, an interim bill to amend the chapter protecting fundamental rights and freedoms in the Jamaica constitution (1962) was tabled before Parliament, but a clear prohibition against gender discrimination, an omission in the existing constitution, was not included in the bill. There was no dispute about the need for reform, but it became a question of priority. The attorney general explained that the issue of gender as a constitutional right would eventually be looked at, but had not been included in the interim bill because "we have put into that Bill *matters which are of the utmost importance* like the right to vote, the right to hold a passport, to have fair treatment". He added: "I am *not saying gender is not important* . . . It is intended that the new charter on fundamental rights will be tabled within weeks and will include the provision that has to do with discrimination on the grounds of gender" (Ansine 1999; emphasis added).

The attorney general describes a hierarchy of rights in which gender equality is "not unimportant" but fails to rank as being "of the utmost importance". By making a distinction between the right to gender equality and the right to vote and have fair treatment, he also alludes to discontinuity between gender equality and citizenship, in that women's rights might not be understood to clearly originate in the concept of citizenship. The rights to vote and have fair treatment are examples of traditional civil and political rights deeply associated with citizenship and participation in the life of the nation. The attorney general first ranks these civil and political rights most highly, then distinguishes women's rights from those civil and political rights. Gender equality thus lies, in this reading, outside the heart of citizenship rights. In this vein, its meaning derives not just from the new provision that will ultimately find its way into the final draft of constitutional amendments, but is shaded by the pause of almost forty years since independence in effecting constitutional reform, the placative tone calling for patience and the resonance of rights of the "utmost importance".

When a constitution is read with an *ear* for nuance, even aspects of constitutional doctrine and tools of constitutional interpretation become visible as gender ideology and practice. The chapter protecting fundamental rights and freedoms in most Caribbean constitutions begins with the assertion that "every person . . . is entitled to the fundamental rights and freedoms . . . whatever his . . . sex",[10] but when moved from the level of abstraction, a hierarchy of rights – those not "unimportant" and those "of the utmost importance" – comes into view. This opening section to the Bill of Rights is the plainest language to be found in most of the Caribbean constitutions speaking to gender equality, and it has been described as merely "a declaratory section, a forerunner of things to come worthy of protection".[11] The logic was that the redress clause in Caribbean constitutions, the one that gives the Supreme or High Court jurisdiction to grant appropriate remedies and redress for breach of the provisions in the Bill of Rights, fails to expressly include this opening section.[12] This argument has always had a tinge of disingenuity, because that very same opening section has been crucial in interpreting the Bill of Rights. Moreover in another context the Privy Council recently gave full effect to the right to "protection of the law" in the introductory section of the Jamaica Bill of Rights.[13]

The notional rights in a constitutional text tell us little about which claims will survive when judges begin the exercise of balancing competing rights and interests. Rights are inherently antagonistic; their authority comes from being able to trump other interests, but they are also structured to yield to the rights of others or if state interest requires it, or if a limitation on the right is reasonably justifiable in a democratic society.[14] In constitutional interpretation this balancing exercise provides larger constitutional meaning and is yet another component that constructs the hierarchy of rights, as illustrated in the St Lucian case *Girard v. Attorney General*.[15] In 1982 the dismissal of two unmarried teachers pregnant with their second children was held by the St Lucia High Court not to violate, among other things, the section in the constitution providing protection against discrimination on the grounds of sex. The dismissals were pursuant to regulations in the teaching service legislation that said an unmarried female teacher was to be suspended on her first pregnancy and dismissed on her second. There were no comparable regulations dealing with married female teachers or unmarried male teachers. The High Court judge started from the presumption that the dismissals were constitutionally permissible and held that the applicants failed to shift that presumption of constitutionality. The judge went further: even if this were a case of discriminatory treatment on the basis of sex, it was one in which the constitution permitted the state to limit that right because the teaching service regulations were "reasonably justifiable in a democratic society".[16]

Surprisingly, the judge failed to explain to what demands of democracy the protection against sex discrimination had to yield. I can only conclude that he was presenting a version of democracy within which were embedded fundamental assumptions about the roles of men and women as citizens in the post-independence Caribbean and in particular, a sentiment that women as citizens have a special responsibility to the nation as purveyors and guardians of the moral code and producers and reproducers of true citizens – a job that pregnant unmarried teachers could not properly perform. Since men have a different role as citizens, what was considered unacceptable behaviour for women could be tolerated from men, giving the double standard constitutional imprimatur.

By saying that the construction of citizenship creates shades of meaning on notional rights such as equality I am not suggesting that citizenship is the original concept that then gives substance to rights thereafter, because citizenship and rights implicate each other in ways that are hardly unidirectional. In essence I am arguing that theoretical debates about models of citizenship, especially the liberal vision of citizenship as a bundle of rights, are misconceived if in the first instance we view rights as having some indubitable meaning, stabilized in law, that we can then quantify in degrees of personhood. Narratives of life unfold the contradictions in concepts such as equality, just as they conceal them too, signalling the futility of uncritically deriving citizenship from rights. What I have been emphasizing is how aspects of constitutional discourse and equality talk lie in uncontested terrain, that eye of law that appears unwaveringly tranquil but is a shifting locus of larger oppositions and conflict. The need to theorize the deceptive landscape of constitutionalism has been the centre of my reflections here, but later on in this chapter it will be much more apparent that I believe in constitutionalism and do not disavow rights discourse, and ultimately I will offer the mining of this under-explored terrain as critical feminist practice.

On Being the Object of Rights

I have just argued that we can see shades of equality and grades of citizens within constitutional doctrine and reasoning, in places where we rarely look. There, I was speaking most like a lawyer, by which I mean from within the law and surrounded by legal devices – texts, case-law and doctrines. Law gives its best show of internal coherence and autonomy from this position; nevertheless I attempted, even from this orientation as an insider, to question the presumed neutrality of law and demonstrate the interconnectedness between law and life. Now I plan to step out into what might be considered a thinner layer of law as abstraction and mysticism – from law as technique and method reified through inscription and encasement in legislation, written judgements and law journals, to the rawer element of law as process, as it is enacted, for example, in courtrooms, courtyards, police stations and police lock-ups. Here we are able to move beyond identifying a *viewpoint* of women in law to actually catch a *view* of women in law.

In this other space, which I am about to describe through a story that begins for us in a courthouse in Jamaica, continues in a jail yard and then spills out into the houses and yards of Jamaica, women find their disembodied selves in the middle of a rights discourse to which they are marginal, and silent and silenced women capture the nation's imagination. When we do hear women, they are subordinated to the status of mere witnesses in the matters that affect them most. These are moments when almost everyone appears to be talking about women's lives and it seems that the call for gender justice has achieved universal support, but during these periods the nation chooses to see women most when they can hear them least.

In January 1997 in Jamaica the case of the "soft-spoken" rape complainant received widespread public attention. A twenty-two-year-old woman from a rural parish came to Kingston to give evidence for the prosecution against a man accused of raping her. Her voice was barely perceptible during her evidence and the judge repeatedly asked her to speak louder. Increasingly annoyed at his inability to hear what she was saying, he threatened to detain her if she did not speak up. At the lunchtime adjournment, he ordered that she be examined by a doctor overnight and told the police to "take her safely, give her food and keep her at a safe place" (*Gleaner* 1997b, 1). Less euphemistically, she was being remanded in custody to the Fort Augusta Prison, where she spent the night while the accused was out on bail.

There was a huge public outcry, spontaneous demonstrations were held outside the Supreme Court building in Kingston, and numerous civic, political and professional organizations registered their outrage and condemnation of the judge's action (*Gleaner* 1997a, A3).[17] Anonymous because of confidentiality rules, and inaudible, the young woman in this case was a body devoid of personhood, ready to be filled with meaning by those talking around her, about her and even for her. She was made to embody and symbolize the injustice experienced by all Jamaicans. "The Jamaican people have suffered enough injustice," said the Citizens' Initiative Organisation, "and cannot suffer further injustice in institutions where justice is expected to be obtained" (*Gleaner* 1997a, A3).[18] This young woman's story was co-opted into a universal narrative. The principles of justice and fairness became vested with a life of their own, divorced from the specific experiences they should address (Majury 1991, 331). The story was bigger than her, and in a short time had little to do with her. She represented everyone but herself and her own reality.

The power of the woman's story in the hands of its interpreters lay in the fact that, unlike the amorphous state, here injustice had a discernible face – that of the trial judge. The injustice to her was localized in one person, or at most in the judicial system. By focusing on the actions of the judge, everyone else was free to use her body for righteous articulation by placing themselves on the outside of the systematic forces that oppress poor women. The judge was demonized for what was undoubtedly a deplorable decision, but little thought was given to the less invidious complicity of life and law around her – including the noisy outrage – in silencing her (Robinson 2000).

Talking about women does not equal greater awareness of women's gendered lives. Many of the times when it seems as if everyone is talking about the condition of women, their experiences are made generic, and gender becomes less consequential as a way of analysing life in the nation. The feminist narrative is completely inverted. Part of the feminist goal is to preserve women as "active and intentional subjects" (Grbich 1991, 75), but during these moments of public engagement, the bodies of silent and silenced women are given over to valorize civic sensibilities that define woman-centred work and thought outside the national good. We as feminists have insisted that women experience a specific kind of injustice that has its origins in the hierarchical relations of gender, and that this implicates all institutions of society, including the interpreters. But here the public interest tends to be premised on exactly the opposite: the experiences of women gain wide appeal because they are described as typical of the injustice others in society face, but in their own facts those same experiences are newsworthy because they are treated as exceptional. Women's reality comes to represent every form of injustice other than what it is, and its intrinsic meaning is eroded and classified as unusual. The antagonism between feminist goals and the national good is pressed into and absorbed by women's bodies, but this does not make the conflict any less authentic than when, as I later discuss in the case of Antigua, women reject civicism by demanding attention be given to their particular concerns and needs.

The question of citizenship is no more resolved by locating it in the constitution rights that may benefit women than it is by identifying women within rights talk. Both the *viewpoints* on women discerned from constitutional discourse and the *views* we caught of women within the broader public conversation about rights convey a marginality for women in citizenship terms, itself in part a reflection of the graded shades of equality.

Regarding the Meaning of "Feminine Emancipation": The Liberated Feminine Woman

I have been trying so far to extract the idea of the citizen from conversations about the organization of social and political life in the Caribbean – a dialogue that was in one case circumscribed by the constitution but in the other less contained and defined. I have up till now presented only glimpses of women in and through the law, and in this exercise I may have left an impression that the present construction of citizenship does not contemplate any agency in women. In this section I want to say more about construction of citizenship for women through a more materialized image that offers a constricted space for women to participate as citizens: that of the liberated feminine woman.

Making sense of what citizenship means for women in the Caribbean today requires an understanding of and regard for the meaning of "feminine emancipation"– the idea that Massiah JA articulated in the *Nielsen* case. I believe that what feminine emancipation does is venerate femininity in political terms; it redefines feminine identity – the primary source of which in the Caribbean is motherhood, and marriage to a lesser extent (Powell 1986, 83; Mohammed and Perkins 1999, 121) – as service to the nation and the basis of citizenship for women. Even if women do not have children themselves, they are expected to parent the children of other women (Powell 1986, 87). Motherhood and marriage no longer set women apart from politics and citizenship. Through feminine emancipation these now form bases for participation (Pateman 1992). This is, as Carol Pateman (1992) puts it, the paradox of women's political standing, because motherhood represents all that excluded women from citizenship, but it is also the central mechanism through which women have been incorporated into the modern political order. Alternatively, as articulated by Nira Yuval-Davis and Pnina Werbner, "the denial of women's role as equal citizens in the public sphere arises not only from their relegation to the familial sphere but also from their simultaneous elevation as reproducers of the nation" (1999, 1). In this way, feminine emancipation provides opportunities for women's progress and participation in the life of the nation, but it necessarily circumscribes them with ideals of femininity.

In examining the idea of the liberated feminine woman, my goal is not to present a comprehensive picture of Caribbean womanhood – that is neither possible nor desirable – but to offer strategic examples. The discussion centres around *married women* and *unmarried mothers* because these images afford me an opportunity to focus on marriage and motherhood separately, albeit somewhat artificially, as key sites where women prove that they are good citizens or not. In the first of my illustrations the liberated feminine woman who evolves from feminine emancipation is married and she gets involved in the formal political life of the nation, but does so behind the scenes. In the second example we meet the woman, commonly termed "the powerful matriarch", whose mothering has a particular political meaning. This woman rises to citizenship through her leadership in the family, but often against a backdrop of economic disadvantage and disempowerment.

Law is not in the foreground of my analysis here, but neither is it far from it. Notions of legitimacy and illegitimacy, grounded in legal and social meaning, construct and reconstruct feminine identity, thereby contributing to a common-sense perception of women's distinctive nature (Smart 1990, 201). That "natural" difference or distinctive nature is then used to justify and constrain access to citizenship for women. Through his analysis of citizenship and law in the British Virgin Islands, Bill Maurer (1997) describes how social status is over-determined, a moral order that stresses equality of persons and belonging to the nation and explains inequality and failing to belong with reference to people's "nature". He explains that law and nature are mutually constitutive but give the illusion of separateness and internal coherence. In considering the "naturalness" of motherhood and marriage for women – the idea that "it is a selfish woman who really would not want to get married and have children and look after a man . . . [because] that's what we women were made for" (Powell 1986, 83) – and its translation into "mothers of the nation", we must pay keen attention to how law helps to institute and reproduce organizing concepts such as motherhood and wifehood. Here I am alluding, especially as I go on to look at married women and unmarried mothers, to how we in the Caribbean talk about "*legal* marriage" and "*illegitimate* children" as emblematic of life, and with seeming indifference to the role of law.

The political mobilization of some married women in Antigua during law-reform debates is one example of the method of the emancipated or liberated feminine woman. These women played a significant role in delaying the passage of the Status of Children Act and the Births Act, which, among other things, removed legal discrimination based on birth status and gave children born outside of marriage the same rights to inherit their father's property as those born inside marriage. The women also ensured that a new Intestate Estates Act, which would strengthen the rights of surviving spouses on intestacy, was put before Parliament. These women wielded their political power quietly and outside the formal system; they spoke to their husbands and ministers, made personal phone calls to officials and arranged a private appointment with the prime minister (Lazarus-Black 1994, 232). The assertion of political power by these women was to protect their feminine identity as wives and mothers and, as Mindie Lazarus-Black (1994, 234) explains, they did so within the confines of everyday norms prescribing gender hierarchy. The political sensibilities of the liberated feminine woman are exercised within a traditional account of femininity and deference to men. She is understood to be a citizen, but her inclusion in "We the People" emanates from her relationship as wife and mother to the archetype citizen – man – which in turn dictates the substance and manner of her political action.

Most thinkers correctly point to the primacy of motherhood over marriage as the defining element of Caribbean femininity; nevertheless there is a singularity, seen in the Antiguan example, with which married women are expected to defend the "protective shield of the title of Mrs." (Durant-Gonzalez 1982, 6) that is not fully captured in the generalization. True enough, Caribbean women generally begin their reproductive life without marriage, but that reality cannot deny the considerable force that marriage still has as an ideal for women. Being able to define oneself socially and legally by reference to a man through marriage provides a distinct form of legitimacy and acceptance for women in the eyes of the community that should not be underestimated. The legitimating force also constrains, because marriage for women is still associated with ideas of social and political dependence that are constituted in ideologies of femininity.

Notwithstanding this, the actions of this liberated feminine woman can have a transforming effect, as seen in Antigua. It is not just that her interests coincide with her feminine identity; also critical is that she understands motherhood and marriage in political terms – therein lies the liberation. That these women were representing their own interests and not those of their husbands (even though defending a pre-eminent status for wives) was the whole point of their advocacy. The Antiguan women worked through men and used their status through men, but in the process they articulated their own specific concerns and needs as a group of women, as distinct from their husbands or married men in general, who were anxious to have their *de facto* families recognized. These women received censure and were characterized by others as being jealous and selfishly motivated by financial considerations (Lazarus-Black 1994, 233). They challenged an ideology that good women do not pursue narrow individual interests but commit themselves to the good of others; masculinity is the proper domain for such individualism. The very women whose method of operating was distinctly feminine treaded perilously close to the edge of femininity in their substantive goals.

The crux of the matter is that the idea of the liberated feminine woman is inherently unstable. We already know that liberation mediated through femininity provides access to citizenship for women, but that ideals of femininity constrain women's possibilities as citizens. Citizenship in these terms is no comfort zone for women. The dynamism generated by the emancipatory possibilities within liberated femininity place women in the ordinary course of engaging it on a swinging tightrope, with one foot on the slender rope of "good citizen" and the other dangling over the abyss of "transgressive citizen", trying to find its footing. Maintaining a balance is an impossible undertaking.

The counterpoint to the liberated feminine woman I have just described – married and privately involved in traditional political activity – is the unmarried mother whose mothering is over-politicized. Paradoxically, she too can be a liberated feminine woman, but this time it is the status of *il*legitimacy that helps produce legitimacy in the public domain. We can recall how the early Caribbean constitutions gave unmarried women rights to pass on citizenship to their children born outside of the jurisdiction, superior rights to those of married women or unmarried men. The child born to an unmarried woman resided in the realm of the illegal – at common law, belonged to no one – and the mother acquired superior rights as a parent. Even if by default, unmarried mothers gained the right to govern their children and to head a household – the very things that initiate men's authenticity as citizens.

When I speak of the unmarried mother as a liberated feminine woman, I am pointing to the image of a woman who is presently romanticized as a powerful matriarch, who "could work miracles, she would make a garment from a square of cloth in a span of time. Or feed twenty people on a stew made from fallen-from-the head cabbage and a carrot and a cho-cho and a palmful of meat" (Lorna Goodison, "My Mother", quoted in Senior 1991, ii). Her liberation comes from her leadership, but she maintains her femininity by sacrificing everything, even herself, for her children. The emphasis is always on the "miracles" she performs for others, and an investigation of her own vulnerability, disadvantage and gendered life only detracts from her mythical image. The bitter irony of her visibility as a citizen is that the household she heads is likely to be among the poorest in the nation. It is a cruel joke to describe her daily struggles for economic survival on behalf of herself and her family as "enjoying economic independence" in an environment where women still generally earn less, often experience higher levels of unemployment and bear a disproportionate amount of the burden of work in the home.

The unmarried mother, not unlike the married women discussed earlier, has to negotiate a delicate balance between the potential of liberation and the expectations of femininity. Her leadership in the home places her within the traditional meaning of true citizenship, except that it is family headship by *men* that is the wellspring of citizenship. The ideology of men's right to rule their families is not destroyed. As a result, women's visibility as citizens in this regard is never far from the reproach of transgressive citizenship. The flip side of the romanticization of mothers' strength and their characterization as matriarchs is always the complaint that women are beginning to look *too much* like citizens and that they are behaving like men, beginning to emasculate men. I will return to this theme later. The domain of the illegal operates in a similar way for unmarried mothers as the legal does for married women – it opens access but limits it as well. What is valued is not the matriarch's leadership itself, but that it produces valuable citizens. To maintain her femininity she must remain selfless and ego-less, gain her reward through what her offspring become and leave the leadership of the nation to the "heirs of the indomitable spirit and unconquerable will of our forefathers" (Guyana 1980).

The avenue for legitimacy founded in illegitimacy never quite escapes its origins. This was the upshot of the *Girard* case I discussed earlier. The unmarried pregnant women who were suspended and dismissed from the teaching service were excluded from full participation in the nation as citizens. They were cast as immoral women who failed to meet the appropriate standard for instructing children. The construction of citizenship for women within feminine identity has given women a special role as guardians of the moral code. As citizens women are expected to fiercely defend the nation by protecting their own honour, by guarding the conjugal family and "culture", which is defined as the transmission of a fixed set of proper values to children (Alexander 1994, 13). Teaching children is the professional embodiment of citizenship for women. Some notion of morality was used to explain the legal response in *Girard* – dismissal or suspension under the legislation – but less visible was the way in which law helped to constitute that immorality through the concept of illegitimacy.

There is an incongruous aspect of the St Lucian case *Girard*. Prior to the legal action taken by the teachers who were dismissed, their union and the government had negotiated and signed a collective agreement, one of the terms of which was that all female teachers, married and unmarried, would be entitled to maternity leave. Ironically, the teachers were dismissed after applying for this benefit. The Court of Appeal ultimately held that the collective agreement was not binding because it had not been properly ratified, and the dismissals were therefore justifiable.[19] These two contradictory faces of state desire – one giving maternity leave to unmarried pregnant teachers, the other dismissing or suspending those same teachers – underscore the complexity of the state's politicization of motherhood and marriage for women. The St Lucian teachers were making a plea for sexual autonomy and privacy in reproduction, but evidently one consequence of emphasizing motherhood and marriage as the medium through which to effect women's liberation is increased surveillance of women's reproductive and familial lives and policing of women's bodies. If women are incorporated into the life of the nation as reproducers of citizens and as the supportive partners of real citizens, then it comes as no surprise that state scrutiny of those functions can be intense.

Wide-ranging reforms over the past twenty-five years that have focused on women's roles as wives and mothers are the product of state initiatives and feminist activism and have resulted in important practical benefits for women. Throughout the Caribbean, working mothers are generally entitled to some form of maternity leave. Unmarried mothers now have better rights to child support and married women are more likely than ever to receive an equitable division of matrimonial property on divorce. And greater protection is available against domestic violence. The danger is that some of these reforms have tended to stereotype women as dependants or clients of the state (Thornton 1995, 198), as the "perennial supplicant, permanently grateful, and . . . as guardians of the minimal" (Alexander 1997, 78). In this mode, women are treated as a special interest group and are therefore not seen to be challenging the basic structures of society or raising any important new political questions (Diamond and Hartsock 1998, 193). At the same time, the state gains legitimacy through these initiatives by, as Jacqui Alexander (1997, 73) suggests, usurping the popular narrative of struggle and converting it into a hegemonic narrative of deliverance initiated by the state as benign patriarch. Alexander further argues that the state draws on women's political mobilizations as evidence that democracy is working, of its own advanced political governance and political and constitutional mature evolution.

In such moments, the liberated *feminist* woman who stands in the forefront of struggles for women's equality looks little different from the liberated *feminine* woman who works from the background. While the liberated feminine woman depends on men to represent her interests in the outside world, for the liberated feminist it is the state that emerges as the patriarch upon whom she relies greatly for emancipation. This existence is fraught with contradictory prospects generated by the frictions in liberated femininity. Women can be granted maternity leave on one hand and be fired for being pregnant without benefit of marriage on the other. Some women are romanticized for their strength as mothers, and in less than a moment castigated for emasculating their sons and lovers. Other women will get respect for exercising feminine decorum in politicking but in the same breath receive reprobation for looking out only for themselves. Liberated femininity is always in the neighbourhood of transgressive citizenship, and that is key to understanding the politics of gender in the Caribbean today, which I am about to discuss.

The Politics of Gender: Strife at the Front Lines and Uncontested Terrain

The discourse on the relation between law and life that I have engaged in so far has been formulated through the project of theorizing citizenship. I have been trying to unearth the idea of the citizen from narratives of law and life in the Caribbean, but more to urge its value than to describe its present-day relevance. I want now to shift register somewhat to do more of the latter: to understand and describe the current political landscape in the Caribbean within which *citizenship linked to gender* is buried and depoliticized, even though questions of gender are at the fore of national attention. Quite simply, I want to contend that the earlier exercise of theorizing is critical to giving meaning to the latter – the nature and quality of the current politics of gender. At the front lines of gender politics in the Caribbean today, "woman questions" have become so contentious that they can hardly be discussed. While acknowledging women's progress, finding a space today to have a meaningful conversation about the ways in which women continue to be systematically disadvantaged is often like navigating a minefield. Caribbean feminists have been put squarely on the defensive, criticized for continuing to characterize women as having some unique claim on victimization, and rebuked for ignoring what is described as women's present-day dominance and the predicament of male marginalization.

The male marginalization thesis presented by professor of education Errol Miller (1991) has helped to script the public debate and has confirmed education's place of prominence within it. Persistently, success for men and for women is presented as inherently antagonistic because "the same forces which push black women forward in education, hold back black men; the same forces which emasculate black men advance the power of black women in society as an alternative to black men holding power" (Espeut 1998). Women's gain is commensurate with men's loss, as a matter not of coincidence but of logic.

What is astonishing is not so much that Miller's thesis has been substantially discredited by other scholars (Bailey 1997; Lindsay 1997; Figueroa 1997; Chevannes 1999; Barriteau 2000a), but that this critique has had virtually no impact on public consciousness. To some degree, the tenacity of the claims of male marginalization is linked to the idea that men are the paradigm of a citizen and women are included as citizens through their relationship to men; women then become secondary citizens with responsibility for producing and reproducing real citizens. Education is central because in the nationalist struggles one issue was whether black men could *learn* to become true citizens and leaders of the nation – education was seen as the performance and articulation of citizenship (see Unterhalter 1999). Some have described Dr Eric Williams, who self-consciously engaged pedagogical practices in engendering citizenship, as having given women a "feeling of nationhood" (Nesta Patrick, quoted in Reddock 1998c, 41). While prime minister of Trinidad and Tobago, he put it in these terms to the Nineteenth Convention of the Federation of Women's Institutes in 1965: "The young men of this country are only as strong or as weak as their mothers and wives have helped to make them . . . Whether they have a decent degree of discipline or not is so only to the degree their women-folk are prepared to tolerate, accept, condone . . ." (quoted in Brodber 1982, 50).

His was a description of women's role as citizens in the early post-independence period. Thirty-five years later, a radio advertisement in Barbados sponsored by Carlton's Supermarket captures the same sentiment. After castigating women for allowing men to act irresponsibly, it concludes: "Thank God for women, you are the only ones who can bring our men to their senses." Notice the "natural" order of things, how the strengths or weaknesses of men dominate imaginings of the nation. It is men in the first instance who are described as "We the People"; women come in not just through their relationship to men, but also through their responsibility to men. To be sure, the environment and the way we talk about the nation has changed. Williams captivated an audience in Woodford Square at the high point of nationalistic sentiment; today the arena is the market and comrades have become consumers and the voice of a supermarket owner now has a particular type of resonance. But there is continuity in the ideology that women collectively bear responsibility for the moral fibre of the nation and for reproducing and producing exemplary citizens. This is not simply about mothers raising sons or women in the family; it has become a burden of womanhood, of citizenship for all females, including girl children in coeducational schools, childless professional women, young women pursuing higher education and poor women working for very low wages in free-zone factories. Its end result is that the blame or the praise for what men achieve rest with womenfolk.

Amidst the hostility of anti-feminist rhetoric at the front lines is territory less explored by feminist theorists, where "woman questions" are deemed to be so uncontroversial as not to warrant any serious investigation. When the issue of women's general right to equality or to equal citizenship has been raised in recent debates on constitutional reform in the Caribbean, it is often given short shrift, not out of disagreement, but because the point is understood to be so well-established as not to warrant extensive discussion. During its tenure, the Barbados Constitution Review Commission, which was set up in 1996 and gave its report in 1998, was repeatedly urged by members of the public to recommend reform to the citizenship provisions that discriminated against Barbados women married to foreigners. At a public session held by the

Commission in Toronto, Canadian men married to Barbadian women raised the issue of citizenship again and spoke about the hardships suffered by their families because of the discriminatory laws. The members of the Commission pointed out that change in this regard was incontrovertible and that a recommendation for reform had been made by the National Commission on the Status of Women many years earlier (NCSW 1978). Norma Forde, a member of the Constitution Review Commission, had also been a member of the National Commission on the Status of Women, and she had filed a minority report against the recommendation by the latter commission for equality in transmitting citizenship. At the meeting in Toronto, Forde indicated that she was worried about the implications reform would have on Barbados and its services, because "everybody now wants to be a Barbadian". Now even she acknowledged that "the recommendations have already been made and . . . in Barbados everybody agrees with you, so we have to consider it seriously again". Another member of the Constitution Review Commission put it in stronger terms: "the door [for constitutional change of these citizenship provisions] is open and so many people are pushing against it that if anyone stands behind the open door they're in trouble" (Constitution Review Commission 1997, 49).

This image of annihilation for those who dared to challenge the assertion of women's right to equality from the weight of consensus on the matter looks like the antithesis of gender politics at the front lines. Nevertheless, what is taken to be an uncontroversial concept such as equality functions rhetorically in much the same way as the disputed "male marginalization" thesis. At the front lines, public discussion is obstructed by intense disputation and feminists are accused of behaving "as if women are the only gender needing liberation" (Espeut 1998), and in the distance it is averted by the appearance of consensus. I must add that the distinction between the front lines and the non-contentious background is not necessarily ideological. The resistance of the male marginalization discourse, just like the certitude about what equality means, can be located in largely uncontested assumptions, partly constituted through law, about the nature of men and women and their roles in the life of the nation.

The comparisons being made today between male and female achievement and performance many times signify a false dichotomy. The converse is true of equality, which gives what is often an erroneous impression of clarity and coherence. Male and female achievement and gender equality are superimposed on an uneven background of engendered citizenship, which in turn stabilizes benchmarks within which women can enjoy qualified equality, and beyond which they become overachievers at the expense of men. The comfort zone provided by the idea of equality rarely reveals the tensions arising from women's struggle to balance the possibilities for progress provided by liberation within ideals of femininity. Nor does the fierceness of the discourse about male marginalization lend itself to an interrogation of those indicators that determine when women's doing well turns subversive and emasculating, and when disappointment in men evidences marginalization.

Open Doors and Spaces for Engagement

Caribbean feminists face a quandary in responding to gender politics at the front lines. Feminist theorizing today requires introspection and a capacity for self-criticism, but also participation in the public debate. The dilemma now is how to be really heard, not just dismissed as women screaming loudly,[20] and how to contribute to public conversations about gender and maintain the legitimacy of women as the subject of analysis. I believe that the question of citizenship, currently neglected and under-explored and not yet affected by the volatility of the front lines, is a valuable place in the present landscape to do this. To be more precise, I believe that Caribbean constitutions, which define citizenship from a legal standpoint, and the ongoing process of constitutional reform can provide a distinct locus for engagement within public discourse.

The Commonwealth Caribbean has entered the twenty-first century with constitutional reform firmly established on regional and national agendas. Discussions are well advanced for the establishment of a Caribbean Court of Justice to replace the Privy Council, many are seriously considering moving towards republicanism, and dissatisfaction with the present system of parliamentary democracy continues to mount. We may be on the precipice of the most important wave of constitutional reform in the Caribbean since independence, and yet, although women and their concerns have in a few instances featured in the debate, they do not appear to have a central place in the process.

The distinction between the space in national life consumed with constitutional reform, which is almost indifferent to gender issues, and the front lines of intense dispute about gender may not be ideological but it has key strategic value. In the former there is a "door" the Barbadian Constitution Review commissioner refers to as "open" and against which "so many people are pushing" that provides a unique opportunity for engagement by feminists. For the most part Caribbean women have concentrated their energies on changing ordinary legislation when laws and state practice compromise gender equality, not on constitutional reform and litigation. They have had some good reasons, not least of all the specificity of statute law, as contrasted with a constitution, in targeting and dealing with areas of disadvantage. Constitutional litigation is not just expensive but also fraught with inherent uncertainty in interpreting the broad language found in constitutional documents. Changing the constitution is necessarily more difficult than ordinary legislative reform, requiring greater levels of parliamentary support and, in some cases, referenda. But I believe that the abstractness of the constitution should not deter us. To the contrary, it provides powerful reasons for engagement because the written constitution "contains not only the design and disposition of the powers of the state which it established but embodies the hopes and aspirations of the people".[21]

I am suggesting a far more comprehensive involvement in the reform process than securing women's rights in the texts of Caribbean constitutions, although this is without doubt an important goal. But it is the forum for discussion offered by the process of reform – the means to the end, and not simply the possibility of a better text – that presents women with a unique opportunity for exploring citizenship. The rhetoric about women's overachievement and male marginalization has made it very difficult to have a conversation in the Caribbean about the totality of women's lives or to have honest talk about what has actually been achieved in the post-independence era, how women are perceived today and how we understand their role in nation-building. The process of constitutional reform is necessarily protracted and provides the possibility of engaging the public in women's issues on an ongoing basis, as compared with the brief life span of most stories about women that now capture public attention. Citizenship, as Mary Dietz (1998, 391) asserts, is a continuous activity, a demanding process that never ends, not a momentary engagement with an eye to a final goal or societal arrangement. She explains that exploring citizenship does not require abandoning pursuit of specific social and economic ends, but she cautions that feminist citizenship must do more than centre on social and economic issues of concern to the community.

Investigating the construction of citizenship within the process of constitutional reform can be used to forge a new relation between life and law. The starting point for feminist intervention must be women's lives and experiences. If at present the relevance of women's experiences to the constitutional reform process looks tenuous and the concept of citizenship appears to be an abstraction, this is not a justification for non-involvement, but precisely the reason for engagement. Until we consider how we can embody the citizen (Thornton 1995) and understand what women's lives have to do with the document – and the process leading to the document – that defines national vision, structures the management of a country, articulates the most fundamental values of a society and sets up standards based on notions of justice that all must have reference to, the rights women appear to have will not have nearly as much significance as we think. This is a critical part of engendering and enlivening law.

Conclusion

In concluding I readily admit that citizenship is a contested concept. I am aware that there are serious questions about whether an ideal premised on the exclusion of women can be re-visioned to truly incorporate women and work to women's benefit (Lister 1997). In addition, I do not want to suggest that citizenship holds some final truth, is determinative of everything else – the meaning of equality, femininity, liberation, marginalization, overchievement – because the processes are interconnected and mutually constitutive (Maurer 1997, 34). We always take the risk that in trying to investigate the under-explored we reify it and fail to capture the full extent of the dynamism between our subject and its environment. Having said this, I am still urging the value of theorizing citizenship as a Caribbean feminist project, in addition to, not at the expense of, other feminist practice. Plainly said, I think this moment in the life of Caribbean nations, consumed as it is by constitutional imaginings in a way that has not been seen since independence, demands it and cannot be understood without it.

Notes

1. A number of scholars have explored in interesting ways the question of citizenship through Caribbean practices of migration. See Razack 1995, Maurer 1997, Lewis 1997 and Berry n.d.
2. *Dow v. Attorney General* [1992] LRC (Const) 623, at 632, *per* Amissah JP. Court of Appeal, Botswana.
3. Jamaica and Trinidad and Tobago were the first British Caribbean colonies to gain independence in 1962. Guyana and Barbados followed in 1966. The Bahamas gained independence in 1973 but its constitution bears similarities to older model constitutions.
4. See, for example, Barbados 1966, ss. 5 and 6.
5. Notably, Guyana and Trinidad and Tobago repealed their independence constitutions when they later became republics.
6. See the recommendations of the Constitution Review Commission that children born of Barbadian males and females should be equally treated (rec. 6.20) and that the non-national spouses of Barbadian-born persons should be treated equally (rec. 6.26) (Barbados, Constitution Review Commission 1998, 28–29).
7. (1982) 32 WIR, 254.
8. Ibid., 263.
9. Ibid., 290.
10. See for example, St Lucia 1978, s. 1.
11. *Girard v. Attorney General* (unreported), 17 December 1986, High Court, St Lucia, Nos. 371/1986, 372/1986, 17, discussed below in the text.
12. The equality clause of the 1980 Republican Constitution of Guyana, article 29, suffers a fate similar to that of the opening clause of the Bill of Rights in other Caribbean constitutions. This provision forms part of a chapter "Principles and Bases of the Political, Economic and Social System". In 1989 the constitution was amended to provide that this chapter contained only directory principles and did not give rise to any enforceable rights (see Demerieux 1992, 421, n. 22). In article 149(1) of the same constitution, certain forms of discrimination are prohibited, but "sex" is not included as a prohibited form of discrimination. The

Guyanese courts in *Nielsen v. Barker* have held that this category, which includes race, place of origin and political beliefs, among others, is closed and "sex" cannot be implied within it.

13. See *Neville Lewis et al. v. Attorney General of Jamaica et al.* (unreported), 12 September 2000, Privy Council, Jamaica, PCA Nos 60/1999, 65/1999, 69/1999, 10/2000.

14. See, for example, the opening section to the Bill of Rights of St Lucia 1978, s. 1, which states that the rights enumerated therein are subject to such limitations of that protection as are contained in the provisions of the chapter, "being limitations designed to ensure that the enjoyment of the said rights and freedoms by a person does not prejudice the rights and freedoms of others or the public interest". The specific rights enumerated thereafter also impose limitations on the rights if the law or government action in question is "reasonably required" for some legitimate state objective or if it is shown to be "reasonably justifiable in a democratic society". See, for example, St Lucia 1978, s. 11(2).

15. (Unreported) 17 December 1986, High Court, St Lucia, Nos. 371/1986, 372/1986.

16. St Lucia 1978, s. 13(4). The High Court found for the plaintiffs on the ground that there was an enforceable collective agreement between the union and the government that three months' maternity leave with full pay would be given to all women regardless of marital status. On appeal by the State, the Court of Appeal reversed that decision, holding that the collective agreement, which was never ratified by Cabinet or passed into law, could not override the clear provisions of regulation 23(3). The Court of Appeal however did not interfere with the decision of Matthew J on the constitutional questions raised in the High Court.

17. Fathers Incorporated expressed "disgust and condemnation of the thoughtless and insensitive judicial order" and described the action as an embarrassment to "all decent men". The Nurses Association said it was a "blatant disregard for our women folk". For the Jamaica Council for Human Rights, the action demonstrated the "undisguised contempt" with which some members of the judiciary held the basic human rights of citizens of a certain class of society. The National Democratic Movement said the decision was inhuman and inexplicable and that the judge had disqualified himself to preside over any cases in the future. There were calls for patience and sensitivity in dealing with rape complainants giving courtroom testimony, and the absence of a public address system in the courts to assist "soft-spoken" witnesses was widely debated.

18. The Jamaica Junior Chamber wondered "when our citizens see treatment like this they are placed in a predicament as to the fairness that may be meted out to them".

19. *Attorney General v. Girard and St Lucia Teachers Union* (unreported), 25 January 1988, Court of Appeal, St Lucia, Civ. App., Nos. 12/1986, 13/1986.

20. Espeut offers the view that males are being marginalized by our education system, and that "if females were being disadvantaged, the screams would be loud and prolonged" (2000, A4).

21. *Dow v. Attorney General* [1992] LRC (Const) 623, at 632, *per* Amissah JP.

Chapter 12

Theorizing the Gendered Analysis of Work in the Commonwealth Caribbean

ANN DENIS

Introduction

The sociology of work has been one of the areas in which feminism since the 1970s has raised conceptual issues and has been making important theoretical contributions aimed at allowing for an adequate analysis of the experiences of women within the field of work. The nature of the social relations of gender in Commonwealth[1] Caribbean societies has meant that these societies offer a particularly fertile site for the study of work. As Joycelin Massiah has pointed out, "Women in the Caribbean have always worked" (1986b, 177), while Christine Barrow (1993) has underlined the continuity that Barbadian women farmers felt existed between their productive and their reproductive work. More generally she notes that "[i]n the Afro-Caribbean context women's social reproduction is defined to incorporate productive money-making work" (1993, 190). Grappling with the ways in which the social relations of gender intersect with those of class and ethnicity/race continues to pose conceptual challenges to feminists interested in the study of work and to "malestream" sociologists of work. Here too the study of Caribbean societies encourages us to challenge and refine the theoretical tools at our disposal. To date these critical analyses, both in the Caribbean and elsewhere, have been more fully developed in relation to women than to men, reflecting, no doubt, the effects of the gendered division of labour in these societies.

I will begin by discussing what may be considered work, both traditionally and using a gender lens. I will then critically review selected feminist theoretical approaches and conceptual contributions to the study of work and their adequacy for addressing the social relations of gender in the context of Commonwealth Caribbean societies. I will conclude by considering recent theorizing that is informed by a consideration of Caribbean realities and which, I argue, can offer fruitful approaches to the gendered study of work both in the Commonwealth Caribbean and elsewhere.

What Is Work?

The traditional, if often implicit, concept of work refers to income-generating activity, mainly waged, that in industrialized societies is carried out in a formal organization. Attention has focused almost exclusively on what occurs in the place of employment and on workers who engage in one (normally full-time) job at a time. This concept and its attendant limitations are reflected in the official statistics collected in most societies.

What are its limitations? Apart from the fact that this concept refers exclusively to the "productive" or "public" sphere, a problem to which we will return, several types of revenue-generating activity are missing: multiple concurrent activities; sequential activities, including seasonal activities, within a single reference period[2]; activity in the informal sector,[3] whether sporadic or regular; outwork; and activity as unpaid family workers.[4] Self-employment and entrepreneurial activity have also received much less attention from sociologists than salaried and waged activity (Barriteau 1994). Illegal income-generating activities, including prostitution, tend to be treated as "deviance", not work.[5] These conceptual gaps are the result of a limited vision of income-generating activity, based on a "westocentric"[6] model of work that assumes an industrialized, bureaucratized structure of employment.

It is feminists, beginning with such pioneers as Lopata (1971) and Oakley (1974), who have argued that the concept of work needs to be broadened to include unpaid reproductive work in the private sphere, such as housework, child care and activities of sociability, including the maintenance of contact with the extended family. This type of work can involve planning, execution and the supervision of execution, usually for pay, by others. Although in the westocentric literature child care has usually referred to care by the biological mother, and more recently by a stepmother, especially in the case of blended families, the realities of Caribbean societies remind us that child care can equally be the work of others, most frequently grandmothers and biological or social aunts (Barrow 1998b; Momsen 1993; *Social and Economic* 1986a, 1986b). The fact that unpaid child care is not necessarily carried out by the biological mother raises questions about explanations of the gendered allocation of this work that are couched in terms of biological determinism.

Conceptualizing work as both productive (paid) and reproductive (unpaid household), although an improvement over an exclusive focus on productive (revenue-generating) activity, is not sufficiently comprehensive. It still excludes activities that might appropriately be considered work. Further training for oneself is one such activity, systematic fitness activities are a second and participation in voluntary activities a third. This last can be carried out through such formal organizations as churches, hospital auxiliaries, parent–teacher associations, service clubs, occupational or business associations and unions. Voluntary activities can also be much more informal, without entailing any less obligation. Elder care, whether in a situation of co-residence or not, is a case in point. And what of the provision of cash or goods to others – such as the remittances sent home from abroad that have played an important role in the Caribbean domestic economy, or assistance to non–co-resident local family members, for instance. Is doing this not work?

These considerations lead me to propose a definition of work (as distinct from non-work, or leisure) in terms of *intentionality* or *obligation*, including activities both *paid* and *unpaid* (revenue generating or not) done in both the *public* and *private* spheres, and including the possibility of *multiple concurrent* activities of work. In a similar vein work has been said to indicate "that the activities are costly in time and energy and are undertaken as obligations (contractual or social)" (UNIFEM 2000, 24). These definitions are in continuity with the criteria – obligation, income generation, expenditure of time and energy – that synthesized those mentioned by women in the Women in the Caribbean Project

(WICP) in explaining what constituted "work" for themselves. Work was any activity that is "functionally necessary to maintain themselves and their households" (Massiah 1986b, 186). One could argue therefore that the definitions respect the feminist epistemological tenet of treating people being researched as *subjects,* whose subjective understanding is valid information, rather than their being merely objects to be fitted into the researcher's predetermined model or set of categories. This tenet could be seen as building on but going beyond the Weberian concept of *verstehen,* or interpretative understanding. They can also include what Nancy Folbre (1995) has identified as caring labour – "labour undertaken out of affection or a sense of responsibility for other people, with no expectation of immediate pecuniary reward" (quoted in Peacocke 1998, 201).

Theorizing Work with Feminist Lenses

Against this preliminary backdrop of empirical issues that must be dealt with when proposing ways of theorizing a gendered analysis of work in the Caribbean, I will critically review a number of theoretical approaches,[7] returning afterwards to a consideration of work in the Caribbean in order to assess the strengths and weaknesses of the approaches for this task. I will begin by considering liberal feminism and Marxist/socialist feminism, since they have been used quite extensively in analyses of work. I will subsequently consider three other approaches – neo-Weberian analysis, materialist feminism and post-modern feminism – which, although focusing less explicitly on work, nevertheless offer some useful conceptual insights.

Liberal Feminist Analyses

The liberal feminist, or idealist, analysis of work developed as a feminist critique within functionalist analysis of society and its institutions. It focuses primarily on the ideological barriers to women's labour-force participation that characterize the Enlightenment ideal of gender specialization: men in the "public" sphere of the economy and politics, and women in the "private" family sphere. The gendered division of labour between the public and private spheres was considered by such functionalist theorists as Talcott Parsons to represent the shared values of members of society, with this role specialization being functional in an industrialized society. Consistent with dichotomies derived from Enlightenment thinking, the "female, private" sphere was described in terms of meeting emotional needs, with no recognition of the more instrumental tasks that are also accomplished within the household. Furthermore the fact that the same phenomenon could be functional for some (typically men) and dysfunctional for others (often women) was not considered. The maintenance of a state of equilibrium is considered to be the fundamental goal for the society.

Like the functionalist theories it criticizes, most liberal feminist theorizing of work concentrates on paid employment, pointing out existing barriers, both legal and attitudinal, to women's participation, together with the potential for greater autonomy that such participation could afford women. It highlights the contradictions between the democratic ideology of equal opportunity and the ideology of separate spheres, the latter legitimizing unequal employment opportunities and pay for women, who would be, after all, according to the dominant ideology, at best temporary participants in the labour force, working for "pin money" until marriage and childbearing. Needless to say, liberal feminists reject the "separate spheres" ideology, arguing that it denies women the opportunity to participate in the more highly valued public sphere and escape from the constraints and isolation of the private sphere. At the same time, the separate-spheres ideology misrepresents and undervalues (in terms of the values of the public sphere) the activities of the private sphere.

Much of the liberal feminist analysis has been at the macro level, documenting the occupational segregation, wage inequality and barriers to promotion that women experience. A few authors, however, have also applied the tools of a traditional sociology of work analysis to housework, examining its contradictory character: the lack of formal training, the social isolation, the diversity of tasks, the autonomy and lack of supervision, the twenty-four-hour-a-day responsibility . . . (for example, Lopata 1971; Oakley 1974). Others, often economists (Cook 1976; Waring 1990), have introduced quantification, estimating the cost of paid labour to do all the tasks of a housewife. Both approaches seem intended to legitimize housework as a "serious" endeavour, serious because of the skills and responsibilities involved and because of the cost that replacing the free labour of the housewife would entail. In so doing they seem to be reinforcing and legitimizing the higher value accorded to the monetarized public sphere. Unlike analyses informed by Marxism, however, no argument is really advanced to the effect that women's unpaid housework is underwriting capitalism. Rather it is argued that it is "only fair" that housework's value be measured – however incompletely – by, for instance, the cost of replacing it, and its importance thus be acknowledged.

Although rejecting gender hierarchies in employment as inefficient for the society and inconsistent with principles of equal opportunity, liberal feminism does not question the principle of hierarchy as such within society, including hierarchies based on social class or race/ethnicity, nor on the whole does it question the greater value associated with the monetarized activities of the public sphere. Within the field of development, liberal feminist theory informs the Women in Development (WID) approach, whose major policy preoccupation has been the integration of women into work in the formal economy.

In summary, these analyses of work and the theorizing that underpins them posit a divide between the public and the private spheres, with the former more highly valued; treat the male-breadwinner family as the norm, with women's labour-force participation as relatively exceptional but liberating; and could be characterized as largely universalizing and ahistorical, informed by a Western, industrialized, middle-class ethnocentrism. Even if the public–private divide and the male-breadwinner family have been part of dominant ideologies in the Caribbean, these features, together with the other overall assumptions of liberal feminism, are at odds with the experience of the majority of women there, and as a result are inadequate as a basis on which to theorize gender and work in the Caribbean. While underlining such inadequacies, the Women in the Caribbean Project (*Social and Economic* 1986a, 1986b; Senior 1991)[8] provided valuable empirical material without proposing alternative theorizing. To the extent that it was theoretically informed, it seems to have been by an implicit liberal feminism, albeit viewed through a critical lens.

Marxist and Socialist Feminist Analyses

Marxist Feminist Analysis

One of the major preoccupations of Marxist feminist analysis was whether housework could be analysed within the Marxist framework of "productive" labour, since so doing was the only way to incorporate it into the Marxist analytic fold. Since the production of (unpaid) use value associated with doing household tasks is not considered "productive" in the Marxist schema, this led to consideration of "wages for housework" (Dalla Costa and James 1972). Such wages, representing exchange value, were conceptualized as a means of incorporating women into capitalist relations of production and thus encouraging the development of their class-consciousness. That their direct employer would be their working-class husband,[9] thus introducing division within the working class, may have contributed to the relatively short life of interest in this approach. Furthermore, no working-class husband could afford a paid wife; the costing of women's domestic activity noted above resulted in a bill far beyond the husband's own wage, a fact that also underlined the indirect exploitation of housewives by capitalism. Like the accounting proposed by liberal feminism, the concept of wages for housework has contributed to the very slow steps that are being taken towards the formal inclusion of housework and caring activities in the calculation of national accounts (Waring 1990). Trinidad and Tobago is a leader in developing the necessary measurement instruments.

An alternative approach to unpaid housework was the socialization of housework – low-cost (that is, non-profit) laundries, cafeterias or take-out food, cleaning services and of course day care – so that women could enter the labour force without the additional burden of the day's "second" labour of housework. It was likely that it would have remained the same women who did the domestic work, although now for pay, and consequently developing at the same time, the theorists argue, a working-class consciousness. Even in such socialist societies as Cuba and China, however, these experiments have been relatively short-lived, apart from a limited amount of non-profit day care (Croll 1985; Smith and Padula 1996).

As far as the "productive" sphere was concerned, women are conceptualized in capitalist society as a reserve army of labour whose low wages and unstable employment would arouse limited objections within society because their primary role was as housewife, complementing their male breadwinner husband. The application of the concept of reserve army to all employed women seems to ignore the widespread occupational segregation that has resulted in a preponderance of women in a limited number of occupations, a generalized phenomenon even if the occupations in which the women are concentrated have varied historically and across societies. The question of unequal wages between men and women is not adequately addressed by the conceptual tools of Marxist feminism. This framework, which has been used primarily for the analysis of working-class women, posits that oppression based on gender will spontaneously disappear when class oppression is eliminated. It has largely been replaced by socialist feminism.

Socialist Feminist Analysis

Socialist feminism was the first feminist theory to incorporate both the public and private spheres in a wide-ranging analysis of society. The various types of socialist feminism draw on a combination of a Marxist analysis of class oppression completed by the radical feminist concept of the gender oppression of patriarchy, although they vary in terms of the primacy accorded to social class and patriarchy or to their interaction as explanatory variables (Juteau and Laurin 1988; Chhachhi 1988). Originally conceptualized by radical feminists as the oppression of women by men and considered to be the fundamental oppression in all societies, patriarchy is understood by socialist feminists as the oppression of women and most men by a minority of men (Fox 1988), a conceptualization that incorporates both class and gender oppression and provides a socio-historical contextualization of gender oppression that is lacking in radical feminism. Chhachhi (1988) notes, however, that some socialist feminists consider that the concept of patriarchy has unacceptably essentialist overtones, which they avoid by using the concept of the *social relations of gender,* to be analysed in conjunction with the social relations of class (including both production and various forms of reproduction).

Rather than pursuing the Marxist feminists' attempt to conceptualize unpaid domestic labour as "productive"– in the sense of producing, even if indirectly, exchange value – socialist feminists introduce the concept of (social) reproduction. This refers to activities carried out in the private sphere, including biological reproduction, the socialization of the young and the material and affective care of adult family members, all of which contribute to the reproduction of the labour force, and thus serve the interests of the dominant class in society. This analysis recognizes that the nature of gender oppression related to both production and reproduction varies by social class, although women of all social classes experience it. It also posits that, on the basis of class relations, women may be the oppressors of other women (and of men).

Typically it has been the oppressed who have been the subjects of study, with imperialism, post-colonialism or world systems theory providing a contextual frame of societal oppression in the case of less economically developed societies. Working within this framework, and considering social class and gender in both more and less economically developed regions of the world, Maria Mies (1986) has introduced the concept of "housewifization", referring to the material and ideological pressures on women of the North to become full-time housewives and consumers and on those of the South to become cheap producers of the consumption goods. The focus in analysing both the public and private spheres is on the ways in which women's work serves the interests of capitalism. Mies's analysis has been criticized for ignoring the importance of consumption as well as production in the case of Caribbean women (Freeman 1997), while Reddock (1989, 1994, 1998b) explicitly discusses the housewifization of Afro- and Indo-Trinidadian women since the late nineteenth century.

Although since the early 1980s some socialist feminists – for instance, Anthias and Yuval-Davis (1983) and Amos and Parmar (1984) – have argued that the variable of race/ethnicity must be integrated as an additional, intersecting source of oppressive relations, it has mainly been during the 1990s that serious attempts have been made to do so, for example in Alexander and Mohanty (1997). On the whole, however, authors have tended to examine two of the three variables, either ignoring the third or holding it constant.

Typically the analysis is macro, while some combines socialist feminism with such micro approaches as ethnomethodology, considering *The Everyday World as Problematic* (Smith 1987) and the perspective of its participants as worthy of integration into the analysis. This feminist standpoint epistemology posits, in continuity with Marxism, that the less powerful members of society are potentially capable of a more complete vision of social reality because of their knowledge (by necessity) of the dominant view, in addition to their knowledge of their own perspective as members of a subordinate group. Although the merits of standpoint epistemology are hotly debated within feminism (Nicholson 1990; Flax 1990b), there is agreement that one of the characteristics of a feminist epistemology is the rejection of the principle of objective, universal truth posited by Enlightenment philosophy (Barriteau 1994; Eichler 1985; Nicholson 1990).

Since the late 1980s socialist feminism, alone or in combination with some of the other approaches I will be discussing, has informed much of the research of women's paid and unpaid work in the economic South, including the Caribbean. It accords explanatory primacy to relations of production, often within a gendered version of world systems theory. Where the informal economy is discussed, it is primarily as a mechanism that, by providing additional revenue to workers, allows capitalist employers to pay low wages or to treat workers as a reserve army, with relative impunity. This oversimplifies the complexity of the informal economy in the Caribbean (Osirim 1997). The emphasis on productive work has resulted in socialist feminism being criticized as "reproduc[ing] the androcentric and ethnocentric bias inherent in the Enlightenment philosophy and privileging the productivist paradigm, which is itself a product of capitalism" (Hirshman 1995, 49). In addition, some feminists reject the concept of patriarchy, preferring instead to use the conceptual tool of social relations between the sexes, or gender relations, in their analysis of the intersecting effects of social class and gender (Chhachhi 1988).

The Potential for Feminism of Neo-Weberian Analysis

Both liberal and Marxist/socialist feminism share the Enlightenment inheritance with its universalizing tendency, its use of absolutes, its conceptual emphasis on dichotomies (dialectical relations) and its assumption of the existence of objective scientific knowledge. Although Parsons' grand theory included a linear model of social change, middle-range functionalist analysis and its feminist derivatives (including its contributions to the sociology of work) have been criticized as ahistorical. Marxism and its feminist derivatives, while more concerned with historical context, also posit a linear model of social change.

Weberian and neo-Weberian analysis, on the other hand, although clearly informed by the Enlightenment, offers fruitful theoretical alternatives. It eschews a grand, universalizing theory of society and social change, being instead firmly rooted in the historical and socio-cultural context. It stresses the interaction of material conditions with ideological or belief systems rather than the automatic primacy of one or the other. A crucial methodological tool is *verstehen,* the interpretive understanding of a phenomenon. It rejects the necessary use of conceptual dichotomies, focusing instead on continua or on the existence of multiple competing groups.

A particularly useful analytical tool for gender analysis is the concept of social closure, which can be exercised by status groups in both exclusionary and usurpatory forms. Exclusionary social closure refers to situations in which a dominant group prevents those who do not share what are considered to be salient status-group characteristics from penetrating its boundaries. Usurpation refers to strategies used by a subordinate status group to acquire access to resources that are being monopolized by another group. While Weber's analysis was gender-blind, neo-Weberian analysts (Parkin 1979; Murphy 1988) identify gender as a basis for status-group formation and thus for the exercise of social closure. This allows us to examine both mechanisms of exclusion and those used in order to attain access to hitherto forbidden resources. It also points out that the same status group may concurrently be attempting usurpation and exercising exclusion relative to different competing status groups within the society. These conceptual insights can be useful in the examination of work, particularly when the complexity resulting from the intersection of diverse types of status groups (based, for instance, on gender, social class, race/ethnicity, age or sexual orientation) is acknowledged, although the theory does not explain *why* particular forms of and changes in social positioning occur, but only *how.* Yelvington suggests this inadequacy could be remedied by keeping "in mind the social identities of individuals and the noneconomic motivations they often induce" (1995, 30). He also suggests that closure theory needs to be grounded by its integration into a theory of relations of production.

Whereas Marx's analysis of hierarchy and power was based on dichotomous and oppositional social relations defined in terms of relation to the means of production, Weber distinguished three bases of hierarchy: class (income),[10] status (lifestyle and prestige) and (political) power, each of which have multiple categories (which may be in competition) or are continua rather than being oppositional dichotomies. Bourdieu's conceptualizations of types of capital and of domination, developed originally as part of his theory of social reproduction, are informed by Weber's tripartite analysis of hierarchies. Bourdieu distinguishes four forms of capital that influence positioning in relations of domination, including those related to work: economic (including money and productive property); social (positions and relations in social groups and networks); cultural (linguistic styles, education, lifestyle, tastes); and symbolic (the use of symbols to legitimate the use of the other types of capital) (Bourdieu 1977; Yelvington 1995, 31). I agree with Yelvington that membership in gender and race/ethnic groups is part of social capital, but feel that his distinction between "embodied" and "generalised" (Yelvington 1995, 31–32) social capital is unnecessary and runs the risk of naturalizing the race/ethnic and gender groups that are included in the former.

A final source of insight that has been developed within the neo-Weberian framework is Blumberg's theory of gender stratification and her discussion, derived from it, of the internal economy of households (1989). In the former she hypothesizes that, of the types of power in society (economic, political, force and ideology), men's and women's *relative* economic power has the greatest effect on gender stratification. Rather than simply referring to the ownership of such economic resources as income, property, labour power and the means of production, her concept of economic power distinguishes *control of surplus* from control of the means of subsistence, and she argues that it is the control of surplus that is more important in determining gender stratification. She hypothesizes that men's and women's relative economic power can vary, not always in the same direction, depending on the level of social organization, from the couple through the household, community, social class and ethnic group to the state, with macro levels having more influence on micro levels than vice versa. With greater relative economic power, women's control of their various life options (marriage, control of fertility and so on) increases. This is consistent with her thesis that households are not monolithic entities, with all members subordinating their own interests to that of household survival under the direction of the household head. One consequence of this is that there will be some combination of communal and separate purses within the household. Furthermore, within cultural constraints women are more likely to allocate labour to activities producing output (such as produce or income) over which they have direct control than those over which they do not have such control. Thus the public–private sphere divide is rejected, but could Blumberg be criticized for "privileging a productivist paradigm" (Hirshman 1995)? I would argue no; at the same time as Blumberg stresses the importance of relative economic power (itself not the same as relations of production), she argues that it is exercised within a complex context in which cultural constraints have, at the least, a limiting or facilitating impact.

Materialist Feminist Analysis

Without adopting Marx's historical materialist analysis of modes of production, this approach is also founded on materialism – the power relation of physical appropriation, which in the case of gender relations Colette Guillaumin (1995) calls "sexage",[11] and its ideological effect, the idea of "nature" that legitimizes this appropriation by referring to an image of what women are supposed to be, as something that is "in their (biological) nature" and thus immutable. This is, then, a theory of how the social construction of a group is used to justify and perpetuate an existing material relation of domination that involves one group's appropriating the producing material unit of labour power of another group, not just its labour power. In the case of sexage this relation of appropriation of the class of women by the class of men can take the forms of appropriation of time (labour power), appropriation of the products of the body and work, sexual obligation and responsibility for the physical needs of members of the group who cannot fully care for themselves and of the able-bodied male members of the group. Women are collectively appropriated by the men in a society in the context of institutional relations as well as interpersonal relations between women and men, and women can also experience private appropriation through the institution of marriage. This offers one way of conceptualizing Afro-Caribbean female-headed households, as well as the Indo-Caribbean family structure in late-nineteenth-century Trinidad.

The theory of sexage is located, according to Juteau and Laurin (1988), through the intersection of a theory of production emphasizing property and a theory of gender/class relations.[12] They contend that sex-class institutions such as the Church and capitalist institutions of production and distribution also represent the interests of the dominant social classes. They argue that since the beginning of industrialization, the paid exploitation of work represents a particular mode of appropriation by the class of men, without excluding this form of appropriation from also being carried out within the class of men. Yet women systematically experience greater appropriation because of their domestic responsibilities, the gendered division of occupations and the additional expectations to which they are subjected in employment. Whereas Juteau and Laurin underline how women's lower pay for employment pushes them to accept the private appropriation of marriage in industrialized societies, without this guaranteeing a respite from poverty for them or children (for whom they typically have primary responsibility), Barrow (1986a) reports concurrent relations of interdependence with a number of others as the strategy preferred by poor women in the Caribbean. This is a strategy that makes them less vulnerable to private appropriation. The uncertainties of serial private appropriation, Juteau and Laurin argue, have made women more dependent on the state, where again they experience sexage, institutional control as a class at the hands of the class of men (through the police, legislation and so on). Is this analysis also applicable in the Caribbean?

Materialist feminist analysis, Guillaumin contends, must be historically contextualized by those applying it and, in principle, is not limited to industrialized or capitalist societies. Like neo-Weberian feminism, but unlike Marxism and its derivatives, this approach does not assume a grand theory of history and social change. It has the merit of not assuming a split between the private and public spheres – appropriation has no such boundaries – and of not assuming, as Christine Delphy (1984), another materialist feminist, does with her concept of the domestic mode of production, that all women are wives and/or mothers, actual or in waiting. Furthermore, a wide variety of "work" activities can be analysed using this approach. There is debate, however, about whether collective and private appropriation should be conceptualized as being in tension (Guillaumin 1995) or in continuity, with the private deriving from the collective (Juteau and Laurin 1988). Guillaumin argues that a second source of tension is between the appropriation of women and their reappropriation of themselves, including the possibility of their selling their labour power *on their own authority*. It is unfortunate that Guillaumin has not more fully theorized this potential for women's agency, including the conditions for its occurring. One must also question whether women's reappropriation of their own labour power is a condition necessary for liberation from collective appropriation or only from private appropriation.

Post-Modern Feminism

Post-modern feminism is the final theoretical approach that will be discussed. Post-modern feminism is informed by post-modernism's critique of the Enlightenment assumptions shared by liberal and Marxist approaches (including their feminist derivatives) of "privileged access to objectivity, reason and reality based on a belief in a supra rational mind . . . [that] allows discourses . . . to marginalize social groups and localized knowledges" (Barriteau 1994, 81–82). It criticizes post-modernism, however, for its failure to account for the continuing presence of relations of domination based on gender. Deconstructing concepts of gender underlying various aspects of social organization is then a key part of post-modern feminist analysis. Another key element is a post-modern articulation, informed by Foucault, of the concept of power. As in neo-Weberian analysis, power is conceived of as plural and as relational, something that is exercised by individual or collective actors, rather than an abstract entity that can be possessed. Examining the relationship between knowledge and power reveals "how rules about what constitutes knowledge are an expression of the practice of power in areas not traditionally regarded as sources of power" (Barriteau 1994, 86).

Foucault's approach to power has been criticized, however, as overemphasizing the discursive at the expense of the social structural, and thus not attending adequately to how "power is implicated in the ways in which structures are created in the first place" and to how individuals' relations to the production of resources (economic or other) are linked to the kinds of power they can use through social resources (for example, Yelvington 1995, 15–22). Thus analyses of work informed by postmodern feminism would be less subject to the criticism of "privileging a productivist paradigm" that Hirshman (1995, 49) has levelled at socialist feminism.

Brooks (1997) provides a useful overview of arguments advanced by both proponents and critics of the intersection of post-modernism with feminism. As she also points out, some of the aspects of post-modernism that have been particularly attractive for feminism – notably the challenging of a single epistemological truth and an emphasis on difference – were also being articulated within Western feminism, in the case of the challenging of a single epistemological truth (Eichler 1985), or by those marginalized by feminism's modernist heritage, in the case of the emphasis on difference (Amos and Parmar 1984; Chhachhi 1988).

In fact Flax argues that all feminist theory is post-modern because it "reveals and contributes to the growing uncertainty within Western intellectual circles about the appropriate grounding and methods for explaining and interpreting human experience" (Flax 1990a, 40–41). In developing this argument she rejects as flawed the epistemological position of some feminists, including standpoint theorists, that posits that "feminist theorists can uncover truths about the whole as it 'really is' " (Flax 1990b, 140), arguing that this position uncritically adopts Enlightenment assumptions of reason and privileged access to truth, which contradict the underlying assumptions of feminism. Although within feminism there is debate about the merits of standpoint epistemology, of the principle of epistemic privilege and of what the consequences (for the legitimacy of feminist knowledge) are of the thoroughgoing relativism that post-modernism can imply, there does seem to be agreement within feminist epistemologies that one cannot conceive of a single, monolithic truth. Rather, the location of the individual within the social structure will affect how she or he constructs reality.

Since the early 1980s feminists in the Caribbean (whether self-identified as such or not) have criticized the inadequacies of westocentric theories and concepts for the analysis of Caribbean society. Gill and Massiah (1984) and Barrow (1986a) provide early examples of such criticism with respect to work. More recently Caribbean feminists have begun developing tools for theorizing about gender relations in their societies, incorporating elements from both the political economy and post-modern approaches. Two important concepts are identity and difference, particularly with regard to gender and ethnicity (Mohammed 1998; Baksh-Soodeen 1998), with the emphasis, as far as ethnicity is concerned, having been largely Afrocentric (Baksh-Soodeen 1998). Although Mohammed contends that "[t]he question of class differences and privilege among women is a more recently acquired twentieth-century issue among the majority of black, indian and coloured peoples" (1998, 24), Massiah (1984b, 42–44) and Baksh-Soodeen (1998) remind us that the intersection of class and race differences has been evident in relation to women's work since colonial times. Furthermore, the question of class is made more complex by the rapid social mobility experienced by many during the post-colonial period. A solid historical contextualization, situated within a framework of globalization, is *de rigueur* for analyses of both the colonial and post-colonial periods, in view of the important ways in which extra-national and extra-regional economic, political and cultural factors have impinged on societies in the region since the beginning of colonialism. At the same time, women's agency is stressed, and analysis that is perceived as treating women "simply" as victims, totally at the mercy of external forces, is rejected.

Eudine Barriteau's (1995a, 1998b, 1998c) theorizing about how gender systems "operate within the political, social and cultural economy of states . . . [which is intended] to generate a gendered analytical model [for the study of] a wide range of social and economic phenomena inherent in the Caribbean and other societies" (1998c, 187) offers potential for theorizing about work in Caribbean society. Barriteau defines gender as referring "to complex systems of personal and social relations through which women and men are socially created and maintained and through which they gain access to, or are allocated, status, power and material resources within society" (1998c, 188), and she is concerned about theorizing "the multiple contested locations of domination in women's lives" (1995a, 144). Material and ideological dimensions together constitute the network of power relations of a gender system, one aspect of social structure.

> The material dimension reveals how women and men gain access to or are allocated status, power and material resources in a given society . . . The ideological dimension indicates the ways in which a society constructs what it accepts (and contests) as the appropriate expression of masculinity and femininity . . . The material and ideological relations of gender reinforce and complicate each other . . . [These] social relations of gender intersect with other oppressive relations, such as those arising from class, ethnicity. (Barriteau 1998b, 439–40)

Especially in elaborating on the material dimension of a society's gender system, I suggest it is important to situate the society in the broader international (socio-)economic order. This is not explicit in Barriteau's formulation, although she does do so in the historicized analysis of Caribbean gender systems she presents (1998c) to illustrate the application of her theory.

While Barriteau identifies her approach with post-modern feminism, notably because of its rejection of Enlightenment absolutes and dualisms and its insistence on the social construction of gender, it is clear from her emphasis on social structure that she does not espouse a version of postmodernism premised on discourse. Based on her emphasis on the interaction of the material and the ideological, on such concepts as status and power, on the complex effects of social relations arising from such bases of social differentiation as gender, race and class, and on mechanisms for effecting social change (exclusion and usurpation), I would argue that her approach also has affinities with the contributions of neo-Weberian analysis discussed in an earlier section of this paper. Within Barriteau's general theory, Blumberg's theorizing about gender stratification and internal household economy could help inform middle-range hypothesis testing relating to work and gender hierarchies over time or across societies in the Caribbean.

Carla Freeman's underlining of the agency of women working in the informatics industry in Barbados and their ways of establishing their identity as workers *and* as women illustrates the dynamic, if contradictory and constraining, nature of gender systems. "The informatics workers demonstrate . . . that globalization is not enacted in a uniform manner, nor is it simply homogenizing in its effects" (2000, 260). Instead "local actors in specific cultural contexts confront, experience, and give shape to the forms of globalization" (p. 261).

Conclusion

The rich descriptive material about women's work in the Caribbean has demonstrated the inadequacy of liberal and Marxist/socialist feminist theoretical models for the analysis of work that had broad currency in the 1970s and 1980s. There has been limited theorizing specifically about work since then, although during the 1990s there have been more general reflections about theorizing the Caribbean experience(s) ("Rethinking" 1998). What has emerged is the importance of incorporating into any theorizing about work the socio-political and historical context (local, regional and international); an examination of the complex intersection of relations of domination based on gender, class and race/ethnicity (and other bases of differentiation), including mechanisms for imposing (and for challenging) social closure; and a broad conceptualization of work that is not constrained by such dualisms as public/private spheres or production/reproduction. Without necessarily adopting the thoroughgoing standpoint epistemology, which negates any role for the researcher apart from that of scribe, rejection of the notion of a single scientific truth allows for validation of the perspectives of those studied. The relative status of the material and the ideological remains a point of theoretical contention, including in the study of work the primacy accorded by post-modernism to the discursive in shaping the material; the material (not limited to relations of production in the case of materialist feminism) that gives rise to their ideological legitimation; or the interrelation between the two without predetermined primacy, as Barriteau suggests, a position compatible with neo-Weberian analysis.

The gendered study of work in the Commonwealth Caribbean has challenged Western feminism. Dealing with these challenges should strengthen our feminist theorizing.

Notes

1. Despite their diversity in terms of size, geography, history, economy and the present socio-economic characteristics of their populations, the societies of the Commonwealth Caribbean share certain features in common, in comparison with other regions of the world, among others: their colonial history of slavery and plantation economies, a relatively high rate of formal labour-force participation by women, a relatively high proportion of female-headed households and a common regional identity, in addition to individual national ones. We must also acknowledge that social science literature about the Caribbean is based preponderantly on studies of Barbados, Jamaica, and Trinidad and Tobago.

2. For instance, for labour force surveys or censuses, during the previous week or the previous year. Acknowledging the possibility of multiple activities by asking the individual to identify "the most important" one begs the question. "Most important" in terms of what? Hours or weeks worked; revenue; self-identification; preferred activity; prestige . . . ?

3. The informal sector refers to unregistered work. In the economic North it has the connotation of illegal or black market work. In the economic South, however, it does not necessarily have this negative connotation. Instead it can simply be referring to a small-scale (and probably unregistered) enterprise of an individual alone or with up to about four workers (Scott 1991).

4. That such activity may not be conceptualized as work, but rather as "helping out" by those doing it, can result in serious under-reporting of it (Denis 1985).

5. Although there has been some feminist analysis of sex workers, such as in Kempadoo 1999a.

6. I am indebted to Nira Yuval-Davis (1997, 5) for this expression, which I think, in the present context, is more appropriate than "Eurocentric" and more specific than "ethnocentric". At the same time, I must stress that she was not using it in relation to work.

7. Armstrong and Armstrong (1978), Lynch (1989) and Sokoloff (1980) provide useful critical reviews of major theoretical analyses of women's paid and unpaid work through the 1980s by North American and European feminist sociologists. Their reviews go into more detail than is possible to do in the present chapter.

8. Senior's book includes a complete list of WICP publications and conference papers.

9. Marxist feminist analysis concentrated on working-class women. The wives of the bourgeoisie were at best mentioned as parasites.

10. Rather than to position relative to the means of production, of the Marxist concept of social class.

11. The equivalent for gender relations of *esclavage* (slavery) and *servage* (serfdom), other forms of physical appropriation to which both men and women have been subject.

12. Guillaumin (1995) first developed her conceptual framework of the material relations of power legitimized by the ideological in her analysis of the racism whose articulation in Europe dated from the advent of European commerce in slaves from Africa to provide labour on the plantations of the "New World".

Chapter 13

Gender and Power in Contemporary Society
A Case-Study of Student Government

ELSA LEO-RHYNIE

Introduction

The countries of the Caribbean have, like all other societies, inherited complex power structures that reflect gender, race and social class inequities. These inequities are evident in the leadership of the state, the legal system and ownership of the means of production. The challenges to such power hierarchies over the past four decades, particularly by the feminist movement, have created an awareness of the need for change. Although some change is evident, the structures have remained highly resistant to the process of transformation advocated by some groups.

One of the reasons advanced for the slow progress of change is the reluctance of the "power groups" to surrender this power. Power has traditionally been viewed as a quality that resides in persons or groups and is used to control other persons or groups. Schaef (1981) considers this to be a masculine perspective of power conceptualized as a scarcity model based on domination and control of others. Feminists are highly critical of this view, and define power as "Energy and strength rather than domination and control . . . a source of synergy – something to be taught and shared" (Smith 1997, 210).

Such a definition has implications for the structures of institutions and styles of leadership. The model advocated would be characterized by relationships rather than hierarchies (Smith 1997), cooperation and inter-dependence rather than competitiveness and dominance (Hartsock 1979). The language and focus of leadership have changed over the past decades. Traditional models of leadership have focused on the use of power in a strongly hierarchical structure. In this hierarchy the leader is an authority figure at the pinnacle of a pyramid of power, where all com-munication, control, responsibility and resources flow from the top downwards. Leadership in the hierarchy is strongly associated with "position power", that is, the degree of power, control and influence that an individual's position in the hierarchy confers. The change from this model to participative leadership has been spearheaded by concepts such as transformative leadership (Burns 1978) and empowering fol-lowers (Bennis and Nanus 1985), which emphasize the relationship aspect of the act of leadership. Strong interpersonal skills are now seen as being central to effective leadership (Batten 1989).

A number of feminist writers (Schaef 1981; Hartsock 1979; Rosener 1990) who equated the old leadership model with patriarchy and mas-culinity have identified the new paradigm as a feminine leadership model. These writers attribute to feminists the questioning and dismantling of the patriarchal world, with its emphasis on male-oriented values of rationality, competition and independence, and with bringing to the fore the realization of the validity and worth of the values of the female. The "female world" is based primarily on an ethos of love and duty, and is a kinder, more relational, more constructive world than the "male world", which is characterized by power, competition and manipula-tion. Gilligan (1982) points out that men view the world in terms of a hierarchy of power, while women see it as a web of relationships. For women it is more important to maintain that network of relationships than to be separate and "on top". Winning – of primary importance to male leaders – is of secondary importance in a woman's world if the con-sequences are personal isolation. The bases on which the new paradigm of leadership has been developed are considered to validate women's ways of knowing, of living and of leadership.

Educational institutions are usually expected to be agents of social change, to themselves reflect such change and to be the training grounds for future leaders who will carry the message of change. Socialist and radical feminists point out that, in reality, educational institutions do not promote change; instead they reproduce gender and social class inequity (Measor and Sikes 1992). Effecting change in leadership styles and building an institutional climate that regards power in terms of relationship building, rather than hierarchy maintenance, demands that women and men accept the new leadership paradigm. The inclusion of women leaders who subscribe to these views becomes an important part of this strategy to effect change. It is especially important that young leaders, male and female, who are developing through practice and experience their own theories of effective leadership, abandon the old hierarchies and seek to build their leadership styles based on sharing, cooperation and strong interpersonal relationships.

The Context

The University of the West Indies (UWI) is the premier tertiary level institution in the English-speaking Caribbean region, with a mission to unlock the potential of the region generally and a specific focus on the students who are registered there. This potential is not defined in academic terms only, and many opportunities are provided for the development and expression of potential in other areas, including leadership. One such opportunity is participation in student government, and election to the executive and council of the Guild of Students is a significant achievement. Elections are held annually and candidates mount election campaigns and canvass votes in order to secure these posts on the guild council and executive.

The student government has considerable influence in terms of policy and decision making on the campus. Student leaders participate in the deliberations of all the university governing committees and represent the interests of the almost twenty thousand students enrolled in the university across the three campuses. They also have the responsibility of managing a fairly large budget; on the Mona campus this budget was approximately J$4.5 million (US$120,000) in the 1998–99 academic year. The guild executive on the Mona campus is comprised of a president, vice president, secretary, treasurer, cultural and entertainment affairs chairman, games committee chairman, public relations officer, publications secretary and external affairs chairman. The guild council is a wider body, with the executive as its core, but also including faculty representatives as well as the chairpersons and deputy chairpersons of the halls of residence, who represent resident as well as commuting students attached to their halls.

UWI statistics for the 1998–99 academic year record enrolment on the Mona campus at 8,982, with 6,257 (69.7 per cent) of this number being female students. Since 1983 this campus has increasingly had more female than male students, and this gender difference has sparked a great deal of concern, with the annual cry at graduation ceremonies being, "Where are the men?" Data on the differential participation of women and men in the education process have generated the male marginalization thesis proposed by Miller (1994). This has been refuted, as preliminary research suggests that the greater involvement of women in education has so far not translated into women's greater achievements in the workplace, nor their upward mobility relative to men in the society (Bailey 1997).

The larger numbers of women on the campus have also not resulted in any change in the gender composition of the leadership in student government. The executive and council of the Guild of Students remain predominantly male. The student body has not elected a female guild president since the 1986–87 academic year, and in the fifty-year history of the university only four women have been president. Irvine Hall has accommodated male and female students since 1950; in the 1998–99 academic year a woman was elected hall chair for the first time in its history. Male hall chairs are the norm among the three halls that house both male and female students. In the elections for the 1999–2000 and 2000–2001 academic years, the pattern of a male guild president and a male vice president emerged once again, and all the hall chairs save the one for Mary Seacole Hall, the only exclusively female hall, were men. Women do form part of the guild executive and guild council, but there appears to be a level above which they are not elected.

The fact that women are a majority group on the campus, thus having the voting power to control the election of candidates, and the continued absence of women in top leadership positions of the Guild of Students have been puzzling. The issue is of particular interest in terms of the gender dynamic, as one would expect young women of the 1990s to be assertive and involved in seeking leadership, as they are not as bound by tradition as were previous generations.

Objectives

The research investigation was preliminary and exploratory. No hypotheses or even specific research questions were developed; instead the investigation was guided by a need to explore the gender dynamics of student leadership in order to reveal the experiences of female leaders, and to examine any power relationships that might emerge. Specifically the enquiry sought to determine

- female students' motivations in seeking leadership positions
- barriers and facilitating factors in their quest for leadership
- expectations and experience in leadership positions
- lack of female participation in competition for the posts of president and vice president
- the support base for women in seeking leadership and carrying out those roles
- the gender and power implications emerging from these issues

Method

Eight female members of the outgoing and incoming guild councils were invited to a focus group discussion on the role of women students in leadership on the Mona campus. Five persons participated; two were from the outgoing council and the other three were newly elected members. The stimulus questions prepared for the focus group discussion were as shown in appendix 13.1. The discussion lasted for approximately three hours.

The students were very open in voicing their opinions and recounting their experiences. The use of a focus group had advantages in that it allowed for confirmation that an experience of one person had been common to all, and the comments of one respondent often sparked a memory that may not otherwise have been brought to the fore. The disadvantage of this method was that the time available had to be shared among the respondents, and there might have been greater detail and depth of discussion that could be captured only in a one-to-one interview. The discussion was recorded on audiotape and the data were analysed from this recording and from notes taken during the session.

Analysis of the data was guided by the need to identify the major themes that would emerge from the women's stories and to interpret the data as they related to these themes. The case is sited in a restricted environment and the data emerge from a very small sample; explanations can therefore be applied only to the specific context, but they can be useful in stimulating and guiding research in other situations. Hartman endorses the use of women's stories and experiences, noting that they are very often "narratives that have explanatory power" (1991, 12).

Data Presentation

Four major themes emerged from the data: difficulty of access, persistence of hierarchy and power, autocratic styles of leadership and the importance of support bases.

Difficulty of Access

All the women spoke of the difficulties involved in gaining access to leadership positions. The culture of leadership on the campus is, they insist, a male one. They point out that the UWI administration implicitly sends a message to the student body that the president is expected to be male, by providing the flat for the guild president's residence in the only exclusively male hall of residence, Chancellor. This situation, they say, reinforces the belief held by members of this hall that not only is the guild president to be male, but that he must be a member of that hall. Where, they ask, would a female guild president live? Respondents had come to the campus with leadership experience in either their schools or communities, and were strongly motivated to try to make a difference. One of the women, who described herself as an introvert, said that she was motivated by the disrespect that she saw on the campus for some categories of students, and she wanted to try to bring about changes in policy. All found that gaining access to leadership at UWI was similar to the rigours of qualifying for membership in an exclusive club, and for women it was made even more difficult, as the club was an exclusively male one.

A woman seeking a leadership position places herself in a vulnerable position. She is seen as trying to "rock the boat" and change the status quo. Her declaration of intent to vie for certain posts on the council or executive is seen as a challenge to the male leadership, and immediately, the women state, the "can't-lose machinery" of Chancellor Hall is put in gear and an organized process of intimidation is implemented. The strategy is to discredit the woman, so her past is investigated in detail, and any indiscretion, including intimate details of her personal life, is made public and used to eliminate her candidacy. One woman spoke of the times when she sat and cried because of the opposition's pressure and contemplated giving up, as many other women have done. She recounted that her opponent went to the high school where she had been head girl and tried to find out whether or not she had performed creditably in that role. When he could find nothing adverse, he went to a nearby boys' school to ask what the "dirt" was on her. When nothing surfaced, he turned to an examination of her personal life, interrogated her friends and told lies to her boyfriend about sexual alliances of which she knew nothing. Rumour-mongering is a basic strategy used to dissuade and exclude women from running for office, and any woman who decides to do so knows that she will have to live through the lies and the rumours circulated about her.

Persistence of Hierarchy and Power

Respondents spoke emphatically of the "greed for power" demonstrated by the male student leaders and those with aspirations to that leadership. They noted that within the executive there is a certain status hierarchy. Women are "allowed" to take their chances in running for positions such as secretary and external affairs coordinator, but definitely not for president or vice president. One respondent said that a woman could possibly become deputy hall chair of Taylor Hall (a mixed-sex hall) if she was a high-profile person and a very hard worker, but no woman should even consider the possibility of being the chair.

The women recalled two occasions when a woman ran for the post of vice president of the guild and the "Chancellor machinery" succeeded in excluding her, despite the fact that she was an excellent candidate. They explained that the men establish a "succession line" based on patronage and cliquishness, and the top posts of the guild executive are a "package" decided in advance. The person being groomed for leadership is voted into a position on the guild executive the year before so that he can become a visible challenger in the community, known to both students and staff. They admit that the person identified to be the leader is usually a hard worker, but describe Chancellor Hall as a "political garrison", with the fight not being merely one between the sexes, but one against all challengers.

Women who aspire to be leaders have to earn their chance to compete for one of the posts assessed as being appropriate for a woman by working hard and advancing up the ranks, being appointed block representative on a hall of residence, for example, and demonstrating an ability to undertake and competently handle the many tasks involved. If a woman appears to be getting too much public notice and she is recognized as a potential threat to the machinery, the subversive tactics begin so as to eliminate her challenge before she starts getting any "lofty ideas". The men do not have to earn their election nominations in this way.

All the women admitted that they felt competent to perform the role of guild president, and one indicated that she had seriously thought of taking up the challenge. She decided against it when she realized all that she would have to endure, asking herself, "Why would I want to go through that?" When asked why they would not think of running for the top post, one of the women said, "I would be crazy, and would be ridiculed. We really just accept the culture." Another said, "A woman would never *dare* win!" They all agreed that the character assassination that would accompany the political campaign would be devastating. They said that it would be like the "Lewinsky thing"[1] and that their names would be "dragged in the dirt".

They resented the double standard that was practised during campaigns: slogans used to describe female candidates were often demoralizing and of a sexual nature, and details of the candidate's personal life were usually up for debate. This is a common practice used by men to intimidate women; they resort to defining the women in terms of their bodies and their sexuality rather than in terms of the skills they possess and their potential for success.

The respondents also pointed to the defacing of posters of female candidates with embarrassing comments, the close scrutiny applied to the profiles of female candidates and the highlighting of any slight inaccuracy in order to humiliate the candidate. At the same time, the profiles of the men were often padded to the point where they contained blatant lies, but these were not challenged.

Autocratic Styles of Leadership

The respondents agreed that an autocratic style of leadership was usually practised, control was stressed and there was a great deal of cliquishness. Women members of the council were often sidelined and not made privy to many important issues facing the guild or the hall. The men dominate the discussions at meetings and usually agree on their position prior to the meeting, and they expect that position to be accepted. The women pointed out that very often the men's position was very high-flown and unrealistic, and they had to be the voices of reason and realism. They emphasized, however, that they had to very assertive in order to make their voices heard.

In illustration of the point of being marginalized, one of the women recounted an incident when the hall chair called a meeting of the entire hall membership. Although she was the deputy hall chair, she received a notice of the meeting minutes before it was due to start, and this notice gave no indication of the purpose of the gathering. The hall chair arrived one hour late, and during the waiting period she suffered great embarrassment at not being able to say or do anything to begin the discussion, as she had been kept entirely in the dark.

The women also noted the gender bias in terms of delegation of tasks. When considering their plans for the year, for example, the guild council considered the introduction of a day-care facility for part-time students and a homework centre. Both were assigned to the female members of the guild. The men also try to pass to the women work that is considered to be less important and tasks that do not attract media attention.

The Importance of Support Bases

The men build strong supportive networks among other male students, but women students neither support nor vote for female candidates. When male candidates came to Mary Seacole Hall (the only female hall) they were warmly welcomed by the women and allowed to present their campaign speeches, yet when female candidates tried to address the men of Chancellor, the men walked out of the room. This blatant act of disrespect did not create any resentment on the part of the women, who still voted for the men.

The women reported that they were embarrassed by the criteria used by some women to select their representatives. A candidate was favoured because he looked "so cute" in his glamour photograph, or because he was "very handsome". The young women hang the posters with these glamour photographs in their bedrooms, and the male candidates assume the status of pin-ups in their eyes. The respondents felt that they had a duty to educate the women on the campus about the serious issues facing the student body, and guide them in making their decisions more responsibly.

An interesting incident took place immediately following the focus group discussion. When the young women who took part were leaving my office, coincidentally a male member of the guild council had come to see me.[2] He sought out the women afterwards and wanted to know whether they were "plotting to overthrow we [the men]" and reminded them that they were "weak" and "could do nothing".

Discussion

The findings of this preliminary investigation demonstrate the importance of understanding the way power is structured and expressed, and the influences these have on women; without such understanding it is very difficult to effect change. Several researchers have been trying to recover women's voices from the historical record; it is equally important to listen to the voices of our contemporary women, whose message is indicative of the very political nature of gender relations at this time.

In 1992, at a seminar staged by the Women and Development Studies groups of the UWI, one of the deans warned that women must not expect men to yield power and authority without a fight. Several years later this warning is being clearly borne out in this case-study among students, which demonstrates

- retention by young men of traditional concepts of patriarchy, power and dominance, and the use of psychological warfare to ensure the maintenance of a male-dominated power system of student leadership;

- acceptance by young women of traditional concepts of patriarchy and dominance, and a lack of motivation to effect change.

The data indicate how difficult it is to change the culture of leadership and undo the practices of relations of gender. The male students are obviously not prepared to accept the legitimate claims that women have on access to and occupancy of leadership positions. The traditions of male power and patriarchy are deeply entrenched, and there is strong resistance to any attempt to bring about change. Cockburn explains that "[m]ale power is not occasional, incidental or accidental. It is *systemic* . . . it is adaptive, with a tendency to self reproduction. To interrupt that reproductive process calls for active and conscious contradiction" (1991, 220; author's emphasis). She warns, as did the UWI dean, that men will resist that interruption; they fear the loss of their power as women compete with them for status and, in some cases, money. The men recognize also that with women occupying leadership positions, the change will transform the status quo, and they are not prepared for this. Cockburn also points out that "[m]en are obliged, therefore, to do more cultural work to ensure the reproduction of male power . . . Without that active and continual cultural labour by men, to be a woman might be a very different thing" (1991, 169).

The cultural work being done by the male students to ensure the reproduction of male power demonstrates the extent of their resistance to change. It is expressed through assertions of power, intimidation and reinforcement of a traditional understanding of woman's place. They employ controlling behaviours to diminish any sense of power women may see themselves acquiring, assigning women low-status tasks, for example, and ensuring that no media attention is paid to women, thus trying to guarantee public invisibility.

Their intimidation has the effect of getting women to decide that the repercussions of challenging the existing situation are just not worth it; that the aggravation and harassment that go with seeking leadership are not compensated for even by gaining the top post. This strategy of undermining a woman's confidence, and usually attacking her sexuality and personal life to accomplish this, is reported in other situations, and very often in organizations (Cockburn 1991; Rosener 1990). Also, as Gilligan (1982) indicated, women place less emphasis than men on being "at the top", especially if this results in personal isolation.

Social cognition is a psychological concept used to explain how gender and gender inequity develop and are maintained. Tajfel (1982) uses an in-group/out-group analysis to explain how this maintenance of inequity takes place. Members of the in-group(s) tend to process information in a way that bolsters their own self-esteem, and they do this by derogating members of the out-group(s) while being strongly supportive of their own group members. This is particularly so in situations where the in-group and the out-group do not have equal power. Thus we see the strategy of ensuring a "succession sequence" among the in-group of male leaders and the building of support for those members. Lowering the self-esteem of the women who constitute the out-group, and who have strong potential power in terms of their numbers, also gives them a certain security.

Interestingly, it seems that more than one out-group exists in this case. The claims that Chancellor Hall is a "political garrison" suggest that the political manoeuvring and the power-seeking are not exclusively gender based, but are targeted at other groups who must also be kept from acquiring power through leadership.[3] This calls to mind the tribal identification and competitive nature of men and the need to define and protect territory from "the enemy" (Hart 1989a). Women in this case may be seen as one of the "enemy tribes", their gender identification determining more easily the strategies used to eliminate their claims to the territory being protected.

The reaction of the women demonstrates some degree of acceptance of the traditional and patriarchal concepts of leadership and, in the context of the Caribbean, raises a number of questions. Why have the women not resisted these strategies to keep them in out-groups? Why have they not come together to bring about the change? Are we seeing a new generation of Caribbean women who see themselves as powerless to effect change? By not participating are the women making a statement about the culture of the institution?

Beckles (1989b) entitled his book on enslaved black women *Natural Rebels* and analysed the active rebellion, historical resistance and tactical use of negotiation by women during the period of slavery. The women are described as "persistent rebels", with this rebellion having both a violent and a non-violent, subversive nature. Has there been a change in the basic historical strategy of Caribbean women? Is their numerical dominance on the campus resulting in competition for the scarce intelligent, educated Caribbean men and a reluctance to demonstrate behaviours that may seem to be confrontational and "non-feminine" – non-acceptable to these men?

Cockburn borrows a definition of hegemony from Bocock (1986) to describe "an apparent right to govern accorded a dominant group by the active consent of the governed" (1991, 168). This is achieved, in her view, by political and cultural work. And the men are certainly doing their work. This work involves rewarding women for being sexually different from men when they are in their "proper" place, but punishing them for this difference when they try to step out of that place into men's places. This is how men control women. Given the masculine cultural hegemony obviously at work among the students on the Mona campus, it appears unlikely that women would be willing to give up the approval of men, or to identify with each other and so work together to bring about change.

Another factor operating on the campus, as well as in the wider society, which may have an effect on the expression of women's leadership qualities, is the paucity of role models for women who aspire to leadership. At the UWI in 1998–99 the academic staff complement was 655 men and 324 women, with a 7:1 ratio of male to female professors. The chancellor, vice chancellor, campus principals and all but one of the eight pro vice chancellors were male.[4] The university registrar and the university librarian are female; the university bursar is male. This predominance of men in leadership reflects the situation in Jamaican society, where political leadership is almost exclusively male.

This brief case-study points to the limitations of a liberal feminist theoretical perspective, which emphasizes provision of equal access for women and development of legal frameworks to ensure both equity of access and equal opportunity. Here women do have access, but it is clearly not enough to overcome the strength of the patriarchal system of male dominance that has developed over the years. Socialist feminist and radical feminist perspectives, which advocate social change and transformation of the power relationships between men and women, see educational institutions such as the university as reproducing the status quo. Education in its widest sense, as well as its practice in lecture rooms, are seen as agents of reinforcement of inequity rather than of change. The development of methods to resist and/or change this situation is a vital component of the feminist agenda.

How much change is possible? Fukuyama scathingly dismisses the possibility of change or transformation as proposed by socialist and radical feminists as "Utopian". He comments, "Liberal democracy and market economies work well because, unlike socialism, radical feminism and other Utopian schemes, they do not try to change human nature. Rather they accept biologically grounded nature as a given and seek to constrain it through institutions, laws and norms" (1998, 21).

In his essay discussing the origin of gender roles and female versus male leadership, Fukuyama strongly advises attention to the biological origins of sexual behaviour, and stresses that people cannot free themselves entirely from this behaviour. He points to the evidence of the new biology and notes that the revolution in the life sciences has almost totally escaped the notice of the social sciences and humanities, particularly feminism, post-modernism and cultural studies. He urges a correction of this situation and use of the "lens of sex and biology" to see the pervasive and irrefutable evidence of the biological nature of sex differences. Fukuyama observes that

> Male attitudes on a host of issues, from child-rearing to housework to "getting in touch with your feelings", have changed dramatically in the past couple of generations due to social pressure. But socialisation can accomplish only so much. Male tendencies to band together for competitive purposes, seek to dominate status hierarchies and act out aggressive fantasies towards one another can be rechannelled but never eliminated. (1998, 21)

Even accepting this view, the challenge is the re-channelling process. Using Cockburn's words, what "active and conscious contradiction" can take place to "interrupt the reproductive process" of male power? Although changing regulations or instituting disciplinary procedures for sexist behaviour (the liberal feminist solution) educates and may gradually change cultural attitudes by establishing boundaries of an acceptable level, they do not necessarily change the beliefs held and the practices adopted. The attitudes, values and behaviours of students have to change.

Bringing about the transformation that the radical and socialist feminist solution demands and the new leadership paradigm advocates will not be easy. Generations of women and men have been so socialized into the traditional ways of leadership that, despite the activism of the feminist movement, it is clear that the role of leader is still automatically perceived in masculine, hierarchical terms. The method of effecting change, however, ought not to employ the traditional male strategies of domination, intimidation, competitiveness and aggression. Current female student leaders have to assess their own power bases and use these to build effective alliances, to harness the energies of other women on campus and to devise creative strategies to bring about change. It is clear that there is a great need for education and awareness training among many female students, and this may be a good place to start building support from the bottom up. The concepts of empowerment of all women and building relationships would be demonstrated in such an initiative. Female members of the guild executive and council should also examine how their posts can be used to advantage in reaching other female students. A female guild secretary, for example, controls the dissemination of information – how can this role be used strategically to reach other women and to dispel the apathy that they now display?

The influence of women on the campus is being controlled through blatant as well as subtle use of power to deny them access to certain leadership positions. They have the power to effect change; they need to harness the "energy and strength" of this power, and use it.

Appendix 13.1
Points for Focus Group Discussion

1. What were your reasons, what was your motivation for seeking a leadership post in the Guild?
2. Were you faced with any barriers? Or assisted by any facilitating factors?
3. What were your expectations as a woman – especially in terms of inclusion/equity?
4. What have been your experiences – especially in terms of inclusion/equity? Have you experienced anything that you would consider sexual discrimination? Sexual harassment?
5. Why did you seek election in the specific area you chose? Why did you not run for the post of president?
6. Is there anything in the role of president that you feel that you would not be able to do?
7. Why is it that women do not seek election to that post?
8. What were/have been the reactions of men/women to your election?
9. Why do women not support/promote other women in leadership?
10. What are your views of the challenges for student leadership *now* in UWI?

Notes

1. A reference to the 1998 sex scandal in the United States involving the president of the United States, Bill Clinton, and Ms Monica Lewinsky.
2. Editor's comment: Elsa Leo-Rhynie is first professor of gender and development studies at the UWI. At the time the study was done she was the deputy principal (similar to vice president) of the Mona campus of the UWI. Hence the young women leaders' meeting with her would be perceived as threatening by young men opposed to women's leadership. She is currently pro vice chancellor, Board for Undergraduate Studies.
3. In the 2000–2001 academic year, a male Taylor Hall candidate successfully challenged the Chancellor Hall candidate for the presidency of the Guild of Students.
4. Two women are now pro vice chancellors: the author and Pro Vice Chancellor Professor Marlene Hamilton. Both are on the Mona campus.

⁂Part VI⁂

Gender and Power in the Public Domain: Deconstructing Masculinity and Marginality

Chapter 14

Gender and the Elementary Teaching Service in Barbados, 1880–1960

A Re-examination of the Feminization and Marginalization of the Black Male Theses

AVISTON DOWNES

Introduction

In the historiography of education in the English-speaking Caribbean, the gendered nature of the colonial education system has been established for some time (Cole 1982; Mohammed 1982; Drayton 1984; Mayers 1995; Hamilton 1997). Education has been acknowledged as the principal vehicle of mobility and social change, especially for non-whites in the region. Consequently, education case studies can provide the empirical base to assess the extent to which colour, class and gender circumscribed social rewards. Caribbean studies on gender and education to date have tended to focus principally on issues such as gender-differential curricula and access – in other words, on students more than on teachers.

Over the past twenty-five years the international historiography on teaching has given much attention to what is termed the "feminization" of the teaching profession since the nineteenth century (Prentice 1975; Grumet 1981; Strober and Lanford 1986; Clifford 1991).[1] In the Caribbean, one of the most contentious conceptualizations of this so-called feminization is Errol Miller's *Marginalization of the Black Male:*

Insights from the Development of the Teaching Profession (1994). Miller's work is based on an impressive empirical analysis of elementary schoolteachers and teachers' college students in Jamaica in the period 1837 to 1990. Miller posits what he terms "place theory" to account for social inequality in Jamaica in terms of "the relative positions of individuals and groups with respect to power, resources, status, belief and culture" (1994, 12). Colour/race, class, gender and age are the operational absolutes that are used to justify inequity in the social structure and are the bases that tend to locate individuals and groups along an axis of centrality or marginality. Gender, then, is one of those operational absolutes that, in interaction and combination with others, determine the place structure of the society. Miller has restated his thesis in *Men at Risk* (1991), a work that attempts to demonstrate an even wider application of his hypothesis. It is a hypothesis that cannot be ignored and has the potential for influencing conceptualization of gender relations in the Caribbean and beyond.

The purpose of this chapter, then, is to offer an empirical study of the elementary teaching service in Barbados between 1880 and 1960 as a case-study to test the validity of the feminization and black male marginalization hypotheses. The study will begin by revisiting the concept of feminization, which has been widely used in the historical literature, to determine its analytical usefulness. It will also test the socio-economic explanations of this perceived phenomenon. This analysis will not explore the many varied dimensions of the marginalization/place theory of Miller but will concentrate on those major interpretations advanced in support of the thesis. Finally, the contention of this work is that the reordering of the elementary teaching service, from the 1890s well into the twentieth century, may be interpreted as a classic case of the construction and consolidation of hegemonic masculinity, with its implied ordering of competing masculinities and the further subordination of women. This reordering was nonetheless fundamentally circumscribed by the structural limitations of society and economy in the region.

Methodology

The study is limited to an examination of the elementary teaching service in the period 1880 to 1960. Secondary education has been excluded because of the generally acknowledged fact of very limited access – in colour, class and gender terms – to this level of education in this period. Moreover, it was at the elementary level where popular access across colour, class and gender lines held the greatest potential for social transformation.

The study draws principally on the annual official reports on elementary education, the minutes of the Board of Education and all the Education Commission reports and policy papers since the Mitchinson Report of 1876. These documents provide the statistical base for a number of the study's conclusions. While the Barbados censuses were consulted and were useful in providing some crude indication of the number of males and females in the public teaching service, the censuses did not assist in the assessment of the structure of allocation of women and men in the service.

Caveats

Comparative history is fraught with pitfalls. While Barbados and Jamaica were British West Indian territories subject to British imperial policies, the imposition of Crown colony government in Jamaica after 1865 provided the imperial centre with greater influence over colonial education policy than in the case of Barbados, with its almost unbridled assembly controlled by merchants and planters. Moreover the education system in Barbados was almost entirely financed by central government, even though the denominations played a critical supervisory role. Nonetheless there are similar enough patterns in job allocation to suggest certain basic common gender assumptions within imperial and colonial education policies, providing then a reasonable base for comparison and criticism.

"A Petticoat System of Education": The Concept of Feminization

In a letter published in the *Times* of Wednesday, 3 April 1889, "A Barbadian Abroad" described the island's elementary school system as "the Barbados Petticoat System of Public Elementary Instruction". "Indeed! Fancy," the writer noted, "the training of our youths – the future men of the country left in the hands of *irresponsible girls*" (emphasis in the original). The Mitchinson Commission had pointed out in 1876 that virtually all primary schools were taught by men and that women tended to be confined to infant schools. By the 1880s little had changed. Although "A Barbadian Abroad" implies that there was a preponderance of females in the elementary schools, the 1884 *Report on Primary and Combined Schools* indicated that there were 105 schools headed by 97 masters and only 8 mistresses (Barbados LC 1886a, 8). There were an additional 86 public infant schools, but these employed males as well as female teachers (Barbados LC 1886b). What is clear is that the elementary teaching service was predominantly male up to the beginning of the past century.

It is also significant that while the letter characterized the female teachers as "irresponsible" and incompetent, the 1884 report on the primary and combined schools reported that all eight female teachers were certified but that there were still six masters who remained unqualified even after repeated examinations (Barbados LC 1886a, 8). So the imagery of an elementary teaching service being overrun by incompetent females and threatening the future of the island's young men was far from factual. Nevertheless, the sentiments of the letter from "A Barbadian Abroad" illustrate the significance of *perception* in many of the arguments about feminization of teaching and its impact.

The Feminization Hypothesis

Analyses of teaching services in societies as diverse as the United States, Canada, England, Wales, Denmark, Germany and Australia from the mid-nineteenth century demonstrate that women constituted a highly visible and growing component of those services. The concept of feminization has been widely employed to describe, if not explain, this phenomenon. However the concept itself continues to elude adequate definition. Incredibly, a publication entitled *The Feminisation of the Teaching Profession,* which is a selection of papers presented to the Conference on Equal Opportunities in Strasbourg, 1995, hardly throws light on the meaning of the term. One of the papers suggests that teaching is in a state of feminization "when more than half of the group concerned are women" (ETUCE 1995, 45). Strober and Lanford have linked (if not conflated) feminization and occupational segregation. They contend that teaching is occupationally segregated "when women are more than 50–55 percent of all teachers" (1986, 212).

But studies from Germany, Denmark and Belgium have purported to analyse the feminization of teaching in situations where women were just 20 to 49 per cent of the service (Albisetti 1993, 255). Clearly, then, the pursuit of percentages in this regard leads only to an explanatory cul-de-sac. Numerical predominance *per se* possesses no obvious theoretical or explanatory usefulness because there is neither inherent power nor lack thereof in a numerical majority. The preoccupation of this scholarship with numerical ratios too often obscures the more fundamental issues of how gender ideologies were and are mobilized to justify the inequitable allocation of power, authority, resources and rewards within formal education structures. I suggest that apart from its crude descriptive value and its capacity to capture the perception and prejudices of perceived female encroachment on heretofore male-dominated spaces, the concept cannot provide an adequate theoretical approach. The following empirical evidence will confirm this.

While it is true that male teachers were in the majority by the early nineteenth century, there is little evidence to suggest that elementary teaching was promoted as an exclusively male domain. Even then the role of women in education was promoted as an extension of their nurturing role in the home. Consequently, women's presence in the formal elementary education system was not ideologically problematic. Still, there seemed to have been an international trend from the mid-nineteenth century towards employing increasing numbers of women in the teaching service. This trend has been explained by one or more of the following arguments:

- the cost-efficiency hypothesis, which contends that more women were employed as a justification for paying lower salaries;
- the argument that men could secure more financially attractive employment elsewhere;
- increased provision of education and teacher-training for women;
- the development of single-sex schools;
- the reservation of infants' and girls' schools for women;
- the sponsored mobility of women by elite white males to effect the marginalization of challenging subordinate black males (Miller's marginalization hypothesis).

Table 14.1 Proposed Rationalization of Elementary Schools and Teachers, Barbados, 1895

Parish	Current Arrangement					Proposed Changes				
	Schools	Male Teachers	%	Female Teachers	%	Schools	Male Teachers	%	Female Teachers	%
St Michael	40	23	57.5	17	42.5	26	12	46.2	14	53.8
St George	15	9	60	6	40	13	5	38.5	8	61.5
Christ Church	25	18	72	7	28	21	9	42.9	12	57.1
St Philip	17	12	70.6	5	29.4	17	6	35.3	11	64.7
St John	15	5	33.3	10	66.7	12	5	41.7	7	58.3
St Joseph	10	7	70	3	30	10	4	40	6	60
St Thomas	16	11	68.8	5	31.2	12	6	50	6	50
St Andrew	10	10	100	0	0	10	6	60	4	40
St James	16	10	63	6	37.5	11	4	36.4	7	63.6
St Peter	14	10	71.4	4	28.6	11	4	36.4	7	63.6
St Lucy	10	7	70	3	30	10	3	30	7	70
Totals	188	122	64.9	66	35.1	153	64	41.8	89	58.2

Source: Adapted from Barbados EC 1897.

The Economic Arguments

It has been suggested that more women – especially single females – were employed by education officials for cost efficiency. A variant of this argument is that men were drawn away from the relatively low-paying teaching occupation to more lucrative options that were not similarly available to women (Albisetti 1993, 254). Bacchus points out that in the early post-slavery period in the West Indies, missionary societies sought to increase the complement of female teachers as a cost-cutting measure, even though parents said they preferred male teachers (1990, 302). On the other hand, while there is evidence of the withdrawal of whites – males and females – on account of poor pay, elementary teaching remained one of the very few white-collar, "respectable" occupations open to black men and women. Moreover, one would have to ask what lucrative alternatives were available to educated blacks within West Indian societies characterized by serious socio-economic strictures.

There is, however, no doubt that government expenditure on elementary education provided primarily for the black masses was always a soft target for reduction whenever West Indian economies were in difficulty, as in the beet-sugar crisis years of the 1880s and 1890s (see Gordon 1963, chapter 6). For instance, following the collapse of sugar prices in 1884, the Barbados government restricted expenditure on education in 1885 in spite of a petition from 2,701 teachers and parents and a mass meeting at the Albert Hall in Bridgetown.[2] In 1894, when the fortunes of sugar took another dip, retrenchment in education was again placed on the legislative agenda (Barbados LC 1894, 1–2). Consequently, in March 1894, the governor appointed an education commission headed by Bishop Herbert Bree of the Anglican Church to review the entire system of education. By far the majority of its sixty-three meetings, held over a two-year period, deliberated on the elementary education system.

The cost efficiency of delivering this level of education was a major preoccupation of the commission; table 14.1 underscores the its gendered approach to cost efficiency.

Implementation of these proposals would have witnessed the emergence of women as the majority in the service, but the exclusion of men by women was never envisaged. Indeed, the gap between the sexes in the service was to be significantly narrower (by 16.4 per cent) than what

Table 14.2   Distribution of Schools, Barbados, 1900–1940

Year	Boys' Schools	Girls' Schools	Mixed Schools	Infant Schools	Total
1900	46	44	30	49	169
1905	63	60	9	34	166
1910	65	62	7	32	166
1916	58	59	4	25	146
1920	55	55	7	18	135
1925	54	54	8	17	133
1930	54	53	8	12	127
1937	53	53	8	12	126
1939–40	52	53	9	12 Jnr	126

Source: Barbados reports on elementary education, 1900–40 (Barbados LC).

obtained when men were predominant (29.8 per cent). What these raw figures obscure is the process of gender segregation based on a policy of creating exclusively boys' and girls' schools and the reservation of all infant schools for women.

From Coeducation to Single-Sex Policy and Back

The idea of single-sex elementary schools had been mooted since the 1870s. When the Mitchinson Commission reported in 1876, virtually all elementary schools in Barbados were mixed, but some clergymen were already expressing concerns about the moral implications (Barbados LC 1894, 1–2). In 1884, out of 105 combined and primary schools, there were just ten single-sex schools – seven for boys and three for girls. However, R.P. Elliot urged the supervisors to step up the separation of the sexes in the interest of morality (Barbados LC 1886a, 10). Six years later it was reported that the mixed schools that operated best were those where the boys and girls sat on separate benches (Barbados LC 1892, 4). In this regard officials were attempting to bring Barbados in line with the pattern set in Victorian England. The stereotype of pathological black sexuality added fuel to the concern of local education officials. By the 1890s cost rationalization was but an added factor; from 1894 the Board of Education began to rigorously implement the policy of separating the sexes and a gender division of labour in the schools.[3]

Table 14.2 illustrates the implementation of the policy. The number of mixed schools declined dramatically between 1900 and 1905. By the latter date, women would have emerged as the majority (certainly at the level of head teacher) provided that the policy of allocating girls' and infant schools to women was strictly observed.

In 1943 Howard Hayden was appointed as the first director of education, with a mandate to reorganize the island's education system. At that time 106 of the 126 elementary schools in Barbados were single-sex. In his *Policy for Education* (1945), Hayden recommended that the elementary schools be reorganized according to age cohorts rather than on the all-age single-sex system (pp. 16–17). He believed that "the mixed unit is the realistic and family unit" and that "the community of the school should reflect the larger community of life" (p. 17d). In January 1947 the Alleyne School became the first coeducational secondary school in the island. By 1954, 43 of the 124 elementary schools were also coeducational, and by 1960 the figure was 48 out of a total of 116 primary schools (Barbados DE 1954, 10; Barbados ME 1960, 17). Even though the implementation of the policy advocated by Hayden witnessed some reintegration of senior boys and girls, he was firmly of the view "that infants of both sexes should be taught by women" (Hayden 1945, 17c). In practice, then, men continued to dominate the administrative and senior levels of the system while the most junior levels continued to be reserved for women. The emergence of coeducation did not change the ideological perspective that women were principally nurturers and should be confined to the lowest salary round.

Migration and the Feminization Hypothesis

It has also been argued that the departure of men to more lucrative pursuits was a factor that accounts for the employment of more women as teachers. In the Caribbean context, few alternatives for higher pay existed for black men. However, migration had provided alternative opportunities since the nineteenth century, especially for men. There is some evidence to indicate that many of the assistant male teachers were emigrating to Panama and the United States during the first two decades of the twentieth century. The Education Report of 1905 took note that

> A steady stream of Emigration among the male assistant teachers has begun. There are not many districts from which assistants have not left, either for the United States of America or Panama but especially the former place. In several cases there has been some difficulty in finding suitable lads to fill the vacancies thus created. (Barbados BE 1907, 25)

The Swaby Education Commission Report of 1907–9 observed that poor pay created much difficulty in recruiting pupil teachers and keeping assistant teachers, especially males, from seeking work in the Canal Zone. It was said to pose a challenge in respect to replenishing the ranks of the headmasters (Barbados LC 1909, 9). Given the long and parsimonious apprenticeship under which most assistant teachers served before receiving an appointment as a teacher, it is not surprising that male assistants were taking the opportunity to emigrate to greener pastures. Although Massiah contends that the emigration of Barbadian men up to 1921 "served to strengthen the bias of the labour market towards female employment" (Massiah 1984a, 21–22), education authorities made valiant efforts to avoid abrogating the gender division in the teaching service. One strategy was to augment the reserve of pupil and assistant teachers wherever possible. For instance, the number of all assistants – male and female – increased from a total of 207 in 1905 to 283 by 1914. In boys' primary schools alone the total number of male pupil teachers and assistants increased from 114 in 1911 to 137 by 1919.

In spite of these efforts, by 1919 the inspectors of schools reported that it was becoming nearly impossible to recruit young men to the teaching service (Barbados LC 1919, 2). That year the governor sought an increase for assistant teachers and pupil teachers after observing that their salaries ranged from $2 to $4 – reportedly less than what trained domestics were receiving (Barbados LC 1919, 2). However, in the 1920s education officials were still plagued by "a steady exodus" of some of their best assistants to the United States (Barbados LC 1924, 8; 1925, 8), so much so that the Board of Education began to permit the appointment of some female assistant teachers in the boys' schools. This was not, however, a retreat from the principle of gender segregation, for these women were apparently being appointed only in schools sufficiently large to have infant departments, where they could be employed under the supervision of a headmaster (Barbados LC 1921, 16). In any case, by 1924 changes to US immigration policy put the brakes on the exodus of young male teachers to that country (Barbados LC 1926, 9). Moreover, the increase in 1928 of the salaries of male assistants from £66 to £75 and of females from £53 to £60 was intended to be a further incentive to check the exodus from the service (Barbados LC 1929, 4). By 1934 some male assistants could work for £85 to £100, while female assistant teachers were offered a maximum of £75.

Large-scale male emigration placed education authorities under some pressure to fill the positions in the system reserved for males. Officials were forced to employ "inexperienced lads" (Barbados LC 1913, 4) and to offer more attractive remuneration packages. However, while the system was under stress, there is no evidence to indicate that women were allowed to take over those positions reserved for men – for example, headships of boys' schools. As Miller concludes, the market forces of lucrative alternative opportunities for men cannot account for the growing number of women in the teaching service (1994, 116).

Discriminatory Salaries and Marriage Restrictions

The Bree Commission recommended that those female teachers who would be retained in the infants' and all-girls' primary schools should have their salaries reduced to 25 per cent below those of their male counterparts in the boys' schools. W.H. Greaves, the attorney general, was convinced that the proposals of the Commission in respect to discriminatory pay and the reservation of infant schools for female teachers would have yielded the most significant cost reductions. However, he objected to the proposal that women should be paid any less than men when filling similar posts. "I cannot see the justice," he said, "of paying a woman less for the same work" (Barbados LC 1897, 3). A year later, when his colleagues on the Board of Education ratified the resolution that "Female Teachers hereafter appointed shall receive only three-fourths of the amount of the salary which would be paid to a male Teacher in a similar position", Greaves dissented and walked out of the meeting (Barbados BE 1898).

The board proceeded to set out its revised rules, which excluded married teachers from the service and restricted the salary of the remaining single women. These rules were clearly aimed at reinforcing and protecting the dominance of the male teacher. According to Rule 1(c) "Married women [are] not to be regarded as suitable persons to be Teachers" because "Schools suffer by frequent absence, and the Board considers that after marriage a wife's proper place is her husband's household and hers".[4]

> Masters will in the majority of cases marry and have families to support. Mistresses must remain single if they continue in the service: they therefore cannot have the same claims on the salaries that a man with a wife and children would have. The grant from the Legislature being limited, it is necessary to make this distinction in the pay of Masters and Mistresses otherwise in the future the salary of a master would be very much less than it is at present. (Barbados 1898, 2311)

Under the Education (Amendment) Act passed the previous year, expenditure on elementary education was limited to £11,000 (Barbados LC 1897, s. 9). The rules reflected the objectives of keeping the cost of elementary education in check while protecting in the long run the salary levels of men, partly at the expense of their female colleagues. One way to do this was to promote the concept of the family wage and the patriarchal nuclear family.

Although the *Report of the West India Royal Commission* (1945) endorsed this family model, it admitted that in the Caribbean "the woman so often is the supporter of the home" (United Kingdom 1945, 220). But this acknowledgement did not reverse colonial pay policy. Elementary teachers were made civil servants starting in October 1945; by then the salary of a female teacher was about 80 per cent of her male counterpart's. Grantley H. Adams, who was appointed in 1948 to review the conditions and emoluments of civil servants, did not challenge the salary differential or the claims of the education officials who reiterated that women teachers were more frequently absent and could not perform the same duties as men (Adams 1945, 141–42). In addition, Adams expressed the view that, given the high unemployment in the island, women would be more susceptible to retrenchment should the principle of equal pay be implemented (p. 142). In effect the Adams Report upheld the principle that had first led to the implementation of differential pay fifty years before. That is, in the context of limited economic resources, priority should be given to securing the salary levels of the male bread-winner. The Dos Santos Commission Report (1952) and the Godsall Report (1956) made no recommendation to equalize the salaries of women and men in the teaching service (Dos Santos 1952, 8–9, 48–49; Godsall 1956, 68–77). Godsall felt that other anomalies demanded a higher degree of priority (1956, 68). It was only during the period of deliberation by Commissioner K.C. Jacobs in 1961 that the government accepted the principle of equal pay in the teaching service (Jacobs 1961, para. 10.31). Even so, for financial reasons this was adopted incrementally, so that by 1966 there was still a disparity in pay based on gender (Gardner-Brown 1966, 50).

The Marginalization Hypothesis

The Lumb Commission of Jamaica made a recommendation similar to that of the Bree Commission in Barbados to lower the pay of women teachers. However, the governor of Jamaica and a Mr Capper of the Education Department opposed this recommendation. The Colonial Office accepted their argument that the offer of equal pay would better serve the objective of attracting females into the service (Miller 1994, 91–92).

Harry Goulbourne has suggested that if the Lumb Commission's proposal to increase the employment of female teachers in Jamaica was "a deliberate attempt to keep salaries down, release men for agricultural work, or even prevent teachers' militancy, the more immediate consideration seems to improve the moral standing of the community and teachers themselves and to encourage the teaching of domestic subjects" (1988, 73–74). But Miller is convinced that out of all of these considerations the principal motivation was to eliminate the political threat of Jamaica's male teachers by reducing their numbers. Miller contends that

> Primary school teaching and teacher education shifted from being male dominated to being female dominated as a result of the intention of those holding central positions in the society to restrict black men to occupations related to agricultural and industrial labour; to stifle the possible emergence of militant black educated men who could possibly overthrow the power structure;

to loosen the hold of the church on the education system; and to limit the upward mobility of black men in the society. In a real sense the black woman was deliberately used against the black man. In essence the logic seems to have been that if social advantage must be conceded to Blacks through teacher education and elementary school teaching, then allow black women such advancement instead of black men. (1994, 125)

Miller's approach serves to remind us that gender represents a site of struggle not only between men and women but also between different groups of men. However, he not only privileges the struggle between the dominant white males and the challenging black males, but also virtually negates the agency of Caribbean women and excludes them from the terrain of resistance. Miller dismisses Afro-Caribbean women as simply "pawns in the conflicts between men" (1991, 289), "foot soldiers" in a "reserved army" in what is essentially a struggle for power and material resources by men (pp. 168, 170). In the fallout women become "innocent beneficiaries". "They were the only innocents in the matter. Unknowingly, the black woman was being recruited by the ruling minority as an ally against the black man" (Miller 1994, 95). Miller's contention that women were the principal beneficiaries of colonial education policy is not supported by any other known study. Moreover, as Mayers demonstrates, women were far from passive pawns in a male struggle; women too engaged in the struggle for equity in the teaching service (1995, 271).

Even if one were to accept Miller's thesis that more women teachers were being recruited because black male teachers were perceived by the establishment as potential political threats, the fact remains that men continued to have a significant presence in the elementary teaching service. Even when women constituted the majority in the teaching service, that numerical majority status did not translate into a threat to male teachers' dominance and privilege.

It is interesting that while Miller has argued for the political militancy of Jamaica's male teachers, he does not offer an adequate explanation why this group of militant men should have allowed themselves to be progressively marginalized without a battle. His contention that the Jamaica Union of Teachers did not foresee the long-term impact of the gendered education policy on its members is unconvincing (1994, 94). Men were invariably at the helm of teachers' professional organizations or unions, and even when women were the majority of the membership, their concerns were inadequately addressed or ignored.

Indeed, when the Marriott–Mayhew Commission investigated education in Trinidad, Barbados, the Windward Islands and the Leeward Islands in 1931–32, it was revealed that women comprised an average of 57 per cent of the teachers across the region but were being paid on a lower scale than men. Marriott and Mayhew said that they heard no complaints about this obvious discrimination, but quickly qualified their statement by observing that women teachers were so marginalized in the various teachers' associations that their views were not really canvassed (1933, 73). The commissioners therefore strongly recommended the appointment of women to every board of education in order to have women's concerns better articulated (p. 109).

When the Moyne Commission met in Queen's Park, Barbados, on Saturday, 28 January 1938, an all-male delegation of the Barbados Elementary Teachers Association appeared to give testimony on behalf of the teachers. This was the first such royal commission sent to the West Indies that set out to receive representation from women, and two women, Dame Rachel Crowdy and Dr Mary Blacklock, sat as commissioners. The latter was an expert in tropical medicine and an advocate for improved educational opportunities for women. The following exchange between Dr Blacklock and the Barbados Elementary Teachers

Table 14.3 Proportion of Gainfully Occupied Population (10 years and over) 1891–1946

Colony	1981		1911		1921		1946	
	Male	Female	Male	Female	Male	Female	Male	Female
Barbados	79.1	78.3	78	77.1	79.5	76.9	78.1	49.2
British Guiana	89	78.2	89	89	86	67.9	79.2	29.4
Trinidad & Tobago	87.4	73.9	85.8	64.6	85.4	62.7	78.6	26.1
Jamaica	81.3	75.4	78.4	60	78.4	64.7	72.5	33.9
Four Colonies	83.8	76.2	82.2	67.6	81.7	66.1	75.5	32.9

Source: West Indian census for 1946 in Harewood 1975, 134.

Association delegation illustrates the professional marginalization of women teachers. Mr C.F. Broome and Mr Taylor were respectively president and secretary of the association.

> *Dr Blacklock:* How many women have you in your Association?
>
> *Mr Taylor:* The majority are women, sorry to say.
>
> *Dr Blacklock:* Mr Secretary why have you no women representative in your deputation?
>
> *Mr Broome:* The women in Barbados are very slow to speak in public. They are very slow to take public offices. They rather sit down and take it quietly. I am sure I would not have got one of them to come here.
>
> *Dr Blacklock:* Do you mean to say women teachers would rather sit down and keep quiet in the schools?
>
> *Mr Broome:* Oh no they teach in the schools. I mean in the Association.
>
> *Dr Blacklock:* I thought women teachers would have plenty of experience in speaking. Did you ask any of them to come?
>
> *Mr Broome:* It surprises me. I ask *one* [emphasis added] of them to sit on a Committee they do not.
>
> *Dr Blacklock:* It surprises me. Women teachers who are generally accustomed to speak would not wish to sit on committees and would not wish to come and represent their point of view here and I am sorry that they are not represented. (WIRC 1939, 117)

It was no surprise, then, that while Broome and Taylor raised the perennial issue of inadequate pay for teachers before the commission, at no stage did they address the peculiar discrimination faced by women teachers.

The preoccupation with numerical "feminization" of the teaching service and, in Miller's case, the interpretation of that process as male marginalization, represent a failure to assess the overall participation of women in the colonial economies and the ideologies that underpinned the gender divisions of labour. While the number of single women in teaching expanded, the general participation of women in paid labour had declined significantly by 1946 – and not only in Barbados.

In Barbados by 1960 the female worker rate had declined to 36.6 per cent, compared to 62.5 per cent for men (Massiah 1984a, 23). This pattern reflected in part the "housewifization" of some women or their relegation to marginal economic pursuits. The expansion of opportunities in "nurturing" activities such as teaching and nursing was entirely consistent with the gendered colonial development policy in which women were to play supportive roles. Based on an analysis of the teaching service, therefore, it is highly problematic to conclude that black males were or are being marginalized.

Hegemonic Masculinity

I have elsewhere contended that education in the late nineteenth-century British West Indies was a site around which hegemonic masculinity was constructed (Downes 1997). Hegemonic masculinity is a discursive construct of masculinity that gains and maintains pre-eminence through its ideological linkages with socially dominant men. Messner and Sabo point out that "Hegemonic masculinity is constructed in relation to various subordinated masculinities as well as in relation to femininities" (1990, 12). I argue that socio-political leadership, economic dominance, heterosexuality, headship of the nuclear family unit and chivalric defence of empire were the cornerstones of colonial hegemonic masculinity. Only elite men had full access to masculinity so constructed, but subordinate men were allowed to share, albeit as "secondary patriarchs", in the spoils of male dominance. It was in part the limited concessions to "lesser" men that were intended to secure their consent to the ideological bases of hegemonic masculinity.

I contend that upwardly mobile black men in the elementary teaching service welcomed the opportunity to share in a respectable masculinity defined in terms of being chief breadwinner with a dependent housewife. As early as 1897 G. Daniel, a journalist and former schoolmaster testifying before the West India Royal Commission, gave his blessing to the policy of employing women as infant teachers. He argued that women were "far better fitted for such work" and could be paid at a much cheaper rate (WIRC 1897, pt. 3, para. 895). Daniel was a member of a delegation of black men, including a shipwright, a homeopathic doctor and a peasant, who expressed their concern with the impact the economic crisis was having not only on the average working-class man, but also on skilled and educated men like themselves.

While from 1898 education policy lowered the salaries of women teachers in the interest of the male teachers, there are indications that economic constraints tempered the ideals of hegemonic masculinity. For instance, there is some evidence suggesting that from the early 1900s the so-called family wage of male teachers was being supplemented by small enterprises such as shopkeeping – an activity through which their spouses could contribute to the family income. The Board of Education banned teachers from operating rum shops for moral reasons,[5] but no doubt grocery shops continued to be operated.

During the first decade of the twentieth century the Board of Education's attention was often drawn to a number of cases of male elementary schoolteachers who were brought before the Petty Debt Court.[6] The Board of Education report of 1902 expressed concern over the growing tendency among some teachers to get into debt (Barbados BE 1904, 84). Although these debt cases have not been studied in detail, their association with failed small shopkeeping enterprises is without doubt. The operation of these enterprises may also give some indication of modification of the male breadwinner ideal; undoubtedly spouses operated these shops while the men were in school. Schoolmasters were therefore learning the painful lesson that Victorian notions of masculinity had to be modified. Colonial education, it has been argued, served to create a black middle stratum who would act as a social buffer between the elite and the masses, and who would serve as a conduit for hegemonic value systems (Downes 1997). Colonial officials, and the local white elite, acknowledged the significant influence that elementary teachers had over the masses. This was underscored by Hayden when he alluded to the importance of providing residences for head teachers in the community (1945, 22). Moreover, colonial education officials expected that the reorganized elementary teaching service would itself serve as a model for gender relations in the Afro-Caribbean family.

White colonial observers had for some time been concerned about what they perceived to be "abnormal" Caribbean family structures characterized by peculiar gender relations. For instance, Rev Alfred Caldecott, a former principal of Codrington College, wrote that Afro-Caribbean women held greater control in their relationships with their partners than their European counterparts. He stated:

> there is in the Negro race a nearer approach to equality between the sexes than is found in European races. The woman is almost as capable a bread winner

as the man; at any rate she can, in early and middle life, easily earn enough to keep a house for herself and two or three children; and not infrequently it is the woman whose affection cools or changes, and from whom arises the abandonment of the connection and the choice of another mate. (1970, 195)

According to Caldecott, black female economic and sexual autonomy was not healthy for society, and his prescribed cure was domestication. He argued for the extension of more domestic skills to "enable a woman to make a home in which she finds her happiness so much involved that the vagaries of the lower passions finding a controlling influence, and the waywardness of affection receives a check" (1970, 195).

The view that women ought to be anchored to the home and that men should be allowed to exercise their "rightful" place in the Afro-Caribbean home, as chief breadwinners, continued to be an article of faith for development planners. T.S. Simey, social welfare adviser to Colonial Development and Welfare, noted:

> But it is nevertheless true that enduring family relationships which bring with them a sharing as well as a division of moral obligations and economic responsibilities between husband and wife and their children are the exception rather than the rule in West Indies. The individual personality undoubtedly suffers from the absence of the father in the typical West Indian family group. (Quoted in Reddock 1994, 214–15)

Social planners and anthropologists studying the Caribbean through the 1950s and 1960s still perceived the "marginal" status in the family of black working-class men as a defining feature of Caribbean society and a fundamental social ill to be corrected (see Barrow 1998a, 339–58).

Miller has contended that

> patriarchs, men of the dominant group, in defending their group's interests from challenges from the men of other groups in society, will relax their patriarchal closure over education, employment, earning and status symbols, thus allowing their women and the women of the challenging groups most of the opportunities that otherwise would have gone to the men of the challenging group. The double purpose of this strategy is to punish the male challengers by keeping them in their traditional place and to defuse the challenge by dividing the challenging group at the most fundamental level of social organization, the family. (1991, 166)

A closer reading of colonial policy seems to suggest that Miller's thesis needs to be turned on its head. While it is true that ruling-class males in the Caribbean have sought to neutralize all challenging groups, I have suggested that this minority ruling class has had to encourage educational policies that were conducive to the creation of middle-status functionaries and ideologues who would lend legitimacy to the status quo. There was some relaxation of patriarchal closure, as Miller suggests, but principally men, not women, were identified to share in the benefits of patriarchy – albeit a secondary and subordinate one.

Conclusion

This case-study has attempted to contribute to an ongoing debate in the international literature on the interpretation of the numerical preponderance of women in the elementary teaching service, and its social implications. I have argued that the concept of feminization, though possessing some perceptive value, offers no meaningful theoretical departure from which to interpret the experiences of men and women in the teaching service or the society at large. More important is the need to account for gender specialization through occupational segregation and to assess the ideological base for inequitable distribution of status and rewards along gender lines.

I have also attempted to analyse the serious conceptual flaws in Miller's black male marginalization thesis. The empirical evidence that I have adduced is generally consistent with the major body of feminist research in the Caribbean over the past twenty-five years. That research points to a colonial socio-economic development policy that privileged education and occupational opportunities for men at the expense of women. Finally, I advance the concept of hegemonic masculinity as a useful paradigm to explain the process of selective and differential incorporation of subordinate men (in this case, black male teachers) into the rank of "men" as defined in terms of leadership, and of socio-economic dominance of women in the patriarchal family. While this study focuses on the colonial period, it is intended to stimulate further research into connections between the quest for gender equality and the structure and operation of post-independence education systems of the Caribbean.

Notes

1. For a good overview of the literature on the nineteenth century see Albisetti 1993, Fultz 1995 and Basten 1997.
2. See "Public Meeting at the Albert Hall", *Times* (Barbados), 25 March 1885; 28 March 1885.
3. By 1895 women teachers were in charge of 60 per cent of the 54 infant schools (Barbados LC 1896).
4. See "Principal Changes Made by the New Code for Elementary Schools and the Reasons for the Same" (Barbados 1898). The objection to married female teachers was expressed from 1890. "We would like to take the opportunity too of drawing to the attention of managers to the unsatisfactory condition of many schools under the charge of married female teachers. We find that the work of a school under such a teacher almost always suffers, and we are of the opinion that as soon as a female teacher gets married it would be for the advantage of the school that she should be called upon to resign her appointment. In addition to frequent absences and late attendances the trials and duties inseparably connected with maternity must tend to render a Teacher less efficient however conscientious she may be, and the school while under her charge is sure sooner or later to suffer" (Barbados LC 1892, 4).
5. See "They Shall Not Sell Liquor", *Barbados Agricultural Reporter,* 17 May 1900, 3.
6. See Barbados BE 1902–11: case of R.M. Cummins of Hinck's Infant School (22 September 1902., fol. 34; 15 December 1902, fol. 47; case of St C. Blackman of St Mary's Boys' and Joseph Thompson of St John the Baptist Boys' (18 May 1903, fol. 71); case of J.T. Blackman of St Barnabas (20 March 1905, fol. 170); case of Mr Gale of Holy Trinity Boys' (24 January 1910, fol. 381–82;14 March 1910, fol. 386).

⊰ Chapter 15 ⊱

Requiem for the Male Marginalization Thesis in the Caribbean
Death of a Non-Theory

EUDINE BARRITEAU

Primary school teaching and teacher education shifted from being male dominated to being female dominated as a result of the intention of those holding central positions in the society to restrict black men to occupations related to agricultural and industrial labour; to stifle the possible emergence of militant, black educated men who could possibly overthrow the power structure; to loosen the hold of the church on the education system; and to limit the upward social mobility of black men in society. In a real sense the black woman was used against the black man. (Miller 1991, 125)

Are males being marginalized? Certainly not, if the main factor being considered is power. Despite the increasing percentage of women at the University of the West Indies, it is the men who are elected to the seat of student power. At community level, whether the issue is dons or youth club leaders, there is no marginalization of males. And as far as the churches are concerned, women's over-representation in the membership and ministering groups, but under representation in the leadership echelons is well documented . . . The marginalization discourse always ignores these facts. (Chevannes 1999, 33)

Introduction

This chapter argues that the thesis of the marginalization of the black Caribbean male as developed by Errol Miller is flawed in its construct, rendering its core assumptions more political than epistemological. I examine the thesis and the construction of Caribbean masculinity against the background of changes in Caribbean political economy and gender systems in the late twentieth century (see Barriteau 2001). I demonstrate that among the several weaknesses of Miller's thesis are that it places too much emphasis on coeducation (which is not universal in the region) and on changes in material and ideological gender relations affecting Caribbean women, without examining men's gender identities and the construct and content of Caribbean masculinities. I construct a framework for assessing marginalization and maintain that Caribbean masculinities are yet to be adequately theorized. Rather than produce an epistemological breakthrough offering new knowledge about Caribbean men, Miller's thesis posits the notion that men have a priori rights to the resources of the state as clients and citizens, and therefore any measures that create conditions that move women towards equality are interpreted as men's being further marginalized. This false construct creates an inaccurate, deeply flawed examination of the issues confronting Caribbean men.

The debate on the marginalization thesis is taking place while Caribbean societies are experiencing economic, social, cultural and political transitions. Academics and popular commentators are trying to grapple with these changes for both men and women. In the context of this particular thesis it has been presented as a definitive theory, when in fact its basic assumptions have not been subject to a sustained, rigorous interrogation. Epistemologically the thesis does not advance our understanding of what is ontologically different in the lives of Caribbean men, although it warns us repeatedly to note (with alarm) the changes for women. As developed in the works of Errol Miller,[1] social commentators and the general public, the thesis has predetermined that Caribbean men have been wilfully or deliberately marginalized as an outcome of adjustments introduced into gender systems to benefit women.

My analysis investigates existing discourses on Caribbean men by dissecting the major contributions to the discourse on marginality and masculinity in order to isolate its core assumptions and concerns. I examine the assumptions of the earlier marginality thesis by structural functionalists and contrast this with the thesis of the marginalization of the black male as developed by Miller. I identify the sharp divergences between the two notions of marginality and marginalization and then present and classify the contributions of others to this debate. As the examination unfolds I make explicit the foundational assumptions underlying the theorizing in this field. Education (that is, access, enrolment, participation, performance and achievement[2]) emerges as the arena in which both academic analyses and popular perception locate male marginalization. Coeducation in particular is identified as the main contributing factor to the marginalization of males. However, the marginalization thesis is firmly located in an expressed disapproval of changing economic and social roles for Caribbean women. Public commentators hold that women are

> responsible for the destruction of families, high rates of divorce, male economic and social marginalization, and the comparatively poorer performance of boys and men at every educational level. Repeated newspaper articles and editorials warn of the damage done to boys by being raised in female-headed households, attending coeducational schools and being taught primarily by female teachers. (Barriteau 1998b, 437; 1994, 283)

It is not accidental or incidental that coeducation has been singled out as the main contributing factor to the marginalization of Caribbean men. While there is very little credible evidence that coeducation positions men outside of the currency of resource distribution, coeducation did bring more women into the mainstream of resource allocation. Through coeducation women gained access to a better quality and greater variety of educational goods. This enhanced their capacity to transform their new qualifications into labour force participation, theoretically at higher levels of pay, even though the latter frequently remain lower than those of men with similar levels of qualifications (see Bailey 1997).

It is this location of the analysis of men's marginality in changes for Caribbean women that I find problematic. This does a disservice to theorizing Caribbean masculinity, one result being that the analysis is not yet centred on men as full socially constructed beings whose ontology needs to be thoroughly examined against the background of history, contemporary political economy and culture.[3]

Intrinsically there is nothing inherently wrong in using changes in gender identities for Caribbean women as an entry point to investigate men's lives. Unfortunately this approach has ossified into what passes for an analysis of masculinity and marginalization. The popular analysis of men and masculinity begins with women and remains there, so frequently public discussions that ostensibly address issues of masculinity just quarrel about women.[4] I am not suggesting that women stand outside of the practices, relations and beliefs that make up gender ideologies in our societies and that may hold specific penalties for men. This situation exists and yet Caribbean societies are resiliently patriarchal. Some men are positioned in hierarchical, disadvantageous relationships to other men, but women remain with secondary, inferiorly ranked gender identities in relation to both elite and subordinate men. Men who experience the power of other men in many dimensions of their lives and who subscribe to patriarchal relations are not automatically less patriarchal in dealing with women. This is so irrespective of the class position and experiences of these men.[5] It has become far too easy to hold women responsible, to blame women for everything that is wrong for men, introducing closure to an area of study that is in need of serious investigation.

A Framework for Assessing Male Marginalization

If Caribbean men are marginalized, how can we determine this marginalization and what would we need to know to introduce policies that would create conditions of gender justice? The concept of gender justice is pivotal to any discussions of marginalization. The analysis requires measures to determine male marginalization and some means of assessing attempts to attain gender justice. Towards attempting to produce some answers I apply a comprehensive model of gender analysis that I developed when I theorized Caribbean gender systems (Barriteau 1998c). In this model I define a just gender system as one in which there are no asymmetries of access to or allocations of status, power and material resources in a society. In a just gender system there are no inequalities in the control over and capacity to benefit from these resources.[6] In a just gender system there are no hierarchies of gender identities or of the meanings society gives to masculinity and femininity. Alternatively, in an unjust gender system there is unequal access to and distribution of material resources and power (Barriteau 1998c, 192). To work towards gender justice not only means closing the gaps and removing the injustices exposed by gender analysis but actively promoting conditions in which women and men are not penalized or unduly privileged for the gender identities with which they clothe their biological, physiological selves. Accordingly, the thesis of the marginalization of the male implies that gender systems are unjust for men.

If institutions and practices are marginalizing men, that is, they are unjust for them, then a theorization of marginalization should seek to determine the following:

- What are the policies, legislation, prejudices and practices that penalize or reward men?
- What are the deeply entrenched policies of the state and its institutions that marginalize men?
- What are the contents and effects of the gender identities men subscribe to?
- What part do these play in expressions of masculinity that are viewed as problematic?
- What recommendations are in the literature for dealing with marginalization if it exists?
- How do these address concerns for gender justice and equality?

Miller's attempts at theorizing marginalization do not answer any of these questions.

Men's Marginality in Families or the Marginalization of the Caribbean Male?

The opening quotations identify divergent views on the notion of a problem that has engrossed the Commonwealth Caribbean for the past decade. If in terms of state interests the 1980s belonged to Caribbean women, the decade of the 1990s was dominated by popular and academic debates on ideas that Caribbean men were in crisis and that they were increasingly marginalized in their homes and in the policies and practices of states. For the first time there was a sustained interest in exploring how men experienced their lives in both the private and public domains. Yet what seemed a significant point of departure in examining men's gender identities stultified at the point of showing men as victims. Why?

In the 1980s other independent Caribbean states joined Jamaica, Barbados, Trinidad and Tobago, and Grenada in institutionalizing state mechanisms to monitor gender inequalities for women. Several countries introduced legislation to remove the more blatant aspects of institutionalized discrimination against women. Women increasingly participated in the labour force in larger numbers. This was influenced by the diversification of Caribbean economies that began in the 1960s with various industrialization strategies of development and expanded educational opportunities. Women began to penetrate professions that were once historically and traditionally male-dominated. A more politicized, organized women's movement (evident in the growth of several women's organizations and NGOs with an explicit concern for women's well-being) became very vocal and very visible. The Caribbean Association for Feminist Research and Action became the best expression of this. Within the University of the West Indies, a women's studies programme was emerging out of Women and Development Studies groups. This was an outcome of the Women in the Caribbean Project (WICP) of 1979 to 1982 and the establishment of the Women and Development Unit (WAND) in the School of Continuing Studies at the University of the West Indies in 1978.

Internationally the United Nation world conferences on women called attention to deplorable conditions existing for women and developed strategies for monitoring their improvement. Some donor countries made the existence of women in development programmes a condition for qualifying for foreign aid (USAID 1978). Others used their development agencies to promote programmes to assist women. However, by the end of the 1980s there was fear that Caribbean states had gone too far. They had surrendered too much to the interests of women at the expense of men, and the first rumblings of "men in crisis" and "the marginalization of the black male" were being heard (Miller 1991, 1994).[7]

Miller's Male Marginalization Thesis

Errol Miller was the first and only Caribbean scholar to theorize the idea of men at risk and the marginalization of the black Caribbean male. The marginalization of the male thesis should be called "Miller's Male Marginalization Thesis". Outside of his attempt to theorize the marginalization of the black Caribbean male, no one else has done so. Several public commentators and men's rights advocates[8] have accepted his assumptions and premises as givens and have contributed analyses based on his foundational arguments. However, they have not tried to devise an explanatory framework for male marginalization. In 1986 Miller published *Marginalization of the Black Male: Insights from the Teaching Profession*, which was revised within a more theoretical analysis and republished in 1994. He followed this with *Men at Risk*, published in 1991. He offers the following as evidence of what is happening to men in the Caribbean:

> The description of Caribbean societies points to lower-strata men's marginal positions in the family, role reversal in a small but increasing number of households, boys' declining participation and performance in the educational system, the greater prospect of men inheriting their fathers' position in the social structure, the decline in the proportions of men in the highest-paying and most prestigious occupations and the decrease in men's earning power relative to women's especially in white collar occupations. While some men, particularly in the highest social strata, have been able to maintain their traditional position in the family, educational system and labour force, the majority are being eclipsed by women rising in all these areas. (1991, 93)

In the 1980s Miller developed the notion of men's marginality as victimhood, as he acknowledges that analyses of the idea of the marginalization of the black Caribbean male have existed since the 1950s in anthropological and sociological studies of Caribbean families (1991, 70–71). However, these differ substantively from Miller's conceptualization of marginalization.

In a review of the earlier literature on Caribbean men and families, Christine Barrow reminds us of the anthropological and sociological roots of an idea of men's marginality that is vastly different to how it is posed today:

> "Male marginality" emerged in the structural functional studies of the "matrifocal family" among the "lower class negroes". Accordingly, the familial roles of men, defined as father and conjugal partner, are perceived as limited to providing economic support and occasional discipline and as woefully inadequately performed. Men are peripheral to the family – their place is everywhere. (1998a, 339)

Barrow challenges the early thesis of male marginality in family life. In the process she unearths a much larger, overlooked role of men in kinship systems. She states, "Perhaps in their anxiety to disassociate themselves from the theme of matrilineal African origin, functionalists searched for men as fathers and husbands and ignored their insertions into the kinship system as brothers and uncles" (1998a, 341). Barrow does not accept that men have been as marginal to family structures as the structural functionalists concluded. She thinks these social scientists misunderstood Caribbean family structures, kinship networks and types of relationships and therefore men's roles within them.

The structural functionalist discussion of men and marginality identifies men as choosing to limit their roles to those of economic provider and disciplinarian. Barrow summarizes the three dominant premises of this view that shaped mid-twentieth-century notions of Caribbean masculinity:

- kinship relations which fall beyond the boundaries of nuclear units and household boundary are of no consequence
- that the significant male family roles are those of co-resident conjugal partner and father, and that, as such, Caribbean men are "irresponsible"
- that men have no real place within the family, they are "marginal" (Barrow 1998a, 343)

Barrow states that the functionalists found only those roles and came to those conclusions because they confined their focus to investigating nuclear-type family structures, which are notoriously problematic for Caribbean women and men. For Barrow the roles men chose involved much more expanded involvement. To challenge the premises of the functionalist literature, she cites evidence from a study of ninety-two black Barbadian males. She concludes:

> Although the problem of marginal fathers and "outside" children persist, social fathering of a few emerges at least as importantly as the biological fathering of many. Within his family, the extended family, the real man strikes a balance between potentially conflicting identities, roles and relationships. Although men receive validation of their masculinity outside of the family, their masculinity is also located within it. Virility is central to their identities but some also spoke of "resisting temptation". (1998a, 356)

Table 15.1 Characteristics Shaping the Values of Reputation and Respectability in the Mid-Twentieth-Century Caribbean

	Reputation	Respectability
Social Actor	**Man**	**Woman**
Main characteristics	virility, sexual promiscuity	chastity, sexual morality, faith
Family involvement	marginal to family	central to family
Main family roles	defence of family, provider, disciplinarian	care of family, nurturer
Family involvement	marginal	central to family, matrifocal
Main type of union desired	visiting	legal marriage
Main social group	peer group, crews (block)	family, kinship networks
Source of validation	community/peer group	church, wider society
Main site where roles are carried out	community	home/household

Source: Constructed from information presented in Wilson 1969.

Barrow highlights a significant fact that has been overlooked. A key point in understanding the earlier analysis of men's marginality is that this phenomenon was analysed as men *choosing* their roles. Whether the man had a narrow or a more extended role, the key point is that his behaviour was interpreted as an exercise of choice. He was perceived as an agent of his actions. He defined the expression of his gender identity as "Caribbean man" to encompass roles that he felt were appropriate expressions of his masculinity. Although there is some degree of agency, I maintain that the prevalent gender roles women and men fulfil are socially constructed and sanctioned and reflect prevailing gender ideologies. The idea of choice really refers to a range of sanctioned behaviours that society and individuals determine are appropriate to men's gender identities, irrespective of the actual outcomes to men. For example, in his study of the black middle-class Jamaican family man, Jack Alexander quotes a respondent as saying that once men attain a higher socio-economic status they are expected (by whom? other men? women?) to have "outside women", that is, additional sexual relationships (Alexander 1977, 379).

Peter Wilson's review of the anthropological literature and his location of Caribbean men in informal networks at a midpoint between the family and formal institutions again underscores men's "choosing" to be minimally involved in family life. Wilson summarized the characteristics of men's social, sexual and economic behaviour. He noted that they were driven to establish reputations while women were concerned with establishing respectability. I summarize these outstanding traits in table 15.1. Wilson's work reinforces the point that men were marginally involved in family life beyond the roles of provider and disciplinarian, but they enhanced their status and reputation by extensive involvement in their informal communities. Wilson was quite clear that marginal involvement in households did not mean marginal involvement in the wider community (Wilson 1969).

Like Wilson, Barrow sees men in a wider variety of roles than those identified by the structural functionalists. The structural functionalist anthropologists saw only *provider* and *disciplinarian* within the nuclear family. They understood men's marginality as minimal involvement in the family. The issue of men's marginal role in families involving selecting among a range of sanctioned roles or activities and the extent of involvement is critical. In contrast, when Errol Miller theorizes marginality in the 1980s and 1990s, the Caribbean working-class man is the victim of an overarching conspiracy that leaves him a pawn in the hands of those conspiring to bring about his ultimate demise.

Several notable points converge. Miller does not seem to find problematic men's minimal roles in families, which is what structural functionalists focus on and criticize. Christine Barrow takes exception to this as a misunderstanding of men's involvement in non-nuclear family forms. We notice that the public–private divide of traditional liberal ideology continues to haunt gender relations. In objectifying Caribbean men and families, structural functionalists perceived men as marginal in the private domain, and declared this socially pathological. We may not want to ignore the fact that in both the European and Caribbean context, European men were not exactly exemplary fathers (Hall 1989). Yet out in the colonial periphery, the "lower-class Negro family" became a perfect anthropological field in which to discover aberrant and dysfunctional expressions of masculinity.

Although Miller is concerned about men's being circumscribed by minimal roles within families, his writings reveal greater anxiety about their being marginalized in the public domain of the state and the economy. What Miller forces us to focus on is the recurring belief about who really has a right to the public domain. Although he does not state this, there is an implicit position in his work that men have a right over and beyond women. So an additional implication of Miller's work is that it insists on maintaining hierarchies of relevance for public participation. Even though the state claims a neutrality in its formal juridical position, one of the gendered effects of the male marginalization thesis is to argue for a ranking of relevance on sex-based distinctions.

Conspiracy Theory of Marginalization and Regressive Masculinity

I label Miller's work a conspiracy theory of marginalization and analyse it as promoting a regressive notion of Caribbean masculinity. The outcomes flowing from Miller's theorizing of changes in gender systems for men is masculinity in retreat, regressing. In his 1994 work Miller states that his purpose is to probe the situation of black men in America and the Caribbean and in particular to uncover the causes of the marginalization of so many black males in the society (1994, 3). He examines the teaching profession in Jamaica but offers generalizations for the Commonwealth Caribbean.

Miller arrives at a number of conclusions in his case-study of the black male in Jamaica. He does so very cautiously by seeking to qualify each of these statements:

Primary school teaching and teacher education shifted from being male dominated to female dominated because "those holding central positions in the society" wanted to restrict black men to agricultural and industrial labour occupations. They wanted to loosen the hold of the church on the education system. They wanted to limit the upward mobility of black men in the society. They wanted to stifle the emergence of militant black educated men who could overthrow the power structure. "In a real sense the black woman was used against the black man. In essence the logic seems to have been that if social advantage must be conceded to Blacks through teacher education and elementary school teaching, then allow black women such advancement instead of black men." (1994, 125)

Miller's underlying thesis – that men have an a priori right to the resources of the state and society over and above women– is clearer here. He seems to interpret attempts to correct for the explicit denial of women's political and economic relevance as being designed instead to punish men. He concludes that the experience of black Jamaican men in being marginalized will become the experiences of all males of subordinate groups in patriarchal societies, and goes on to list seven different groups of men regionally and internationally who can expect to share the fate of Jamaican black men. He credits the creation of the women's lobby to the process that marginalizes the black male rather than to any adverse conditions in women's lives forcing them to organize and articulate. This contradicts his statement that "these [men] holding central positions" were responsible for advancing black women at the expense of black men. His arguments have been construed in popular discussions to mean women are to blame for all the educational problems that men, especially young men, are experiencing (Miller 1994, 124–31).

Miller's theorizing has a curious mixture of fixed, static assumptions and elements of dynamism. He inserts some core ideas into his theory because subsequent arguments depend on their being embedded in its foundational structure. This seems like a *deus ex machina* device. He has already solved the dilemma of men's marginalization. What is required are some untested assumptions that point towards his conclusion. However, Miller provides no justification as to why a particular course of action (which is pivotal to the internal coherency and therefore the working of the theory) is more preferable:

The marginalization hypothesis is that patriarchs, men of the dominant group, in defending their group's interests from challenges from the men of other groups in society, will relax their patriarchal closure over education, employment, earning and status symbols, thus allowing their women and women of the challenging groups most of the opportunities that would have gone to the men of the challenging group. The double purpose of this strategy is to punish the male challengers by keeping them in their traditional place and to defuse the challenges by dividing the challenging group at the most fundamental level of social organization, the family. The unintended consequences are: the creation of circumstances which would lead to the liberation of women and the regression of men of the challenging group to patriarchy practised in the personalistic idiom. (1991, 166)

It would be useful if Miller could explain why it is more satisfying for men of the dominating group to reward women and not men of the challenging group. He also needs to clarify the cohesion that his hypothesis implies in the family structures of the black working class, the challenging group. What Miller really wants to explain and warn about is women's seemingly rapid advancement. He approaches this by talking about men's marginalization, with the result that the theory offers very little internal analysis of what is actually happening for or to men.

He blames international development institutions, UN agencies and the World Bank for marginalizing black men in Jamaica:

Certainly UNESCO, the World Bank, USAID, and CIDA, which aided and assisted successive Jamaican governments since 1962 in expanding education, cannot stand aloof from the fact that their interventions have left black males in Jamaica more marginal in the Jamaican society than their grandfathers were. The full implications of this are still to be experienced. The recency of these interventions makes it still early to realize fully the entire extent of the social repercussions for family life, employment, religion, relations between the sexes, and the social structure. (1994, 124–31)

In 1997 Miller states that the essence of his work is not to deny feminist scholarship in respect to findings and claims concerning the marginalization of women within patriarchy. Rather it is to add the dimension of the marginalization of men of subordinate groups within societies in which race and class have been actively contested as criteria for organizing society (1997, 36). Women are also members of subordinate groups in which gendered asymmetric relations further distort their experiences of race and class exploitation. In this essay Miller seems to modify his earlier position, and his conclusions are closer to feminist analyses of gender relations in the region. He states that he does not hold the view that male underachievement is caused by the pedagogical approaches of female teachers in schools or the socialization practices of single mothers in the homes (all popular arguments). Rather he views the feminization of teaching, the matrifocal form of an increasing number of households, the poor participation of boys in school and the underachievement of men in the workplace as symptoms of the intense conflict and competition among various groups that comprise society. Miller's final statement is that the observed patterns are not the result of the absence or presence of male role models but of the changing definition and apportionment of the roles themselves (1997, 44).

He prioritizes race/racism in his analysis and insists that black women were deliberately used against black men (1994, 129). Miller attributes to black male teachers the potential to liberate Caribbean societies. He identifies them as the targeted enemies of racist white elites that denied them social, economic and political power by giving it to black female teachers. Without citing the evidence, he states, "Co-education in Jamaica and the Caribbean cannot continue to ignore the research findings that conclude that both boys and girls perform better academically in single sex schools" (1994, 127). In so doing he targets coeducation as the main contributor to the marginalization of Caribbean men.

Whether this is so or not, many people believe it. This belief is now so deep-seated it is within the realm of popular ideology. In Barbados, two male principals, one of whom was educated at a coeducational school, called for a study of the real effects of coeducation on boys. "I don't think that these single sex schools were prepared enough for the change. I'll not stick my neck out and say it is co-ed because I've been in co-ed for many years and I never felt intimidated by girls" (*Daily Nation* 2000, 5).

Miller's arguments continue to be used to advocate limiting access to public resources for women. The supporters of this position recommend a return to single-sex schools, closing women's bureaux, excluding girls from extracurricular programmes and blaming women for high divorce rates and a variety of social ills. It continues the deep-rooted myth that men's misfortunes originate from women's transgressions (Koven and Michel 1993, 1).

A Feminist Response: What Marginalization?

> To argue that women can overpower men simply on the basis of increased income or occupational status is to incorrectly presume that income or occupational dominance form the sole basis of men's control over women. (Lindsay 1997, 14)

Keisha Lindsay's work represents a systematic, sustained critique of all the arguments that Miller offers in his marginalization construct. She presents a re-analysis of the data surrounding women's participation in the family, the workplace and the classroom, casting doubts on both the extent and significance of women's participation in these arenas (1997, 1). Further, Lindsay maintains that male marginalization stems not from any concrete material reality, but from a gender-biased methodological frame that recognizes some data sources and ignores, or invalidates, others (p. 1). She suggests that, far from advancing any fundamental reordering of gender constructs, the marginalization thesis perpetuates the age-old patriarchal mandate – that of woman as "lesser", inferior being (p. 1). Lindsay argues that to make sense of Caribbean women's apparent dominance over men in education, employment and the family, one should examine the wealth of statistical data addressed by neither Miller nor other proponents of the marginalization thesis (p. 1). In response to Miller's using the family to locate the beginning of men's marginalization, Lindsay effectively destabilizes the seeming coherency of his assumptions (p. 4).

Women and the Family

Keisha Lindsay states the Caribbean family has long been characterized as matrifocal. Miller and others give as evidence the number of female-headed households in the region. However, Lindsay comments that these scholars often fail to recognize that there is no implicit correlation between female headship and actual social and economic power within the family structure, or in the wider society. Lindsay reminds us that headship status itself is not economically empowering for Caribbean women, and that the opposite may be true. She reports that Jamaican female-headed households were more likely to experience economic deprivation. While female heads are as involved in work as male heads, the pattern of their occupational distribution is markedly different (1997, 5).

Lindsay concludes that the "marginalization of the black male" thesis is fundamentally flawed at the epistemological level. Accordingly, its limitations are not just in its inadequate (and selective) use of existing data but also in the way it systematically (and wilfully) invalidates women and women's experiences (1997, 10).

The cumulative effect of Miller's theorization is to assign to men as a group a priori rights to whatever resources are available. If citizens are distinguished from non-citizens by rights, a core assumption in Miller's theory is the belief that male citizens have a right of the first-born, the right of primogeniture as citizens.

Miller's theorizing of men's marginality does a disservice to our understanding of how material and ideological relations of gender affect and are affected by Caribbean men. By commenting on changing material and ideological relations for women, he seems to recognize the significance of gender identities in shaping gender roles. But again his approach ossifies and becomes the analysis. Women remain the entry point and the real focus of analysis. The discourse on men and marginality in the region is not yet about men. Miller never extends this insight into examining how the gender identities of men influence their gender roles. The insights gained in examining how women interact with and are affected by changes in the political economy of post-independence states quickly degenerate into blaming women for men's problems. Miller and others[9] do not turn the lens on men's gender identities and how these influence the behaviours of men, irrespective of adverse or other outcomes.

This practice is particularly worrisome as it relates to the coeducation and male underperformance debate. To the extent that boys and men may face particular challenges in current educational systems, the constant carping about girls and women yields no insights, but does breed resentment. In a very timely study, *Male Underachievement in High School Education* in three Caribbean countries, Odette Parry states that her main finding "is that the current construction of male sex gender identity in the Caribbean has implications for educational underachievement of Caribbean males" (2000, 56). What passes for an analysis of changing gender relations is still an approach to understanding gender dynamics. According to this analysis the answer to men's problems is to change the educational structure. Yet if we continue to maintain this myopic gendered approach we end up emphasizing structures while ignoring changing gender relations. We also miss another opportunity to generate new knowledges about changing gender relations for men. This places the responsibility for the underperformance of boys on the structures through which the educational product is delivered, rather than on the ways boys are socialized to view academic work and achievement (Parry 2000).

If policy-makers accept that coeducation is the problem and move to single-sex schools, girls may still continue to perform more competitively than boys. What will the new policy approach then be? We need to pay some attention to what boys learn from men and women about what it means to be male and masculine in our societies.

We need to theorize configurations of Caribbean masculinity using gender as an analytical frame. It is time to analyse the content of the gender identities that societies expect boys to acquire as a way of proving that they have copied the right model of manhood. Many of the problems men experience flow from the gender identities that boys and men acquire as part of the larger gender ideologies circulating in gender systems in our societies.[10] These gender ideologies are embedded in relations of dominance. They are relations of power that play out between women and men, but also, significantly, between men and men. Men who subscribe to these ideologies pay a price, just as those do who try to resist the popular but punitive renderings of masculinity. The Men's Forum of Barbados correctly yet perversely states that feminists are complaining about violence against women, but only 20 per cent of violence committed by men affects women. This suggests that there is some statistically acceptable level of male-to-female violence and that feminists should not be concerned, because 80 per cent of this violence affects other men.[11] They miss the unfortunate point that violent behaviour is an acceptable expression of dominant masculinity.[12] The focus should not be on which sex suffers the most but on eradicating violent behaviour as an acceptable expression of masculinity and finding acceptable means for women and men to deal with conflict.

Male Gender Identities and Changing Gender Roles

Writing extensively on Jamaican and Caribbean masculinity, Barry Chevannes does not accept the hypothesis of the marginalization of the black or other male (1999, 33). What concerns him primarily is the negative stereotypes of Jamaican and Caribbean masculinities, most of which he sees as exaggerated or contradictory of the realities he discovered in a range of national and regional research initiatives. He has produced research on Caribbean men and fatherhood, sexuality and the construction of masculine gender identities. His findings force a nuancing and often a rethinking of some of the generalizations of men and gender relations. Where Miller sees Caribbean men as the victims of a conspiracy of elite male power brokers, international development institutions and a compliant, even if powerless, pawn-like women's movement, Chevannes identifies the problematic character of Caribbean masculinities as originating in the gender identities that men cultivate and the deliberate distortions of their social behaviour. He assigns part of the responsibility for these negative stereotypes to the women's movement. Chevannes's work is compensatory and corrective. It is dedicated to redeeming and correcting what he identifies as distortions of masculinity and to creating a gender agenda for men. It is similar to earlier feminist works that seek to reclaim aspects of the feminine that are dismissed as inferior. That type of validation, undertaken primarily by radical feminists, seeks to validate women's way of doing and to refuse political and epistemological pressures to have women's contributions, lives and social relevance determined by using an androcentric lens.

In 1998 Janet Brown and Chevannes published a report on a two-year research project that they conducted in six communities in Jamaica, Guyana and Dominica. The project sought to correct a deficiency in the literature on men's family roles and provide material that would facilitate an understanding of gender-related issues within Caribbean communities (Brown and Chevannes 1998, 6). They identified five clusters of tensions and distrust that emerged in discussions with women and men: .

- double standards of fidelity for men and women and the modes of behaviour which result;
- meanings ascribed to "manhood" and their inherent contradictions;
- challenges to the "natural order" of male headship posed by economic hardships, women's liberation, media images, and the incursions of North American values and norms, with their resultant power struggles;
- issues concerning family finances;
- mixed messages about men's roles in the domestic division of labour; debates on levels of domestic violence. (Brown and Chevannes 1998, 7)

Brown and Chevannes identified eight areas of evidence to substantiate their conclusion that men possess a detailed understanding of their contributions and perceptions of their roles in family life. This corresponds with Christine Barrow's research on Barbadian men. However, there are several contradictory areas in the findings and analysis that, while not eroding the contributions of the overall observations, indicate a need to rethink some of the positions. These are especially apparent when Brown and Chevannes attempt to articulate different (that is, beyond the conventional and stereotypical) understandings of the behaviour and roles of boys and men in families. For example, the mother–son bond is often perceived as having the effect of sons remaining "sons" as adults, while daughters are raised to become independent, resourceful helpmates. I have heard public commentators blame women for coddling sons and sowing the seeds for irresponsible adult partners. Yet Brown and Chevannes found that the number of abandoned male children far exceeds that for girls, and that street children are more often male (1998, 9). Where is the pervasive mother–son bond for these abandoned boys and male street children? Their findings indicate that regional gender ideologies governing the division of labour transcend religion and culture. In an Indo-Guyanese Hindu community and a rural Christian black Jamaican community they found identical sharp gendered divisions of labour affecting boys and girls (1998, 17–21).

Of the three areas that Chevannes examines on the question of what is wrong with Jamaican males, I focus on the first two: sexual behaviour and education (Chevannes 1999).[13] He concludes with some unexpected findings and imaginative recommendations. These underscore his position that men are not marginalized, even though there are areas where intervention is necessary to alter negative inputs into the cultivation of men's gender identities.

Sexual Behaviour and Fatherhood

On male sexual behaviour Chevannes accepts "that in Jamaica multiple partnerships are a feature of male sexual behaviour" (1999, 5). In a 1985 survey, "I found *that only fifty percent of the males I interviewed acknowledged that they had more than one partner.* However, many more indicated that they would have liked to have had more, implying that lack of finance was the limiting factor" (pp. 5–6; emphasis added). In a 1991 survey with Claudia Chambers he found that women also had multiple partners and that those partnerships were motivated by the need for money and feelings of sexual independence (Chambers and Chevannes 1991).

Chevannes argues that the available data do not substantiate the charge that Jamaican men are sexually irresponsible. The data do not reveal any information about sexual responsibility or irresponsibility. Instead his research shows that men may provide higher levels of material and moral support for pregnant partners than is popularly perceived (1999, 9). He rejects the idea that it is characteristic of Jamaican men to run from commitment of any sort, in particular, paternity. In other words, men may have had multiple sexual partners, but that did not mean they did not want to father their children (p. 5). In fact fatherhood was an important dimension of the construction of male gender identity that men regarded with pride (p. 7). The two key components of fatherhood that his respondents identified – "providing" and discipline – are the same two elements the structural functionalists defined as men's key roles in families over forty-five years ago.

In the construct of masculinity and the gender identities boys and men acquire as they learn what is acceptable behaviour, they receive and act upon many conflicting and contradictory messages. Prevailing gender ideologies define masculinity in opposition to femininity and rank the feminine as consistently less valuable. Accordingly, in popular perception women have everything to gain by acquiring characteristics and professions associated with masculinity, while men have everything to lose by pursuing professions seen as female-dominated or, worse yet, displaying characteristics associated with women. This is why Figueroa states that no one cares if males underperform in humanities or nursing, since gender ideologies posit these as feminine (and therefore lesser-ranked) areas of study. Boys who want to succeed in an area defined as feminine are seen as behaving in a "gender inappropriate fashion" and also as displaying a lack of ambition (Figueroa 1997, 14).

More insidious and damaging for young men is the notion that academic work itself is feminine and to like to study, to enjoy books, to want to do well in schools is "girlish", effeminate and not the stuff that makes good men. Even while many public commentators are bemoaning girls' taking over in academic performance, none of them say to young men that they have to put in a one hundred per cent effort at school, that they have to take their school life seriously. Instead they concentrate on demonizing coeducation, female teachers, female-headed households and the minority of women employed in visible, high-profile professions. They do want boys and young men to perform better, but by sending contradictory messages they create a view of wounded masculinity that seems an almost inevitable fate.

Speaking at the opening of the All Saints Primary School, Barbadian Prime Minister Owen Arthur told his audience he knew every cave, gully and field and when every fruit tree was in season. "It seems to me that boys need to be allowed to develop their identity at a time when girls are developing more quickly than themselves" (*Barbados Advocate* 1999, A3).

The significance of these beliefs about appropriate expressions of masculinity does not remain in the realm of ideology but also has material outcomes. These affect women and men and cumulatively either impede or facilitate societal change. Chevannes correctly states that Caribbean males and females are socialized to identify domestic (reproductive) work as women's work, and activities outside of the domestic sphere as male. That is the reality of the existing gender ideologies. It also represents an area that has to change. This need for change is not because of any feminist agenda to emasculate men or effeminize boys, but because changes in Caribbean political economy in the last thirty years require a reorganization of work in the domestic sphere. After centuries of denial and exclusion, Caribbean women have gained entry into the public sphere and are acquiring skills in areas that were once legally or in terms of ingrained prejudices out of bounds. As a sex group they already have skills to perform effectively in the domestic sphere. Boys and men must acquire and value those skills as necessary for the organization of life.

I do not agree with Chevannes's characterization of chores associated with the household as "female" tasks or chores traditionally associated with the outside as "male" tasks. His naming the performance of these as "cross-gender tasks" is also problematic. There is a distinction between how phenomena are perceived in society and how intellectuals explain or theorize their existence. These chores do not belong to females or males, and their performance should not be conceptualized as cross-gender. They are chores that are required for the running of households.

Fathers and Partners

Chevannes has theorized fatherhood in particular and masculinity in general to produce a more complex, richer understanding of how Caribbean men construct their gender identities. He concludes that fatherhood is a critical component of men's gender identity. They regard it with pride. Two defining elements revolve around providing. As fathers they believe their role is to supply resources for their children and to provide discipline. There may be contradictions in that the actual delivery of these may fall short of their expectations of fulfilment. The basic point is that men believe this is what makes a man a father and in turn reinforces manhood. The core expressions of fatherhood that Chevannes discovered were observed by anthropologists some four decades ago. This indicates that these features do reinforce some core, self-identified beliefs about masculinity and fatherhood.

Men's relationships with women as boyfriends, partners, husbands or common-law spouses are still a very problematic area and require serious investigation and intervention strategies. More men need to begin to identify with or claim being responsible, loving partners as part of their gender identities.[14] Barrow and Chevannes uncovered how critical the role of father is to men. There is a great deal of ambivalence around the role of lover, partner, friend. Not enough Caribbean children see their mothers and fathers negotiating life's problems together. Both women and men need to learn how to build stable relationships based on trust and respect. Just as Fathers Incorporated has been helping men negotiate fatherhood, there is need for a similar intervention to help men negotiate "partnering" from a position of trust and security. Many men assume it is their right to engage in multiple relationships, with financial capability being the only restraint (Chevannes 1999). The double standards in society guarantee greater tolerance and acceptance for men doing this, even though, as Chevannes has pointed out, women also engage in multiple partnering.

One of the major contributions of theorizing gender and methodologies of gender analysis was to break apart the belief in a simplistic unity between biology and an inherent, static naturalized sex identity (see chapter 2, this volume). Gender analysis reveals that several characteristics, beliefs and behaviours assumed to be biologically and rigidly male or female are instead the product of gender ideologies that serve particular purposes at particular junctures in a society's development. The best proof of that is the changes in the gender identities of Caribbean women over the course of the twentieth century. As Lindsay and Figueroa demonstrate, the discourse on male marginalization is fed more by fear of the changes in the gender identities of Caribbean women than by any solid evidence that men are being marginalized in Caribbean society.

If what it means to be a woman were fixed in biology it would not have been possible for women to undertake the multiplicity of roles and responsibilities they now do. In disagreeing with the suggestion that special incentives should be created to attract boys into schools, Figueroa notes, "the evidence shows that it is the readiness of girls and women to be flexible and adjust their identities that has enabled them to benefit from new opportunities" (2000, 9). The challenge facing us as a society is to have boys and men, girls and women see masculinity also as a much more fluid concept than currently understood. One of the major changes taking place is that many young men are seeing masculinity as a much more fluid set of behaviours and practices than did men of previous generations. It is unlike the rigid, static understanding of masculinity the marginalization thesis suggests. Many younger men are altering the content of what constitutes masculinity for them, and this is misunderstood. I do not agree with many of the practices they are substituting, because

I believe several create harm for themselves, their families and their societies. However, they are stating that they reject their fathers' generation's definition of masculinity, as other generations before them have done. We have to understand this and seek interventions that recognize how they are redefining masculinity.

I sense there is a foundational shift in renderings of masculinity by younger Caribbean men that begs for specific research. There is greater freedom and play with what a man looks like. For example, some young heterosexual men will dress in ways that older Caribbean women and men regard as feminine. They will wear large gold earrings in both ears, often in the popular shapes of a gun or a cluster of grapes. They tie their heads with brightly coloured bandanas and wear around their necks several very large gold chains with huge pendants. Their upper body jewellery and head wraps are almost identical to those worn by older Caribbean women in St Lucia, Dominica, Martinique and Guadeloupe. However, the men wear them with very fashionable, very baggy, low-slung jeans. In Barbados during the annual Crop Over celebrations, a group of young men called the Grass Skirt Posse perform at shows and large parties. They wear grass skirts over boxer shorts, are naked to the waist and gyrate "whine" in sexually explicit ways while singing songs to women indicating the sexual pleasures that await them.

Much of what are considered appropriate expressions of masculinity are burdensome to men, especially when economic circumstances prevent their fulfilment. The ideology of man the breadwinner is pervasive even when difficult to meet, and even though Caribbean women have also been performing this role. Boys and girls should be socialized to see the significance of everyone's contributing to the well-being of the family. They should understand that contributions to the well-being of the family include women as breadwinners and men as nurturers. The irony is that this situation already exists, and has existed for a long time (Mintz 1981; Sutton and Makiezy-Barrow 1981), but the gendered ideology lingers that this is an aberration. Caribbean economies are increasingly dependent on tourism. Several jobs in this sector will seem like women's work, especially at the lower-end skill level. Young men and women should not exclude themselves from gaining skills in new or expanding economic sectors because of archaic, erroneous understandings of gender identities.

Migration, Marginality and Masculinity in the Region

An area of the political economy that has been overlooked is changes in migration patterns in the Caribbean and their effect on men materially and ideologically. Chevannes comments on one dimension of this problem. It is from the perspective of schools graduating students largely uncertified, with no apparent employment prospects. "I wish to call attention to the veritable army of fourteen and fifteen-year-olds who are, as it were, demobilized every year, but who, unlike Caesar's army, are without land or pay, and must fend for themselves" (1999, 11). In Jamaica this group of students is too young to enter vocational academies or the country's national youth service. According to Chevannes they are socially immature, with no fully developed skills, entering a society unprepared to absorb them (p. 11).

In Barbados this group is sixteen years old, and a fresh group is disgorged into the society every July. Mass-migration outlets for Caribbean unskilled labour have dried up. Many of the young men in this group of school-leavers turn up on the blocks, unemployed and eventually unemployable. Many young women do too, but that statistic is less interesting.

I have argued that contemporary Caribbean governments seem unaware of the significance of migration in Caribbean societies (Barriteau 2001). They seem unaware because there is no public policy that explicitly addresses this. Migration has been an institutionalized aspect of Caribbean society (Momsen 1987, 346) and male migration has had a significant impact on the character of Caribbean society. Male migration dominated from the 1900s to the 1950s. It contributed to the growth of female-headed households, women's comparative economic autonomy and the much misunderstood phenomenon of matrifocality in the region (Newton 1984, 170; Mondesire and Dunn 1995, 11; Momsen 1987, 346). The World Bank reported in 1993 that the Caribbean region has the highest rate of migration in the world (Mondesire and Dunn 1995, 11), underscoring the critical economic role of migration in Caribbean societies. Perhaps its most singular contribution is that migration absorbed surplus labour and acted as a safety valve for social pressures on narrow state sectors with restricted welfare and employment-generating capacities.

Caribbean governments have yet to devise a comprehensive policy to deal with the thousands of young women and men who swell the ranks of the unemployed yearly and who, unlike their grandparents' generation, cannot as easily migrate in search of work (Barriteau 2001). When Miller states that young Jamaican men are even more marginal in their societies than their grandfathers were, he does not factor in this critical dimension, but instead blames the investments of international development institutions in building an educational infrastructure in Jamaica that somehow favours women. Chevannes is aware of the social, economic and gendered dimensions of this challenge to the long-term stability of Caribbean societies and, more immediately, to the future of these young men and women.

Historically the impact of migration has been greater or manifests itself differently in different territories. Whereas all Caribbean people migrate, smaller territories such as Carriacou and Montserrat experience a different type of migration. In the former, women have traditionally played the breadwinner roles in the absence of seafaring men. In the latter, the population has been dislocated because of the eruption of the Soufrière volcano. How has this affected men, women and families there? A phenomenon of the Caribbean in the 1980s was the greater migration of women in search of work (Mondesire and Dunn 1995). Have men taken up the caregiver roles in families? The societies in the British Dependencies or Overseas Territories are affected by intra-regional migration; the implications for women and men and, of course, for children, are different. Are men of those territories disadvantaged by these migration patterns and by the laws governing citizenship, "belonger" status and the right of children to inherit their father's property?

Coeducation and Educational Performance

On education Chevannes reveals findings that contradict many of Miller's assertions as well as popular beliefs within the region on male performance, male underachievement and education. His findings validate or support research conducted by Odette Parry (2000), Barbara Bailey (1997), Mark Figueroa (1997, 2000), Marlene Hamilton (1999) and Keisha Lindsay (1997).[15] Chevannes questions the general perception that "Females are outperforming males. Females are more conscientious in their school attendance, graduate with higher marks and are preparing themselves better for life by going on to institutions of higher learning. There they win proportionately more honours and graduate in larger numbers than the males" (1999, 10). He discovered higher attrition rates for boys throughout the school system and higher attrition ratios for all students in rural schools. Attendance and attrition were directly affected by the type of school, its location and the sex of the student, with boys in rural all-age schools at the greatest possible disadvantage (p. 11). He concludes that there are gender biases operating in the selection of certain subjects as opposed to others, and that there is no evidence to substantiate the belief that girls routinely outperform boys, "but ample evidence of gender performance both ways" in specific subject areas (p. 15).

Barbara Bailey reaches similar conclusions in a study of the performance of boys and girls in secondary schools. She states that the results indicate the typical sex-linked patterns reported universally (1997, 28). Mark Figueroa links the recent interest in male academic underperformance to the emergence of women in non-traditional academic and professional areas. He declares that

> A lot of the popular discussions and some of the research on "Male Academic Under Performance" have been rooted in male supremacist consciousness. That is it is taken for granted that males have the right to the preeminent positions they have held in patriarchal societies. As such when women come to challenge men in a field that men formally dominated, this is a matter for concern. If the field has no prestige attached to it or if it is in decline then it can be handed over to women with little or no regret. (1997, 5)

Like Chevannes and Bailey, Figueroa concludes that it is not true to say that males are underperforming at all levels and with respect to all courses of study. He states that an examination of statistics for entries and passes at various levels of the educational system will demonstrate that the main characteristic evident is that boys and girls perform differently in different areas (1997, 2). Figueroa observes,

> males have been underperforming for years in certain areas and continue to do so but those areas have never been a matter of concern; when male academic under performance is being discussed concern is never expressed in the areas where their performance is weakest; startling areas of female academic

under performance receive little or no comment from those who are headlining male academic under performance. (pp. 2–4)

Chevannes makes an observation that is problematic. "I would like to propose that under-performance of the males in English Language has far more important consequences for them than the under-performance in Mathematics for the females" (1999, 15). English language is a core subject for all subjects, requiring in-depth reading and sound language skills. Similarly, mathematics is a core subject for the sciences, and many women who do not hold certification in high-school mathematics cannot proceed to careers in medicine and other related fields. Chevannes's comment is even stranger when he admits that the English results for girls are also routinely weak (pp. 15–16).

As it relates to analysing data from the University of the West Indies, Figueroa states that a major defect is that we do not really know how many Caribbean nationals are studying abroad or their gender ratios. "It is possible that more men go abroad and as a result the gender imbalance among tertiary students is not as strong as it appears at first sight" (1997, 9).

Figueroa theorizes the gender-privileging dialectic to replace Miller's marginalization thesis. Although he uses the term "male underachievement", Figueroa suggests the problem is really one of highly differentiated gender achievement. He is the only male scholar to explicitly call for solutions that challenge the structures of male privilege that encourage inequalities and result in negative outcomes for women.

In attempting to ensure that young men participate fully in reaping the benefits of education and becoming socially developed, well-rounded citizens, we should be careful about generalizing from particular disadvantages and prejudices that may or do exist, to a generalized position that boys and men are doomed to conditions of marginality and irrelevance in Caribbean societies. Chevannes reminds us that male unemployment has high visibility. A well-kept secret, and for ideological reasons of gender less interesting, is the fact that female unemployment in Caribbean countries has been higher historically than male unemployment, and continues to be so. Barbados provides an illustration. In 1998 the overall employment rate fell from 12.2 per cent to 11.8 per cent. Male unemployment fell by two percentage points to 8.3 per cent

(Central Bank 1999). However, female unemployment actually rose, and closed the year at above 15 per cent (Central Bank 1999, 8). According to a fourth-quarter survey, in 1999 the unemployment ratio fell to single digits at 9.8 per cent. Female unemployment also declined, but while for men it was 6.7 per cent, for women it was 13.1 per cent.[16] There are proportionately more unemployed young women than there are young men. Unemployed young women do not hang out on the block or in town squares. Neither do unemployed young men spend free time working in their yards or around the homes where they live.

Race and class relations often intersect with those of gender to produce entirely different manifestations of patriarchal power. Although all anglophone Caribbean countries have some percentage of their populations of European origin, one cannot determine the unemployment status of white Caribbean men by observing them "hanging out" on street corners. In Barbados about 4 per cent of the population is white Barbadian. Even though there are no statistics to refute or substantiate this, it is a common belief among black Barbadians there is no white unemployment. The private sector is dominated by white-owned businesses and corporations (Beckles 1989a) and black Barbadians believe white men and women are automatically absorbed into these companies, creating conditions of full employment.

Conclusion

The male marginalization thesis is a deeply flawed, one-dimensional reading of manhood in the region. It gives us Caribbean man as victim, with a wounded, regressive masculinity. It does a disservice to understanding the many manifestations of Caribbean masculinity, and therefore it is inadequate in providing guidelines for further research and policy on issues affecting and affected by Caribbean men in relation to changing gender identities and roles. If we were to answer the questions posed within the framework for determining the existence or extent of male marginalization, we would have to conclude that men are not marginalized. Yet this answer may be more a reflection of the poverty of the attempt to create an explanatory model for changes affecting Caribbean men that is based only on external factors and an undeclared desire to preserve a pristine past, rather than on a gender analysis of the juncture where Caribbean men interact with a changing political economy. The weaknesses of the current thesis underscore the need for a rigorous examination of the issues shaping masculinity. This has to be undertaken against an appreciation of changes in Caribbean political economy and changing gender identities for Caribbean women. This examination must engage with the issues of gender justice and inequities in our societies. It requires opening several Pandora's boxes that, in true mythological fashion, will never again be shut. For example, researchers have to be aware that much of what constitutes studies of Caribbean societies, economies, politics and political systems are studies of male power and practices that are unnamed and generally unrecognized as such. These new investigations should not be motivated by an impulse to recreate some golden age of Caribbean manhood. Not only is the past never available, its romanticization seriously obscures the problems it bequeaths to the present. These necessary studies of Caribbean masculinities should be informed instead by desire to reveal how changing gender ideologies reproduce shifts in gender identities for both men and women and to decipher the implications of these for our societies.

Notes

1. The review of the literature reveals that only Errol Miller as a scholar has theorized the marginalization of the Caribbean male. Most academics (feminist or other) reject it. See Chevannes 1999, Figueroa 1997, Lindsay 1997 and Bailey 1997. However, the Caribbean public and some academics who admit to not researching the area accept the thesis as an article of faith. See Bennett 20002a–d.
2. These terms are critical and are defined as follows:
   access – the proportion of existing places in relation to the age cohort in the population
   enrolment – being registered in and pursuing a course of study
   participation – active involvement
   performance – level of attainment in relation to set criteria
   achievement – academic achievement is an overall measure of the extent of participation and levels of performance in relation to the age cohort. See UWI 2000.

3. My aim is to expose the flawed construct of the male marginalization thesis rather than to provide detailed evidence on how the convergence of Caribbean history, contemporary gender relations, political economy and culture reconfigure men's gender identities. This requires a separate, but necessary, research project. See the work in this area by Linden Lewis (1994, 1996–2000). However while I do recognize how capitalist relations exploit tensions in gender relations, I have reservations about the extent to which the belief that Caribbean men are now marginalized can be explained through the processes of the economic global restructuring of capitalism.

4. See Men's Forum, "Pity Caribbean Men, Cricketers" *Daily Nation* (Barbados), 7 March 2001, A17.

5. Working-class men have considerably less access to the structural and material dimensions of power. This also holds for minority men in racist societies. Still, this does not mean they are automatically less willing and less able to exert other forms of control and dominance over the women they interact with. Not all men are driven to exert control over women, but for those who subscribe to patriarchal ideologies, antagonistic and/or racist relations do not prevent patriarchal behaviour, and may frequently exacerbate it. Black feminists in the United States during the civil rights movement were especially aware of these complications.

6. I thank Gemma Tang Nain for pointing out the need to add control over and benefiting from resources to a discussion of the material dimensions of gender.

7. See also "Where Have All the Men Gone?", *Gleaner* (Jamaica), 15 August 1989, A6.

8. For example, see the statements of the Men's Forum of Barbados in various newspaper articles. A recent sampling of newspaper headlines in Barbados includes: "Men Fear Female Strides: Gains for Women Seen as Loss for Men", *Barbados Advocate*, 30 June 1998, 2; "Men 'in Danger . . .': Two Politicians Have Say on Gender Roles", *Sun on Saturday* (Barbados), 21 March 1998, 2; "Caribbean Boys in Crisis" *Sunday Sun*, 20 December 1998, A20; "Female Edge: Men Wasting Crucial Time", *Barbados Advocate*, 1 January 1999, 8; "Concern for Boys: Single Sex Schools May Be Better, Says [Prime Minister] Arthur", *Daily Nation*, 24 June 1999, 2, 48; "PM: Schools Need Proper Male Figures", *Barbados Advocate*, 24 June 1999, 4; "Women Taking Over?", *Sunday Sun*, 17 August 1997, A7; "Males Crippled by Slavery", *Barbados Advocate*, 24 February 1998, 7; "Men Say Law Courts Favour Women", *Barbados Advocate*, 24 February 1998, 7.

9. I see Chevannes's work as an exception here.
10. For example, Odette Parry found that male gender identity as currently constructed runs counter to the academic ethos of education; see Parry 2000.
11. See Men's Forum, "Pity Caribbean Men, Cricketers", *Daily Nation* (Barbados), 7 March 2001, A17.
12. They also miss the point that it may be only 20 per cent of all violent acts by men that target women, but that may very well represent over 90 per cent of all violence that women experience. It is puerile to make this argument. Even if only 10 per cent of men rape women, they still represent the 100 per cent of rape that women are forced to endure. Note that I am not suggesting that men are genetically predisposed to be violent. Rather, societal expectations and personal constructions of men's gender identities include violent behaviour as an acceptable expression of masculinity. Women conduct violent acts too, yet violent behaviour is not viewed as a core, "required" or defining characteristic of women's gender identities, as it is for men.
13. The third area is crime. Chevannes examines these in the 1999 Grace Kennedy Lecture. The intersection of crime and violence in the shaping of male gender identities is extremely critical and merits a separate treatment, which is beyond my focus here.
14. This is an area that both women and men have to pay attention to; however, women more willingly claim being loving and supporting partners as part of their gender identity, even though their actual behaviour may contradict the ideologies they subscribe to.
15. These are all academics at the University of the West Indies, Mona campus, working in different disciplines but arriving at very similar conclusions on the intersection of gender and education.
16. See "Jobless Record: Unemployment Falls below Ten Percent", *Sunday Sun* (Barbados), 27 February 2000, 1, A3.

References

Compiled by Jo-Ann Granger

Abraham-Van der mark, Eva. 1993. "Marriage and Concubinage among the Sephardic Merchant Elite of Curaçao". In *Women and Change in the Caribbean,* edited by Janet Momsen, 38–49. Kingston, Jamaica: Ian Randle.

Adams, G.H. 1945. *Report of the Commission Appointed to Review and Make Recommendation upon the Structure of the Civil Service of Barbados and the Remuneration and Conditions of Service of all Government Servants.* Barbados: n.p.

Afigbo, A.E. 1973. "The Indigenous Political System of the Igbo". *Tarikh* 4, no. 2: 13–23.

Agarwal, Bina. 1997. " 'Bargaining' and Gender Relations: Within and Beyond the Household". *Feminist Economics* 3, no. 1: 1–51.

Agonito, Rosemary. 1977. *History of Ideas on Woman: A Source Book.* New York: Putnam.

Ahmed, Leila. 1992. *Women and Gender in Islam: Historical Roots of a Modern Debate.* New Haven: Yale University Press.

Albisetti, James C. 1993. "The Feminization of Teaching in the Nineteenth Century: A Comparative Perspective". *History of Education* 22, no. 3: 253–63.

Albuquerque, Klaus de. 1998. "Sex, Beach Boys, and Female Tourists in the Caribbean". *Sexuality and Culture* 2, no. 1: 87–112.

Albuquerque, Klaus de, and Sam Ruark. 1998. " 'Men Day Done': Are Women Really Ascendant in the Caribbean?" In *Caribbean Portraits: Essays on Gender Ideologies and Identities,* edited by Christine Barrow, 1–13. Kingston, Jamaica: Ian Randle.

Alcoff, Linda, and Elizabeth Potter. 1993. "When Feminisms Intersect Epistemology". Introduction to *Feminist Epistemologies,* edited by Linda Alcoff and Elizabeth Potter, 1–14. New York: Routledge.

Alexander, Jack. 1977. "The Role of the Male in the Middle-Class Jamaican Family: A Comparative Perspective". *Journal of Comparative Family Studies* 8, no. 3: 369–89.

Alexander, M. Jacqui. 1994. "Not Just (Any)body Can Be a Citizen: The Politics of Law, Sexuality and Postcoloniality in Trinidad and Tobago and the Bahamas". *Feminist Review,* no. 48: 5–23.

———. 1997. "Erotic Autonomy as a Politics of Decolonization: An Anatomy of Feminist and State Practice in the Bahamas Tourist Economy". In *Feminist Genealogies, Colonial Legacies, Democratic Futures,* edited by M. Jacqui Alexander and Chandra Talpade Mohanty, 63–100. New York: Routledge.

Alexander, M. Jacqui, and Chandra Talpade Mohanty, eds. 1997. *Feminist Genealogies, Colonial Legacies, Democratic Futures.* New York: Routledge.

Allen, S. 1972. "Plural Society and Conflict". *New Community* 1, no. 5: 389–92.

Alloula, Malek. 1986. *The Colonial Harem.* Minneapolis: University of Minnesota Press.

Amadiume, Ifi. 1987. *Male Daughters, Female Husbands: Gender and Sex in an African Society.* London: Zed Books.

Amos, Valerie, and Pratiba Parmar. 1984. "Challenging Imperial Feminism". *Feminist Review,* no. 17: 3–19.

Anderson, Patricia. 1986. "Conclusion: Women in the Caribbean". *Social and Economic Studies* 35, no. 2: 291–324.

Ansine, Janice. 1999. "Women's Rights Ignored". *Gleaner* (Jamaica) [online], 15 March. [Cited 3 February 2002.] <http://www.jamaica-gleaner.com/gleaner/19990315/index.html>.

Anthias, Floya, and Nira Yuval-Davis. 1983. "Contextualising Feminism: Gender, Ethnic and Class Divisions". *Feminist Review,* no. 15: 62–75.

Antoni, Robert. 1991. *Divina Trace.* Woodstock, NY: Overlook Press.

———. 1997. *Blessed Is the Fruit.* New York: Henry Holt.

Antonius-Smits, Christel C.F. 1999. "Gold and Commercial Sex: Exploring the Link Between Small-Scale Gold Mining and Commercial Sex in the Rainforest of Suriname". In *Sun, Sex and Gold: Tourism and Sex Work in the Caribbean,* edited by Kamala Kempadoo, 237–59. Lanham, Md.: Rowman and Littlefield.

Antrobus, Peggy. 1989. "The Empowerment of Women". In *The Women and International Development Annual,* vol. 1, edited by R.S. Gallin, M. Aronoff and A. Ferguson, 189–208. Boulder: Westview Press.

———. 1993. "Setting the Context". In *Women at the Center: Development Issues and Practices for the 1990s,* edited by Gay Young, Vidyamali Samarasinghe and Ken Kusterer, 9–14. West Hartford, Conn.: Kumarian Press.

Appiah, Kwame Anthony. 1993. *In My Father's House: Africa in the Philosophy of Culture.* New York: Oxford University Press.

Ardener, Shirley. 1975. "Sexual Insult and Female Militancy". In *Perceiving Women,* edited by Shirley Ardener, 29–53. New York: Wiley.

Aristotle. 1885. *The Politics of Aristotle,* vol. 1. Translated by Benjamin Jowett and edited by W.D. Ross. Oxford: Clarendon Press.

Armstrong, Pat, and Hugh Armstrong. 1978. *The Double Ghetto: Canadian Women and Their Segregated Work.* Toronto: McClelland and Stewart.

Atanda, J.A. 1973. "Government of Yorubaland in the Pre-colonial Period". *Tarikh* 4, no. 2: 1–12.

———. 1980. *An Introduction to Yoruba History.* Atanda: Ibadan University Press.

Atluri, Tara L. 2001. *When the Closet Is a Region: Homophobia, Heterosexism and Nationalism in the Commonwealth Caribbean.* Working Paper no. 5. Cave Hill, Barbados: Centre for Gender and Development Studies, University of the West Indies.

Awe, Bolanle. 1977. "The Iyalobe in the Traditional Yoruba Political System". In *Sexual Stratification: A Cross-Cultural View,* edited by Alice Schlegel, 144–59. New York: Columbia University Press.

Bacchus, M.K. 1990. *Utilization, Misuse and Development of Human Resources in the Early West Indian Colonies.* Waterloo, Ont.: Wilfrid Laurier University Press.

Bailey, Barbara. 1997. "Not an Open Book: Gender Achievement and Education in the Caribbean". Working Paper no. 1, edited by Patricia Mohammed, 21–44. Mona, Jamaica: Centre for Gender and Development Studies, University of the West Indies.

Baksh-Soodeen, Rawwida. 1998. "Issues of Difference in Contemporary Caribbean Feminism". *Feminist Review,* no. 59: 74–85.

Barbados. 1898. "Principal Changes Made by the New Code for Elementary Schools and the Reasons for the Same". *Official Gazette,* 14 July, 2310–11.

———. 1966. *Constitution of Barbados.*

Barbados Advocate. 1999. "PM: Let Boys Be Boys", 19 January, A3.

Barbados. Board of Education (BE). 1898. "Minutes of Special Meeting, 22 March 1898". Fol. 276. Barbados Department of Archives, ED 1/9.

———. 1902–11. Minutes, 9 January 1902–16 January 1911. Fol. 34, 47, 71,170, 381–82, 386 Barbados Department of Archives, ED 1/10.

———. 1904. Report for 1902. In *Minutes of Proceedings of the Honourable Board of Legislative Council and Honourable House of Assembly for Session of 1903–1904.* Barbados Legislature, doc. 77.

———. 1907. Report for 1905. In *Minutes of Proceedings of the Honourable Board of Legislative Council and Honourable House of Assembly for Session of 1906–1907*. Barbados Legislature, doc. 32.

Barbados. Colonial Office (CO). 1897. "Education Commission: Minutes of the Attorney General". *Sessional Papers*. Barbados, CO 31/86, doc. 66.

Barbados. Constitution Review Commission (CRC). 1997. "Verbatim Transcript of Public Session of the Constitution Review Commission, North York Community Hall, Ontario, Canada". Barbados: n.p.

———. 1998. *Report of the Constitution Review Commission*. St Michael, Barbados: Government Printing Department.

Barbados. Department of Education (DE). 1954. *Report of the Department of Education for the Year Ended on the 31st August 1954*. Barbados: Advocate.

Barbados. Education Commission (EC). 1876. *Education Commission Report, 1875–76*. Barbados: n.p.

———. 1897. *Education Commission Report, 1894–96*. Barbados, doc. 176.

Barbados. Legislative Council (LC). 1886a. "Report on Primary and Combined Schools for the Year 1884". In *Minutes of Proceedings of the Honourable Board of Legislative Council and Honourable House of Assembly for Session of 1884–85*. Barbados: Legislature, doc. 163.

———. 1886b. "Report on the Public Infant Schools for the Year 1884". In *Minutes of Proceedings of the Honourable Board of Legislative Council and Honourable House of Assembly for Session of 1884–85*. Barbados: Legislature, doc. 97.

———. 1892. "Report on the Elementary Schools for the year 1890". In *Minutes of Proceedings of the Honourable Board of Legislative Council and Honourable House of Assembly for Session of 1891–92*. Barbados: Legislature, doc. 53.

———. 1894. "Report on the Elementary Schools for the Year 1893". In *Minutes of Proceedings of the Honourable Board of Legislative Council and Honourable House of Assembly for Session of 1893–1894*. Barbados: Legislature, doc. 126.

———. 1896. "Report on Elementary Schools for 1895". In *Minutes of Proceedings of the Honourable Board of Legislative Council and Honourable House of Assembly for Session of 1896–97*. Barbados: Legislature, doc. 101.

———. 1897. *An Act to Amend the Education Act, 1890*. Barbados Department of Archives.

———. 1899. "Report of the Education Board on the General Working of the Educational System for the Year 1897". In *Minutes of Proceedings of the Honourable Board of Legislative Council and Honourable House of Assembly for Session of 1898–99*. Barbados: Legislature, doc. 99.

————. 1909. "Report of the Education Commission, 1907–1909". In *Minutes of Proceedings of the Honourable Board of Legislative Council and Honourable House of Assembly for Session of 1908–1909*. Barbados: Legislature, doc. 252.

————. 1913. "Report of the Education Board on the Working of the Education System for the Year 1911". In *Minutes of Proceedings of the Honourable Board of Legislative Council and Honourable House of Assembly for Session of 1912–1913*. Barbados: Legislature, doc. 150.

————. 1919. "His Excellency the Governor to the Honourable the House of Assembly". In *Minutes of Proceedings of the Honourable Board of Legislative Council and Honourable House of Assembly for Session of 1918–1919*. Barbados: Legislature, doc. 263.

————. 1921. "Report on the Elementary Schools for the Year 1920". In *Minutes of Proceedings of the Honourable Board of Legislative Council and Honourable House of Assembly for Session of 1920–1921*. Barbados: Legislature, doc. 303.

————. 1924. "Report of the Elementary Schools for the Year 1922". In *Minutes of Proceedings of the Honourable Board of Legislative Council and Honourable House of Assembly for Session of 1923–1924*. Barbados: Legislature, doc. 181.

————. 1925. "Report on the Elementary Schools for the Year 1923". In *Minutes of Proceedings of the Honourable Board of Legislative Council and Honourable House of Assembly for Session of 1924–1925*. Barbados: Legislature, doc. 167.

————. 1926. "Report of the Elementary Schools for the Year 1924". In *Minutes of Proceedings of the Honourable Board of Legislative Council and Honourable House of Assembly for Session of 1925–1926*. Barbados: Legislature, doc. 168.

————. 1929. "Report on the Elementary Schools for the Year 1928". In *Minutes of Proceedings of the Honourable Board of Legislative Council and Honourable House of Assembly for Session of 1928–1929*. Barbados: Legislature, doc. 353.

Barbados. Ministry of Education (ME). 1960. *Report of the Ministry of Education for the Period 1st September, 1957, to 31st August, 1960*. Bridgetown, Barbados: Government Printing Office.

Barnes, Natasha. 1997. "Face of the Nation: Race, Nationalisms and Identities in Jamaican Pageants". In *Daughters of Caliban: Caribbean*

Women in the Twentieth Century, edited by Consuelo López Springfield, 285–306. Bloomington: Indiana University Press.

———. 1999. "Reluctant Matriarch: Sylvia Wynter and the Problematics of Caribbean Feminism". *Small Axe* 5: 34–47.

———. 2000. "Body Talk: Notes on Women and Spectacle in Contemporary Trinidad Carnival". *Small Axe* 7: 93–105.

Baron, Dennis. 1986. *Grammar and Gender.* New Haven: Yale University Press.

Barrett, Michelle. 1992. "Words and Things: Materialism and Method in Contemporary Feminist Analysis". In *Destabilizing Theory: Contemporary Feminist Debates,* edited by Michele Barrett and Anne Phillips, 201–19. Cambridge, UK: Polity Press.

Barriteau, Eudine. 1992. "The Construct of a Postmodernist Feminist Theory for Caribbean Social Science Research". *Social and Economic Studies* 41, no. 2: 1–43.

———. 1994. "Gender and Development Planning in the Post Colonial Caribbean: Female Entrepreneurs and the Barbadian State". PhD diss., Howard University.

———. 1995a. "Postmodernist Feminist Theorizing and Development Policy and Practice in the Anglophone Caribbean: The Barbados Case". In *Feminism/Postmodernism/Development,* edited by Marianne H. Marchand and Jane L. Parpart, 142–58. London: Routledge.

———. 1995b. "Socialist Feminist Theory and Caribbean Women: Transcending Dualisms". *Social and Economic Studies* 44, no. 2–3: 25–63.

———. 1998a. *Engendering Local Government in the Commonwealth Caribbean.* Working Paper no. 1. Cave Hill, Barbados: Centre for Gender and Development Studies, University of the West Indies.

———. 1998b. "Liberal Ideology and Contradictions in Caribbean Gender Systems". In *Caribbean Portraits: Essays on Gender Ideologies and Identities,* edited by Christine Barrow, 436–56. Kingston, Jamaica: Ian Randle.

———. 1998c. "Theorizing Gender Systems and the Project of Modernity in the Twentieth-Century Caribbean". *Feminist Review,* no. 59: 186–210.

———. 2000a. *Examining the Issues of Men, Male Marginalisation and Masculinity in the Caribbean: Policy Implications.* Working Paper no. 4. Cave Hill, Barbados: Centre for Gender and Development Studies, University of the West Indies.

———. 2000b. "Feminist Theory and Development: Implications for Policy, Research and Action". In *Theoretical Perspectives on Gender and*

Development, edited by Jane L. Parpart, M. Patricia Connelly and Eudine Barriteau, 161–77. Ottawa, Ont.: International Development Research Centre.

———. 2000c. "Re-examining Issues of 'Male Marginalisation' and 'Masculinity' in the Caribbean: The Need for a New Policy Approach". Paper presented to the Sixth Meeting of the Commonwealth Ministers Responsible for Women's Affairs, New Delhi, India, 16–19 April 2000.

———. 2001. The Political Economy of Gender in the Twentieth-Century Caribbean. New York: Palgrave.

Barrow, Christine. 1986a. "Autonomy, Equality and Women in Barbados". Paper prepared for the Eleventh Annual Caribbean Studies Association Conference, Caracas, Venezuela, May 1986. Main Library, University of the West Indies (Cave Hill).

———. 1986b. "Finding the Support: A Study of Strategies for Survival". Social and Economic Studies 35, no. 2: 131–76.

———. 1986c. "Male Images of Women in Barbados". Social and Economic Studies 35, no. 3: 51–64.

———. 1993. "Small Farm Food Production and Gender in Barbados". In Women and Change in the Caribbean, edited by Janet Momsen, 181–93. Kingston, Jamaica: Ian Randle.

———. 1998a. "Caribbean Masculinity and Family: Revisiting 'Marginality' and 'Reputation'". In Caribbean Portraits: Essays on Gender Ideologies and Identities, edited by Christine Barrow, 339–58. Kingston, Jamaica: Ian Randle.

———, ed. 1998b. Caribbean Portraits: Essays on Gender Ideologies and Identities. Kingston, Jamaica: Ian Randle.

Barry, Kathleen. 1984. Female Sexual Slavery. New York: New York University Press.

Bartelmus, Peter. 1994. Environment, Growth and Development: The Concepts and Strategies of Sustainability. London: Routledge.

Bartky, Sandra Lee. 1975. "Toward a Phenomenology of Feminist Consciousness". Social Theory and Practice 3, no. 4: 425–39.

Basten, Carolyn. 1997. "A Feminised Profession: Women in the Teaching Profession". Educational Studies 23, no. 1: 55–62.

Batten, Joe D. 1989. Tough Minded Leadership. New York: AMACON.

Baudrillard, Jean. 1997. "The Illusion of the End". In The Postmodern History Reader, edited by Keith Jenkins, 39–46. London: Routledge.

Beck, Tony. 1994. The Experience of Poverty: Fighting for Respect and Resources in Village India. London: Intermediate Technology.

Beckles, Hilary McD. 1989a. *Corporate Power in Barbados: The Mutual Affair, Economic Injustice in a Political Democracy.* Bridgetown, Barbados: Lighthouse Communications.

———. 1989b. *Natural Rebels: A Social History of Enslaved Black Women in Barbados.* London: Zed Books.

———. 1989c. *White Servitude and Black Slavery in Barbados, 1627–1715.* Knoxville: University of Tennessee Press.

———. 1993. "White Women and Slavery in the Caribbean". *History Workshop Journal* 36: 66–82.

———. 1996a. *Black Masculinity in Caribbean Slavery.* WAND Occasional Paper no. 2. Cave Hill, Barbados: Women and Development Unit, School of Continuing Studies, University of the West Indies.

———. 1996b. "Property Rights in Pleasure: The Marketing of Slave Women's Sexuality in the West Indies". In *West Indies Accounts: Essays on the History of the British Caribbean and the Atlantic Economy in Honour of Richard Sheridan,* edited by Roderick A. McDonald, 169–87. Kingston, Jamaica: University of the West Indies Press.

———. 1997. "Centering Women: Gender Ideologies and Female Enslavement in the Caribbean". Paper presented to the UNESCO/SSHRC Summer Institute, York University, Toronto.

———. 1999. *Centering Woman: Gender Discourses in Caribbean Slave Society.* Kingston, Jamaica: Ian Randle.

———. 2000. "Female Enslavement and Gender Ideologies in the Caribbean". In *Identity in the Shadow of Slavery,* edited by Paul E. Lovejoy, 163–82. London: Continuum.

Bell, Diane, and Renate Klein, eds. 1996. *Radically Speaking: Feminism Reclaimed.* North Melbourne, Australia: Spinifex.

Belly. 1998. Produced by Big Dog Films. Directed by Hype Williams. Santa Monica: Artisan Entertainment.

Belsey, Catherine, and Jane Moore, eds. 1989. *The Feminist Reader: Essays in Gender and the Politics of Literary Criticism.* London: Macmillan.

Beneria, Lourdes, and Shelley Feldman, eds. 1992. *Unequal Burden: Economic Crises, Persistent Poverty and Women's Work.* Boulder: Westview Press.

Benhabib, Seyla. 1995. "Cultural Complexity, Moral Interdependence and the Global Dialogical Community". In *Women, Culture and Development: A Study of Human Capabilities,* edited by Martha C. Nussbaum and Jonathan Glover, 235–59. Oxford: Clarendon Press.

Bennett, Dawne. 2000a. "B'dos' Biggest Mistake! NDP Leader Says Co-ed Schools Bad for Boys". *Barbados Advocate,* 13 March, 7.

———. 2000b. "Boys to Men: Co-ed Way a Mixed Adventure". *Barbados Advocate*, 6 February, 8.

———. 2000c. "Co-ed Error: A Mountain of Evidence". *Sunday Advocate* (Barbados), 19 March, 8.

———. 2000d. "Co-ed School One Big Mistake, Says Fraser". *Daily Nation* (Barbados), 9 March, 7.

Bennis, Warren, and Burt Nanus. 1985. *Leaders: The Strategies for Taking Charge*. New York: Harper and Row.

Berkovitch, Nitza. 1999. *From Motherhood to Citizenship: Women's Rights and International Organizations*. Baltimore: Johns Hopkins University Press.

Berktay, Fatmagul. 1993. "Looking from the 'Other' Side: Is Cultural Relativism a Way Out?" In *Women's Studies in the 1990s: Doing Things Differently?* edited by Joanna De Groot and Mary Maynard, 110–31. London: Macmillan.

Berleant-Schiller, Riva. 1999. "Women, Work and Gender in the Caribbean: Recent Research". *Latin American Research Review* 34, no. 1: 201–11.

Berry, David S. n.d. "International Law and the Violation of Women's Right to Nationality: A Caribbean Perspective". Unpublished document.

Blackburn, Robin. 1997. *The Making of New World Slavery: From the Baroque to the Modern, 1492–1800*. London: Verso.

Blumberg, Rae Lesser. 1989. "Toward a Feminist Theory of Development". In *Feminism and Sociological Theory*, edited by Ruth A. Wallace, 161–99. Newbury Park, Calif.: Sage Publications.

Bocock, Robert. 1986. *Hegemony*. Chichester, UK: Ellis Horwood.

Bolles, A Lynn. 2001. "Grassroots MBAs: Women Craft Vendors in Negril, Jamaica". Paper presented to the twenty-sixth annual conference of the Caribbean Studies Association, 27 May–2 June 2001, St Martin.

Boserup, Ester. 1970. *Women's Role in Economic Development*. New York: St Martin's Press.

Boulding, Kenneth E. 1993. "The Economics of the Coming Spaceship Earth". In *Valuing the Earth: Economics, Ecology, Ethics*, edited by Herman E. Daly and Kenneth N. Townsend, 297–309. Cambridge, Mass.: MIT Press.

Bourdieu, Pierre. 1977. *Outline of a Theory of Practice*. Cambridge: Cambridge University Press.

Boxill, Ian. 2002. "Class System: Has Barbados Changed?" *Sunday Sun* (Barbados), 24 March, A3, A12.

Braidotti, Rosi. 1991a. *Patterns of Dissonance: A Study of Women in Contemporary Philosophy*. Translated by Elizabeth Guild. Oxford, UK: Polity Press.

————. 1991b. *Theories of Gender or, Language Is a Virus.* Utrecht, The Netherlands: Faculteit der Letteren, Universiteit Utrecht.

Brana-Shute, Rosemary. 2000. "Liberating Women: Female Manumitters in Late Eighteenth and Early Nineteenth Century Suriname". In *Differentiating Caribbean Womanhood,* Working Paper no. 3, edited by Jacquelin Stevens, 38–48. Mona, Jamaica: Centre for Gender and Development Studies, University of the West Indies.

Brathwaite, Kamau. 1984. *The Black Woman of the Caribbean during Slavery.* Elsa Goveia Memorial Lecture, 1984. Cave Hill, Barbados: Department of History, University of the West Indies.

Brereton, Bridget. 1979. *Race Relations in Colonial Trinidad, 1870–1900.* Cambridge: Cambridge University Press.

————. 1988. "General Problems and Issues in Studying the History of Women". In *Gender in Caribbean Development: Papers Presented at the Inaugural Seminar of the University of the West Indies Women and Development Studies Project,* edited by Patricia Mohammed and Catherine Shepherd, 123–41. St Augustine, Trinidad: Women in Development Studies Project, University of the West Indies.

————. 1994. *Gendered Testimony: Autobiographies, Diaries and Letters by Women as Sources for Caribbean History.* Elsa Goveia Memorial Lecture, 1994. Mona, Jamaica: Department of History, University of the West Indies.

————. 1998. "Gendered Testimonies: Autobiographies, Diaries and Letters by Women as Sources for Caribbean History". *Feminist Review,* no. 59: 143–63.

————. 1999. "Family Strategies, Gender and the Shift to Wage Labour in the British Caribbean". In *The Colonial Caribbean in Transition: Essays on Postemancipation Social and Cultural History,* edited by Bridget Brereton and Kevin A. Yelvington, 77–107. Kingston, Jamaica: University of the West Indies Press.

Brodber, Erna. 1982. *Perceptions of Caribbean Women: Towards a Documentation of Stereotypes.* Women in the Caribbean Project no. 4, edited by Joycelin Massiah. Cave Hill, Barbados: Institute of Social and Economic Research (Eastern Caribbean), University of the West Indies.

————. 1988. *Myal.* London: New Beacon.

Brooks, Ann. 1997. *Postfeminisms: Feminism, Cultural Theory and Cultural Forms.* London: Routledge.

Brown, Janet, and Barry Chevannes. 1998. *"Why Man Stay So": An Examination of Gender Socialization in the Caribbean.* Mona, Jamaica: University of the West Indies.

Brown, Stewart. 1999. Introduction to the *Oxford Book of Caribbean Short Stories,* edited by Stewart Brown and John Wickham, xiii–xxxiii. Oxford: Oxford University Press.

Burgess, Norma J. 1994. "Gender Roles Revisited: The Development of the 'Woman's Place' among African American Women in the US". *Journal of Black Studies* 24, no. 4: 391–401.

Burns, James MacGregor. 1978. *Leadership.* New York: Harper and Row.

Bush, Barbara. 1981. "White 'Ladies', Coloured 'Favourites', and Black 'Wenches': Some Considerations on Sex, Race, and Class Factors in Social Relations in White Creole Society in the British Caribbean". *Slavery and Abolition* 2, no. 3: 245–62.

———. 1990. *Slave Women in Caribbean Society, 1650–1838.* Kingston, Jamaica: Heinemann (Caribbean).

Bush-Slimani, Barbara. 1993. "Hard Labour: Women, Childbirth and Resistance in British Caribbean Slave Societies". *History Workshop Journal* 36: 83–99.

Butler, Judith. 1990. *Gender Trouble: Feminism and the Subversion of Identity.* New York: Routledge.

Cabezas, Amalia L. 1999. "Women's Work Is Never Done: Sex Tourism in Sosua, the Dominican Republic". In *Sun, Sex and Gold: Tourism and Sex Work in the Caribbean,* edited by Kamala Kempadoo, 93–123. Lanham, Md.: Rowman and Littlefield.

Caldecott, A. 1970. *The Church in the West Indies.* London: Frank Cass.

Campbell, John. 2001. "Single White Female . . . Reconsidering the Dialectic of White Women, Power and Sugar Management on Eighteenth Century British West Indian Caribbean Sugar Estates". Paper presented at the seminar Conversations with Gender 5, University of the West Indies, Mona, Jamaica, 22 February.

Carby, Hazel V. 1987. *Reconstructing Womanhood: The Emergence of the Afro-American Woman Novelist.* New York: Oxford University Press.

Cave, Michelle, and Joan French. 1995. "Sexual Choice, a Human Rights Issue: Women Loving Women". Paper presented to the Caribbean Association for Feminist Research and Action (CAFRA) Conference on Critical Perspectives on Human Rights Issues, Port of Spain, Trinidad, 26–28 January 1995.

Central Bank of Barbados. 1999. *1998 Annual Report.* Barbados: Central Bank of Barbados.

Chadha, Kumkum. 2000. " 'Male Marginalisation' Clause Dropped". *Hindustan Times Online* (New Delhi). 21 April. [Cited 13 May 2001.] <http://www.hindustantimes.com/nonfram/220400/detNAT14.htm>.

Chambers, Claudia, and Barry Chevannes. 1991. *Report on Focus Groups: Sexual Decision-Making Project*. Kingston: Institute of Social and Economic Research, University of the West Indies.

Chambers, Robert. 1988. *Poverty in India: Concepts, Research, and Reality*. IDS Discussion Paper no. 241. Brighton, UK: Institute of Development Studies.

Chanel, Ives Marie. 1994. "Haitian and Dominican Women in the Sex Trade". *CAFRA News* 8: 13–14.

Chevannes, Barry. 1997. "Helping Men Become Better Fathers: A Case Study of Jamaica". In *Caribbean Social Structures and the Changing World of Men*, 24–26. Port of Spain, Trinidad: United Nations Economic Commission for Latin America and the Caribbean, Subregional Headquarters for the Caribbean.

————. 1999. *What We Sow and What We Reap: Problems in the Cultivation of Male Identity in Jamaica*. Grace, Kennedy Foundation Lecture Series, 1999. Kingston, Jamaica: Grace, Kennedy Foundation.

Chhachhi, Amrita. 1988. "Concepts in Feminist Theory: Consensus and Controversy". In *Gender in Caribbean Development: Papers Presented at the Inaugural Seminar of the University of the West Indies Women and Development Studies Project*, edited by Patricia Mohammed and Catherine Shepherd, 76–96. St Augustine, Trinidad: Women in Development Studies Project, University of the West Indies.

Chodorow, Nancy. 1978. *The Reproduction of Mothering: Psychoanalysis and the Sociology of Gender*. Berkeley: University of California Press.

Christian, Barbara. 1985. *Black Feminist Criticism: Perspectives on Black Women Writing*. New York: Pergamon Press.

————. 1990. "The Race for Theory". In *Making Face, Making Soul, Haciendo Caras: Creative and Critical Perspectives by Women of Color*, edited by Gloria Anzaldua, 335–45. San Francisco: Aunt Lute Foundation Books.

Chude-Sokei, Louis. 1997. "The Sound of Culture: Dread Discourse and Jamaican Sound Systems". In *Language, Rhythm, and Sound: Black Popular Cultures into the Twenty-first Century*, edited by Joseph K. Adjaye and Adrianne R. Andrews, 182–202. Pittsburgh: University of Pittsburgh Press.

Cixous, Helénè. 1981. "The Laugh of Medusa". In *The New French Feminisms: An Anthology*, edited by Elaine Marks and Isabella De Courtivon, 245–64. New York: Schocken Books.

Clarke, Maria Donoso. 1998. Statement to the World Bank NGO Meeting, Montego Bay, Jamaica, 1–4 June 1998.

Clarke, Roberta. 1986. "Women's Organisations, Women's Interests". *Social and Economic Studies* 35, no. 3: 107–55.

Clifford, Geraldine Joncich. 1991. " 'Daughters into Teachers': Educational and Demographic Influences on the Transformation of Teaching into 'Women's Work' in America". In *Women Who Taught: Perspectives on the History of Women and Teaching,* edited by Alison Prentice and Marjorie R. Theobald, 115–35. Toronto: University of Toronto Press.

A Clockwork Orange. 1971. Produced by Warner Brothers. Directed by Stanley Kubrick. Los Angeles: Warner Brothers.

Cockburn, Cynthia. 1991. *In the Way of Women: Men's Resistance to Sex Equality in Organizations.* Basingstoke, UK: Macmillan.

Cohen, William B. 1980. *The French Encounter with Africans: White Response to Blacks, 1530–1880.* Bloomington: Indiana University Press.

Cole, Joyce. 1982. "Official Ideology and the Education of Women in the English-speaking Caribbean, 1835–1945, with Special Reference to Barbados". In *Women and Education,* edited by Joycelin Massiah, 1–31. Women in the Caribbean Project, vol. 5. Cave Hill, Barbados: Institute of Social and Economic Research (Eastern Caribbean), University of the West Indies.

Collingwood, R.G. [1946] 1994. *The Idea of History.* Revised ed. Oxford: Oxford University Press.

Cook, Gail C.A., ed. 1976. *Opportunity for Choice: A Goal for Women in Canada.* Ottawa, Ont.: Statistics Canada.

Cox, Robert. 1981. "Social Force, States and World Order: Beyond International Relations Theory". *Millennium: Journal of International Studies* 10, no. 2: 126–55.

Crash. 1997. Produced by Fine Line Features. Directed by David Cronenberg. Los Angeles: Fine Line Features.

Craton, Michael. 1979. "Changing Patterns of Slave Families in the British West Indies". *Journal of Interdisciplinary History* 10, no. 1: 1–35.

Crick, Malcolm. 1989. "Representations of International Tourism in the Social Sciences: Sun, Sex, Sights, Savings and Servility". *Annual Review of Anthropology* 18: 307–44.

Croll, Elizabeth. 1985. *Women and Rural Development in China.* Women, Work and Development, no. 11. Geneva: International Labour Office.

Cumber Dance, Daryl. 1993. "Matriarchs, Doves and Nymphos: Prevalent Images of Black, Indian and White Women in Caribbean Literature". *Studies in Literary Imagination* 26, no. 2: 21–31.

Curtin, Philip D. 1969. *The Atlantic Slave Trade: A Census.* Madison: University of Wisconsin Press.

———. 1990. *The Rise and Fall of the Plantation Complex: Essays in the Atlantic History*. Cambridge: Cambridge University Press.

Dagenais, Huguette. 1993. "Women in Guadeloupe: The Paradoxes of Reality". In *Women and Change in the Caribbean,* edited by Janet Momsen, 83–108. Kingston, Jamaica: Ian Randle.

Daily Nation (Barbados). 2000. "Heads Want Probe into Co-education", 27 March, 5.

Dalla Costa, Mariarosa, and Selma James. 1972. *The Power of Women and the Subversion of the Community*. Bristol, UK: Falling Wall Press.

Davies, Carole Boyce, and Elaine Savory Fido, eds. 1990. *Out of the Kumbla: Caribbean Women and Literature*. Trenton, NJ: Africa World Press.

Davis, David. 1966. *The Problem of Slavery in Western Culture*. Ithaca: Cornell University Press.

de Beauvoir, Simone. 1949. *The Second Sex*. London: Penguin Books.

———. 1953. *The Second Sex*. New York: Alfred Knopf.

Decker, Jeffrey Louis. 1994. "The State of Rap: Time and Place in Hip Hop Nationalism". In *Microphone Fiends: Youth Music, Youth Culture,* edited by Andrew Ross and Tricia Rose, 99–121. New York: Routledge.

Delphy, Christine. 1984. *Close to Home: A Materialistic Analysis of Women's Oppression*. London: Hutchinson.

———. 1991. "Rethinking Sex and Gender". *Women's Studies International Forum* 16, no. 1: 1–9.

Demerieux, Margaret. 1992. *Fundamental Rights in Commonwealth Caribbean Constitutions*. Cave Hill, Barbados: Faculty of Law Library, University of the West Indies.

Denis, Ann. 1985. " 'Helping Out' in the Family Enterprise". Paper presented at the Women and the Invisible Economy Conference, Simone de Beauvoir Institute, Concordia University, Montreal, 1985.

Diamond, Irene, and Nancy Hartsock. 1998. "Beyond Interests in Politics: A Comment on Virginia Sapiro's 'When Are Interests Interesting? The Problem of Political Representation of Women'". In *Feminism and Politics,* edited by Anne Phillips, 193–202. Oxford: Oxford University Press.

Dietz, Mary G. 1992. "Introduction: Debating Simone de Beauvoir". *Signs: Journal of Women in Culture and Society* 18, no. 1: 74–88.

———. 1998. "Context Is All: Feminism and Theories of Citizenship". In *Feminism and Politics,* edited by Anne Phillips, 378–400. Oxford: Oxford University Press.

di Leonardo, Micaela. 1998. *Exotics at Home: Anthropologies, Others, American Modernity*. Chicago: University of Chicago Press.

Dos Santos, Errol. 1952. *Report of the Salaries Commissioner.* Bridgetown, Barbados: Advocate.

Downes, Aviston D. 1997. "'Boys of the Empire': Elite Education and the Socio-cultural Construction of Hegemonic Masculinity in Barbados, 1875–1920". Paper presented to the History Forum, Department of History, University of the West Indies, Cave Hill, Barbados, January 1997.

Drayton, Kathleen. 1984. "The Development of Higher Education for Women in the Commonwealth Caribbean with Special Reference to Barbados". Paper prepared for the Sixth Berkshire Conference on the History of Women, Smith College, Massachusetts, 1–3 June.

Durant-Gonzalez, Victoria. 1982. "The Realm of the Female Familial Responsibility". In *Women and the Family,* edited by Joycelin Massiah, 1–27. Women in the Caribbean Project, vol. 2. Cave Hill, Barbados: Institute of Social and Economic Research (Eastern Caribbean), University of the West Indies.

Edmondson, Belinda. 1999a. "Jamaica Kincaid and the Genealogy of Exile". *Small Axe* 5: 72–79.

———. 1999b. *Making Men: Gender, Literary Authority, and Women's Writing in Caribbean Narrative.* Durham: Duke University Press.

Edwards, Bryan. 1966. *The History, Civil and Commercial, of the British West Indies, with a Continuation to the Present Time,* vol. 2. 5th ed. New York: AMS Press.

Eichler, Margrit. 1985. "And the Work Never Ends: Feminist Contributions". *Canadian Review of Sociology and Anthropology* 22, no. 5: 619–44.

Ellman, Mary. 1968. *Thinking about Women.* New York: Harcourt, Brace and World.

Elster, Jon. 1982. "Sour Grapes: Utilitarianism and the Genesis of Want". In *Utilitarianism and Beyond,* edited by Amartya Sen and Bernard Williams, 219–38. Cambridge: Cambridge University Press.

Eltis, David. 2000. *The Rise of African Slavery in the Americas.* Cambridge: Cambridge University Press.

Eltis, David, Stephen D. Behrendt, David Richardson and Herbert S. Klein, eds. 1999. *The Trans-Atlantic Slave Trade: A Database on CD-ROM.* Cambridge: Cambridge University Press.

Eltis, David, and David Richardson. 1997. "West Africa and the Transatlantic Slave Trade: New Evidence of Long-run Trends". *Slavery and Abolition* 18, no. 1: 16–35.

Emmanuel, Patrick A.M. 1992. *Elections and Party Systems in the Commonwealth Caribbean 1994–1991.* St Michael, Barbados: Caribbean Development Research Services.

Engineer, Asghar Ali. 1992. *The Rights of Women in Islam*. New York: St Martin's Press.

Escobar, Arturo. 1995. *Encountering Development: The Making and Unmaking of the Third World*. Princeton: Princeton University Press.

Espeut, Peter. 1998. "Woman Time Now!" *Gleaner* (Jamaica), 11 March, A4.

———. 2000. "Marginalising Males". *Gleaner* (Jamaica), 26 January, A4.

Espinet, Ramabai. 1993. "Representation and the Indo-Caribbean Woman in Trinidad and Tobago". In *Indo-Caribbean Resistance*, edited by Frank Birbalsingh, 42–61. Toronto: TSAR.

European Trade Union Committee for Education (ETUCE). 1995. *The Feminisation of the Teaching Profession*. Bruxelles: CSEE, ETUCE.

Evans, Mary. 1990. "The Problem of Gender for Women's Studies". *Women's Studies International Forum* 13, no. 5: 457–62.

Fierlbeck, Katherine. 1995. "Getting Representation Right for Women in Development: Accountability and the Articulation of Women's Interests". *IDS Bulletin* 26, no. 3: 23–30.

Figueroa, Mark. 1997. "Gender Differentials in Educational Achievement in Jamaica and Other Caribbean Territories". Paper presented at the Conference on Intervention Strategies to Address Male Underachievement in Primary and Secondary Education, Port of Spain, Trinidad.

———. 2000. "Making Sense of Male Experience: The Case of the Academic Underachiever in the English Speaking Caribbean". Department of Economics, University of the West Indies, Mona, Jamaica. Typescript.

Firestone, Shulamith. 1970. *The Dialectic of Sex: The Case for Feminist Revolution*. New York: Morrow.

Flax, Jane. 1990a. "Post Modernism and Gender Relations in Feminist Theory". In *Feminism/Postmodernism*, edited by Linda J. Nicholson, 39–62. New York: Routledge.

———. 1990b. *Thinking Fragments: Psychoanalysis, Feminism, Postmodernism in the Contemporary West*. Berkeley: University of California Press.

———. 1992. "The End of Innocence". In *Feminists Theorize the Political*, edited by Judith Butler and Joan W. Scott, 445–63. New York: Routledge.

Foucault, Michel. 1972. *The Archaeology of Knowledge and the Discourse on Language*. New York: Pantheon Books.

———. 1981. *Power/Knowledge: Selected Interviews and Other Writings, 1972–1977*. New York: Pantheon Books.

Fox, Bonnie. 1988. "Conceptualizing Patriarchy". *Canadian Review of Sociology and Anthropology* 25, no. 2: 162–82.

Fox-Genovese, Elizabeth, and Eugene Genovese. 1983. *The Fruits of Merchant Capital: Slavery and Bourgeois Property in the Rise and Expansion of Capitalism.* New York: Oxford University Press.

Fraser, Nancy. 1997. *Justice Interruptus: Critical Reflections on the "Postsocialist" Condition.* New York: Routledge.

Fraser, Nancy, and Linda Gordon. 1997. "Decoding 'Dependency': Inscriptions of Power in a Keyword of a US Welfare State". In *Reconstructing Political Theory: Feminist Perspectives,* edited by Mary Lyndon Shanley and Uma Narayan, 25–47. Cambridge, UK: Polity Press.

Fraser, Nancy, and Linda J. Nicholson. 1990. "Social Criticism Without Philosophy: An Encounter Between Feminism and Postmodernism". In *Feminism/Postmodernism,* edited by Linda J. Nicholson, 19–38. New York: Routledge.

Fredrickson, George M. 1995. "From Exceptionalism to Variability: Recent Developments in Cross-National Comparative History". *Journal of American History* 82, no. 2: 587–604.

Freeman, Carla. 1997. "Reinventing Higglering across Transnational Zones: Barbadian Women Juggle the Triple Shift". In *Daughters of Caliban: Caribbean Women in the Twentieth Century,* edited by Consuelo López Springfield, 68–95. Bloomington: Indiana University Press.

———. 1998. "Island-Hopping Body Shopping in Barbados: Localising the Gendering of Transnational Workers". In *Caribbean Portraits: Essays on Gender Ideologies and Identities,* edited by Christine Barrow, 14–27. Kingston, Jamaica: Ian Randle.

———. 2000. *High Tech and High Heels in the Global Economy: Women, Work, and Pink-Collar Identities in the Caribbean.* Durham, NC: Duke University Press.

Fukuyama, Francis. 1998. "How Women Could Rule the World". *The Times,* 10 October, 21.

Fultz, Michael. 1995. "African-American Teachers in the South, 1890–1940: Growth, Feminization and Salary Discrimination". *Teachers College Record* 96, no. 3: 544–68.

Gardner-Brown, A.G.H. 1966. *Report of the Commission Appointed to Examine the Structure and Remuneration of the Civil Service.* Bridgetown, Barbados: Government Printing Office.

Gaspar, David Barry, and Darlene Clark Hine, eds. 1996. *More than Chattel: Black Women and Slavery in the Americas.* Bloomington: Indiana University Press.

Gautier, Arlette. 1983. "Les esclaves femmes aux Antilles Françaises, 1635–1848". *Historical Reflections/Reflexions historiques* 10, no. 3: 409–33.

Gearing, Jean. 1995. "Fear and Loving in the West Indies: Research from the Heart (As Well As the Head)". In *Taboo: Sex, Identity, and Erotic Subjectivity in Anthropological Fieldwork,* edited by Don Kulick and Margaret Wilson, 186–218. London: Routledge.

Geggus, David P. 1996. "Slave and Free Colored Women in Saint Domingue". In *More than Chattel: Black Women and Slavery in the Americas,* edited by David Barry Gaspar and Darlene Clark Hine, 259–78. Bloomington: Indiana University Press.

Gemery, Henry A., and Jan S. Hogendorn, eds. 1979. *The Uncommon Market: Essays on the Economic History of the Atlantic Slave Trade.* New York: Academic Press.

Gilbert, Sandra M., and Susan Gubar. 1979. *The Madwoman in the Attic: The Woman Writer and the Nineteenth-Century Literary Imagination.* New Haven: Yale University Press.

Gill, Margaret, and Joycelin Massiah, eds. 1984. *Women, Work and Development.* Women in the Caribbean Project no. 6, edited by Joycelin Massiah. Cave Hill, Barbados: Institute of Social and Economic Research (Eastern Caribbean), University of the West Indies.

Gilligan, Carol. 1982. *In a Different Voice: Psychological Theory and Women's Development.* Cambridge: Harvard University Press.

Giroux, Henry A. 1992. *Border Crossings: Cultural Workers and the Politics of Education.* New York: Routledge.

Godsall, W.D. 1956. *Report of the Commission Appointed to Review the Remuneration of Public Officers and Government Employees of Barbados.* Barbados: n.p.

Goody, Jack, and Joan Buckley. 1973. "Inheritance and Women's Labor in Africa". *Africa* 43, no. 2: 108–21.

Gordon, Linda. 1991. "On 'Difference'". *Genders* 10: 91–111.

Gordon, Shirley. 1963. *A Century of West Indian Education: A Source Book.* London: Longmans.

Goulbourne, Harry. 1988. *Teachers, Education and Politics in Jamaica, 1892–1972.* Basingstoke, UK: Macmillan.

Goveia, Elsa V. 1965. *Slave Society in the British Leeward Islands at the End of the Eighteenth Century.* New Haven: Yale University Press.

Gray, Obika. 2001. "Rethinking Power: Political Subordination in Jamaica". In *New Caribbean Thought: A Reader,* edited by Brian Meeks and Folke Lindahl, 210–31. Kingston, Jamaica: University of the West Indies Press.

Grbich, Judith E. 1991. "The Body in Legal Theory". In *At the Boundaries of Law: Feminism and Legal Theory,* edited by Martha Albertson Fineman and Nancy Sweet Thomadsen, 61–76. New York: Routledge.

Greene, Sandra E. 1996. *Gender, Ethnicity and Social Change on the Upper Slave Coast: A History of the Anlo-Ewe.* Portsmouth, NH: Heinemann.

Greer, Germaine. 1970. *The Female Eunuch.* London: Macgibbon and Kee.

Grosz, Elizabeth. 1990. "Contemporary Theories of Power and Subjectivity". In *Feminist Knowledge: Critique and Construct,* edited by Sneja Gunew, 59–120. London: Routledge.

Grumet, Madeleine. 1981. "Pedagogy for Patriarchy: The Feminization of Teaching". *Interchange* 12, no. 2–3: 165–84.

Guillaumin, Colette. 1995. *Racism, Sexism, Power and Ideology.* London: Routledge.

Guyana. 1980. *Constitution of Guyana.*

Hall, Catherine. 1995. "Gender Politics and Imperial Politics: Rethinking the Histories of Empire". In *Engendering History: Caribbean Women in Historical Perspective,* edited by Verene Shepherd, Bridget Brereton and Barbara Bailey, 48–59. Kingston, Jamaica: Ian Randle.

Hall, Douglas. 1989. *In Miserable Slavery: Thomas Thistlewood in Jamaica, 1750–86.* London: Macmillan.

Hall, Stuart. 1994. "Cultural Identity and Diaspora". In *Colonial Discourse and Post-colonial Theory: A Reader,* edited by Patrick Williams and Laura Chrisman, 392–403. Hertfordshire, UK: Harvester Wheatsheaf.

———. 1997. "What Is This 'Black' in Black Popular Culture?" In *Representing Blackness: Issues in Film and Video,* edited by Valerie Smith, 123–33. London: Athlone Press.

Hamilton, Marlene. 1997. "The Availability and Suitability of Educational Opportunities for Jamaican Students: An Historical Overview". In *Gender: A Caribbean Multi-Disciplinary Perspective,* edited by Elsa Leo-Rhynie, Barbara Bailey and Christine Barrow, 133–43. Kingston, Jamaica: Ian Randle.

———. 1999. *Women and Higher Education in the Commonwealth Caribbean. UWI: A Progressive University for Women?* Working Paper no. 2. Cave Hill, Barbados: Centre for Gender and Development Studies, University of the West Indies.

Handler, Jerome S. 1998. "Life Histories of Enslaved Africans in Barbados". *Slavery and Abolition* 19, no. 1: 129–40.

Harewood, Jack. 1975. *The Population of Trinidad and Tobago.* Paris: CICRED Series.

Harsanyi, John C. 1982. "Morality and the Theory of Rational Behavior". In *Utilitarianism and Beyond*, edited by Amartya Sen and Bernard Williams, 39–62. Cambridge: Cambridge University Press.

Hart, Keith. 1989a. Introduction to *Women and the Sexual Division of Labour in the Caribbean*, edited by Keith Hart, 1–8. Kingston, Jamaica: Consortium Graduate School of Social Sciences, University of the West Indies.

———, ed. 1989b. *Women and the Sexual Division of Labour in the Caribbean*. Mona, Jamaica: Consortium Graduate School of Social Sciences, University of the West Indies.

Hartman, Joan E. 1991. "Telling Stories: The Construction of Women's Agency". In *(En)gendering Knowledge: Feminists in Academe*, edited by Joan E. Hartman and Ellen Messer-Davidow, 11–34. Knoxville: University of Tennessee Press.

Hartsock, Nancy C.M. 1979. "Feminism, Power, and Change: A Theoretical Analysis". In *Women Organizing: An Anthology*, edited by Bernice Cummings and Victoria Schuck, 2–24. Metuchen, NJ: Scarecrow Press.

Hawkesworth, Mary. 1997. "Confounding Gender". *Signs: Journal of Women in Culture and Society* 22, no. 3: 649–85.

Hayden, Howard. 1945. *A Policy for Education*. Bridgetown, Barbados: Department of Education.

Henriques, Fernando. 1965. *Prostitution in Europe and the Americas*. New York: Citadel Press.

———. 1974. *Children of Caliban: Miscegenation*. London: Secker and Warburg.

Hentsch, Thierry. 1992. *Imagining the Middle East*. Montreal: Black Rose Books.

Hermsen, Joke J., and Alkeline van Lenning. 1991. *Sharing the Difference: Feminist Debates in Holland*. London: Routledge.

Herskovits, Melville J. 1948. *Man and His Works: The Science of Cultural Anthropology*. New York: Knopf.

Higman, Barry. 1973. "Household Structure and Fertility on Jamaican Slave Plantations: A Nineteenth Century Example". *Population Studies* 27, no. 3: 527–50.

———. 1979. "Growth in Afro-Caribbean Slave Populations". *American Journal of Physical Anthropology* 50, no. 3: 373–86.

———. 1984. *Slave Populations of the British Caribbean*. Baltimore: Johns Hopkins University Press.

Hirshman, Mitu. 1995. "Women and Development: A Critique". In *Feminism/Postmodernism/Development*, edited by Marianne H. Marchand and Jane L. Parpart, 42–55. London: Routledge.

Hoffman, Mark. 1987. "Critical Theory and the Inter-Paradigm Debate". *Millennium: Journal of International Studies* 16, no. 2: 231–49.

hooks, bell. 1989. *Talking Back: Thinking Feminist, Thinking Black*. London: Sheba Feminist.

———. 1993. "Dreaming Ourselves Dark and Deep: Black Beauty". In *Sisters of the Yam: Black Women and Self-Recovery*, 79–98. Boston: South End Press.

Hopkinson, Nalo. 1998. *Brown Girl in the Ring*. New York: Warner Aspect.

Hopkinson, Slade. 1976. "The Madwoman of Papine: Two Cartoons with Captions". In *The Madwoman of Papine: Poems*, 17–18. Georgetown, Guyana: Ministry of Education and Social Development.

Hosein, Shaheeda. 1996. "Towards a Re-examination of the Indian Woman in Trinidad, 1870–1945". Paper presented to a staff/graduate seminar, Department of History, University of the West Indies, St Augustine, Trinidad.

How Stella Got Her Groove Back. 1998. Produced by 20th Century Fox. Directed by Kevin Rodney Sullivan. Los Angeles: 20th Century Fox Film Corporation.

Humm, Maggie. 1990. *The Dictionary of Feminist Theory*. Columbus: Ohio State University Press.

Inikori, Joseph E., ed. 1982. *Forced Migration: The Impact of the Export Slave Trade on African Societies*. London: Hutchinson.

———. 1992. "Export versus Domestic Demand: The Determinants of Sex Ratios in the Transatlantic Slave Trade". *Research in Economic History* 14: 117–66.

Jackson, Cecile. 1997. "Post Poverty, Gender and Development". *IDS Bulletin* 28, no. 3: 145–55.

———. 1998. "Rescuing Gender from the Poverty Trap". In *Feminist Visions of Development: Gender, Analysis and Policy*, edited by Cecile Jackson and Ruth Pearson, 39–64. London: Routledge.

Jacobs, K.C. 1961. *Report of the Commission Appointed to Review the Structure of the Civil Service and the Remuneration of Public Officers and Government Employees of Barbados*. Barbados: n.p.

Jain, Shobhita, and Rhoda Reddock, eds. 1998. *Women Plantation Workers: International Experiences*. Oxford: Berg.

Jamaica. 1962. *Constitution of Jamaica*.

Jayasinghe, Daphne. 2001. " 'More and More Technology, Women Have to Go Home': Changing Skill Demands in Manufacturing and Caribbean Women's Access to Training". *Gender and Development* 9, no. 1: 70–81.

Jeffreys, Sheila. 1997. *The Idea of Prostitution*. North Melbourne, Australia: Spinifex.

John, Mary E. 1996. *Discrepant Dislocations: Feminism, Theory and Post Colonial Histories*. Berkeley: University of California Press.

Jubilee. 1978. Produced by Magalovision Film. Directed by Derek Jarman. London: Cinegate.

Junega, Renu. 1996. *Caribbean Transactions: West Indian Culture in Literature*. London: Macmillan Caribbean.

Juteau, Danielle, and Nicole Laurin. 1988. "L'evolution des formes de l'appropriation des femmes: des religieuses aux 'meres porteuses'". *Canadian Review of Sociology and Anthropology* 25, no. 2: 183–207.

Kabbani, Rana. 1988. *Europe's Myths of Orient: Devise and Rule*. London: Pandora Press.

Kabeer, Naila. 1992. "Feminist Perspectives in Development: A Critical Review". In *Working Out: New Directions in Women's Studies,* edited by Hilary Hinds, Ann Phoenix and Jackie Stacey, 101–12. London: Falmer Press.

Kandiyoti, Deniz. 1988. "Bargaining with Patriarchy". *Gender and Society* 2, no. 3: 274–90.

Kane, Stephanie C. 1993. "Prostitution and the Military: Planning AIDS Intervention in Belize". *Social Science and Medicine* 36, no. 7: 965–79.

Kanhai, Rosanne, ed. 1999. *Matikor: The Politics of Identity for Indo-Caribbean Women*. St Augustine, Trinidad: School of Continuing Studies, University of the West Indies.

Kassim, Halima Saadia. 1999. "Education, Community Organisations and Gender among the Indo-Muslims of Trinidad, 1917–1962". PhD diss., University of the West Indies.

Kelly, Joan. 1984. *Women, History and Theory: The Essays of Joan Kelly*. Chicago: University of Chicago Press.

Kempadoo, Kamala. 1996. "Prostitution, Marginality and Empowerment: Caribbean Women in the Sex Trade". *Beyond Law* 5, no. 14: 69–84.

———. 1999a. "Continuities and Change: Five Centuries of Prostitution in the Caribbean". In *Sun, Sex and Gold: Tourism and Sex Work in the Caribbean,* edited by Kamala Kempadoo, 3–33. Lanham, Md.: Rowman and Littlefield.

————. 2001. "Women of Color and the Global Sex Trade: Transnational Feminist Perspectives". *Meridians: Feminism, Race, Transnationalism* 1, no. 2: 28–51.

————, ed. 1999b. *Sun, Sex and Gold: Tourism and Sex Work in the Caribbean*. Lanham, Md.: Rowman and Littlefield.

Kempadoo, Kamala, and Jo Doezema, eds. 1998. *Global Sex Workers: Rights, Resistance and Redefinition*. New York: Routledge.

Kerns, Virginia. 1982. "Structural Continuity in the Division of Men's and Women's Work among the Black Carib (Garifuna)". In *Sex Roles and Social Change in Native Lower Central American Societies,* edited by Christine A. Loveland and Franklin O. Loveland, 23–43. Urbana: University of Illinois Press.

————. 1983. *Women and Their Ancestors: Black Carib Kinship and Ritual.* Urbana: University of Illinois Press.

Kerr, Paulette A. 1995. "Victims or Strategists?: Female Lodging-house Keepers in Jamaica". In *Engendering History: Caribbean Women in Historical Perspective,* edited by Verene Shepherd, Bridget Brereton and Barbara Bailey, 197–212. Kingston, Jamaica: Ian Randle.

Kincaid, Jamaica. 1985. *Annie John.* New York: Farrar, Straus and Giroux.

Kinnaird, Vivian, and Derek Hall, eds. 1994. *Tourism: A Gender Analysis.* Chichester, UK: Wiley.

Kitzinger, Celia. 1991. "Feminism, Psychology and the Paradox of Power". *Feminism and Psychology* 1, no. 1: 111–29.

Kopytoff, Igor. 1979. "Indigenous African Slavery: Commentary One". *Historical Reflections* 6, no. 1: 62 –64.

Koven, Seth, and Sonya Michel. 1993. "Mother Worlds". Introduction to *Mothers of a New World: Maternalist Politics and the Origins of Welfare State,* 1–42. New York: Routledge.

Kruks, Sonia. 1992. "Gender and Subjectivity: Simone de Beauvoir and Contemporary Feminism". *Signs: Journal of Women in Culture and Society* 18, no. 1: 89–110.

Kutzinski, Vera M. 1993. *Sugar's Secrets: Race and the Erotics of Cuban Nationalism.* Charlottesville: University Press of Virginia.

Lacey, Nicola. 1998. *Unspeakable Subjects: Feminist Essays in Legal and Social Theory.* Oxford: Hart Publishing.

Lagro, Monique, and Donna Plotkin. 1990. *The Suitcase Traders in the Free Zone of Curaçao.* Port of Spain, Trinidad: Economic Commission for Latin America and the Caribbean, Subregional Headquarters for the Caribbean.

Lamming, George. 1953. *In the Castle of My Skin.* London: Michael Joseph.

————. 1960. *The Pleasures of Exile*. London: Michael Joseph.

Lazarus-Black, Mindie. 1994. *Legitimate Acts and Illegal Encounters: Law and Society in Antigua and Barbuda*. Washington, DC: Smithsonian Institution Press.

Leo-Rhynie, Elsa, Barbara Bailey and Christine Barrow. 1997. *Gender: A Caribbean Multi-Disciplinary Perspective*. Kingston, Jamaica: Ian Randle.

Lerner, Gerda. 1986. *The Creation of Patriarchy*. New York: Oxford University Press.

Lewis, Hope. 1997. "Lionheart Gals Facing the Dragon: The Human Rights of Inter/national Black Women in the United States". *Oregon Law Review* 76: 567–632.

Lewis, Linden. 1994. "Constructing the Masculine in the Context of the Caribbean". Paper presented to the Nineteenth Annual Caribbean Studies Conference, Merida, Mexico, 23–28 May.

————. 1996. "Caribbean Masculinity at the Fin de Siècle". Paper presented at the Centre for Gender and Development Studies, University of the West Indies, St Augustine Symposium on the Construction of Caribbean Masculinity: "Towards a Research Agenda". St Augustine, Trinidad, 11–13 January.

————. 1998. "Masculinity and the Dance of the Dragon: Reading Lovelace Discursively". *Feminist Review*, no. 59: 164–85.

————. 2000. "Nationalism and Caribbean Masculinity". In *Gender Ironies of Nationalism: Sexing the Nation*, edited by Tamar Mayer, 261–83. London: Routledge.

————. 2001. "The Contestations of Race in Barbadian Society and the Camouflage of Conservatism". In *New Caribbean Thought: A Reader*, edited by Brian Meeks and Folke Lindahl, 144–95. Kingston, Jamaica: University of the West Indies Press.

Lewis, Reina. 1996. *Gendering Orientalism: Race, Femininity and Representation*. New York: Routledge.

Lim, Lin Lean, ed. 1998. *The Sex Sector: The Economic and Social Bases of Prostitution in Southeast Asia*. Geneva: International Labour Office.

Lindsay, Keisha. 1997. "Caribbean Male: An Endangered Species?" Working Paper no. 1, edited by Patricia Mohammed, 1–20. Mona, Jamaica: Centre for Gender and Development Studies, University of the West Indies.

Lister, Ruth. 1997. *Citizenship: Feminist Perspectives*. Houndsmills: Macmillan.

Long, Edward. 1970. *The History of Jamaica, or General Survey of the Antient and Modern State of That Island: With Reflections on its*

Situations, Settlements, Inhabitants, Climate, Products, Commerce, Laws and Government. London: Frank Cass.

Look Lai, Walton. 1993. *Indentured Labour, Caribbean Sugar: Chinese and Indian Migrants to the British West Indies, 1838–1918*. Baltimore: Johns Hopkins University Press.

Lopata, Helena Znaniecka. 1971. *Occupation: Housewife*. New York: Oxford University Press.

López Springfield, Consuelo, ed. 1997. *Daughters of Caliban: Caribbean Women in the Twentieth Century*. Bloomington: Indiana University Press.

Lovejoy, Paul E., and Jan S. Hogendorn. 1993. *Slow Death for Slavery: The Course of Abolition in Northern Nigeria, 1897–1936* . Cambridge: Cambridge University Press.

Lovell, Terry. 2003. "Toril Moi, *What Is a Woman*". *Feminist Theory* 4, no. 1: 93–95.

Lynch, Roslyn. 1989. "Gender and Labour Market Theories: A Review". In *Women and the Sexual Division of Labour in the Caribbean*, edited by Keith Hart, 29–45. Kingston, Jamaica: Consortium Graduate School of Social Sciences, University of the West Indies.

Lyotard, Jean-Francois. 1997. "The Post-Modern Condition". In *The Postmodern History Reader*, edited by Keith Jenkins, 36–38. London: Routledge.

MacKinnon, Catharine A. 1987. *Feminism Unmodified: Discourses on Life and Law*. Harvard: Harvard University Press.

———. 1989. *Towards a Feminist Theory of the State*. Cambridge: Harvard University Press.

Macklem, Patrick. 1988. "Constitutional Ideologies". *Ottawa Law Review* 20: 117–56.

MacMillan, Terry. 1996. *How Stella Got Her Groove Back*. New York: Signet.

Mahase, Anna, Sr. 1992. *My Mother's Daughter: The Autobiography of Anna Mahase Snr., 1899–1978*. Claxton Bay, Trinidad: Royards Publishing.

Mair, Lucille Mathurin. 1986. "Women Field Workers in Jamaica during Slavery". Elsa Goveia Memorial Lecture, Department of History, University of the West Indies, Mona, Jamaica.

———. 1987. *Women Field Workers in Jamaica During Slavery*. Mona, Jamaica: Department of History, University of the West Indies.

———. 1988. Foreword to *Gender in Caribbean Development: Papers Presented at the Inaugural Seminar of the University of the West Indies Women and Development Studies Project*, edited by Patricia Mohammed and Catherine Shepherd, x–xi. St Augustine, Trinidad: Women in Development Studies Project, University of the West Indies.

Majury, Diana. 1991. "Strategizing in Equality". In *At the Boundaries of Law: Feminism and Legal Theory*, edited by Martha Albertson Fineman and Nancy Sweet Thomadsen, 320–37. New York: Routledge.

Mangru, Basdeo. 1987. "The Sex-Ratio Disparity and Its Consequences under the Indenture in British Guiana". In *India in the Caribbean*, edited by David Dabydeen and Brinsley Samaroo, 211–30. London: Hansib.

Marchand, Marianne H., and Jane L. Parpart, eds. 1995. *Feminism/Postmodernism/Development*. London: Routledge.

Marglin, Frederique Apffel. 1990. "Smallpox in Two Systems of Knowledge". In *Dominating Knowledge: Development, Culture and Resistance*, edited by Frederique Apffel Marglin and Stephen A. Marglin, 102–44. Oxford: Clarendon Press.

Marriott, F.C., and Arthur Mayhew. 1933. *Education in the West Indies: Report of a Commission Appointed to Consider Problems of Secondary and Primary Education in Trinidad, Barbados, Leeward Islands and Windward Islands, 1931–32*. London: HMSO.

Marshall, Paule. 1982. *Brown Girl, Brownstones*. London: Virago Press.

Massiah, Joycelin. 1984a. *Employed Women in Barbados: A Demographic Profile, 1946–1970*. Cave Hill, Barbados: Institute of Social and Economic Research (Eastern Caribbean), University of the West Indies.

———. 1984b. "Indicators of Women in Development: A Preliminary Framework for the Caribbean". In *Women, Work and Development*, edited by Margaret Gill and Joycelin Massiah, 41–129. Cave Hill, Barbados: Institute of Social and Economic Research (Eastern Caribbean), University of the West Indies.

———. 1986a. "Women in the Caribbean Project: An Overview". *Social and Economic Studies* 35, no. 2: 1–29.

———. 1986b. "Work in the Lives of Caribbean Women". *Social and Economic Studies* 35, no. 2: 177–239.

Mathurin, Lucille. 1974. "A Historical Study of Women in Jamaica from 1655 to 1844". PhD diss., University of the West Indies.

———. 1977. "Reluctant Matriarchs". *Savacou* 13: 1–6.

Maurer, Bill. 1997. *Recharting the Caribbean: Land, Law and Citizenship in the British Virgin Islands*. Ann Arbor: University of Michigan Press.

Mayers, Janice. 1995. "Access to Secondary Education for Girls in Barbados, 1907–43: A Preliminary Analysis". In *Engendering History: Caribbean Women in Historical Perspective*, edited by Verene Shepherd, Bridget Brereton and Barbara Bailey, 258–75. Kingston, Jamaica: Ian Randle.

Maynard, Mary. 1994. " 'Race', Gender and the Concept of 'Difference' in Feminist Thought". In *The Dynamics of "Race" and Gender: Some Feminist Interventions,* edited by Haleh Afshar and Mary Maynard, 9–25. London: Taylor and Francis.

Mead, Margaret. 1935. *Sex and Temperament in Three Primitive Societies.* New York: William Morrow.

———. 1949. *Male and Female: A Study of the Sexes in a Changing World.* New York: Dell.

Measor, Lynda, and Pat Sikes. 1992. *Gender and Schools.* London: Cassell.

Mernissi, Fatima. 1991. *The Veil and the Male Elite: A Feminist Interpretation of Women's Rights in Islam.* Reading, Mass.: Addison-Wesley.

Messner, Michael A., and Donald F. Sabo, eds. 1990. *Sport, Men, and the Gender Order: Critical Feminist Perspectives.* Champaign, Ill.: Human Kinetics.

Miers, Suzanne, and Richard Roberts, eds. 1988. *The End of Slavery in Africa.* Madison: University of Wisconsin Press.

Mies, Maria. 1986. *Patriarchy and Accumulation on a World Scale: Women in the International Division of Labour.* London: Zed Books.

Mill, John Stuart. 1995. *The Subjection of Women.* Cambridge: MIT Press.

Miller, Errol. 1991. *Men at Risk.* Kingston, Jamaica: Jamaica Publishing House.

———. 1994. *Marginalization of the Black Male: Insights from the Development of the Teaching Profession.* 2d ed. Kingston, Jamaica: Canoe Press, University of the West Indies.

———. 1997. "The Caribbean Male in Perspective". In *Caribbean Social Structures and the Changing World of Men,* 35–46. Port of Spain, Trinidad: United Nations Economic Commission for Latin America and the Caribbean, Subregional Headquarters for the Caribbean.

Millett, Kate. 1970. *Sexual Politics.* New York: Doubleday.

Mintz, Sidney W. 1981. "Economic Role and Cultural Tradition". In *The Black Woman Cross-Culturally,* edited by Filomina Chioma Steady, 515–34. Cambridge, Mass.: Schenkman Publishing.

Moglen, Helene. 1983. "Power and Empowerment". *Women's Studies International Forum* 6, no. 2: 131–34.

Mohammed, Patricia. 1982. "Educational Attainment of Women in Trinidad-Tobago, 1946–1980". In *Women and Education,* edited by Joycelin Massiah, 35–77. Women in the Caribbean Project, vol. 5. Cave Hill, Barbados: Institute of Social and Economic Research (Eastern Caribbean), University of the West Indies.

———. 1994a. "Nuancing the Feminist Discourse in the Caribbean". *Social and Economic Studies* 43, no. 3: 135–67.

———. 1994b. "A Social History of Post-migrant Indians in Trinidad 1917–1947: A Gender Perspective". PhD diss., Institute of Social Studies, The Hague, The Netherlands.

———. 1995. "Writing Gender into History: The Negotiation of Gender Relations among Indian Men and Women in Post-indenture Trinidad Society, 1917–47". In *Engendering History: Caribbean Women in Historical Perspective,* edited by Verene Shepherd, Bridget Brereton and Barbara Bailey, 20–47. Kingston, Jamaica: Ian Randle.

———. 1996. "Unmasking Masculinity and Deconstructing Patriarchy: Problems and Possibilities within Feminist Epistemology". Paper presented at the Centre for Gender and Development Studies, University of the West Indies, St Augustine Symposium on the Construction of Caribbean Masculinity: "Towards a Research Agenda". St Augustine, Trinidad, 11–13 January.

———. 1997. "*Midnight's Children* and the Legacy of Nationalism". *Small Axe* 2: 19–37.

———. 1998. "Towards Indigenous Feminist Theorizing in the Caribbean". *Feminist Review,* no. 59: 6–33.

———. 2000a. " 'But Most of All Mi Love Me Browning': The Emergence in Eighteenth and Nineteenth-Century Jamaica of the Mulatto Woman as the Desired". *Feminist Review,* no. 65: 22–48.

———. 2000b. " 'But Most of All Mi Love Me Browning': The Emergence of the Mulatto Woman as the Desired in Eighteenth and Nineteenth Century Jamaica". In *Differentiating Caribbean Womanhood,* Working Paper no. 3, edited by Jacquelin Stevens, 18–37. Mona, Jamaica: Centre for Gender and Development Studies, University of the West Indies.

———. 2001. *Gender Negotiations among Indians in Trinidad, 1917–1947.* Basingtoke, UK: Palgrave.

Mohammed, Patricia, and Althea Perkins. 1999. *Caribbean Women at the Crossroads: The Paradox of Motherhood among Women of Barbados, St Lucia and Dominica.* Kingston, Jamaica: Canoe Press, University of the West Indies.

Mohammed, Patricia, and Catherine Shepherd, eds. 1988. *Gender in Caribbean Development: Papers Presented at the Inaugural Seminar of the University of the West Indies Women and Development Studies Project .* St Augustine, Trinidad: Women in Development Studies Project, University of the West Indies.

Mohanty, Chandra Talpade. 1991. "Under Western Eyes: Feminist Scholarship and Colonial Discourses". In *Third World Women and the Politics of Feminism,* edited by Chandra Talpade Mohanty, Ann Russo and Lourdes Torres, 51–80. Bloomington: Indiana University Press.

Mohanty, Chandra Talpade, Ann Russo and Lourdes Torres, eds. 1991. *Third World Women and the Politics of Feminism.* Bloomington: Indiana University Press.

Moi, Toril. 1985. *Sexual/Textual Politics: Feminist Literary Theory.* London: Methuen.

Molyneux, Maxine. 1985. "Mobilisation without Emancipation? Women's Interests, the State and Revolution in Nicaragua". *Feminist Studies* 11: 227–54.

———. 1998. "Analysing Women's Movement". In *Feminist Visions of Development: Gender, Analysis and Policy,* edited by Cecile Jackson and Ruth Pearson, 65–88. London: Routledge.

Momsen, Janet, ed. 1993. *Women and Change in the Caribbean.* Kingston, Jamaica: Ian Randle.

———. 1987. "The Feminization of Agriculture in the Caribbean". In *Geography of Gender in the Third World,* edited by Janet Henshall Momsen and Janet G. Townsend, 344–47. Albany: State University of New York Press.

Momsen, Janet Henshall, and Janet G. Townsend, eds. 1987. *Geography of Gender in the Third World.* Albany: State University of New York Press.

Mondesire, Alicia, and Leith Dunn. 1995. *Towards Equity in Development: A Report on the Status of Women in Sixteen Commonwealth Caribbean Countries.* Georgetown, Guyana: Caribbean Community Secretariat.

Moore, Henrietta L. 1994. *A Passion for Difference.* Cambridge, UK: Polity Press.

Moore, Robert J. 1999. "Colonial Images of Blacks and Indians in Nineteenth Century Guyana". In *The Colonial Caribbean in Transition: Essays on Postemancipation Social and Cultural History,* edited by Bridget Brereton and Kevin A. Yelvington, 126–58. Kingston, Jamaica: University of the West Indies Press.

Mootoo, Shani. 1998. *Cereus Blooms at Night.* London: Granta Books.

Morgan, Dawn. 2000. "Yuh Daddy Ain't Yuh Daddy". *Weekend Nation Extra* (Barbados), 24 March, 10.

Morikang, Irene. 1999. "Two Laws, Two Conflicting Extremes for Widows". *Cameroon Tribune,* 17 May.

Morrisey, Marietta. 1989. *Slave Women in the New World: Gender Stratification in the Caribbean.* Lawrence, Kan.: University Press of Kansas.

Moser, Caroline O.N. 1989. "Gender Planning in the Third World: Meeting Practical and Strategic Gender Needs". *World Development* 17, no. 11: 1799–825.

————1993. *Gender Planning and Development: Theory, Practice and Training.* London: Routledge.

Murphy, Raymond. 1988. *Social Closure.* Oxford: Clarendon Press.

Nash, June, and Maria Patricia Fernandez-Kelly, eds. 1983. *Women, Men, and the International Division of Labour.* Albany: State University of New York Press.

National Commission on the Status of Women. 1978. *Report of the National Commission on the Status of Women in Barbados,* vol. 1. Bridgetown, Barbados: Barbados Government Printing Office.

Nederveen Pieterse, Jan. 1990. *Wit over zwart: Beelden van Afrika en zwarten in de westerse populaire cultuur.* Amsterdam: Koninklijk Instituut voor de Tropen.

Newton, Velma. 1984. *The Silver Men: West Indian Migration to Panama 1850–1914.* Mona, Jamaica: Institute of Social and Economic Research, University of the West Indies.

Nicholson, Linda, ed. 1990. *Feminism/Postmodernism.* New York: Routledge.

————. 1994. Interpreting Gender. *Signs: Journal of Women in Culture and Society* 20, no. 1: 79–105.

Northouse, Peter G. 1997. *Leadership: Theory and Practice.* Thousand Oaks, Calif.: Sage Publications.

Nurse, Keith. 1997. "Masculinities in Transition: Gender and the Global Problematique". Paper presented at the conference Caribbean Masculinities, Centre for Gender and Development Studies, University of the West Indies, St Augustine, Trinidad, November.

Nussbaum, Martha. 1993. "Non-relative Virtues: An Aristotelian Approach". In *The Quality of Life,* edited by Martha Nussbaum and Amartya Sen, 242–69. Oxford: Clarendon Press.

————. 1995. "Human Capabilities, Female Human Beings". In *Women, Culture and Development: A Study of Human Capabilities,* edited by Martha C. Nussbaum and Jonathan Glover, 61–104. Oxford: Clarendon Press.

————. 1998. "Public Philosophy and International Feminism". *Ethics* 108: 762–96.

———. 1999. *Sex and Social Justice*. New York: Oxford University Press.

Nye, Andrea. 1989. *Feminist Theory and the Philosophies of Man*. New York: Routledge.

Nzimiro, Ikenna. 1972. *Studies in Ibo Political Systems: Chieftaincy and Politics in Four Niger States*. London: Cass.

Nzomo, Maria. 1995. "Women and Democratization Struggles in Africa: What Relevance to Post-Modernist Discourse? In *Feminism/Postmodernism/Development*, edited by Marianne H. Marchand and Jane L. Parpart, 131–41. London: Routledge.

O'Connell Davidson, Julia. 1998. *Prostitution, Power and Freedom*. London: Polity.

O'Connell Davidson, Julia, and Jacqueline Sanchez Taylor. 1999. "Fantasy Islands: Exploring the Demand for Sex Tourism". In *Sun, Sex and Gold: Tourism and Sex Work in the Caribbean*, edited by Kamala Kempadoo, 37–54. Lanham, Md.: Rowman and Littlefield.

O'Neill, Onora. 1989. "Justice, Gender and International Boundaries". WIDER Working Papers no. 68. Helsinki: World Institute for Development Economics Research of the United Nations University.

Oakley, Ann. 1974. *The Sociology of Housework*. London: Martin Robinson.

Okin, Susan Moller. 1989. *Justice, Gender and the Family*. New York: Basic Books.

———. 1995. "Inequalities Between the Sexes in Different Cultural Contexts". In *Women, Culture and Development: A Study of Human Capabilities*, edited by Martha C. Nussbaum and Jonathan Glover, 274–97. Oxford: Clarendon Press.

———. 1998. "Feminism and Multiculturalism: Some Tensions". *Ethics* 108, no. 4: 661–84.

Osirim, Mary Johnson. 1997. "We Toil All the Livelong Day: Women in the English-Speaking Caribbean". In *Daughters of Caliban: Caribbean Women in the Twentieth Century*, edited by Consuelo López Springfield, 41–67. Bloomington: Indiana University Press.

Parker, Richard, Regina Maria Barbarosa and Peter Aggleton. 2000. "Framing the Sexual Subject". Introduction to *Framing the Sexual Subject: The Politics of Gender, Sexuality and Power*, 1–25. Berkeley: University of California Press.

Parkin, Frank. 1979. *Marxism and Class Theory: A Bourgeois Critique*. London: Tavistock.

Parpart, Jane L., M. Patricia Connelly and Eudine Barriteau, eds. *Theoretical Perspectives on Gender and Development*. Ottawa, Ont.: International Development Research Centre.

Parpart, Jane L., and Marianne H. Marchand. 1995. "Exploding the Canon: An Introduction/Conclusion". In *Feminism/Postmodernism/Development*, edited by Marianne H. Marchand and Jane L. Parpart, 1–22. London: Routledge.

Parry, Odette. 2000. *Male Underachievement in High School Education in Jamaica, Barbados, and St Vincent and the Grenadines*. Kingston, Jamaica: Canoe Press, University of the West Indies.

Pateman, Carole. 1992. "Equality, Difference, Subordination: The Politics of Motherhood and Women's Citizenship". In *Beyond Equality and Difference: Citizenship, Feminist Politics and Female Subjectivity*, edited by Gisela Bock and Susan James, 17–31. London: Routledge.

———. 1995. *The Disorder of Women: Democracy, Feminism and Political Theory*. Cambridge, UK: Polity Press.

Patterson, Orlando. 1967. *The Sociology of Slavery: An Analysis of the Origins, Development and Structure of Negro Slave Society in Jamaica*. London: MacGibbon and Kee.

Pattullo, Polly. 1996. *Last Resorts: The Cost of Tourism in the Caribbean*. Kingston, Jamaica: Ian Randle.

Peacocke, Nan. 1998. "Meditation on 'The Subject': Rethinking Caring Labour". In *Caribbean Portraits: Essays on Gender Ideologies and Identities*, edited by Christine Barrow, 194–207. Kingston, Jamaica: Ian Randle.

Peake, Linda, and Alissa D. Trotz. 1999. *Gender, Ethnicity and Place: Women and Identities in Guyana*. London: Routledge.

Phillips, Grenville. 2002. "Sexes Are Just Different". *Barbados Advocate*, 31 July, 8.

Phillips, Joan L. 1999. "Tourism-Oriented Prostitution in Barbados: The Case of the Beach Boy and the White Female Tourist". In *Sun, Sex and Gold: Tourism and Sex Work in the Caribbean*, edited by Kamala Kempadoo, 183–200. Lanham, Md.: Rowman and Littlefield.

The Players' Club. 1998. Produced by New Line Cinema. Directed by Ice Cube. Los Angeles: New Line Cinema.

Pohlmann, Lisa. 1995. "Ambivalence about Leadership in Women's Organizations: A Look at Bangladesh". *IDS Bulletin* 26, no. 3: 117–24.

Postma, Johannes Menne. 1990. *The Dutch in the Atlantic Slave Trade, 1600–1815*. Cambridge: Cambridge University Press.

Potter, Elizabeth. 1993. "Gender and Epistemic Negotiation". In *Feminist Epistemologies*, edited by Linda Alcoff and Elizabeth Potter, 161–86. New York: Routledge.

Pouchet Paquet, Sandra. 1995. "The Fifties". In *West Indian Literature.* 2d ed. Edited by Bruce King, 51–62. London: Macmillan Education.

Powell, Dorian. 1986. "Caribbean Women and Their Response to Familial Experiences". *Social and Economic Studies* 35, no. 2: 83–130.

Poynting, Jeremy. 1987. "East Indian Women in the Caribbean: Experience and Voice". In *India in the Caribbean,* edited by David Dabydeen and Brinsley Samaroo, 231–63. London: Hansib.

Prentice, Alison. 1975. "The Feminization of Teaching in British North America and Canada, 1845–1875". *Histoire sociale/Social History* 8: 5–20.

Pruitt, Deborah, and Suzanne La Font. 1995. "For Love and Money: Romance Tourism in Jamaica". *Annals of Tourism Research* 22, no. 2: 422–40.

Puri, Shalini. 1993. "East Indian/West Indian: Discourses of Race and Place in Trinidad". Typescript.

Quillen, Carol. 2001. "Feminist Theory, Justice and the Lure of the Human". *Signs: Journal of Women in Culture and Society* 27, issue 1: 87–122.

Radtke, H. Lorraine, and Henderikus J. Stam. 1994. Introduction to *Power/Gender: Social Relations in Theory and Practice,* 1–14. London: Sage.

Ragsdale, Kathleen, and Jessica Tomiko Anders. 1998. "The Muchachas of Orange Walk Town and Sex Work in Belize". Typescript.

Ramchand, Kenneth. 1970. *The West Indian Novel and Its Background.* London: Faber.

———. 1976. *An Introduction to the Study of West Indian Literature.* Middlesex, UK: Nelson Caribbean.

Rathgeber, Eva M. 1995. "Gender and Development in Action". In *Feminism/Postmodernism/Development,* edited by Marianne H. Marchand and Jane L. Parpart, 204–20. London: Routledge.

Razack, Sherene. 1995. "Domestic Violence as Gender Persecution: Policing the Borders of Nation, Race and Gender". *Canadian Journal of Women and the Law* 8: 45–88.

Red Thread Women's Development Programme. 1999. " 'Givin' Lil Bit fuh Lil Bit: Women and Sex Work in Guyana". In *Sun, Sex and Gold: Tourism and Sex Work in the Caribbean,* edited by Kamala Kempadoo, 263–90. Lanham, Md.: Rowman and Littlefield.

Reddock, Rhoda. 1985a. "Freedom Denied: Indian Women and Indentureship in Trinidad and Tobago, 1845–1917. *Economic and Political Weekly* 20, no. 43: 79–87.

———. 1985b. "Women and Slavery in the Caribbean: A Feminist Perspective". *Latin American Perspectives* 12, no. 1: 63–80.

———. 1986. "Indian Women and Indentureship in Trinidad and Tobago 1815–1917: Freedom Denied". *Caribbean Quarterly* 32, no. 3–4: 27–49.

———. 1989. "Historical and Contemporary Perspectives: The Case of Trinidad and Tobago". In *Women and the Sexual Division of Labour in the Caribbean,* edited by Keith Hart, 47–65. Kingston, Jamaica: Consortium Graduate School of Social Sciences, University of the West Indies.

———. 1994. *Women, Labour and Politics in Trinidad and Tobago: A History.* London: Zed Books.

———. 1998a. "Contestations over National Culture in Trinidad and Tobago: Considerations of Ethnicity, Class and Gender". In *Caribbean Portraits: Essays on Gender Ideologies and Identities,* edited by Christine Barrow, 414–35. Kingston, Jamaica: Ian Randle.

———. 1998b. "The Indentureship Experience: Indian Women in Trinidad and Tobago 1845–1917. In *Women Plantation Workers: International Experiences,* edited by Shobhita Jain and Rhoda Reddock, 29–48. Oxford: Berg.

———. 1998c. "Women, the Creole Nationalist Movement and the Rise of Eric Williams and the PNM in Mid Twentieth Century Trinidad and Tobago". *Caribbean Issues* 8, no. 1: 41–65.

"Rethinking Caribbean Difference". 1998. *Feminist Review* (special issue), no. 59.

Robertson, Claire. 1996. "Africa into the Americas? Slavery and Women, the Family, and the Gender Division of Labor". In *More Than Chattel: Black Women and Slavery in the Americas,* edited by David Barry Gaspar and Darlene Clark Hine, 3–40. Bloomington: Indiana University Press.

Robertson, Claire C., and Martin A. Klein, eds. 1983a. *Women and Slavery in Africa.* Madison: University of Wisconsin Press.

———. 1983b. "Women's Importance in African Slave Systems". In *Women and Slavery in Africa,* edited by Claire C. Robertson and Martin A. Klein, 3–25. Madison: University of Wisconsin Press.

Robinson, Tracy S. 2000. "Fictions of Citizenship, Bodies Without Sex: The Production and Effacement of Gender in Law". *Small Axe* 7: 1–27.

Rodney, W. 1968. "Jihad and Social Revolution in Futa-Djalon in the Eighteenth Century". *Journal of the Historical Society of Nigeria* 4, no. 2: 269–84.

Rogers, J.A. 1972. *The New World.* 6th ed. Vol. 2 of *Sex and Race.* New York: Helga M. Rogers.

Rohlehr, Gordon. 1988. "Images of Men and Women in 1930s Calypsoes: The Sociology of Food Acquisition in a Context of Survivalism". In *Gender in Caribbean Development: Papers Presented at the Inaugural Seminar of the University of the West Indies Women and Development Studies Project*, edited by Patricia Mohammed and Catherine Shepherd, 232–306. St Augustine, Trinidad: Women in Development Studies Project, University of the West Indies.

Rosener, Judy B. 1990. "Ways Women Lead". *Harvard Business Review*: 119–25.

Ross, Leone. 1999. *Orange Laughter*. London: Angela Royal Publishing.

Ross, W.D., ed. 1912. *The Oxford Translation of Aristotle*. Oxford: Clarendon Press, 1912.

Rouse, Irving. 1964. "Prehistory of the West Indies: The Indians Columbus Encountered When He Discovered the New World Were Moving up from South America". *Science* 144: 499–513.

———. 1992. *The Tainos: Rise and Decline of the People Who Greeted Columbus*. New Haven: Yale University Press.

Rousseau, G.S., and Roy Porter, eds. 1990a. *Exoticism in the Enlightenment*. Manchester: Manchester University Press.

———. 1990b. Introduction to *Exoticism in the Enlightenment*, 1–22. Manchester: Manchester University Press.

Rubin, Gayle. 1975. "The Traffic in Women: Notes on the 'Political Economy' of Sex". In *Toward an Anthropology of Women*, edited by Rayna R. Reiter, 157–210. New York: Monthly Review Press.

Sacks, Karen. 1979. *Sisters and Wives: The Past and Future of Sexual Equality*. Contributions in Women's Studies no. 10. Westport: Greenwood Press.

Safa, Helen. 1995. *The Myth of the Male Bread Winner: Women and Industrialization in the Caribbean*. Boulder: Westview Press.

Said, Edward W. 1979. *Orientalism*. New York: Vintage Books.

St Lucia. 1978. *Constitution of St Lucia*.

Sapiro, Virginia. 1998. "When Are Interests Interesting? The Problem of Political Representation of Women". In *Feminism and Politics,* edited by Anne Phillips, 161–92. Oxford: Oxford University Press.

Savory, Elaine. 1995. "Returning to Sycorax/Prospero's Response: Kamau Brathwaite's Word Journey". In *The Art of Kamau Brathwaite*, edited by Stewart Brown, 208–30. Brigend, Wales: Seren.

Schaef, Anne Wilson. 1981. *Women's Reality: An Emerging Female System in a White Male Society*. Minneapolis: Winston Press.

Schartz, Stuart B. 1985. *Sugar Plantations in the Formation of Brazilian Society.* Cambridge: Cambridge University Press.

Schwartz, Rosalie. 1997. *Pleasure Island: Tourism and Temptation in Cuba.* Lincoln: University of Nebraska Press.

Scott, Alison MacEwen. 1991. "Informal Sector or Female Sector? Gender Bias in Urban Labour Market Models". In *Male Bias in the Development Process,* edited by Diane Elson, 105–32. Manchester: University of Manchester Press.

Scott, Joan W. 1986. "Gender: A Useful Category of Historical Analysis". *American Historical Review* 91, no. 5: 1053–75.

———. 1988. *Gender and the Politics of History.* New York: Columbia University Press.

Scott, Lawrence. 1998. *Aelred's Sin.* London: Allison and Busby.

Sen, Amartya. 1990. "Gender and Cooperative Conflicts". In *Persistent Inequalities: Women and World Development,* edited by Irene Tinker, 123–49. New York: Oxford University Press.

———. 1992. *Inequality Reexamined.* New York: Russel Sage Foundation.

———. 1993. "Capability and Well-Being". In *The Quality of Life,* edited by Martha Nussbaum and Amartya Sen, 30–53. Oxford: Clarendon Press.

———. 1995. "Women's Equality: Justice, Law, and Reason. Gender Inequality and Theories of Justice". In *Women, Culture and Development: A Study of Human Capabilities,* edited by Martha C. Nussbaum and Jonathan Glover, 259–73. Oxford: Clarendon Press.

Sen, Gita, and Caren Grown. 1987. *Development, Crises and Alternative Visions: Third World Women's Perspectives.* New York: Monthly Review Press.

Senior, Olive. 1991. *Working Miracles: Women's Lives in the English-Speaking Caribbean.* London: James Currey.

Sewell, Tony. 1997. *Black Masculinities and Schooling: How Black Boys Survive Modern Schooling.* Stoke-on-Trent, UK: Trentham Books.

Shaffer, Paul. 1998. "Gender, Poverty and Deprivation: Evidence from the Republic of Guinea". *World Development* 26, no. 12: 2119–35.

Shepherd, Verene. 1993. "Emancipation through Servitude: Aspects of the Condition of Indian Women in Jamaica, 1845–1945". In *Caribbean Freedom: Society and Economy from Emancipation to the Present,* edited by Hilary McD. Beckles and Verene Shepherd, 245–50. Kingston, Jamaica: Ian Randle.

———. 1994. *Transients to Settlers: The Experience of Indians in Jamaica, 1845–1950.* Leeds: Peepal Tree Press.

———. 1995. "Gender, Migration and Settlement: The Indentureship and Post-Indentureship Experience of Indian Females in Jamaica, 1845–1943". In *Engendering History: Caribbean Women in Historical Perspective*, edited by Verene Shepherd, Bridget Brereton and Barbara Bailey, 233–57. Kingston, Jamaica: Ian Randle.

———, ed. 1999. *Women in Caribbean History: The British-Colonised Territories*. Kingston, Jamaica: Ian Randle.

Shepherd, Verene, Bridget Brereton and Barbara Bailey, eds. 1995. *Engendering History: Caribbean Women in Historical Perspective*. Kingston, Jamaica: Ian Randle.

Showalter, Elaine. 1977. *A Literature of Their Own: British Women Novelists from Brontë to Lessing*. Princeton: Princeton University Press.

Shrage, Laurie. 1994. *Moral Dilemmas of Feminism: Prostitution, Adultery and Abortion*. New York: Routledge.

The Silence of the Lambs. 1991. Produced by Orion Pictures Corporation. Directed by Jonathan Demme. Los Angeles: Criterion Pictures.

Silvera, Makeda, ed. 1992. *Piece of My Heart: A Lesbian of Colour Anthology*. Toronto: Sister Vision Press.

Smart, Carol. 1990. "Law's Power, the Sexed Body, and Feminist Discourse". *Journal of Law and Society* 17, no. 2: 194–210.

Smith, Abdullahi. 1971. "The Early States of the Central Sudan". In *History of West Africa*, vol. 1, edited by J.F.A. Ajayi and Michael Crowder, 158–201. London: Longman.

Smith, Dayle M. 1997. "Women and Leadership". In *Leadership: Theory and Practice,* edited by Peter G. Northouse, 204–38. Thousand Oaks, Calif.: Sage Publications.

Smith, Dorothy E. 1987. *The Everyday World as Problematic: A Feminist Sociology*. Toronto: University of Toronto Press.

———. 1990. *The Conceptual Practices of Power: A Feminist Sociology of Knowledge*. Boston: Northeastern University Press.

Smith, Lois M., and Alfred Padula. 1996. *Sex and Revolution: Women in Socialist Cuba*. New York: Oxford University Press.

Social and Economic Studies. 1986a. Vol. 35, no. 2. Special issue on the Women in the Caribbean Project. Kingston, Jamaica: Institute of Social and Economic Research, University of the West Indies.

———. 1986b. Vol. 35, no. 3. Special issue on the Women in the Caribbean Project. Kingston, Jamaica: Institute of Social and Economic Research, University of the West Indies.

Sokoloff, Natalie J. 1980. *Between Money and Love: The Dialectics of Women's Home and Market Work*. New York: Praeger.

Spivak, Gayatri Chakravorty. 1994. "Can the Subaltern Speak?" In *Colonial Discourse and Post-colonial Theory: A Reader,* edited by Patrick Williams and Laura Chrisman, 66–111. Hertfordshire, UK: Harvester Wheatsheaf.

———. 1999. *A Critique of Postcolonial Reason: Toward a History of the Vanishing Present.* Cambridge: Harvard University Press.

Stacey, Judith. 2001. "The Empress of Feminist Theory Is Overdressed". *Feminist Theory* 2, no. 1: 99–103.

Statham, Anne. 1987. "The Gender Model Revisited: Differences in the Management Styles of Men and Women". *Sex Roles* 16, no. 7–8: 409–29.

Steady, Filomina Chioma, ed. 1981. *The Black Woman Cross-Culturally.* Cambridge, Mass.: Schenkman Publishing.

Strange Days. 1995. Produced by Lightstorm Entertainment. Directed by Kathryn Bigelow. Los Angeles: 20th Century Fox.

Strober, Myra H., and Audri Gordon Lanford. 1986. "The Feminization of Public School Teaching: Cross-sectional Analysis, 1850–1880". *Signs* 11, no. 2: 212–35.

Sturtz, Linda. 2000. "The Eighteenth Century 'Bokcorah Woman' in Jamaica". In *Differentiating Caribbean Womanhood.* Working Paper no. 3, edited by Jacquelin Stevens, 1–17. Mona, Jamaica: Centre for Gender and Development Studies, University of the West Indies.

Sun on Saturday (Barbados). 1999. "Lashley on Gender Affairs", 6 March, 5.

Sunday Advocate (Barbados). 2000. "Boys in Peril: Squeezed by Gender Trap", 12 March, 8.

Sunday Sun (Barbados). "Jobless Record: Unemployment Falls below Ten Percent", 27 February, 1, A3.

Sutton, Constance, and Susan Makiesky-Barrow. 1981. "Social Inequality and Sexual Status in Barbados". In *The Black Woman Cross-Culturally,* edited by Filomina Chioma Steady, 469–98. Cambridge, Mass.: Schenkman Publishing.

Taitt, Edna. 1998. "A Policy Recommendation with Reference to Specific Implementation Issues to Assist the Needs of Women in the Informal Sector". Typescript. Centre for Gender and Development Studies, University of the West Indies (Cave Hill, Barbados).

Taitt, Ria. 2000. "Women Dominance Posing Serious Challenge Says PM". *Trinidad Express,* 21 March. Reported in *Gender Dialogue* 1 (July 2000): 5 [ECLAC/CDCC, Port of Spain, Trinidad].

Tajfel, Henri, ed. 1982. *Social Identity and Intergroup Relations.* Cambridge: Cambridge University Press.

Tamir, Yael. 1996. "Hands Off Clitoridectomy: What Our Revulsion Reveals about Ourselves". *Boston Review* 21, no. 3: 12–20.

Terborg-Penn, Rosalyn, Sharon Harley and Andrea Benton Rushing, eds. 1989. *Women in Africa and the African Diaspora*. Washington, DC: Howard University Press.

Thomas, Deborah. 2001. "Seasonal Labor, Seasonal Leisure: The Gruntwork, Goals and Gains of Jamaican Hotel Workers in the United States". Paper presented to the twenty-sixth annual conference of the Caribbean Studies Association, St Maarten, 27 May–2 June.

Thornton, Margaret. 1995. "Embodying the Citizen". In *Public and Private: Feminist Legal Debates*, edited by Margaret Thornton, 198–220. Melbourne: Oxford University Press.

Tinker, Irene, ed. 1990. *Persistent Inequalities: Women and World Development*. New York: Oxford University Press.

Tinker, Irene, and Michelle Bo Bramsen, eds. 1976. *Women and World Development*. Washington, DC: Overseas Development Council.

Tong, Rosemary. 1992. *Feminist Thought: A Comprehensive Introduction*. London: Routledge.

Travel Industry World Yearbook, 1996–7. 1997. New York: Child and Waters.

Trinidad Guardian. 2000. "Men Belittled in Dominica – Minister", 18 March, 7.

Trinidad and Tobago. n.d. *Men and Women Working Together to Build a Stronger Trinidad and Tobago*. Information Brochure no. 1. Port of Spain, Trinidad: Gender Affairs Division, Ministry of Culture and Gender Affairs.

———. 1997. *A Proposal to Effect the Name Change of the Ministry of Community Development, Culture and Women's Affairs, Port of Spain, March 27, 1997*. Port of Spain, Trinidad: Ministry of Community Development, Culture and Women's Affairs.

———. 1999. *Training and Sensitization in Gender and Development: A Training Manual*. Port of Spain, Trinidad: Gender Affairs Division, Ministry of Culture and Gender Affairs.

Truong, Thanh-Dam. 1990. *Sex, Money and Morality: The Political Economy of Prostitution and Tourism in South East Asia*. London: Zed Books.

Udayagiri, Mridula. 1995. "Challenging Modernization: Gender and Development, Postmodern Feminism and Activism". In *Feminism/Postmodernism/Development*, edited by Marianne H. Marchand and Jane L. Parpart, 159–77. London: Routledge.

UNICEF and Planning Institute of Jamaica (PIJ). 1997. *Situation Analysis of Children and Women in Jamaica, 1995*. Kingston, Jamaica: UNICEF.

UNIFEM. 2000. *Progress of the World's Women 2000*. New York: United Nations Development Fund for Women.

United Kingdom. West India Royal Commission (WIRC). 1897. *Report of the West India Royal Commission*. Appendix C, vol. 2 (parts 2–5): *Proceedings, Evidence, and Documents Relating to Barbados, Trinidad, and Tobago*. London: HMSO.

———. 1939. *Proceedings of Investigations in Barbados*. Bridgetown, Barbados: Advocate.

———. 1945. *West India Royal Commission Report*. London: HMSO.

United Nations. 1995. *The World's Women 1995: Trends and Statistics*. New York: United Nations.

United Nations Development Programme (UNDP). 1992. *Human Development Report*. New York: Oxford University Press.

———. 1999. *Human Development Report 1999*. New York: Oxford University Press.

United States. Agency for International Development (USAID). 1978. "The Percy Amendment". In *Report on Women in Development: Submitted to the Committee on Foreign Relations, US Senate and the Speaker, US House of Representatives, in Fulfillment of Section 113(b) of the Foreign Assistance Act of 1961 as Amended August 3, 1977*. Washington, DC: Office of Women in Development, US Agency for International Development.

University of the West Indies (UWI). Centre for Gender and Development Studies. 2000. "Report on the Workshop to Review the Draft Proposal for the Study of Gender-Based Imbalances at the Secondary and Tertiary Levels of Education Systems of the Borrowing Members of the Caribbean Development Bank". Kingston, Jamaica, 23–25 February.

University of the West Indies. Office of Planning and Institutional Research. n.d. *Official Statistics, 1998–99*. Mona, Jamaica: University of the West Indies.

Unterhalter, Elaine. 1999. "Citizenship, Difference and Education: Reflections Inspired by the South African Transition". In *Women, Citizenship and Difference*, edited by Nira Yuval-Davis and Pnina Werbner, 100–117. London: Zed Books.

van Allen, Judith. 1972. "Sitting on a Man: Colonialism and the Lost Political Institutions of Igbo Women". *Canadian Journal of African Studies* 6, no. 2: 165–81.

Visweswaran, Kamala. 1994. *Fictions of Feminist Ethnography*. Minneapolis: University of Minnesota Press.

Walcott, Derek. 1970a. "Ti-Jean and His Brothers". In *Dream on Monkey Mountain and Other Plays,* by Derek Walcott, 81–166. New York: Farrar, Straus and Giroux.

———. 1970b. "What the Twilight Says: An Overture". In *Dream on Monkey Mountain and Other Plays,* by Derek Walcott, 1–40. New York: Farrar, Straus and Giroux.

Walvin, James. 1992. "Selling the Sun: Tourism and Material Consumption". *Revista/Review Interamericana* 22, no. 1–2: 208–25.

Waring, Marilyn. 1989. *If Women Counted: A New Feminist Economics.* London: Macmillan.

———. 1990. *If Women Counted: A New Feminist Economics.* San Francisco: Harper and Row.

Washington, Patricia A., and Lynda Dixon Shaver. 1997. "The Language Culture of Rap Music Videos". In *Language, Rhythm, and Sound: Black Popular Cultures into the Twenty-first Century,* edited by Joseph K. Adjaye and Adrianne R. Andrews, 164–77. Pittsburgh: University of Pittsburgh Press.

Watson, Hilbourne. 1990. "Beyond Ideology: The Question of the Black Middle Class in Barbados". *Bulletin of Eastern Caribbean Affairs* 15, no. 6: 16–31.

West, Cornel. 1993. "Black Sexuality: The Taboo Subject". In *Race Matters,* by Cornel West, 81–91. Boston: Beacon Press.

Wieringa, Saskia, ed. 1995. *Subversive Women: Historical Experiences of Gender and Resistance.* London: Zed Books.

———. 2002. "Essentialism versus Constructivism: Time for a Rapprochement?" In *Gendered Realities: Essays in Caribbean Feminist Thought,* edited by Patricia Mohammed, 3–21. Kingston, Jamaica: University of the West Indies Press.

Wilkie, Angus. 1997. "Slow, Silent Take-Over: Men Uncertain of Role in Society". *Daily Nation* (Barbados), 26 March, 10C–11C.

———. 1999. "No Equality Between Genders". *Sunday Advocate* (Barbados). 30 May, 12.

Wilson, Peter. 1969. "Reputation and Respectability: A Suggestion for Caribbean Ethnology". *Man* 4, no. 1: 70–84

Wiltshire-Brodber, Rosina. 1988. "Gender, Race and Class in the Caribbean". In *Gender in Caribbean Development: Papers Presented at the Inaugural Seminar of the University of the West Indies Women and Development Studies Project,* edited by Patricia Mohammed and Catherine Shepherd, 142–55. St Augustine, Trinidad: Women in Development Studies Project, University of the West Indies.

Wipper, Audrey. 1995. "Women's Voluntary Associations". In *African Women South of the Sahara*. 2d ed. Edited by Margaret Jean Hay and Sharon Stichter, 164–86. New York: Longman.

Woolf, Virginia. 1989. *A Room of One's Own*. New York: Harcourt Brace Jovanovich.

Yeğenoğlu, Meyda. 1998. *Colonial Fantasies: Towards a Feminist Reading of Orientalism*. Cambridge: Cambridge University Press.

Yelvington, Kevin A. 1995. *Producing Power: Ethnicity, Gender and Class in a Caribbean Workplace*. Philadelphia: Temple University Press.

Young, Iris Marion. 1998. "Polity and Group Difference: A Critique of the Ideal of Universal Citizenship". In *Feminism and Politics*, edited by Anne Phillips, 401–29. Oxford: Oxford University Press.

Young, Kate. 1988a. "Notes on the Social Relations of Gender". In *Gender in Caribbean Development: Papers Presented at the Inaugural Seminar of the University of the West Indies Women and Development Studies Project*, edited by Patricia Mohammed and Catherine Shepherd, 97–109. St Augustine, Trinidad: Women in Development Studies Project, University of the West Indies.

———. 1988b. "Reflections on Meeting Women's Needs". Introduction to *Women and Economic Development: Local, Regional and National Planning Strategies*, 1–30. Oxford: Berg.

———. 1993. *Planning Development with Women: Making a World of Difference*. London: Macmillan.

Yuval-Davis, Nira. 1997. *Gender and Nation*. London: Thousand Oaks.

Yuval-Davis, Nira, and Pnina Werbner. 1999. "Women and the New Discourse of Citizenship". Introduction to *Women, Citizenship and Difference,* 1–38. London: Zed Books.

Zuhur, Sherifa. 1992. *Revealing Reveiling: Islamist Gender Ideology in Contemporary Egypt*. Albany: State University of New York Press.

Zulu, Samu. 1999. "Zimbabwe Court Rules Women are 'Teenagers' ", *Daily Mail and Guardian* (Johannesburg), 7 May [online]. <http://www.aegis.com/news/dmg/1999/MG990503.html>

Contributors

Eudine Barriteau is Senior Lecturer and Head of the Centre for Gender and Development Studies, University of the West Indies, Cave Hill, Barbados. She is the author of *The Political Economy of Gender in the Twentieth-Century Caribbean*. Her most recent publications include "Confronting Power and Politics: A Feminist Theorizing of Gender in Commonwealth Caribbean Societies", *Meridians: Feminism, Race, Transnationalism* 3, no. 2: 57–92, and "Women Entrepreneurs and Economic Marginality: Rethinking Caribbean Women's Economic Relations", in *Gendered Realities: Essays in Caribbean Feminist Thought*, edited by Patricia Mohammed. She has published several articles on feminist theorizing and is currently coordinating three research projects that collectively examine Caribbean political economy and social change from the perspective of gender. She is the inaugural Dame Nita Barrow Women in Development Fellow, Ontario Institute for Studies in Education, University of Toronto (1997).

Hilary McD. Beckles is Principal, Pro Vice Chancellor and Professor of History at the University of the West Indies, Cave Hill, Barbados. He has a major research interest in gender in Caribbean slavery and has published several books and articles on the subject, including *Natural Rebels: A Social History of Enslaved Black Women in Barbados* and *Centering Woman: Gender Discourses in Caribbean Slave History*.

Jane Bryce was born and brought up in Tanzania, and lived in Italy, the United Kingdom and Nigeria, before moving to Barbados in 1992 to teach at the University of the West Indies. She worked as a teacher, a freelance editor and a journalist before becoming an academic, and she still contributes to newspapers and journals. She did her doctoral research on Nigerian women's writing at Obafemi Awolowo University in Nigeria, and her current appointment is as a specialist in African literature and film. Since moving to the University of the West Indies, she has extended her interest in popular culture to the Caribbean and now works in the areas of feminist and postcolonial theory, popular culture, film, and creative writing. She has published in all these areas.

Ann B. Denis is Professor of Sociology, University of Ottawa, Canada, and has been Visiting Professor (Research) in the Department of Sociology, University of the West Indies, St Augustine, Trinidad, and Visiting Research Fellow in the Centre for Gender and Development Studies, University of the West Indies, Cave Hill, Barbados. Her research has focused on a feminist analysis of the intersection of gender, class and ethnicity/race, particularly in relation to work and education. Recent publications include *Femmes de carrières: Carrières de femmes* (with Caroline Andrew and Cécile Coderre); "Le corps des femmes dans la construction des savoirs et des savoirs-faire. Éducation et travail rémunéré des femmes au Canada, 19e et 20e siècles" (with Ruby Heap); "Rethinking Development from a Feminist Perspective" (in press); and "Multiple Identities . . . Multiple Marginalities: Franco-Ontarian Feminism" in *Gender and Society*.

Aviston Downes is Lecturer in History and Coordinator of the Oral History Project in the Department of History and Philosophy, University of the West Indies, Cave Hill, Barbados. He is a Commonwealth scholar and completed his doctorate at the University of York in 1995. His specialization is Commonwealth Caribbean social and cultural history, with particular focus on gender, sport and fraternal organizations. He has delivered many papers at international conferences and is the author of a number of articles in scholarly books and journals.

Margaret Gill is presently pursuing her Master of Philosophy/Doctor of Philosophy degree at the University of the West Indies, Cave Hill, Barbados, where she received her Master of Arts degree in 1996, and her Bachelor of Science degree in 1978. In 1983–84 she was the recipient of the Tinker Fellowship to the University of Florida, Gainesville, and the 1982–83 Inter-American Foundation Fellowship to same university. She has received several other honours. She devotes her time to a number of organizations, including the Barbados Association of Literary Artists; Voices: Barbados Writers Collective; the Caribbean Association of Feminist Research and Action (CAFRA), for which she is the Barbados national representative; the Women's Forum of Barbados, of which she is a founding member. She has published several poems as well as academic work. Her current research interests are in nationhood and identity in Barbados and Bermuda, industrial relations in Barbados, and women and the informatics sector in Barbados.

Richard A. Goodridge is Lecturer in the Department of History and Philosophy at the University of the West Indies, Cave Hill, Barbados. He has published articles on teaching African history and on women in twentieth-century anglophone Cameroon. He teaches courses on African history at the University of the West Indies.

Jo-Ann Granger is Librarian III at the University of the West Indies, Cave Hill, Barbados, where her duties include cataloguing and the management of the main library's VTLS system. Her interests include computer applications for library services and functions. She is currently working on a bibliography on gender in the Commonwealth Caribbean.

Kamala Kempadoo is Associate Professor in Social Science at York University, Toronto, Canada. She has been engaged over the past decade with research on the intersections of racialized, gendered and international economic relations in the configuration of the global sex trade. She is specialized in sociology, race and ethnic studies, prostitution studies, and feminist theory, and presently teaches Caribbean studies. She has been attached to the women's studies programme at the University of Colorado–Boulder, and the Centre for Gender and Development Studies at the University of the West Indies, Mona, Jamaica, and is active in political struggles of Third World, black and migrant women. Her publications include *Global Sex Workers: Rights, Resistance and Redefinition* and *Sun, Sex and Gold: Tourism and Sex Work in the Caribbean,* and she has a new book forthcoming on Caribbean sexuality, race and sex work. Currently, she is compiling a manuscript about political and theoretical directions on trafficking in Asia.

Elsa Leo-Rhynie is Professor of Gender and Development Studies at the University of the West Indies, Mona, Jamaica. She was appointed Pro Vice Chancellor and Chair of the Board for Undergraduate Studies at the University of the West Indies in August 2002. Prior to this she served for six years as deputy principal of the Mona Campus and for four years as regional coordinator of the Centre for Gender and Development Studies at the University of the West Indies. She has published extensively on education, training and gender concerns, and has edited a number of publications including, with Barbara Bailey and Christine Barrow, *Gender: A Caribbean Multi-Disciplinary Perspective.* In 2000 she received the Order of Distinction, Commander Class, from the Government of Jamaica for her contribution to the field of education.

Patricia Mohammed is Senior Lecturer at the Centre for Gender and Development Studies, University of the West Indies, St Augustine, Trinidad, which she joined from August 2002. She headed the Centre for Gender and Development Studies, Mona Unit, University of the West Indies, Jamaica, for eight years. She holds a doctorate from the Institute of Social Studies, The Hague. She has had both an activist and academic relationship to feminism and gender studies and has published extensively on gender and feminist thought. She is the author of *Gender Negotiations among Indians in Trinidad, 1917–1947;* editor of *Gendered Realities Rethinking Caribbean Difference;* co-author (with Althea Perkins) of *Caribbean Women at the Crossroads;* and co-editor (with Catherine Shepherd) of *Gender in Caribbean Development.* In July 2002, she completed a two-year research fellowship at the University of the West Indies, Mona, Jamaica, during which the forthcoming *Imaging the Caribbean* was written. This is work will also be released as a documentary film.

Tracy Robinson is Lecturer in the Faculty of Law, University of the West Indies, Cave Hill, Barbados, and teaches Gender and the Law, Family Law, Constitutional Law, and Administration of Trusts and Estates. She is the editor of the *Caribbean Law Bulletin,* a journal aimed at the legal community in the Caribbean and devoted to examining contemporary legal issues in the region. In her current work, she has been exploring the relation of gender, citizenship and constitutionalism from different angles. She is also interested in the content, process and politics of family law reform, including the place of "culture" within it.

Michelle Rowley received her doctorate in Women's Studies from Clark University, Worcester, Massachusetts. Her doctoral dissertation is "The Politics of (M)Othering: Maternal Centrality and Afro-Trinidadian Women's Subjectivities". Her present research interests include issues of reproductive rights, and gender planning and policy formulation, and cultural constructions of Caribbean femininity. She is presently on staff at the Centre for Gender and Development Studies, University of the West Indies, Cave Hill, Barbados.

Donna St Hill is an international consultant on gender, race and economic governance. She has also served as an advisor to governments and international institutions on socially inclusive labour market policies, gender responsive budgets and equalities mainstreaming. She is a member of the European Union Economic and Social Committee, sitting on the sub-committees for ACP–EU Relations and the economic integration of immigrants into member economies. She is a member of the Women's Budget Group, which advises the UK government on the gender implications of macroeconomic policy, and of the International Association for Feminist Economics. She is the author of several articles and papers on gender and macroeconomic policy, employment equity, race, gender and industrial restructuring, and equalities mainstreaming in public sector reform.